THE MUSLIM BROTHERHOOD

The Muslim Brotherhood is the most significant and enduring Sunni Islamist organization of the contemporary era. Its roots lie in the Middle East, but it has grown into both a local and global movement, with its well-placed branches reacting effectively to take the opportunities for power and electoral competition offered by the Arab Spring.

Regarded by some as a force of moderation among Islamists, and by others as a facade hiding a terrorist fundamentalist threat, the potential influence of the Muslim Brotherhood on Middle Eastern politics remains ambiguous. *The Muslim Brotherhood: The Arab Spring and Its Future Face* provides an essential insight into the organization, with chapters devoted to specific cases where the Brotherhood has important impacts on society, the state, and politics. Key themes associated with the Brotherhood, such as democracy, equality, pan-Islamism, radicalism, reform, the Palestine issue, and gender, are assessed to reveal an evolutionary trend within the movement since its founding in Egypt in 1928 to its manifestation as the largest Sunni Islamist movement in the Middle East in the twenty-first century. The book addresses the possible future of the Muslim Brotherhood, whether it can surprise sceptics and effectively accommodate democracy and secular trends, and how its ascension to power through the ballot box might influence Western policy debates on their engagement with this manifestation of political Islam.

Drawing on a wide range of sources, this book presents a comprehensive study of a newly resurgent movement and is a valuable resource for students, scholars, and policymakers focussed on Middle Eastern politics.

Beverley Milton-Edwards is a professor in the School of Politics, International Studies, and Philosophy at Queen's University Belfast. She is the author of *Islamic Fundamentalism since 1945* (2014), *Contemporary Politics in the Middle East* (2011), and with Stephen Farrell, *Hamas* (2010).

THE MUSLIM BROTHERHOOD

The Arab Spring and its future face

Beverley Milton-Edwards

LONDON AND NEW YORK

First published 2016
by Routledge
2 Park Square, Milton Park, Abingdon, Oxon OX14 4RN

and by Routledge
711 Third Avenue, New York, NY 10017

Routledge is an imprint of the Taylor & Francis Group, an informa business

© 2016 Beverley Milton-Edwards

The right of Beverley Milton-Edwards to be identified as author of this work has been asserted in accordance with sections 77 and 78 of the Copyright, Designs and Patents Act 1988.

All rights reserved. No part of this book may be reprinted or reproduced or utilised in any form or by any electronic, mechanical, or other means, now known or hereafter invented, including photocopying and recording, or in any information storage or retrieval system, without permission in writing from the publishers.

Trademark notice: Product or corporate names may be trademarks or registered trademarks, and are used only for identification and explanation without intent to infringe.

British Library Cataloguing-in-Publication Data
A catalogue record for this book is available from the British Library

Library of Congress Cataloging-in-Publication Data
A catalog record for this book has been requested

ISBN: 978-0-415-66000-6 (hbk)
ISBN: 978-0-415-66001-3 (pbk)
ISBN: 978-1-315-65930-5 (ebk)

Typeset in ApexBembo
by Apex CoVantage, LLC

This book is dedicated to
John William Hunter Andrews
"Semper Fidelis"

CONTENTS

Acknowledgements	*ix*
Introduction	1
1 Roots and ideas	12
2 Egypt – Phoenix	34
3 Palestine – Hamas and the link in the chain	61
4 Jordan – Hashemites and the brethren	86
5 Tunisia – Renaissance	111
6 Yemen – The Muslim Brotherhood and the ties of tribe	137
7 Transnational Brotherhood	161
Epilogue	*187*
Bibliography	*199*
Index	*229*

ACKNOWLEDGEMENTS

My interest in the Muslim Brotherhood commenced in the mid-1980s when, as a graduate and later PhD research student at the University of Exeter, my lecturers Professors Tim Niblock and Nazih Ayubi first introduced me to the topic of political Islam. It was a given then that any study of political Islam and explanations for its rise in the wake of the Iranian Revolution of 1979 would include the study of an organization called the Muslim Brotherhood. Later, as a student, I undertook research in the Middle East involving the Muslim Brotherhood in Egypt, Jordan, the West Bank and Gaza Strip, Lebanon, Syria, and beyond to the UK, others parts of Europe, and the US. I still recall in 1985 buying a copy of Sayyid Qutb's *Milestones* from a backstreet underground bookseller in Cairo and pencilling in my own notes and commentary. Throughout the research process of this book, I was further motivated through interaction with inspiring and leading scholars in the field such as Rema Hammami, James Piscatori, Maha Azzam, Tariq Ramadan, Michael Willis, Nathan Brown, Muhammed Qandil, Nathan Thrall, Clive Jones, John Esposito, Daniel Byman, Robert Gleave, Joas Wagemakers, Bruce Lawrence, David Cook, Saud Al-Sarhan, Ruud Peters, Jonathan Brown, and Atef Alshaer. Their conversations with me and their critical feedback and encouragement were very important in helping shape this work. There are also many other scholars and individuals who helped me with the book but have chosen to remain anonymous or have to stay anonymous in order to protect their safety. I thank them all.

Over the last three decades, numerous hours have been spent in the research orbit of this particular subject and its variants. Meeting the Muslim Brotherhood has led me to an interesting variety of encounters in which my own identity as a white European woman has been highlighted, whether in the polite refusal to shake a hand or the quiet but firm insistence from an office manager that a hijab should be donned, a button be done up, or that a chaperone would join us. I have travelled to war zones, visited segregated campuses, watched summer camp displays,

x Acknowledgements

visited Brotherhood media production offices, attended their conferences, and visited village mosques, refugee camps, professional association offices, medical clinics, town councils, and even national parliaments in my own odyssey with the Muslim Brotherhood. With such an odyssey have come measures of understanding and an insatiable thirst to know more, particularly in countries such as Yemen where the machinations of the Muslim Brotherhood under the banner of the Islah movement collides with one of the most complex and dynamic forms of politics in the modern Middle East.

The patience which my publishers have shown in the genesis and completion of this book has been incredible. I would like to offer my sincere thanks to Joe Whiting and assistant editors Holly Jones and Kathryn Rylance. I was also given unstinting assistance from Drew Mikhael, who brought his own important perspectives to share in this project. Moreover, I am truly indebted to Jake Gutman for his sterling effort and unflagging help as I prepared this manuscript for submission. Jake's assistance with research and copyediting helped transform the writing of this book; otherwise, much of the text would have read like a graduate paper from the Derek Zoolander School For Children Who Can't Read Good And Wanna Learn To Do Other Stuff Good Too! Jake has injected this project with some much-needed enthusiasm and curiosity. To this end, I owe Jake and his mother, Jane Gutman, a great deal of gratitude: to Jake for his skills and scholarship and to Jane for supporting her son while he came away from the sunny climes of California to the cold rains of Belfast.

My final words of thanks, as ever, are to my wonderfully supportive children, Cara and Josh Milton-Edwards.

Beverley Milton-Edwards
Belfast, June 2015

INTRODUCTION

Over a period of more than three decades, the path to Dr Zahar's door has always been a potholed dirt and sand affair. That much was a constant. In the 1980s a visit to this veteran 'Brother' was a low-key affair. The approach was unimpeded by obvious signs of security or surveillance. Once inside his modest home, a meeting with him would entail being an audience to a lengthy diatribe coloured by Islamic commentary and medical analogies. During one such meeting, Dr Zahar lamented the fate of the Muslim Brotherhood and the 'cancer' of Israel's occupation against the Palestinian people. His ire was then apparent as he recalled his early adulthood spent studying medicine at Ain al-Shams University in the Egyptian capital, Cairo, and the punitive repression of President Gamal Abdel Nasser against the Muslim Brotherhood. Zahar outlined his aspirations for his movement: 'We want an Islamic state . . . an Islamic alternative . . . a pan-Islamic state.'[1] He cautioned that much work would still be needed to achieve this goal. And he spoke of the Muslim Brotherhood as 'one movement . . . one entity . . . laws, economics, political life all connected'.[2] But Zahar knew he had a long way to go as he spoke of his fellow Brotherhood leader Sheikh Ahmed Yassin, who was incarcerated and 'shackled' and 'subject to harsh treatment' in Israeli custody, and compared him to Muslim Brotherhood founder Hassan al-Banna. He called both men 'catalysts' who 'evoked the consciousness of the people' and were 'able to arouse a whole nation'.[3] He acknowledged that his movement had many enemies and existed in a political environment that was inimical to its goals, but he cautioned patience and said that all would pay off for the Brotherhood in the end.

Over the succeeding decades, Dr Zahar presided over the rise of the Palestinian wing of the Muslim Brotherhood – Hamas – from incipient supporter of the first Palestinian uprising to winner of an electoral mandate in 2006 and sole governors of the Gaza Strip by June 2007. In 2012, as I approached his door as part of a regular visit to the Gaza Strip, the entrance to this veteran Muslim Brotherhood leader

2 Introduction

and Hamas cofounder's house, however, was covered from public view and heavily protected. The armed guards consisted of a small contingent of bearded men who scanned the skies above my head while simultaneously speaking into radios to coordinate and permit my admission. Inside his house again, sitting in a large and echoing 'reception' room which also appeared to be doubling as a garage because of the vehicle parked inside it, I found Dr Zahar to be in a happy and expansive mood. This was uncharacteristic. Usually Dr Zahar was not disposed to such feelings with a visitor such as me and his conversation would focus on the grim business of death and occupation. On this occasion, however, Dr Zahar wanted to talk about the fulfilment of a long-held vision and a reward for patience which he had long predicted: the victory of the Muslim Brotherhood. He contended that the burden of repression and hostility which the movement had endured for decades with fortitude was worth it to see its dominance in the wake of the Arab Spring. He pointed to elections in the Egyptian parliament, the ballot box victory of Mohammed Morsi as president, votes propelling Ennahda in Tunisia to power, and the regeneration of the Brotherhood in Jordan, Syria, Libya, and Yemen. 'The virtue of decades of patience and hard work and belief in our goal of Islam is visible today,' said Dr Zahar.[4] His eyes literally shone as he spoke of the opportunities that now lay ahead for subscribers to this pan-Islamic project and the ways in which the Middle East region would now be reconfigured for its inhabitants.

A year later, in 2013 as the implications of the events in Cairo including the toppling of Morsi and the killings of Muslim Brotherhood supporters were becoming clear, and the ongoing effects of an Israeli blockade were still biting at Gaza's population, the mood of Dr Zahar had changed once again. His sense of jubilation at the astonishing and apparently unstoppable rise of the Brotherhood had been replaced with a return-to-normal countenance of thinly veiled anger that he had borne for many decades and frustration at the forces at large which had once again halted and stymied the Islamic project as envisioned by the Muslim Brotherhood. 'Time and Allah is always on our side,' said Zahar, 'but for the time being we have to immunise our people against the extreme regional infection.'[5]

There are many reasons why Dr Zahar's views on the Brotherhood and the movement itself matters. In less than two years, the Muslim Brotherhood had risen to the dizzying heights of power in the belief that the Arab Spring would serve as a popular vehicle for the realization of their Islamic-inspired agenda. Its leaders believed that its destiny would be one that was characterized by a transformative experience of government and the Islamization of the state in the Middle East. It was also one in which leaders believed their future face could be set as pan-Islamic in terms of unifying the region to causes and cases which the Brotherhood itself had long championed. It did not come to pass; instead, as Muslim Brotherhood scholar Samer Shehata noted, the Brotherhood was in 'tremendous disarray . . . facing greater repression today than in all of its 85-year history'.[6]

It is because the Muslim Brotherhood is the most significant and enduring Sunni Islamist organization of the contemporary era that in the past attention has been paid to it by scholars, policymakers, and pundits alike.[7] Its roots lie in the Middle

Introduction **3**

East, but today it is both a local and global movement. Under the slogan 'Islam is the solution', the Muslim Brotherhood and its ideologues have impacted the political evolution of the Middle East. The Muslim Brotherhood is variously regarded as a true force for moderation among Islamists or a facade behind which lies a terroristic fundamentalist threat which could undermine global security agendas. The Arab Spring has brought the Muslim Brotherhood to the fore of regional politics once more. As the ambitions of the Muslim Brotherhood were being realized through a reordering of state power in the Middle East, however, a vicious backlash against the movement has taken place.

In this book I shed light on and analyze the evolution of the Muslim Brotherhood in both its historical and contemporary context to account for its evolving nature and its new place in the wake of the Arab Spring. The mass protests that brought down regimes in Tunisia, Egypt, Libya, and Yemen might not have been ignited by the Muslim Brotherhood, but the movement and its branches have been well placed to organize effectively for the transition phase and the opportunities for power it presented. In taking advantage of the openings afforded to it by the Arab Spring, the Brotherhood, however, perhaps failed to take account of the equally substantial risks that these opportunities presented. Like previous studies of the Brotherhood, this book examines the genesis and evolution of the Muslim Brotherhood in the Middle East and North Africa but with chapters devoted to specific cases and localities where the Brotherhood and its ideas have made and continue to make important impacts on society, the state, and politics.[8] Within these chapters I assess in detail the dynamics of particular themes of Islamist politics associated with the Brotherhood such as democracy, equality, pan-Islamism, radicalism, violence, reform, the Palestine issue, and gender. This reveals an evolutionary trend within the movement since its founding in Egypt in 1928 to its manifestation as the largest Sunni Islamist movement in the Middle East in the twenty-first century. The book also questions whether the Muslim Brotherhood can demonstrate to its sceptics that its ideology can be accommodated with democracy and the presence of secularism within the region can be made.

Furthermore, I focus on a history-making moment for the Muslim Brotherhood in evaluation of its future in the Middle East region and beyond. This is because, in many respects, the Muslim Brotherhood has reached a watershed not unlike the Six Day War in 1967 was for the movement of Arab nationalism or specifically pan-Arabism. This conflict between the Arab states and Israel was considered a turning point in the modern political dynamic of the Middle East which ended Arab nationalism and augured the rise of Islamic fundamentalism in the region.[9] Pan-Arabism and its Arab nationalist variants have been marshalled by leaders of Arab states to promote an ideological perspective that transcended modern national (and colonially inspired) boundaries in the Middle East to unify its people. Under the leadership of figures such as President Gamal Abdel Nasser of Egypt, however, the pan-Arab dream was shattered following the defeat in the war of 1967 against Israel. Arab nationalism and its pan-Arab variant were never able to truly recover in the wake of the war. In their place, many have argued, Islamic fundamentalist

4 Introduction

movements, including the Muslim Brotherhood, filled the ideological void and identity crisis experienced across the Arab world.[10] After 1967, however, the Muslim Brotherhood was still largely regarded as a threat to incumbent regimes across the region. The possibility that its message might translate into a genuine challenge to power in mobilizing popular masses was perceived as real in many Arab capitals. Hence, for many decades the Brotherhood and its affiliated organizations were subjected to major state-organized campaigns of suppression designed at best to keep the movement on the margins of state-centred power.

The Arab Spring initially appeared to offer a definitive turning point to change all that. The fall of autocratic rulers and the demands for freedom, democracy, and political reforms accompanied with socioeconomic revolution offered a historic opportunity for the Brotherhood to compete for power. The decades of repression seemed to fall as easily from the shoulders of the Brotherhood as they did for the millions of Arabs who cast off fear by participating in the protests. The Brotherhood, many predicted, was the best placed, the best organized, and the best hope of translating freedom from tyranny to a new Islamist-inspired order for power. The Muslim Brotherhood capitalized on this historic moment like no other grouping in the Arab world, even among their Islamist friends and foes. With lightning speed, the movement appeared to be able to marshal the hopeful and attained power. Yet in power it all unravelled just as rapidly as the delimiters, domestically and externally, moved to cut the Brotherhood back down to size. The prize of state control would not be so easily surrendered, and at the same time the Brotherhood drew criticism for its alacrity in forcing change from its own Islamist-inspired agenda when governing for the people. It is my contention throughout this book that as a result of the roles the Muslim Brotherhood has performed both during and after the Arab Spring, it has played an unprecedented part in altering its own future course. It can no longer, as it did in the past as an opposition movement, remain unaccountable for its own fate and fortunes. This is not to say that the Muslim Brotherhood has been left to its own devices, for it has faced a formidable alliance against it, arising from within its own Sunni ranks. The limits of its power have been tested through both popular mandate and state force and have been found wanting.

Assumptions about the democratic credentials of the movement have proved either false or true, depending on which side of the Islam and democracy argument one comes down on. In terms of a fundamental incompatibility between Islam and democracy, the experience of the Muslim Brotherhood in power seemed to confirm that the ballot box was a vehicle for achieving a monopoly of power once elected to government. No matter what apparent assurances the Brotherhood gave, the movement's disinclination in Egypt to share power or govern in recognition of the plural population it represented was fodder for those who believed Islam to be incompatible with democracy.[11] On the other hand, the Tunisian example of Ennahda striving to build alliances and share power was dismissed as 'unique' and ill suited to the other contexts in which the Muslim Brotherhood has organized over the decades.[12] Other branches of the Brotherhood in the region have struggled to maximize the moment of political opportunity which the Arab uprisings in many countries across the region seemed to offer. They have found, for example, in Syria, that state power remains as elusive as ever and that by siding with the people in protests that have called for reform and even change of power, the resistant regime has sought to repress and damage them. Additionally, the Arab Spring has given rise to a new generation of Islamist competitors within the Salafi and Salafi-jihadi fold who have also challenged particular dimensions of the long-held strategic positions of the Muslim Brotherhood. As Brotherhood senior leader Essam el-Erian noted in January 2012, 'We hope that we can pull the Salafists – not that they pull us – and that both of us will be pulled by the people's needs.'[13] Furthermore, the Brotherhood has had to wrestle with the tensions that have arisen within its own movement as the redundancy of certain approaches, institutional arrangements, and power-holding structures has been exposed by a new generation of youth activists and leaders. Such elements have found some of the 'Old Guard' highly resistant or cautious about the direction in which the young generation of the Brotherhood would like to lead the movement. In turn, there is evidence that the younger generation has, in part, grown frustrated at the traditional and rigid structures which the Brotherhood has built up to endure and protect itself. The outcome of such tensions has been openly public; it has led to defections and splintering which expose the myth of the monolith that the Brotherhood has been considered to represent.

The triumph for the Muslim Brotherhood that was quickly predicted in the wake of the Arab Spring, which critics termed an 'Islamist winter', has turned into an unprecedented tragedy. State leaders in some of the region's most conservative and pro-Western countries have marshalled their energies together to definitively push the Brotherhood from power. Hence, ideas upon which the Brotherhood built its movement of incremental reform and opposition appeared to be overthrown in a headlong rush to seize power for itself at the state level. Although the Brotherhood was always intended to be a religious movement with an abiding social-welfare agenda, this programme was compromised as political power was achieved. The convenient ambiguities about its desire for power, the terms and conditions of its Islamic state project, were jettisoned. Many, and not just authoritarian state incumbents and their external supporters, were determined to act as a bulwark against this.

When one visits the Muslim Brotherhood's own wiki site, Ikhwanwiki, there is a section dedicated to its diverse presence and connections not only across the Middle East and North Africa (Morocco, Algeria, Tunisia, Libya, Egypt, the Palestinian Territories, Jordan, Lebanon, Syria, Iraq, Kuwait, Saudi Arabia, Bahrain, Qatar, and Yemen) but also elsewhere across the globe including Indonesia, the United States of America, Germany, Bosnia Herzegovina, Chechnya, Sudan, Somalia, Djibouti, Senegal, Nigeria, Mauritania, Pakistan, and Afghanistan. This expansive and diverse range of geographic and political environments spotlights the Brotherhood's 'global reach'. The validity of such assertions is interrogated in Chapter 7 of this book, but for the purposes of this study, I have selected five distinct examples of what I consider to be important nationally rooted and inspired manifestations of the Muslim Brotherhood alongside a more detailed account of transnational scope of the movement in the final chapter. The examples of Egypt, the Palestinian Territories,

6 Introduction

Jordan, Tunisia, and Yemen help illustrate the birth and important growth of the movement in both North Africa and elsewhere in the Middle East. They exemplify a variety of relationships which have grown (over nearly a century in some cases) between the Brotherhood and an assortment of state actors including monarchies, authoritarian presidencies, and occupiers alongside attendant regional and external political machinations, the most important for this study being the Arab Spring.

Today, the Muslim Brotherhood can be described as one among many Islamic and Islamist groups that organize and operate in the Middle East and beyond. When the organization was founded in 1928, however, it was very much the first modern organization of its kind to articulate the Islamic as relevant to spheres and realms which went beyond the mosque and the religious courts to include the social, economic, and perhaps most importantly of all, the political realm. This is not to say that the Muslim Brotherhood did not have intellectual forerunners but rather that its founder, Hassan al-Banna, and his colleagues, as we shall explore in Chapter 1, outlined and articulated a widely appealing agenda for Islam which by its nature was populist in rhetoric and a challenge to existing forms of authority. Its core values were associated with preaching, education, and forms of Islamic utopianism imagined for a modern age. In this way, the Brotherhood could be considered as a new vanguard heralding change and, as such, also challenged assumptions about Islam and obedience to authority. The Muslim Brotherhood exposed and represented common distrust and hostility to the imposition of forms of rule considered inauthentic to Muslim understandings of power but was also compelled to engage with the political ideologies of its opponents and thus to contend with nationalism, secularism, and democracy by way of response. In turn, the movement gave rise to its own internal diversity leading it to frequently being described as embracing radical or moderate tendencies. Externally, the Muslim Brotherhood has also appeared to inspire, give rise to, or articulate ideas which others have incorporated into their own visioning of Islamist vanguard and challenges. The fundamental tenets of the movement as conceived by its founders were initially not political, but they were inevitably drawn into the political as it was seen to present a formidable challenge to the status quo at the time. But in its political inclinations, the Brotherhood, like its contemporaries, was less concerned with democracy and free societies. Its plural credentials existed in appealing to and working with the Arab masses including the impoverished, the working classes, and as the decades progressed, the educated and professional classes that burgeoned throughout the Middle East. The movement's concept of pluralism lay in its membership and support which attempted to transcend national and other barriers that were erected in the name of Arab nationalism. And although the Brotherhood did emerge, at least in some ways, as a movement that attempted to promote a pan-Islamic vision, Egypt remained central to the movement's identity formation and power.

In Chapter 2 we will see that the present-day movement took its inspiration from the historic origins of the late 1920s in Egypt when the Brotherhood was formed. Indeed the events since 2011 and the outbreak of the Arab Spring cannot be understood without cognizance of the deep roots that the organization has in

Egypt. The political strategies adopted and pursued by the Brotherhood in relation to its own ambitions, as well as other actors, had an important effect on its internal politics and exposed new pressures and tensions in calibrating the march of the movement to power and its responsiveness to the new political climate. The Brotherhood's route during this period led to a significant abandonment of earlier pledges to participate in the politics of transition rather than dominate. It can be convincingly argued that it was this decision to accelerate to power and then dominate, and thus rescind earlier undertakings, that irreparably damaged the reputation of the Brotherhood in the eyes of the Egyptian people.[14] This, however, does little to explain the levels of violence and state force in evidence against the Brotherhood in July and August 2013 which deposed President Morsi and led to a collapse of power in Egypt. As the chapter demonstrates, since 2013 the future of the Brotherhood in Egypt has become increasingly precarious and its survival uncertain. Under President al-Sisi, in alliance with regional actors, the Egyptian Brotherhood and its sister branches (near and far) chafe under hostile discourses of criminalization and state-imposed strictures declaring them terrorists, killing thousands of supporters, and sentencing hundreds of their leaders to death.[15]

The Muslim Brotherhood in Palestine, otherwise known as Hamas, as Chapter 3 will highlight, owes its inception to the pan-Islamic and anticolonial ideals manifest in the Brotherhood in Egypt. Throughout its existence it has maintained important ties to its brothers in Egypt, but it was also enduringly cemented to the local context when the Zionist movement gained national recognition at the UN in 1947, granting them a Jewish state in Palestine. The symbolic power attached to Palestine by the Brotherhood is apparent throughout its history and has inspired Palestinians to find their own iterations of Islamist identity as a form of resistance against Israel's realization of Zionism through nationhood. This was tellingly apparent in the inception of Palestinian Islamism during the British mandate in Palestine, as well as the revival of the Brotherhood in the establishment of Hamas during the first Palestinian Intifada. It is Hamas and its powerful relationship with the Muslim Brotherhood in Egypt which has played such an important role in determining its survival as governors of the Gaza Strip in the wake of the Arab Spring. While the rise of the Egyptian Muslim Brotherhood to power gave great hope to their Palestinian brethren of better times to come, al-Sisi's decision to crush Morsi and the Brotherhood has had serious implications for Hamas and its ability to govern Gaza and remain connected regionally as well.

By and large the Muslim Brotherhood in Jordan was, until relatively recently, never regarded as anything other than a form of loyal opposition to the Hashemite monarchy, as discussed in Chapter 4. The Brotherhood was almost symbiotically tied into the entire history of the modern state and has been as enduring as its British-installed Hashemite monarchy. By remaining loyal to the royal court, the Brotherhood in Jordan survived the many decades of political repression which the Hashemite regime organized against many of its other opponents. It had managed to remain in step with the regime led by King Hussein even when he moved against his Palestinian opponents (principally in the Palestine Liberation Organization),

8 Introduction

causing an enduring schism in the country, and further when the king took positions against Syria in the 1970s and supported Saddam Hussein in the early 1990s. Indeed it would be fair to say that, for the most part, the Brotherhood fared moderately well in Jordan under King Hussein and avoided the fate of its counterparts in countries such as Syria and Egypt where it was crushed in repressive waves by the ruling regimes. King Abdullah II, however, has presided over a relationship with the Brotherhood that has evolved in an altogether different fashion. Since he acceded to the throne in 1999, Abduallah II has been influenced and, on occasion, even steered by a variety of actors within the Jordanian regime who regard the Brotherhood as a threat that should be suppressed. Such actors have been supported by a variety of external forces who, although enemies in other circumstances, coalesce to convince King Abdullah II to deal firmly with his Brotherhood elements at home. Along with states such as Saudi Arabia, these external forces include Israel, which has long maintained that the Brotherhood in Jordan is a powerful conduit for and extension of the Brotherhood-Hamas in the Palestinian territories and, therefore, part of the existential axis of Islamist terrorism that it must counteract. It is certainly the case that since the Arab Spring and the regional fallout over the Muslim Brotherhood, King Abdullah II, while at first appearing to bow to pro-Brotherhood elements, soon aligned his approach to reflect the positions of antipathy common to Israel and Saudi Arabia. By 2015, the king had ordered substantive measures against the Brotherhood, effectively rendering it weaker than it had ever been before. Not only was the Brotherhood itself split internally, but the state also then permitted a 'new' Muslim Brotherhood to be registered and for it to access the assets of the 'old' and increasingly marginalized organization headed by Hammam Said.

In the case of Tunisia, as I explore in Chapter 5, the role played in the wake of the Arab Spring by the Islamist Ennahda is frequently explained as a form of exception. Given that Tunisia is the birthplace of the Arab Spring and possesses a political culture that is one of the most secularized in the Middle East, there were early expectations, however, that the path carved by Ennahda and Tunisia's other Islamists in the wake of the Arab Spring might determine the future face of the Brotherhood movement. In many respects, Ennahda, even under the leadership of one of the movement's founders, Rachid Ghannouchi, was unable to be a model which other branches in the Muslim Brotherhood family could follow.

When the Arab Spring broke out in Tunisia in December 2010, the waves of protest and demonstration and the mass mobilization of Tunisia's citizens against the sclerotic regime of President Ben Ali were characterized by the plurality of society rather than Islam alone. Ennahda was also absent. By this I mean that, unlike the Muslim Brotherhood in Egypt or Jordan, the movement had been repressed to the point that it was almost disbanded and its leadership was in exile. This denied it the opportunity afforded to other branches of the Brotherhood in the region to build a strong civic profile for itself. This is not to say that there was not a strong residue of support for Ennahda among the Tunisian people. Yet, the Tunisian tradition of secularism was deeply engrained not just at a legislative and constitutional level but also within the political culture of the country. It has proved resistant to particular Islamist pillars

Introduction **9**

especially as they relate to the status of women and their rights. This has required compromise and flexibility of interpretation from the leadership of Ennahda in how it determines the representation of their Islamist agenda to the Tunisian people. After a number of high-profile assassinations of secular political leaders by Salafi-jihadists and as protests mounted against Ennahda, it appeared that the group was heading down the same path as the Brotherhood in Egypt. However, the movement chose to preemptively step down from power to avoid further unrest. It was then dealt an electoral setback in the 2014 elections but remained in power as part of a coalition government with its secularist rivals, its future appearing secure as a legitimate Islamist party in Tunisia moving forward.

One of the most interesting features of the Muslim Brotherhood is its chameleon-like adaptability to its environment, and nowhere is this better illustrated than in Yemen, which I examine in Chapter 6. In many respects, the Yemeni state will never be the sum of its parts and instead has remained vulnerable to the triumph of tribe over politics and the bonds of fealty that this demands. Islah, which brings the Yemeni Muslim Brotherhood in under its banner, reflects these tribal balances to its core, as well as the enduring legacy of a state that only reunified in the 1990s and the powerful ties of dependency forged through the mass migration of male labour to neighbouring Saudi Arabia. Since reunification, Islah had to navigate Yemen's challenging political environment through competition, and at times cooperation, with the Salih regime, as well as confront its own internal factions ranging from radical Salafists to the reformist Muslim Brotherhood. This is further complicated by the complex tribal dynamics of Yemeni society which intersect with the Islah party in terms of the al-Ahmar family members who lead the Hashid confederation, as well as occupy key positions within the leadership of Islah. Following the initial protests of the Arab Spring, the economic and liberties-focussed discourses that resonated with demonstrators across the region were largely undercut by the agendas of the political elite including Islah and President Salih, which took the country to the brink of civil war before mediation by Gulf states led the way to a transition government headed by former Vice President Hadi. The chapter ends by examining the prospects for the Muslim Brotherhood in the wake of the Houthi challenge to power in 2014–15 and the counterresponse from Yemen's Gulf neighbours and Saudi Arabia in particular. The Houthi rebel takeover of power in Sanaa all but dismantled Hadi's government and exposed the Muslim Brotherhood in Yemen to powerful sectarian challenges involving major actors in the proxy contest between Iran and Saudi Arabia. In April 2015, Saudi Arabia launched Operation Decisive Storm against the Houthi rebel leaders amidst fears that they would take control of the Bab al-Mandeb Strait in the Arabian Gulf, threatening vital shipping. Islah offered support to the Saudi assault, but it was too little too late, and by this point it had been repeatedly targeted and weakened by the governing Houthi. Houthi elements had stormed offices belonging to the movement, targeted and attacked their top leadership including Islah chief Mohammed al-Yadoumi, and kidnapped as many as 140 of their members including senior party officials and members of the legislature. The future for Islah looked precarious as it sought to rebuild alliances

10 Introduction

within the country at a time when the region, led by Saudi Arabia, had its face still turned away from the Muslim Brotherhood.

The final chapter examines the extent to which the Muslim Brotherhood can be defined as a transnationalism phenomenon. It explores the issue of unity in the sense that the Brotherhood's founders and ideologues have always sought to create a greater sense of belonging for Muslims who shared their vision. This form of unity also coalesced around a rejection of Western-inspired and Western-imposed state borders, particularly in the Middle East, where the Muslim Brotherhood was founded. It was also evident in the extent to which Brotherhood leaders around the region have appealed to or mobilized around common issues which would unite their supporters and appeal to potential followers. One such issue, both historic and in the present, which has galvanized the Brotherhood in this way is Palestine and Israel's occupation. Additionally, the Brotherhood has always been a transnational organization in character, seeking to realize its agenda beyond the borders of Egypt. Almost from the point of the Brotherhood's foundation, its ambassadors established national branches of the movement in countries across the region and later in Europe and beyond. By the twenty-first century, as I explain later in the chapter, these links were enhanced by the Brotherhood's embrace of new technologies such as the Internet and social media to establish a virtual transnational dimension.

The Muslim Brotherhood: The Arab Spring and Its Future Face places the phenomenon of political Islam in an important regional as well as interconnected global context. By looking at examples of its ideas, its leaders, the countries, the organizations, and the trends it is associated with in relation to the Arab Spring, the diversity of this significant religious-political movement will be explored. Finally, the issues generated by the Muslim Brotherhood and rising conflicts and instability with the changing regional order of the Middle East in the wake of the Arab Spring will be assessed. The challenge here is to discover whether the future face of the Muslim Brotherhood bodes ill or well for the political orders emerging from the seismic shake-up of the region that is the Arab Spring.

Notes

1 Dr Mahmoud Zahar, author interview, Gaza City, 27 November 1989.
2 Dr Mahmoud Zahar, author interview, Gaza City, 27 November 1989.
3 Dr Mahmoud Zahar, author interview, Gaza City, 27 November 1989.
4 Dr Mahmoud Zahar, author interview, Gaza City, 9 July 2012.
5 Dr Mahmoud Zahar, author interview, Gaza City, 2 September 2013.
6 S. Shehata, 'The Military vs. the Islamists', *Woodrow Wilson International Center for Scholars*, 4 November 2013, http://www.wilsoncenter.org/islamists/article/the-military-vs-the-islamists (accessed 28 May 2015).
7 See R.P. Mitchell, *The Society of the Muslim Brothers*, Oxford: Oxford University, 1969; B. Lia, *The Society of the Muslim Brothers in Egypt*, Reading: Ithaca Press, 1998; B. Rubin, (ed.), *The Muslim Brotherhood: The Organization and Policies of a Global Islamist Movement*, Basingstoke: Palgrave Macmillan, 2010.
8 See J. Schwedler, *Faith in Moderation: Islamist Parties in Jordan and Yemen*, Cambridge: Cambridge University Press, 2006; A. Pargeter, *The Muslim Brotherhood: The Burden of*

Tradition, London: Saqi Books, 2010; C.R. Wickham, *The Muslim Brotherhood: Evolution of an Islamist Movement*, Princeton: Princeton University Press, 2013; S. Hamid, *Temptations of Power: Islamists and Illiberal Democracy in a New Middle East*, New York: Oxford University Press, 2014; H. Kandil, *Inside the Brotherhood*, Cambridge: Polity Press, 2014.

9 See F. Ajami, 'The End of Pan-Arabism', *Foreign Affairs*, Vol. 57:2, Winter 1978, pp. 355–73, https://www.foreignaffairs.com/articles/yemen/1978-12-01/end-pan-arabism (accessed 31 May 2015); A.E.H. Dessouki (ed.), *Islamic Resurgence in the Arab World*, New York: Praeger, 1982.

10 See J.P. Piscatori, *Islam in a World of Nation States*, Cambridge: Cambridge University Press, 1986; J.L. Esposito (ed.), *Voices of Resurgent Islam*, New York: Oxford University Press, 1983.

11 See C.R. Wickham, *The Muslim Brotherhood: Evolution of an Islamist Movement*, Princeton: Princeton University Press, 2013; A.M. Abou el-Fotouh, 'Democracy Supporters Should Not Fear the Muslim Brotherhood', *Washington Post*, 9 February 2011, http://www.washingtonpost.com/wp-dyn/content/article/2011/02/09/AR2011020905222.html (accessed 28 May 2015); B. Tibi, *The Sharia State: Arab Spring and Democratization*, New York: Routledge, 2013.

12 S. Hamid, 'Tunisia Field Report: The Islamist Balancing Act', *Brookings Institution*, 12 February 2015, http://www.brookings.edu/blogs/markaz/posts/2015/02/12-tunisia-islamists-ennahda-hamid (accessed 31 May 2015).

13 T.L. Friedman, 'Political Islam Without Oil', *New York Times*, 10 January 2012, http://www.nytimes.com/2012/01/11/opinion/friedman-political-islam-without-oil.html?_r=0 (accessed 31 May 2015); B. Milton-Edwards, 'Revolt and Revolution: The Place of Islamism', *Critical Studies in Terrorism*, Vol. 5:2, 2012, pp. 219–36, http://dx.doi.org/10.1080/17539153.2012.686658 (accessed 12 May 2015).

14 See S. Hamid, *Temptations of Power: Islamists and Illiberal Democracy in a New Middle East*, New York: Oxford University Press, 2014.

15 J. Malsin, 'Egyptian Court Sentences Ousted President Morsi to Death', *New York Times*, 16 May 2015, http://www.nytimes.com/2015/05/17/world/middleeast/egyptian-court-sentences-ousted-president-morsi-to-death.html (accessed 31 May 2015).

1
ROOTS AND IDEAS

No one but God knows how many nights we spent reviewing the state of the nation . . . analysing the sickness, and thinking of the possible remedies. So disturbed were we that we reached the point of tears.

Hassan al-Banna[1]

Introduction

The old man sat outside a crudely whitewashed breeze-block dwelling. It was too hot to sit inside the cramped, stuffy one-room shack he called home. Instead, he sat in an alleyway where sewage water ran in open gullies of the refugee camp. His name was Mohammed, and he was the son of Mohammed and father to his own son named Mohammed. In the slowing of the day amidst the blanket of heat, he was reminiscing about an earlier time when his life was shaped and made relevant through his pious commitment to faith and his political attachment to a movement which offered him hope. Mohammed was a refugee. He and his family had fled their Palestinian village in 1948, and more than forty years later he remained stateless while Israel's Jewish citizens had built a new life in his home. As a young teenager, he had been introduced to the ideas and goals of a new movement which, he claimed, offered him hope that one day he would live again in his home, back in his village, and enjoy the security of a passport. That movement was the *Ikhwan al-Muslimeen*, otherwise known in English as the Muslim Brotherhood. 'These men were simple and pious believers who offered me an education and a dream of Palestine restored,' said Abu Mohammed.[2] Joining this movement in the Gaza Strip in the 1950s, he was educated in the principles of Islam as applied by the Muslim Brotherhood. In the ensuing years, the Egyptian authorities that administered Gaza imprisoned him for his affiliation with the movement. 'But even in this time,' he said, 'I kept faith. I kept faith with the pious men who showed me that the path of Islam would bring me freedom.'[3]

The story of the founding of the Muslim Brotherhood is about faith and the impact, individually and collectively, of a pious attachment and its outworking. It commences with the Brotherhood's establishment in Egypt, in 1928 by a twenty-two year old man named Hassan al-Banna. Born in the small village of Mahmoudiya on the Nile Delta in 1906, this 'preacher's son' would be influenced by his faith and his attachments to it to become recognized as a principal inspiration for modern-day Islamism. He grew up in an age of revolution, anti-imperialism, and rising nationalism in Egypt. Al-Banna himself claimed that as a young village boy in 1919 he had joined his compatriots in demonstrations to support the revolutionary movement that swept the country as its nationalist leaders demanded independence from the British.[4]

In this chapter a historical account of the establishment of the Muslim Brotherhood along with identification of leading thinkers within the movement, such as Hassan al-Banna and Sayyid Qutb, will be presented. The Muslim Brotherhood was initially established, as this chapter will highlight, as a religious movement for social affairs and preaching (*dawa*). Yet within the context of colonial Egypt and the rest of the Middle East where native power was subjugated to European political control, the emergent ideas of Islamist intellectuals embodied by the Brotherhood soon developed a politically responsive hue. This political hue addressed itself to the dilemmas of living in Muslim states in the modern age and the challenges of Muslim solidarity over emergent transnational issues such as Palestine. Almost from its inception, the Muslim Brotherhood became a growing force of opposition with a message that garnered appeal across the Middle East. This chapter accounts for and analyses the roots of the movement and the dominant ideas that its major thinkers conceptualized.

Al-Banna and the rise of a reformist Islamist movement

Al-Banna's early life bore much in common with the majority of Egyptians at the turn of the twentieth century. During this period most Egyptians lived in the rural lands of the Nile Delta in villages and hamlets where livelihoods were derived from centuries-old economic and social relations.[5] Historian Albert Hourani called this period one of 'changing ways and thought' where life in the countryside polarized; populations and cities grew; travel, education, and new media opened new intellectual horizons; and Islam both in its elite and mass form would emerge changed.[6] Al-Banna's father, Sheikh Ahmad Abd al-Rahman al-Banna al-Sa'ati, was the village imam (preacher) and its religious scholar. Historians credit al-Banna's father for introducing his son to a life of religious piety, as well as training in religious scholarship and thought.[7] In his early life al-Banna's fortunes were also inextricably tied to that of his father, and hence in 1923 the family departed from the certainties, traditions, and stability of village life in Mahmoudiya and moved to Egypt's bustling, dynamic, and explosively modern capital city Cairo.

14 Roots and ideas

Anyone who visits Cairo for the first time cannot help but be overwhelmed and overawed by this grand and noisily frenzied city. Cairo in the 1920s was a cosmopolitan and exciting place but one that had been reshaped and modernized since 1882 by British rulers. The gains of Egyptian ruler Mohammed Ali (1769–1849) in terms of winning dimensions of self-rule from the Ottoman powers of Istanbul were rolled back under the British colonial project. And although only a year previously Egyptian nationalists had succeeded in winning a pledge from London that it would pull out of Egypt and grant the country independence, there were few who truly believed that the British would relinquish rule so easily.[8] Such qualms were not misplaced, and it became apparent that behind the throne of Egypt's King Fuad the British would continue to dictate. In 1923 there can be little doubt that the teenage al-Banna's first experiences of the city were staggering, overwhelming, and powerful as he and his family were exposed to heady societal and political upheavals. Al-Banna's father soon ensured that his son was enrolled in a religious teacher–training school that was considered modernist in its pedagogic approach. This exposed al-Banna to the intellectual discourse of a new generation of Islamic scholars often described as reformist or modernist.[9] Such scholars advocated new approaches to Islam to allow for processes of interpretation (*ijtihad*) that would permit the faith to be relevant to a modern context. This distinguished them from traditional Muslim scholars who sought to maintain the status quo. Scholars such as John Esposito contend that the reformists in 'attributing the weakness of Muslim society to its stagnation and tendency to blindly follow and cling to past authority' also had 'one ultimate political purpose' as well.[10] The modern Muslim reformists included emergent and leading intellectuals of the time such as Mohammad Abduh, Jamal al-Din al-Afghani, and Rashid Rida. Al-Afghani, for example, was a highly influential reformist Muslim scholar whose ideas and approaches to the role and place of Islam in modern society were considered to also be in opposition to European colonial and imperial projects across the Middle East and Asia.[11] His approach created opportunities for Muslim nationalists and pan-Islamists to increasingly articulate their demands for freedom and independence from foreign usurpation and domination. Al-Afghani articulated a set of ideas that resonated particularly strongly in British colonial Cairo and were disseminated by his acolyte Mohammad Abduh and Abduh's own protégé, Rashid Rida.

Al-Banna's inquiry brought him into the same circles of Rashid Rida and other Cairo-based Muslim modernist ideologues of the time. Rida was a leading light who not only articulated his ideas within the confines of the mosque or particular study groups. Rida's approach was emphasized when he also began to publish a magazine called *Al-Manar* (The Lighthouse), which covered a gamut of issues and concerns that animated the Islamist modernist reformist movement at the time. In *Al-Manar* (which would later be edited by Hassan al-Banna and the Muslim Brotherhood) its many readers could access the nuances of debate shaped by Abduh and Rida's ideas on how Muslims should interpret their condition of social, political, and economic subjugation, as well as more mundane concerns about modern Muslim life. As a 'mouthpiece of Islamic reform', the ideas and articles contained in the magazine sought to validate to a public audience this new approach to making Islam relevant for purposes of adherence and practice, as well as the contemporary social, economic, and political conditions of the time.[12]

When his studies were complete, al-Banna moved to the city of Ismailia on the Suez Canal and took up a teaching post in a primary school. The city was a product of the building of the canal. Although Khedive Ismail the Magnificent founded the city during the construction of the Suez Canal in 1863, the British established a base there following the Battle of Kafr-el-Dawwar in 1882. Hence, the fabricated city must have appeared as inauthentic to this religious young man as the nature of the city's European-inspired architecture. Al-Banna was struck by the contrasts between foreign wealth and Egyptian poverty in Ismailia. He too was concerned that the Egyptian nationalist movement, spearheaded by the nationalist Wafd party, neglected Islam in favour of a secularist approach.[13] Al-Banna established his new society, called the Muslim Brotherhood, as his response. Allied with some six workers who had raised grievances about their status and the yoke of British control over their lives, al-Banna vowed to act, though it was a crowded stage on which the Muslim Brotherhood would be established. Muslim and Islamic societies in Egypt flourished, but this was also an indication of the capacity that existed in Egypt at the time for the kind of message that al-Banna sought to spread. The Muslim Brotherhood quickly gained supporters and members, and al-Banna was able to establish branches across Egypt within a decade (and shortly after, beyond) attracting thousands to his new credo. The message was simple: improving piety and promoting the call of Islam and its manifestation in Egyptian society.

The rise of the Muslim Brotherhood was part of a more general movement of nationalism and modernism that was influencing the Muslim imagination. The Middle East was no longer unified in Islam but increasingly fragmented under postwar and foreign-inspired forms of power and governance. In Turkey the caliphate had been demolished and attempts to revive it in 1926 failed in the face of the nationalist republic being shaped by Kemal Attaturk. European influence appeared to have an impact on Muslim culture across the region and was apparent in powerful measure in the Cairo and Ismailia of al-Banna's age. This impact was tellingly conveyed to an important audience in 1930 by Rashid Rida, who described the Middle East as engulfed in a time

> afflicted by ideological, intellectual, political, Communist and Bolshevik upheavals; in a time that is strained by religious, literary and social chaos; in a time that is threatened by women's revolution, the violation of marital vows, the disintegration of the family and the bonds of kinship . . . [where] nothing remains stable to raise our youths and teach them respect.[14]

This was al-Banna and Rida's rejection of liberal secular ideas which appeared to prevail in the discourse of thinkers such as Taha Hussein and in the Egyptian nationalist movement for independence. Even the redoubt of Muslim tradition, the venerable Islamic university of al-Azhar in Cairo, appeared to give rise to scholars at the time

16 Roots and ideas

who were reflecting a discourse of ideas which appeared to allow for a separation between politics and faith. This was perhaps best epitomized by the publication of Ali Abd al-Raziq's book titled *Islam and the Foundations of Governance* (*al-Islam wa usul al-hukm*).[15] For al-Banna, state and faith were considered inseparable. Hence, the ideas of anti-imperialism, the promise of an authentic Islamic project, and the challenges of nationalism animated the discourse of the Brotherhood.

When al-Banna formed the Muslim Brotherhood in 1928, he reflected some of these developments in modern Egyptian political thought, allowing the new movement to attract members from across the social and class strata. This approach appealed to the new intelligentsia, resonating with their desire to engage in a form of identity politics that accommodated Islam. Al-Banna's chief appeal, however, lay with other classes in Egyptian society reaching out as he did to ordinary workers, as well as the merchant and artisan classes of the city. By 1932 he had relocated back to Egypt's capital and set up a modest headquarters in Cairo. Al-Banna had hoped to create an organization that was religiously rather than purely politically inspired. The task of the Muslim Brotherhood that he envisioned and strove to realize was to recreate a truly Islamic society that publicly reflected the fundamental tenets of the faith. Yet al-Banna would engage in this task by employing techniques that took advantage of the changes that modernization had wrought on Egyptian society. Under his leadership the Brotherhood quickly established itself as a grass-roots, populist, and media-savvy organization that harnessed the public and political openings in Egypt at the time. In securing the Brotherhood structures into society and scaffolding the new organization onto traditional and existing social and religious institutions such as the mosque and through Muslim welfare activities, al-Banna could mix the old with the new and accommodate the growing sense of dislocation that so many Egyptians were experiencing. The scaffolding of Islam by the Muslim Brotherhood presented the movement and its leader with the means by which to address a variety of contemporary issues.

Although not intended to be established as a political party, the Muslim Brotherhood increasingly found itself compelled by its supporters and opponents to address the political realm. To be or not to be in politics was the question that dogged the Islamic reformist movement as a whole, as well as the Muslim Brotherhood, not to mention a question that remains salient even today among many political Islamist groups. There had been many debates among Muslim modernists and reformers at the time with respect to what their political role or function, if any, should be.[16] Some abjured from politics and urged their fellow thinkers and supporters to instead concentrate on more fundamental preoccupations such as inclining local populations back to the faith system itself. In this realm the Brotherhood found itself in distinction not only to secularist nationalist and socialist opponents but also to the elites of institutional Islam. The religious revivalism of al-Banna and his followers was a challenge to traditionalist Muslim scholars and preachers who sought to preserve the status quo. But the status quo was a problem for al-Banna and his supporters, as it presented the Egyptian people with an image of Islam in decline and increasingly eclipsed from public life by the kinds of secular and licentious

Roots and ideas **17**

practices associated with the West. Islam on the margins was the antithesis of al-Banna's connection to his faith. He lamented the erosion of Muslim principles and warned of the rising tide of Western-inspired ideals and ideologies. Such ideologies, principally secularism among them, were perceived by al-Banna and successive Brotherhood ideologues as a corrosive danger to the influence of Islam and its values. Secularism threatened to relegate Islam to the realm of the private while al-Banna instead sought to encourage Islamic resurgence in all aspects of life, and especially in the public realm. He tied the corrosive impacts of imperialism and secularism together, considering them both to be 'anathema to the true spirit of Islam'.[17] If the individual and the wider Muslim community (*ummah*) were core to al-Banna's project, the principles of *shari'a* law were the means by which the project could be realized. Egypt governed according to Islamic law would, al-Banna contended, provide an authentic alternative to a state governed according to the rules and mores of a foreign occupying power: the British.[18]

As the Muslim Brotherhood grew and flourished, these social and religious ideas soon began to have a substantive political impact. Within a decade of its founding, the Brotherhood had no less than 300 branches across Egypt with as many as 150,000 new members joining the movement and committing themselves to the Islamic resurgence and revivalist project. Though other thinkers, leaders, and ideologues would later attempt to prevail or would actually succeed in prevailing as leaders or principal ideologues of the movement, al-Banna himself was pivotal in determining the nature of the movement and its growing acclaim kudos. As Abu Rabi quotes, al-Banna

> was the Brotherhood in the early stages of its development. He gave his Brethren (Ikhwan) their group characteristics as well as their program; he inspired them with his ardour and sincerity; and his magnetic personality attracted an ever-swelling stream of adherents to his movement. Until within a few months of the end of his life, Hassan al-Banna kept the power in his own hands and personally directed the program and the policies of his organization.[19]

In part, this can be accounted for by the extent to which al-Banna himself epitomized the delicate balance within Egypt's Muslim society at the time between traditional Sufi identity and rootedness, and a contemporary grasp of the quotidian travails of common people that the Muslim Brotherhood could address through its burgeoning welfare, education, and social support.[20] Furthermore, if the influence of al-Banna and his supporters was to grow further and impact the very governing structures of the state, it was impossible for them to ignore Egypt's political environment at the time. Indeed by the late 1930s al-Banna was prepared to publicly identify the Muslim Brotherhood as a political organization. At the group's fifth conference, where the movement celebrated its tenth anniversary, the assembled Brotherhood delegates set out to outline the 'foundations of the ideology of the Society and the substance of its appeal', thus marking a key event in the development of the organization. Accordingly, al-Banna defined the Muslim Brotherhood

18 Roots and ideas

as 'a Salafiyya message, a Sunni way, a Sufi truth, a political organization, an athletic group, and cultural-educational union, an economic company, and a social idea'.[21]

The Brotherhood reflected the public mood and offered a comprehensive approach and solution to the myriad of pressures that the Egyptian people were experiencing at the time. Hence, local nationalists, who were responding to growing antiforeign and in particular anti-British tendencies, the pervasive socioeconomic uncertainty and intermittent crisis that affected the country during this period and the rising regional instability as a result of Zionist ambitions in Palestine, were being met on the same ground by a new challenger who offered an alternative. Al-Banna sought to present the Muslim Brotherhood as a national movement based on the same brotherly ties and emergent solidarities that characterized so many other Arab nationalist groups at the time. To this end, the Zionist settlement of Palestine and ambitions for statehood in a land of important Muslim holy places resonated widely with Arab audiences which the Brotherhood addressed. As the leader of a national movement, al-Banna claimed that his aim was to

> educate young people and mould the souls of the nation around the principle that ensures the good of the public, peace and working for the betterment of all people. This had all the excellence which internationalism had; and it also secures our self respect in adhering to it and defending it in addition to defending our countries and our sacred things. This had all the benefits of nationalism.[22]

New fronts: Politics, Palestine, and militant units

In respect of Zionist ambitions in Palestine, the Muslim Brotherhood was alert to the challenges faced by the Palestinians and created a role for itself in the burgeoning political crisis. By the mid-1940s the Muslim Brotherhood had established branches in Palestine and engaged in aspects of political activism back in Cairo to raise awareness around the issue.[23] El-Awaisi, a scholar of the Muslim Brotherhood, ascribes both religious and 'nationalist and political' factors in accounting for al-Banna's adherence to the Palestinian issue throughout the period of the Brotherhood's founding until the establishment of the state of Israel.[24] Indeed the political crisis in Palestine, involving as it did the British, Zionists, and opposing local Palestinian forces, provided al-Banna's movement with 'the first occasion for active involvement, beyond propaganda, in matters "political"'.[25] Indeed from 1938 to 1948, the political dimension of the Brotherhood's activities would assume even greater domestic and regional (specifically in Palestine) dimensions leading al-Banna down the path of his own demise.

There is evidence that by engaging in the political upheavals of the time, the Muslim Brotherhood developed some of the most important political ideas which

Roots and ideas **19**

would later underpin the movement. Under al-Banna's leadership there were initial overtures to governing authorities and power holders in Egypt, the echoes of which would long reverberate through the annals of the movement's history to the present day. But such overtures proved problematic as power holders perceived the new organization to be an incipient and growing threat. Indeed it was becoming clear that the new movement was developing into a strong and increasingly oppositional force for the governing authorities to contend with. In 1941 the authorities in Cairo moved against al-Banna, and the following year the Wafdist government shuttered branch offices of the movement. The Muslim Brotherhood, it would seem, was to be both feared and embraced by other political actors, which was apparent in unfolding relations with Egypt's nationalists and ambitious military leaders.[26] While other oppositional elements existed, there were a number of features which distinguished al-Banna's movement from these other groups, including its claim to Islamic credentials, as well as an increasing mass or populist national base of up to half a million members.[27] Hence, throughout the 1940s, Muslim Brotherhood leaders and supporters emerged in the public arena. They began promoting their ideas in media and propaganda campaigns and organizing rallies, demonstrations, and sit-ins, as well as agitating against the governing authorities locally and nationally to alter their policies and devise new approaches to the pressing political issues of the day.

Such overt political activities were not envisaged as part of al-Banna's original mandate, and a challenge quickly arose in terms of whether this society of Muslim brothers that he had founded should in fact simply emerge as a political party among many others at the time in Egypt. Al-Banna, however, always resisted such a move and feared this route would limit the wider religious and Islamic ambitions that he nurtured. This was a tension which would endure to the present day with opposing voices in the movement debating the facilitation of al-Banna's goals through the political route. Al-Banna's goal was not parliament or a place in government alone. For him, the Muslim Brotherhood could accommodate or reject such a role or function since its project was much larger than simply political representation. Over half a century later, however, in June 2012 this vision was not echoed or adhered to by the present-day leaders of the Muslim Brotherhood in Egypt who were elected to lead the country after President Hosni Mubarak had been ousted in the January 2011 revolution. In his victory speech in Tahrir Square in Cairo, President Mohammed Morsi of the Muslim Brotherhood instead declared:

> I pledge to God and I pledge to you – I swear by Almighty God to uphold the Republican system; to respect the Constitution and law; to look after the interests of the people fully; and to safeguard the stability and territorial integrity of the homeland.
>
> I pledge to God and I pledge to you, the honourable people of Egypt, to fulfil my promises. I pledge to work with you in order to bolster our unity

20 Roots and ideas

and our strength. I stress my rejection of any attempt to blackmail the people power.

I confirm that I, as president of the Egyptian people, after the legal formal proceedings which I respect, will endeavour to overcome all obstacles. I reiterate my rejection of any attempt to wrest the power of the people, because I am the decision-maker – with your will.[28]

In this respect, al-Banna promoted a comprehensive vision of what his movement could and should achieve in the name of Islam but one that was not bounded by the nature of the state in Egypt – republican, monarchical, or otherwise. Changing politics would not be enough for the kind of Muslim emancipation that he envisaged, and in this respect, al-Banna emphasized the totality of the kind of project that he was promoting. Islam was envisaged as a 'total system, complete unto itself, and final arbiter of life in all its categories', based on the Koran and Sunna and 'applicable to all time and to all places'.[29] Hence, by default the political entered the remit of al-Banna's conception of Islam, but how to engage with the political and the role or function of formal political participation would continue to test the leadership of the organization at the time.

By the late 1940s the Palestine issue would prove to be the testing ground once again for the kind of politics that would become possible for the Muslim Brotherhood. This engagement though would be characterized by secrecy and thus, as perceived by some, a form of insurrectionary politics that would lead to the organization being seen as a potent threat to the authority of the state. Indeed by the 1940s al-Banna had approved the formation of a secret armed wing of the movement known as the Secret Apparatus (*al-Jihaz al-Sirri*). Hence, although the Brotherhood undertook and engaged in a major propaganda effort to support the Palestinian issue and prevent Zionist encroachment in the region, it would be the existence of the Secret Apparatus or paramilitary unit of the Brotherhood for the cause of a jihad that would compel its opponents to declare it a menace that should never be accommodated or approved by the Egyptian state.[30] Even if the declared cause of Palestine was seen as a noble one at home, the Brotherhood's opponents believed that the real intention of the secret wing would be to mount a coup against the government of the day.[31]

The violent intent of the Brotherhood was, many believed, now exposed, and the iterations of al-Banna's ideology that had stressed the gradualist reformist route to change were greeted with increasing suspicion and scepticism. Al-Banna, unlike some of his contemporaries, was not known to promote violence, and yet he presided over a movement in which jihad was advocated. The Brotherhood's formation of the secret armed wing was combined with the message of '*militancy and martyrdom*', which was

elevated to the central virtues in the Society's ethos. Its literatures and speeches were permeated with references identifying it and its purposes in military terms. Al-Banna told members again and again and again that they were 'the army of liberation, carrying on your shoulders the message of liberation; you are the battalions of salvation for this nation afflicted by calamity'. They were the 'troops of God' whose 'armament' was their 'Islamic morality'.[32]

In 2013, following the ouster of Muslim Brotherhood President Mohammed Morsi, the same language permeated the Muslim Brotherhood in Egypt in its confrontations with the military-governed state. 'The struggle to overthrow this illegitimate regime is an obligation, an Islamic, national, moral, and human obligation which we will not steer away from until justice and freedom prevail, and until repression is conquered,' declared the Muslim Brotherhood as it called on its supporters to participate in a 'Day of Rage'.[33]

Al-Banna had also created an important precedent in the movement with the creation of an element called the Rover Troops. El-Awaisi argues that in order to avoid early detection, the unit was formed as a cover for al-Banna's jihadist and military ambitions, but in fact the Rovers were a Brotherhood protection unit created to defend the organization from external threats and enemies.[34] They attracted thousands of members and caught the attention of the governing authorities.[35] The Rover Troops illustrated al-Banna's articulation of the defensive character of Islam and jihad, and the usual ambiguity that he displayed in relation to violence was dissipated. Defensive jihad, and thus violence, was permissible if Muslims were defending their lands in the name of Islam or against the usurpation of a foreign non-Muslim power. The existence of the Rovers and the Secret Apparatus intimated violence and force by the Brotherhood that would overshadow, and continue to do so to the present day, the nonviolent political and social reformist ambitions of the majority attracted to al-Banna's programme and goals. Reconciling such contrasting positions under the same banner of Islam would remain a provocative challenge for al-Banna in both thought and deed.

The cadres of the Secret Apparatus, however, led al-Banna's movement into inevitable confrontation with the state, culminating in the assassination of Egyptian Prime Minister al-Nuqrashi on 28 December 1948 at the hands of a young member of the Muslim Brotherhood. As violence against the state and instability had grown throughout the country in the preceding period, the government had sought to blame the Muslim Brotherhood and outlaw it. Al-Nuqrashi's successor, Ibrahim Abdel Hadi, refused to consider any conciliatory overtures from al-Banna himself as relations deteriorated in the wake of al-Nuqrashi's death. Less than two months after the prime minister's killing, al-Banna himself was gunned down on a Cairo street in a tit-for-tat killing generally considered to be sanctioned by the state. If the state had thought that killing the Brotherhood's sole leader and arresting and imprisoning many thousands of his followers would deal a fatal blow to the movement itself, they were mistaken. Although it took time for the Brotherhood to recover, under its new leader Hassan al-Hudaybi, the task undertaken by al-Banna in 1928 would continue.

Al-Banna's legacy is subject to wide and often contested interpretation, but in terms of his impact and that of the movement he founded, there is agreement among supporters and critics. The consensus rests in the importance of the founding of the Muslim Brotherhood in respect of Islamic modernism, revivalism, fundamentalism, and political Islam. The Muslim Brotherhood, even in al-Banna's lifetime, grew to encompass broad ambitions for the Islamist project in the twentieth century that would endure in the twenty-first. In 2006, when members of the Muslim Brotherhood marked the centenary of al-Banna's birth back in his home village of Mahmoudiya, it was acknowledged that the movement had changed in many respects from its founder's aspirations but that its desire for power remained undiminished. At the gathering, Supreme Guide Mohammed Akef declared, 'When the conditions are ripe, if the people are convinced, then power will be ours.'[36]

After al-Banna: Crackdown, Qutbism, and the Brotherhood's new normal

Al-Banna's successor, Hassan al-Hudaybi, faced a momentous task when he undertook to lead the organization in 1951. He would have to steer the two decade old movement away from politics and violence at a time when Egypt and the wider Middle East was characterized by instability and violent political change. This was the era of national revolt throughout the region, when the certainties of established British colonial power in particular had been tested and found weak and wanting. In neighbouring Palestine, the British had quit their mandate in April 1948 after the UN had voted to recognize the plan to partition the country, thus awarding the Zionists a state in November 1947. In Egypt the political turmoil epitomized by the assassinations of al-Nuqrashi and al-Banna was not quelled by the electoral victory of the Wafd party in the 1950 election. Negotiations with the British to achieve Egyptian independence broke down, the Anglo-Egyptian treaty of 1936 was unilaterally abrogated, and the British refused to accept their declining influence in the face of Egyptian demands. Amidst this Egyptian-inspired turmoil, the Muslim Brotherhood could play a role in localized agitation and attacks against the British, particularly in the Suez Canal zone so vital to British strategic interests.[37]

Though al-Hudaybi wanted to distance the movement from its growing violent reputation and armed cadres, he would, in turn, by supporting the abrogation of the Anglo-British treaty and pledging to enjoin armed struggle and jihad, be compelled to rely on such elements again. Thus, although the Rovers were all but disbanded as violence broke out against the British, the ranks of the attackers and agitators were swelled by some hundreds of members of the Secret Apparatus from the Muslim Brotherhood. By becoming brothers in arms with army officers and other nationalists who seized power in the revolution of July 1952, the leadership of the Brotherhood could have been forgiven for thinking that their role in rebutting British power on behalf of the Egyptian people would make them friends of the Free Officer faction. The Free Officers were led by the populist leadership epitomized by Gamal Abdel Nasser, who became president of Egypt in 1956. But such assumptions would prove to be overly optimistic. With the Free Officers now in power, there was a honeymoon in relations, but it was short and not sweet.

Roots and ideas **23**

There had been prominent figures in the Free Officer Movement who had previously associated with or even been close to the Muslim Brotherhood including the future presidents Nasser and Sadat. Additionally, some of the Free Officers had actually been involved with the Brotherhood and the Secret Apparatus.[38] The Brotherhood had hoped that under the new nationalist dispensation Islam would be elevated in terms of power and governance. Nasser was initially responsive, offering the Brotherhood positions in his government and appearing to be inclusive. Yet many suspicions lingered on both sides with respect to the intent of the other, and Nasser, like his predecessors, grew to regard the contribution, critique, and stands of the Brotherhood as a growing threat to his power and vision for Egypt at home and abroad. In January 1954 matters took a turn for the worse when the Free Officers government issued a proclamation banning membership in the Muslim Brotherhood. The populist military regime considered the Brotherhood a significant internal threat, and a major crackdown on the movement soon confirmed this as thousands of Brotherhood members and supporters were jailed. This would be the first of many occasions when a military regime in charge in Cairo would resort to mass arrests to quell the power and influence of the Brotherhood.[39] In October 1954 al-Hudaybi himself was arrested, and in retaliation an activist from the Muslim Brotherhood attempted to assassinate Gamal Abdel Nasser during a visit to his hometown of Alexandria. As bullets were fired at him, and those sitting on the public stage with him sought cover, Nasser defiantly spoke out, 'Let them kill Nasser. What is Nasser but one among many? My fellow countrymen, stay where you are. I am not dead, I am alive, and even if I die all of you is Gamal Abd al-Nasser.'[40]

In the aftermath of the assassination attempt and as Nasser's monopoly on power in Egypt and regional ambition grew, it became apparent that there would be little political space for the Muslim Brotherhood to occupy. The clampdown that followed would be fundamental in all but destroying the movement in its initial manifestation, in radicalizing and driving underground particular elements and ideologues; in inspiring narratives of opposition, transnationalism, and martyrdom; and in embedding hostility to secularism and nationalism which would affect the movement for many decades to come. Nearly sixty years later, in an eerie repetition of history, the military regime of Supreme Council of the Armed Forces led by General Abdel Fattah al-Sisi would engage in wide-scale repression of the movement designed to all but destroy it as it presided over government and politics in Egypt. Thousands of followers were targeted by the regime in a series of purges throughout the late 1950s and early 1960s in which the Islamists and other opponents such as leftists and communists languished in the same jails and often in the same cells. Among their number was an ideologue of the Muslim Brotherhood named Sayyid Qutb.

Qutb, sometimes referred to as the 'father of al-Qaeda', has come to be considered a leading radical Islamist ideologue influencing not only sections of the Muslim Brotherhood but also other radical Sunni jihadi movements through to the present day. Qutb, like al-Banna, called for a return to Islam but also implied that Muslims should urgently seek power through jihad to realize this project. In 1966,

24 Roots and ideas

after spending more than a decade in prison, Qutb was sentenced to death after the Egyptian courts charged and tried him with plotting to overthrow Nasser. Qutb had been a prolific writer throughout the turbulent decades before his death. He had also spent time in the West, in America, and experienced at a personal level a sense of profound disconnect with Western culture, values, and politics in relation to his view of what Islam had to offer. This Qutbian discourse recognized that true Islamic values had been lost under Western domination, establishing a form of society that was meaningless and pre-pagan in stance (*jahilli*). Qutb demanded that Muslims return to their faith, its practice, and its values and then change society through jihad. In terms of politics, Qutb was perceived as dangerously advocating for a form or forms of revolution rather than reform of the prevailing political system. He did not see how a system so dominated and acculturated to the values of the West and secularism could be reformed enough to return it to an authentic Islamic state. Despite having been a member of the Revolutionary Command Council set up in 1952, Qutb refused the blandishments of the Nasserist regime and, in doing so, unknowingly doomed himself to his 'martyr' death.

Additionally, the regime then set about dismantling the Brotherhood's substantial organizational structure, which had been created over the previous decades. Mitchell refers to this as a process of 'dissolution', 'paralysis and breakdown of the formal structure of the organization'.[41] The organization, by this point, was hierarchical in structure, and this model for the Muslim Brotherhood would endure and be replicated by branches of the movement elsewhere in the Middle East region. At the pinnacle of the organization was the Supreme Guide (*murshid al-'amm*), and beneath him, the Consultative Assembly (*majlis al-shura*) and a Guidance Council (*maktab al-irshad*). The structure presented opportunities for forms of internal organizational competition through elections for positions at the top of the organizational order. Broadening out from the pinnacle of the hierarchy, the Brotherhood structure evolved to include administrative branches and offices at regional and local levels based on the principle that the local branch is composed of a 'family'. The family is made up of no more than ten locally based people who meet regularly. The purpose of the family is primarily one in which the dissemination and indoctrination of the Brotherhood occurs. Every member of the Muslim Brotherhood is supposed to be in regular attendance of a family meeting. The family is not part of the organizational structure but instead is amalgamated as district level into a 'branch'. Branch membership numbers are restricted to no more than one hundred. Branch members then elect from among their number members to serve on the consultative committee. The consultative committee members are responsible for electing a smaller branch administrative committee to run the branch and manage it. The branch will run a number of activities focussed on work in the mosque, preaching, Koran recitation groups, and youth work and may also link to social and welfare support. This organizational structure is replicated right up through the Muslim Brotherhood at both the regional and national level. At the highest level of the organization, the Administrative Office's Consultative Council elects around one hundred members to the General Consultative Council. This council then elects

Roots and ideas **25**

and advises the Guidance Bureau, which in turn elects the Supreme Guide of the Muslim Brotherhood.

It was not just within Egypt's border that the clampdown and attempted destruction of the Brotherhood had its impact. In addition to the targeting of the Muslim Brotherhood in Egypt, the Nasserist government also organized a crackdown on its branches in the Egyptian-controlled Palestinian territory of the Gaza Strip, and in Syria several years later the Brotherhood would experience similar regime-inspired purges. In addition to being driven underground, the remnants of the movement were also radicalized and influenced by the Qutbian narrative. Qutb was considered by many within the Brotherhood as somewhat of an outlier. He was not simply content to echo and ape al-Banna's reformist and largely nonviolent approach to the Islamic project but was considered as introducing a sense of profound tension and radical challenge to the prevailing order. Qutb's seminal work of 1964, *Milestones (Ma'alim fi al-Tariq)*, was perceived as a thinly veiled critique of the Nasserist project in Egypt and a radical call to arms.[42] He argued that the sovereignty of the people should not be permitted to override the sovereignty of Allah (*hakmiyya*) and that in such circumstances God is abandoned and rule is apostate in nature.[43] In contrast to al-Banna's focus on reform and the return of the masses to Islam, Qutb also contended that a vanguard could lead the radical change required to overthrow apostate and *jahilli* regimes if it would secure the Islamic state project and the proper foundation of Islamic law and rule (*shari'a*).[44]

This divergence was an anathema to those who adhered to the founding vision and ideals of al-Banna, particularly as it related to notions of Muslim rule and endurance. Qutb's disturbance of the vision and ideal of al-Banna necessitated a response from his Islamist heirs and in particular the Supreme Guide of the movement, al-Hudaybi. He reacted by countering many of Qutb's fundamental assertions about sovereignty, the nature of society, and Muslim rule in relation to their applicability to Egypt at the time. Al-Hudaybi also cautioned against radical reactions and restated the modernist reformist mantras outlined by the late lamented al-Banna.[45] This included a recognition of the political reality and the political structures and nature of the Egyptian state, and its parliamentary system. In so doing, he rejected Qutb's tense, proto-violent, revolutionary, and radical doctrines in favour of an acceptance of the modern acculturated state. This was the same state that under Nasser would persecute the leadership of the Brotherhood through exile, imprisonment, and execution.[46] This difference of discourse would also highlight a schism within the Muslim Brotherhood and the wider movement of contemporary Islamism that it spawned that remains evident to the present day.

Al-Hudaybi's position reflected to a far greater extent the reality that the Muslim Brotherhood was forced to contend with in the wake of events as they had unfolded in Egypt in the late 1940s through Qutb's own death at the hands of the state in 1966. This was a reality where the aspirations of the movement would have to be scaled back to the social reformist project of calling the people back to Islam rather than through mounting a vanguard to strike at and overthrow the state. The goal for the Brotherhood would have to be confined to working to transform a

26 Roots and ideas

generation of Egyptians to Islam from a societal base rather than top down from an Islamist-controlled state. This elided with al-Banna's position: transform through education, through preaching, through social and welfare support, and through the evolution of the Brotherhood to encompass all aspects of life, including eventually the political. There was an acute realization that in the political arena the Brotherhood was not yet strong enough to go up against the dominant array of nationalist forces. It was not alone in this respect, but this was of little comfort at the time. The Brotherhood under al-Hudaybi had to eschew violence and distance itself from elements under its auspices that espoused it and radical jihadi militancy if it were to survive the tumult of the time. Nevertheless, the militaristic regime of Nasser still targeted the Brotherhood with its own forms of violent suppression treating it as inimical to the state project of building a modern national independent Egypt that could lead the Arab world. Indeed members of the Brotherhood who reflect on this period contend that they had no choice but to remain outside the political arena, the state arena, and the competition for power that was unfolding in order to protect and ultimately maintain their Muslim project. They turned their misfortune into an opportunity to build an organization from the margins, among those often on the margins of the national project themselves or bereft of much-vaunted and promised state support. Al-Hudaybi could envision a society governed by a system of parliament, and elections for a government freely chosen by the people.[47] In this way the Brotherhood could content itself in opposition and, when opportunity arose, enter a contest for power freely. Remaining in opposition was a way of providing natural cover during the period of Nasser's fierce repression of the movement. The leadership came to understand that they would always be perceived by those in power as an inherent threat. The Islamic project of the Brotherhood was not a goal to be easily shared by king, prime minister, or president alike.

In Nasser's Egypt, the Brotherhood became a marginal force. Likewise in Jordan, Palestine, and Syria, the fortunes of the Brotherhood plummeted throughout the 1950s and 1960s. In Syria, the Brotherhood, which had established loosely affiliated branches with the Egyptian movement in the late 1940s, had been seen as a rising political force until the short-lived United Arab Republic union with Egypt in 1958 when Nasser demanded that the group in Syria be dismantled. In 1963, after the union with Egypt had collapsed, the Ba'athist government that had gained power through a coup continued to ban the Brotherhood and identify it as hostile to its pan-Arab secular nationalist objectives. In Jordan, the Brotherhood, formed in 1942, survived the turbulence of the nationalist wave that swept the region in the 1950s, as discussed in Chapter 4. Even when in 1957 King Hussein proscribed all political parties in his kingdom, the Brotherhood was allowed to continue its activities. This was partially as a way for the regime to counterbalance leftist political movements. Nevertheless, the price for survival in Jordan was the maintenance of loyalty even in opposition to its monarch King Hussein.[48] The Brotherhood, however, remained under the constant and watchful eye of the kingdom's intelligence services, its potential for disturbance to the Hashemite project always understood. In Palestine, both in the Jordanian-governed West Bank and Egyptian-administered

Gaza Strip, the Brotherhood almost dissipated to the point of evaporation, as the next chapter documents. Its members, supporters, and former leaders who survived the war of 1948 and the Egyptian crackdown went into exile in the Gulf states or stayed but did not engage outwardly in major political activism. In Gaza, those that survived the Nasserist purges of the late 1950s and 1960s, such as the young Ahmed Yassin, returned to their homes and maintained a low profile for fear of further attack and persecution.[49] Their deliverance would come. But in a form that none had anticipated.

A new vitality: The Muslim Brotherhood after the 1967 war

The Six Day War of 1967 in which the Arab forces, including Nasser's Egypt, intended to defeat Israel and liberate the Palestinians turned out to be a watershed in the fortunes of the Muslim Brotherhood.[50] The Arab defeat was also a personal one for Nasser; the promises of victory he had made to Egyptians and the entire Arab world for years now rang hollow. The Israeli victory over Egypt, Syria, and Jordan was perceived as symbolic of the enduring strength and power of the West over the Arab East. The promises of Arab secular nationalist leaders proved worthless. Palestinians had not been liberated in the war of 1967. In fact, their plight had worsened now that Israel occupied the territories of the West Bank and Gaza Strip, as well as East Jerusalem, where the third most holy site in Islam – the al-Aqsa mosque and Dome of the Rock – was located. Syria had lost the Golan Heights to Israel's occupation and Egypt the Sinai territory. Nasser's offer to resign in front of the popular crowds of Cairo was a form of face-saving from which he never truly politically recovered.

Equally as important as Nasser's undoing, the defeat of the Arabs was seen across the Muslim world as a catalyst for the reexamination of the ideology and associated ideals and promises inherent to the Arab secular, socialist, and nationalist project. As Haddad notes, while the war of 1967 was not responsible for creating 'Islamist ideology' of the type most significantly associated with the Muslim Brotherhood, Islamists concluded that the war was 'punishment for misplaced trust in the promise of alien ideologies that had been fostered as a means of mobilizing for modernization and development'.[51] Indeed some would date the 'new vitality' of Islamism from this period as it appeared to offer an alternative solution to the quest for political currency and legitimacy in the Middle East.[52] There was a form of revival apparent in the raised banners and symbols of Islam, especially those that would soon be hoisted by the Muslim Brotherhood. But the revival would be localized, uneven, and not uniform in character. In Egypt the turning point in the fortunes of the Brotherhood came in the wake of Nasser's death in 1970. Amidst the genuine outpouring of grief of the tens of thousands of mourners who gathered in Cairo to attend Nasser's funeral, there would have been few if any from the Brotherhood among their number. Nasser's successor, Anwar Sadat, would become dependent on the legitimating symbols of Islam to secure his power, strengthening the Islamists

28 Roots and ideas

along the way as he battled political foes among the powerful leftist secularist factions of a now increasingly unstable Egyptian state.

Anwar Sadat, the 'Believer' president, would promote the Brotherhood, along with other Islamists, as a countervailing element against other political forces that he deemed a threat to his power. This form of state-sanctioned Muslim revivalism was premised on Sadat's belief that he could successfully neutralize the Brotherhood by co-optation. He sanctioned the return of Islam to the public realm, and naturally the Brotherhood was part of this process. Gradually members of the Brotherhood were released from their jail cells and permitted to undertake public organization. However, there were limits to Sadat's rapprochement, as he would not legalize the movement again or permit it to rebuild its organizational structure. Their freedom may have been won, but there were many in the Brotherhood and wider Islamist spectrum who found it difficult or impossible to expunge the memory of torture, the humiliation at the hands of the Egyptian authorities, or the martyrdom of others, including leaders like al-Banna and Qutb. They were simply unwilling to pledge their fealty to the Egyptian state presided over by Sadat.

Throughout the 1970s, as Sadat took his country to war again against Israel and then embarked on a diplomatic route that would deliver the country to the United States and a peace treaty with Israel, the Brotherhood maintained a distanced stance from the political machinations of the state. In 1973, while under house arrest, al-Hudaybi died. Four years later his text *Du'at la Qudat* (Preachers not judges), considered a form of response and critique to Qutb's *Milestones*, was published. Zollner contends, however, that Qutb was not the main subject of the text but rather that it was a response to the radical tendency of the movement that he had sought to contain in the late 1950s and 1960s.[53] Al-Hudaybi's reference to *dawa* over jihad continued to officially characterize the Brotherhood even under his successor, leader Umar al-Tilmisani. Behind closed doors, however, it was evident that there were ongoing tensions between those in the organization who gravitated towards Qutb's message of jihadism and radicalism and those that preferred the gradualist *dawa* approach that the movement's leader had expounded. This would be an enduring tension that would characterize the internal dynamic of the Muslim Brotherhood for many decades to come and was evident in its reactions and responses to the Arab Spring when it broke out in Egypt in 2011.

The radical and vanguard potential of Islamism inspired by Qutb but ultimately disavowed by the Brotherhood, however, was apparent in the emergence of the jihadi movements in Egypt in the 1970s and 1980s. These elements were prepared to effect a radical and, if necessary, violent challenge to power holding under Sadat's rule. As political and societal tensions grew, and opposition to Sadat's economic and political policies mounted, those radicals that declared the 'pious president' in a state of ignorance and as an infidel ruler inflamed the situation. In 1981 these radicals struck at the heart of power, assassinating President Sadat and agitating widely among student groups and others in Egyptian society.[54] The Brotherhood had to weather the storm wrought by Sadat's successor, President Hosni Mubarak. Quietly, and while adhering to its apolitical principle of preaching, the movement slowly rebuilt itself through assiduous social and welfare support work, activities, and links to student movements on university campuses.[55]

Al-Hudaybi's successor, al-Tilmisani, was perceived as a powerless figurehead of the Brotherhood, reflecting socially conservative, apolitical, and avowedly nonviolent ends. Yet at the broader base of the movement, as it linked with students who argued for jihad, a new sense of energy and direction became apparent, particularly in the wake of the revolution in Iran in 1979 and the resurgence more generally of Islamic political discourse and activism. As Supreme Guide, al-Tilmisani had to fend off such powerful currents from within his own movement, as well as help the movement survive any backlash mounted by Egyptian authorities. The governing regime under Mubarak made the rules of political play simple: mount a political challenge through the party system or keep quiet. As a result, the Brotherhood began to contest elections. In alliance with other political parties, it variously contested and then boycotted elections in the 1980s and 1990s. This was a precarious route, in some respects, leaving the leadership vulnerable to accusations from hardliners or those sympathetic to the radical current that it was bolstering the legitimacy of the Mubarak regime.

Al-Tilmisani died in 1986 and was soon replaced by Hamed Abu Nasser, who in turn was controversially succeeded a decade later by Mustafa Mashour. Mashour was considered contentious not just because of the way in which he was positioned to power by key individuals such as al-Hudaybi but also because of his more radical-leaning tendencies and association with jihadi elements. For example, Mashour's own views on jihad resonated, at points, with the tension and urgency of the radicals within the Brotherhood and the wider radical Islamist tendency in the region. In his book, *Jihad Is the Way* (*Bayna al-qiyadah wa-al-jundiyah ala tariq al-dawah*), Mashour repeatedly emphasizes the importance of jihad as a solution for 'youth', as a means to liberate those 'subject to oppression or control by Allah's enemies'.[56] Struggle, jihad, and the acceptance of martyrdom for the sake of Allah and the *dawa* of Islam is core to the appeal that Mashour makes, citing past and present sacrifices and examples from across the Middle East. Nevertheless, Mashour was very much viewed as a member of the 'Old Guard' of the Brotherhood rather than the new, reformist generation. These elements challenged the Old Guard when, with little by way of consultation with the leadership, they attempted to form the al-Wasat (Centre) political party.[57] Al-Wasat, as a centrist Islamist party, marked a form of separation from the Muslim Brotherhood and its presiding Old Guard.

Future face

Such fissures became a defining feature of the Brotherhood, and despite the axiomatic view of outsiders of the hegemonic qualities of Islamism, and in particular the Muslim Brotherhood, the reality evident throughout the history of the movement is starkly different. The general ideas and inspiration behind the movement and its founders have always served as a useful banner to which the movement in its various manifestations can rally. The elaboration of 'Islam is the solution', however,

30 Roots and ideas

evinces complex dynamics and ideas expressed within the movement. Additionally, the leaders of the Muslim Brotherhood have always had to contend with the perception by ruling regimes and other actors that it is a menacing, all-encompassing, and inherently violent threat. It is signified as permanently disabling the movement in terms of its interactions with political systems across the Middle East and beyond. There were always various currents and strands of thought apparent in the discourse and activities of the Brotherhood. This was reflected in those strands of the movement that believed in the political insertion of the movement. There also have always been elements of the Brotherhood that contend that the state in relation to Islamizing agendas could or should be altered from within, that the goal of establishing a polity determined by the implementation of *shari'a* law was possible by this route.

It was the Islamizing agenda that would sustain the movement as it developed into a multinational phenomenon and as a crucial spring of opposition to the state in the Middle East, as well as the Western influences of secularism. The Muslim Brotherhood continued to develop its ideas whether it was forced to work under forms of constitutional limit against them as religious-based political parties, as criminalized 'terroristic' elements, or as 'tolerated' ideas so long as its opposition remained loyal to the regime. But the Muslim Brotherhood did also inspire or give rise to militant and violent offshoots or jihadist organizations which promoted jihad through terrorism. Other Muslim Brotherhood groups, such as Hamas, which arose in the Palestinian Territories in the late 1980s, also employed violence defining itself as resistance against Israel's occupation.

Al-Banna's legacy to the Muslim Brotherhood was to define its promotion of Islam as all-encompassing. This was a blessing with respect to its broad and wide appeal. Al-Banna had declared,

> We believe the provision of Islam and its teachings are all inclusive, encompassing the affairs of the people in this world and the hereafter. And those who think that these teachings are concerning only with the spiritual or ritualistic aspects are mistaken in this believe because Islam is a faith and a ritual, a nation and a nationality, a religion and a state, spirit and deed, holy text and sword. . . .The Glorious Quran . . . considers [these things] to be the core of Islam and its essence.[58]

But it was a curse in relation to the challenge it then presented to the emerging nation state in the Middle East. The Muslim Brotherhood was on a crash course with the Arab nationalist ideologues of the age because the movement argued that only a genuine Islamic state could emerge across the region through overcoming Western-inspired secularism and its outworking in the post-independent age. In particular this was evident in the conflict that emerged as an enduring dynamic between the Muslim Brotherhood and the state almost from the point of its inception to the present day. In turn, this means that the Brotherhood can only be understood from a historical perspective of its oppression by the state and challenge and enmity from other actors. Furthermore, the ideas of major figures associated with the Brotherhood such as Sayyid Qutb endured to cast a shadow over the movement and leave it struggling to secure an identity for itself where the constant disavowal of violence was demanded of them. Even after the events of July and August 2013, when the pall of death hung over al-Nahda and Rabaa al-Adawiya Squares after raids mounted by Egyptian security forces killed hundreds of Muslim Brotherhood supporters, the movement was still denounced and considered synonymous with terrorist violence. Here the legend and historical narrative of the Brotherhood as always oppressed and fated to occupy a place in opposition, not power, was reinforced in the full glare of the world's media. This, as the key current throughout the history of the Brotherhood and almost all of its branches across the Arab world, has surely shaped its outlook. Whether in Yemen, Jordan, Tunisia, Egypt, Syria, Lebanon, the UK, or elsewhere, the ambitions of the Brotherhood for power, to be at the centre of the political, have been circumscribed time and time again by patterns of resistance to contain them, suppress them, and make sure they remain on the margins of the opposition.

Notes

1 Hassan al-Banna, as quoted in R.P. Mitchell, *The Society of the Muslim Brothers*, Oxford: Oxford University Press, 1969, p. 5.
2 Abu Mohammed, author interview, Nusseirat refugee camp, Gaza Strip, 6 September 1993.
3 Abu Mohammed, author interview, Nusseirat refugee camp, Gaza Strip, 6 September 1993.
4 P. Vatikiotis, *The History of Modern Egypt from Muhammad Ali to Mubarak*, London: Weidenfeld, 1991, p. 266.
5 A. Hourani, *A History of the Arab Peoples*, London: Faber and Faber, 1991, pp. 333–48.
6 A. Hourani, *A History of the Arab Peoples*, London: Faber and Faber, 1991, p. 333.
7 R.P. Mitchell, *The Society of the Muslim Brothers*, Oxford: Oxford University Press, 1969.
8 D. Hopwood, *Egypt 1945–1990: Politics and Society*, 3rd ed., London and New York: Routledge, 1991.
9 See B. Milton-Edwards, *Islamic Fundamentalism since 1945*, 2nd ed., Abingdon: Routledge, 2014; J.L. Esposito, *Islam: The Straight Path*, New York: Oxford University Press, 1988.
10 J.L. Esposito, *Islam and Politics*, 3rd ed., Syracuse, NY: Syracuse University Press, 1991, pp. 48–9.
11 See H. Enayat, *Modern Islamic Political Thought*, London: I.B. Tauris, 2005.
12 K. Yasushi, 'Al-Manar Revisited, the "Lighthouse" of the Islamic Revival', in S.A. Dudoignon, K. Hisao and K. Yasushi (eds), *Intellectuals in the Modern Islamic World, Transmission, Transformation and Communication*, Abingdon, Oxon: Routledge, 2006; M. Kerr, *Islamic Reform: The Political and Legal Theories of Muhammed 'Abduh and Rashid Rida*, Berkeley and Los Angeles: University of California Press, 1966.
13 See A.A. Ramadan, 'Fundamentalist Influence in Egypt: The Strategies of the Muslim Brotherhood and the Takfir Groups', in M.E. Marty and R.S. Appleby (eds), *Fundamentalisms*

32 Roots and ideas

and the State, Remarking Polities, Economies and Militance, Chicago: University of Chicago Press, 1993.

14 M.R. Rida, M.R. 'Renewal, Renewing and Renewers', in C. Kurzman (ed.), *Modernist Islam, 1840–1940: A Sourcebook*, New York: Oxford University Press, 2002, http://home.zcu.cz/~dkrizek/SBV1/Texty%202/Rida-Renewal_renewing_and_renewers.pdf (accessed 7 May 2015), p. 78.

15 H. Enayat, *Modern Islamic Political Thought*, London: I.B. Tauris, 2005.

16 See Z. Munson, 'Islamic Mobilization: Social Movement Theory and the Egyptian Muslim Brotherhood', *Sociological Quarterly*, Vol. 42:4, Fall 2001, pp. 487–510, http://www.jstor.org/stable/4121130 (accessed 14 May 2015).

17 I. Abu-Rabi, *Intellectual Origins of Islamic Resurgence in the Modern Arab World*, Albany: State University of New York Press, 1996, p. 70.

18 M. Zahid, *The Muslim Brotherhood and Egypt's Succession Crisis: The Politics of Liberalisation and Reform in the Middle East*, London: I.B. Tauris, 2010, pp. 70ff.

19 I. Abu-Rabi, *Intellectual Origins of Islamic Resurgence in the Modern Arab World*, Albany: State University of New York Press, 1996, p. 63.

20 M. Zahid, *The Muslim Brotherhood and Egypt's Succession Crisis: The Politics of Liberalisation and Reform in the Middle East*, London: I.B. Tauris, 2010, p. 73.

21 R.P. Mitchell, *The Society of the Muslim Brothers*, Oxford: Oxford University Press, 1969, p. 14.

22 Hassan al-Banna, as quoted in A. El-Awaisi, *The Muslim Brothers and the Palestine Question, 1928–47*, London: I.B. Tauris, 1998, p. 5.

23 B. Milton-Edwards, *Islamic Politics in Palestine*, London: I.B. Tauris, 1996, p. 33.

24 A. El-Awaisi, *The Muslim Brothers and the Palestine Question, 1928–47*, London: I.B. Tauris, 1998, p. 2.

25 R.P. Mitchell, *The Society of the Muslim Brothers*, Oxford: Oxford University Press, 1969, p. 15.

26 R.P. Mitchell, *The Society of the Muslim Brothers*, Oxford: Oxford University Press, 1969, pp. 19–30.

27 J. Calvert, *Islamism: A Documentary and Reference Guide*, Westport: Greenwood, 2008, p. 24.

28 M. Morsi, 'President Mohamed Morsi's Speech in Tahrir Square', *IkhwanWeb*, 29 June 2012, http://www.ikhwanweb.com/article.php?id=30153 (accessed 3 March 2014).

29 R.P. Mitchell, *The Society of the Muslim Brothers*, Oxford: Oxford University Press, 1969, p. 14.

30 A. El-Awaisi, *The Muslim Brothers and the Palestine Question, 1928–47*, London: I.B. Tauris, 1998, p. 113.

31 A. El-Awaisi, *The Muslim Brothers and the Palestine Question, 1928–47*, London: I.B. Tauris, 1998, p. 113.

32 R.P. Mitchell, *The Society of the Muslim Brothers*, Oxford: Oxford University Press, 1969, p. 206–7.

33 IkhwanWeb, 'Statement: Friday of Rage', *IkhwanWeb*, 16 August 2013, http://www.ikhwanweb.com/article.php?id=31245 (accessed 19 December 2014).

34 A. El-Awaisi, *The Muslim Brothers and the Palestine Question, 1928–47*, London: I.B. Tauris, 1998, p. 106.

35 R.P. Mitchell, *The Society of the Muslim Brothers*, Oxford: Oxford University Press, 1969, p. 203–4.

36 Mohammed Akef, as quoted in Agence France-Presse, 'Hassan Al-Banna, Founding Father of Egypt's Muslim Brotherhood', *IkhwanWeb*, 14 October 2006, http://www.ikhwanweb.com/article.php?id=3272 (accessed 28 February 2014).

37 E. Rogan, *The Arabs: A History*, London: Penguin, 2011, p. 352.

38 L. Wright, *Thirteen Days in September: Carter, Begin, and Sadat at Camp David*, New York: Knopf, 2014, pp. 195–4.

Roots and ideas **33**

39 See Times, 'Many Arrests in Egypt', *Times*, 14 January 1954, p. 8; H. Tomlinson, 'Islamist Leaders Arrested as Egypt's Army Tightens Grip', *Times*, 5 July 2013, pp. 26–7.

40 M. Heikal, *The Cairo Documents*, New York: Doubleday, 1973, p. 25.

41 R.P. Mitchell, *The Society of the Muslim Brothers*, Oxford: Oxford University Press, 1969, p. 159.

42 G. Kepel, *The Roots of Radical Islam*, London: Saqi Books, 2005.

43 See N. Ayubi, *Political Islam: Religion and Politics in the Arab World*, London: Routledge, 2003, pp. 107–8.

44 J. Calvert, *Sayyid Qutb and the Origins of Radical Islamism*, New York: Oxford University Press, 2009, p. 14.

45 G. Kepel, *Muslim Extremism in Egypt: The Prophet and the Pharaoh*, London: Saqi Books, 1985, p. 62.

46 B. Zollner, 'Prison Talk: The Muslim Brotherhood's Internal Struggle during Gamal Abdel Nasser's Persecution, 1954–1971', *International Journal of Middle East Studies*, Vol. 39:3, August 2007, pp. 411–33, http://dx.doi.org/10.1017/S0020743807070535 (accessed 13 May 2015).

47 R.P. Mitchell, *The Society of the Muslim Brothers*, Oxford: Oxford University Press, 1969, p. 247.

48 B. Milton-Edwards, 'Temporary Alliances: The Islamic Response in Jordan', in J. Piscatori, (ed.), *Islamic Fundamentalisms and the Gulf Crisis*, Chicago: University of Chicago Press, 1991.

49 B. Milton-Edwards, *Islamic Politics in Palestine*, London: I.B. Tauris, 1996, pp. 54–5.

50 B. Milton-Edwards, *Islamic Politics in Palestine*, London: I.B. Tauris, 1996, p. 73.

51 Y. Haddad, 'Islamists and the "Problem of Israel": The 1967 Awakening', *Middle East Journal*, Vol. 46:2, Spring 1992, p. 267, http://www.jstor.org/stable/4328433 (accessed 13 May 2015).

52 See F. Ajami, 'The End of Pan-Arabism', *Foreign Affairs*, Vol. 57:2, Winter 1978, pp. 355–73, https://www.foreignaffairs.com/articles/yemen/1978-12-01/end-pan-arabism (accessed 31 May 2015); A.E.H. Dessouki (ed.), *Islamic Resurgence in the Arab World*, New York: Praeger, 1982.

53 B. Zollner, *The Muslim Brotherhood: Hasan al-Hudaybi and Ideology*, London and New York: Routledge, 2009, p. 149.

54 G. Kepel, *Muslim Extremism in Egypt: The Prophet and the Pharaoh*, London: Saqi Books, 1985, pp. 210–13.

55 B. Rutherford, 'Explaining the Ideological Change in Egypt's Muslim Brotherhood during the Mubarak Regime', in S. Arjomand and N. Brown (eds), *The Rule of Law, Islam, and Constitutional Politics in Egypt and Iran*, Albany, NY: State University of New York Press, 2013.

56 M. Mashour, *Bayna al-qiyadah wa-al-jundiyah ala tariq al-dawah (Min fiqh al-dawah)* [Jihad is the way (from the laws of Da'wa)], Cairo: Dar al-Tawziah wal-Nashr al-Islamia, 1995.

57 V. Durac, *Islamic Modernism in Contemporary Egypt: An Evaluation*, PhD thesis, Queen's University Belfast, 2000; D. Shehata, *Islamists and Secularists in Egypt: Opposition, Conflict & Cooperation*, London and New York: Routledge, 2009, p. 59.

58 M. Moaddel, *Islamic Modernism, Nationalism, and Fundamentalism: Episode and Discourse*, Chicago: University of Chicago Press, 2005, p. 97.

2

EGYPT – PHOENIX

In the 1960s, they [the government] were trying to destroy us. . . . They wanted to rid Egyptian society of such a movement. . . . Now, that is impossible. There are more roots than anyone can completely pull out from the streets.

Mohammed Morsi[1]

Introduction

Populist, Muslim, broad based, and historically well organized, the Muslim Brotherhood in Egypt was a force to be reckoned with on the eve of Mubarak's downfall in 2011. The Muslim Brotherhood had few serious rivals, or so they thought, among Egypt's opposition elements. Their leadership believed that they were on a trajectory of power that was divinely inspired to return this Arab state to forms of governance and politics imprinted by Islam. Its leaders believed that they were so firmly rooted into Egyptian society that they were synonymous with the citizens who had grown weary to the point of rebellion against President Mubarak's authoritarian order. This led many to conclude that the Muslim Brotherhood was better positioned than any other political grouping in the Arab world to take advantage of the tumult of political change that would erupt in the wake of the Arab Spring.[2]

As the 'opposition' or opponents of the regime in Egypt, the Muslim Brotherhood had, however, also endured many decades of fierce repression and challenge from the ruling political elite. The organizational breadth of the Brotherhood, drawing as it had historically done on a variety of individuals with competing and dynamic ideological positions on Islamism as a political and social project, also created internal tensions and an outward appearance of ambiguity on certain issues. Thus, while many were concluding that the time had come for the Muslim Brotherhood to reap the political rewards for its enduring patience, few predicted how quickly and brutally the movement would again suffer repression at the mercy of more powerful elites embedded for decades within the Egyptian state. Nor did the Brotherhood and its allies predict the scale of opposition that would rain down on it as part of the new repertoire of protest performance that the Arab Spring had unleashed in Egypt. Nevertheless, as Egypt's President Hosni Mubarak was forced from power by the Egyptian army in February 2011, there was an emerging consensus that the Arab Spring presented unprecedented opportunities for the Muslim Brotherhood in Egypt to steer the country to a new era. The Brotherhood was rapidly empowered by the revolution, but this empowerment would prove to be short-lived.

This chapter begins with the tumultuous events of January 2011 and the subsequent parliamentary electoral victory of the Muslim Brotherhood, alongside Islamist competitors such as the new Salafi and Sufi parties, in the wake of the Mubarak regime. It charts the perilous path that the movement attempted to navigate as it assumed parliamentary power in a country in transition not only from Mubarak's tyranny but also from the absolutist domination of the Egyptian military over core institutions and industries of the state. This was a military overturning its 'accepted subordinate role' in Mubarak's presidential system, which had formerly been considered to 'safeguard its interests'.[3] The chapter will then examine the role of the Muslim Brotherhood as it sought to access power and government in Egypt during a tumultuous period of transition in the country. The chapter will also examine the ways in which the Muslim Brotherhood sought to mobilize its own leadership and cadres towards this momentous national goal. With electoral success came major challenges in terms of governance and the economy, which the Muslim Brotherhood seemed to struggle with and fail at, putting it on a crash course with sections of Egypt's politically emancipated population and the nationalist-military complex at the heart of the transitional order in the post-Mubarak era. It did this at a time when every move it made was amplified by social and other media negatively to highlight the dominance of the Muslim Brotherhood in the Egyptian context as a transnationalized concern across the rest of the Middle East region and in the West. Finally the chapter will assess the trajectory of the Muslim Brotherhood in the post-Morsi era as it has attempted to negotiate its own survival. I will assess the Brotherhood and its future prospects as it continues to navigate its new role in Egypt.

Dawn

As the new year of 2011 dawned on the Muslim Brotherhood in Egypt, the movement faced a daunting political landscape. Parliamentary elections months earlier had been so effectively rigged by President Mubarak that the Brotherhood was on the back foot and reeling from the loss. Despite initially contesting elections, the opposition movement felt compelled to withdraw its candidates from the second-round run-off in December 2010 when the extent to which the state was manipulating the outcome became apparent to all opposition elements.[4] Prior to the election, Mohammed Badie, the General Guide of the Brotherhood since 2009, had initially declared that 'the only way to achieve peaceful change is through the ballot box,' only to be forced into a humiliating climb down weeks later.[5] Many others in the leadership of the Muslim Brotherhood still languished in jail or exile, aware of the hostility of the regime to their powerful and long-standing opposition movement. The marginalization of the movement was all the more apparent in the wake of a terrorist bombing attack on Egyptian worshippers attending a midnight mass on New Year's Eve at the al-Qiddissin Church in the Sidi Bechr district of Alexandria. Speaking to the press, Egyptian President Hosni Mubarak urged Muslims and Christians to unite but pointed the finger at Islamist militants for perpetrating the attack. Leaders of the Muslim Brotherhood publicly condemned the attack, but hours later when Muslims clashed with Christians, it appeared such calls had fallen on deaf ears.

Certainly when protest broke out in Tunisia, Egypt's Brotherhood paid attention. Brotherhood activists used social media to address commentary on the Jasmine Revolution, the fall of President Ben Ali, and the resurgence of Islam. The Brotherhood, like their counterparts in other social movements, such as Kefaya, had already established and used dedicated social media to mobilize their supporters and disseminate their views on Facebook, Twitter, and YouTube.[6] Yet when protest broke out across Egypt, the Brotherhood were not the instigators of events. Following Ben Ali's ouster in Tunisia, on 25 January 2011 huge public protests and occupations of public spaces broke out in Egypt. The government soon mobilized its resources in an attempt to shut down the protest. Not only did they deploy their security forces to the streets and squares where masses had gathered, but they also tried to shut down Internet, cell phone, and other social media services to stop the rebellious ferment that was spreading like wildfire across the country. President Mubarak appeared to be responsive to some demands when he sacked his government and appointed a new vice president, but as the protest grew in scale and demands, Mubarak grew intransigent, refusing to step down from power, and prepared to ferment violence against the crowds of protesting citizens. Within the month, however, Egyptians of all classes, political perspectives, and faiths succeeded in playing their part in forcing President Mubarak from power on 11 February 2011.

Carrie Wickham, author of *The Muslim Brotherhood: Evolution of an Islamist Movement*, contends that there were two reasons why the unfolding events would prove so significant.[7] The first was the scale of public mobilization in Egypt against Mubarak and the speed at which, in part thanks to social media, the notion of protest and the demands for change spread throughout the country. This left the regime ill-equipped to suppress protest because of its sheer size and makeup, and it resorted to desperate measures such as disconnecting the country from the Internet to try and break the protests up.[8] The second reason was that the demands of the protestors soon mushroomed from complaints about police brutality to include broader issues of government reform as it related to public security, the economy, and emergency legislation limiting human rights to regime change. Here was a protest that was propelled into a people's rebellion against an autocratic president and his family entourage but was effectively expedited by the intervention of the Egyptian military that would soon step in to form the intervening governing authority.

Throughout much of these initial events, the Brotherhood was on the sidelines. Certainly when on 25 January 2011 tens of thousands of Egyptians gathered into Tahrir Square to protest and initiate a call to end Mubarak's tyranny, the movement was formally absent.[9] In the quickly gathering momentum of protest and revolt that was breaking out across Egypt, the leadership of the Brotherhood was reluctant to insert themselves on the side of the people. At a time when the fears and hesitations of Egyptians to oppose and confront the regime were finally broken, the Brotherhood remained behind rather than in step. Cautious and uncertain about the way in which the situation would unfold in Egypt, the Brotherhood leadership appeared to prevaricate. Despite the events in Tunisia where President Ben Ali had been overthrown and the Islamists had rapidly emerged from the shadow of repression to embrace the democratic transition, the Egyptian Brotherhood dithered. Decades of severe repression had certainly constrained the Brotherhood's ambition to lead mass revolt against Mubarak. Its leadership was more than aware of the regime's ability to strike back and painfully so, as it had done in earlier eras against the Brotherhood. Survival, not confrontation, was the name of the game, and the Brotherhood was more than prepared to wait for the tide of history to turn in their favour.

Hence, the rapid turn of events in January and February 2011 caught the Brotherhood somewhat unexpectedly. Unlike many other groups or opposition interests at the time, the Muslim Brotherhood did not set up camp in Tahrir Square or direct protest as it began to break out across Egypt. This is not to say that there were not tensions within the movement over the direction in which to go. On an individual basis many younger members of the Brotherhood decided to join and support the protest movement. They were prepared to throw their lot in with the growing swell of the populous defiant against the president and his security forces. The calculation of the Brotherhood's leadership did begin to change when it attempted to mediate the demands of the protestors with the regime, but this gave the regime an opportunity again to point the finger of blame at the Brotherhood.

The dynamic pace of events unfolding in Egypt and the role played by social and political forces and factors such as the labour movement, social media, the young, and women was a challenge for the Muslim Brotherhood. The Brotherhood is a large, cumbersome, and slowly evolving movement where decisions are taken on the principle of consensus and on an agenda of widespread social reform and political change within, not outside, the Egyptian system dominated for so many decades by Mubarak and his predecessors Sadat and Nasser. Egyptian society, however, in January 2011, was forcing a rapid pace of change and revolution, the likes of which had never been witnessed before in contemporary Egyptian history. Mass mobilization was not unusual, the people of Egypt and especially in vast cities like Cairo could be orchestrated to rally in support of the state, but the mobilization of 2011 was simply unprecedented. The Muslim Brotherhood had historically claimed the Egyptian people to their ideological goals and agendas in an all-embracing contemporary Islamist agenda, but it was reluctant to champion such a *political* revolution.

38 Egypt – Phoenix

They were cautious that the winds of change blowing through Egypt in early 2011 would, like the hot summer *khamsin* (wind), blow themselves out all too quickly. It was thus natural that the movement would hesitate as events spiralled out of Mubarak's control, for it knew all too well that with the apparent gain of political opportunity came the risk of significant cost to the wider social and Islamic ambitions of the movement.

This caution was all too apparent as the protest erupted in January 2011 and Egyptians amassed at Tahrir Square, yet the Brotherhood initially stood to one side as it attempted to assess the portent of the situation. Nevertheless, its rank and file began to join the throngs in the square, later forcing it to commit to the revolution in the making on 28 January. The leadership of the Brotherhood meanwhile tried to insert itself in the gamble for political survival being played by Mubarak. Politically it attempted to assert itself in ways it was best suited to – seeing the prospect of an electoral contest for power as its best choice. The group's rank and file, mostly young men and women, were not novices when it came to grass-roots mobilization and stood shoulder to shoulder with other elements of civil society and human rights groups. For them, this was a moment to both live and realize a dream:

> 'You felt you were in utopia,' said Dr. Umaima Kamel . . . [a] member of the MB. She and hundreds of other women went to Tahrir Square every day. The number of overtly religious Egyptians grew each day too. 'On Tuesday, February the 1st, I met Sheikh Emad Effat in the square,' recalled Najah Nadi, a student at the religious al-Azhar university. 'I asked him about our class at al-Azhar and he said, "The lesson is right here."'[10]

The Brotherhood knew how to mobilize the people. This was something that it had experience with, and it also marshalled its social media networks to the protest calls and demands echoing through the cities, towns, and villages of the country.[11] This experience stood the movement in good stead as it worked with counterparts in the secular opposition to better organize the mobilization at Tahrir Square. The Shabab al-Ikhwan (Youth of the Brotherhood) also worked quickly, assiduously, and eventually persuasively to convince the older leadership of the Brotherhood's Guidance Bureau to let them be publicly recognisable as a distinct grouping in Tahrir Square – the generational divide within the movement was palpable.[12] The older generation of the leadership in the Guidance Bureau remained at once removed from the events on the ground, and it was hoped, this would partly inure them if things did not go their way. The *shabab* (youth) of the Brotherhood and their relationship with the leadership at this critical juncture in Egyptian politics was similar to that of the PLO in 1987 and the Palestinian *shabab* who organized and led the first Intifada through the Unified National Leadership of the Uprising. Religious as opposed to secular, the *shabab* of the Brotherhood would find themselves, like their Palestinian youth counterparts, marginalized by their mother movement in the weeks and months after the revolution subsided and power under a new political dispensation was established. As Shahin highlights, 'According to many accounts, the role that the youth of the Muslim Brotherhood played during the first days of the revolution and the early confrontations with the regime's security forces was crucial in saving the revolution.'[13]

As the tide of protest grew and pressure from the Shabab al-Ikhwan of the Brotherhood swelled from within, it became apparent to the leadership that the time for prevarication and studied neutrality would soon come to an end. As Wickham highlights,

> The Brotherhood apparently reached the conclusion that its own fate hung in the balance, knowing that it would be the first target of the regime's wrath if the uprising failed. As one leader put it, 'Our only card is the mobilization in Tahrir Square. It has been our life insurance against the swing of the pendulum if the regime gets back on its feet.' . . . The Brotherhood abandoned its earlier caution and ordered its members into the streets.[14]

It should have come as no surprise that it was the youth of the Brotherhood that ultimately determined its place and prominence in the revolution and the emerging political order. The movement's youth played a decisive role on Friday 28 January, as they joined activists to form 'the crucial front lines of protesters who broke security cordons and later faced attacks from pro-Mubarak loyalists'.[15] The *shabab* played a significant part in also averting the threat of violence emanating from the protestors themselves or the infiltration of agent provocateurs. They, along with other secular civic activists, ensured that the Egyptian revolution would not be marked by the violence of protest.[16] The positions taken by the Muslim Brotherhood during this period reflected an internal divide. On the streets and among the crowds of protestors, Brotherhood *shabab* played a fundamental part in protecting and defending against state thugs (*balatnajajeh*) and other forces when they attempted to disrupt the protests. Meanwhile, the leadership once again appeared to prevaricate when the regime, in an increasingly desperate bid to remain in charge, appeared to offer them, along with other opposition elements, a place at the table of governance.[17]

Additionally, throughout the revolution, as Egyptian scholar Emad Shahin, who in May 2015 was sentenced to death in absentia by al-Sisi's courts,[18] noted,

> The Brotherhood adopted a conciliatory and pragmatic position. It agreed to not raise any of its religious slogans and gave assurances that after Mubarak's ousting, it would not field a candidate nor would it run for more than 35 percent of the seats of the parliament.[19]

Within ten days of protests and occupation of Tahrir square by the Egyptian people, Mubarak had been toppled from power and the Brotherhood had played a role in events with powerful repercussions across the region. As Noueihed and Warren contend,

> Egypt's status had no doubt declined, but its location at the very heart of the region . . . meant that ripples of upheaval in Cairo would be felt on the streets

on Damascus, Benghazi or Sanaa. If Egypt had changed, the whole Arab world had changed. In Bahrain, Libya, and Yemen, opposition activists took heart and began to plan their own revolutions. If Egyptians had overthrown their pharaoh through people power, then so could they.[20]

In the wake of the revolution, however, the Brotherhood was keen to acknowledge that it had not led the revolution but had merely played its part according to its place in the wider Muslim constituency of the country. Such a position was apparent in the statements of Brotherhood leaders such as Essam el-Erian when he reaffirmed 'it was groups of brave, sincere Egyptians who initiated this moment of historical opportunity on Jan. 25, and the Muslim Brotherhood is committed to joining the national effort toward reform and progress.'[21] The Brotherhood was determined to advertise their part in the Arab Spring as motivated by patriotic duty to the nation and the Egyptian people and not simply as a crude power grab. As Brotherhood leader Abdel Moneim Abou el-Fotouh declared,

> Like Egyptians from all walks of life, we in the Muslim Brotherhood are taking part in the popular uprising to depose a repressive dictator. . . . We seek to share in the debate sweeping the country and to be part of the resolution, which we hope will culminate in a democratic form of government. Egyptians want freedom from tyranny, a democratic process and an all-inclusive dialogue to determine our national goals and our future, free of foreign intervention.[22]

They were not alone in this respect. The Supreme Council of the Armed Forces (SCAF), who took control after Mubarak was ousted in February 2011, ensured that its pronouncements and decisions were in the name of the nation, highlighting the role that it too had played in Mubarak's fall from power. When the Egyptian military sided with the protestors and refused to deploy its weapons against them, its role became as decisive as that of the Brotherhood in determining the way ahead.[23] This attempt by both the Brotherhood and the military to speak on behalf of the Egyptian people would inevitably lead to confrontation. The Brotherhood's desire to market its role in the revolution as part of the patriotic groundswell which swept the country was also about attempting to minimize backlash and to open the way forward for it politically to accede to power.[24] Not everyone in the Brotherhood favoured taking a political approach because in the past this had led to episodes of severe repression from the state. Nevertheless, it was unreasonable to expect that the largest opposition movement in the country would disavow democracy and elections for a quietist approach at this turning point in Egypt's political system. Furthermore, even those who had previously taken apolitical positions, such as the Salafists and the Sufis, used the new dispensation to organize political parties to contest elections in a bid for power in the name of Islam.[25]

The promise of democracy, a new constitutional era of governance, and free and fair elections was seductive to the Brotherhood. It was so seductive that previous caution and earlier promises were thrown to the wind. The Brotherhood believed that the powerful political dynamic unleashed by the Arab Spring in Egypt was its opportunity to emerge as a dominant political force in the new political order. It decided to stand candidates in more than 50 per cent of the electoral districts of Egypt for the legislative assembly. It also went for the most powerful political post in Egypt – the presidency. This was the ultimate challenge for the movement and one that it became convinced would be delivered to it through contest at the ballot box. By attempting to gain control during this period of transition, the leadership of the Brotherhood believed that the Islamist project would be expedited and made integral to the new Egyptian political order. But what the Brotherhood was not prepared for was how to safely navigate and share power with a variety of powerful forces in the post-Mubarak era.

Path to power: Participate, not dominate

Mubarak's fall from power was the perfect opportunity for those elements of the Muslim Brotherhood who prized politics over piety. While it was widely acknowledged that the revolution in Egypt was not an Islamic one, there was unease in some quarters and hope in others that Islamists, and principally the Muslim Brotherhood, could benefit from the democratic and constitutional opportunities ahead. This was the moment for the Muslim Brotherhood to move from opposition to power and to play a part in or even lead the attempts to refashion Egypt's political system. SCAF, like the Free Officers of 1952 when they led the coup against the monarchy and eventually installed Gamal Abdel Nasser as head of the Egyptian republic, appeared to be inclusive of popular sentiment by allowing the Brotherhood a place in the emergent transitional dispensation. The Brotherhood was permitted to register as a political party; powerful figures associated with or leading the Muslim Brotherhood, including eminent preacher scholar Yusuf al-Qaradawi, were allowed to return from exile; and Brotherhood leaders were appointed to the constitutional reform committee.[26]

The members of the Old Guard of the movement were nevertheless cautious of their many opponents both internally and externally. Internally the *Shabab al-Ikhwan* wing of the movement began to discover that their inputs were marginalized and ignored, leading to a weakening of internal cohesion and defections. Factions within the Brotherhood, including the youth, began to call for internal restructuring of decision making and authority. Brotherhood youth refused to acquiesce to traditional spheres of power within the movement as their role in the 25 January protests had emboldened and empowered them to raise their voice and make demands within the organization as well. They were worried about being sidelined and concerned that this growing disenchantment with the Brotherhood leadership would lead young followers to defect. Such fears were confirmed when later in the spring a number of key youth activists and figures were reported to have left or been expelled from the movement.[27] The leadership, however, was largely deaf to such appeals at the time, and it would be several years before the root-and-branch

42 Egypt – Phoenix

reform demanded by the *shabab* would come to fruition and their voice within the movement be heard.[28]

In the early weeks after Mubarak stepped down and SCAF took control of the transition, the Brotherhood's General Guide Mohammed Badie made public appearances where he assured audiences that the Muslim Brotherhood wanted to 'participate not dominate' the transition to a new political dispensation in the country. Within such statements were further reassurances that the Brotherhood wanted to 'advance the interests of the nation as a whole' and that its ambition was for a 'civil state based on Islamic references'.[29] Such assurances had to be balanced, as the Brotherhood's critics did, against the acceleration by the Brotherhood in the wake of the revolution to establish its new political party and its emergent positions as constitutional crafting got underway.[30] This was the case particularly around the referendum and Article 2's incorporation of Islam (*shari'a*) as the primary source of legislation.[31] The focus on the Brotherhood's role in a civic rather than Islamic dispensation was again emphasized as work got underway to establish the Freedom and Justice Party (FJP), which drew in many thousands of members, hundreds of branches, and activities across the country. Veteran Brotherhood leader and FJP Secretary General Mohammed Saad al-Katatni assured his audiences that the FJP was 'not a religious party but a civil party, rejecting a religious country government by Imams' and stated that the FJP desired 'modern democracy'.[32] The appearance of civic inclusion was bolstered when it was announced that Christians and women would be part of the FJP.

In many respects the incipient FJP resembled the approach of Hamas in the Palestinian Territories when it formed the Change and Reform Party to contest the legislative elections of January 2006 and the Jordanian Brotherhood's formation of the Islamic Action Front (IAF) in the early 1990s in its quest for parliamentary representation. Hamas leaders were all too aware of the parallels, pointing out the pitfalls and perils of contesting free and fair elections in a region where other forces within society would be externally supported against any form of Islamist challenge. Another parallel that was also apparent between the FJP and the IAF was the desire to present their agenda in a wider pan-Islamist framework, though eventually both failed to do so and became just a reflection of the narrower interests of the Muslim Brotherhood in their respective countries. Nevertheless, it was clear that the Egyptian Brotherhood hoped to use the FJP as the vehicle to obtain political power while retaining the wider organizational structure of the Brotherhood as separate and distinct from the new institutions of the FJP. Although membership of other political parties was forbidden, for the Muslim Brotherhood the movement itself would always trump political party. In many respects this was evident in the attempts by the leadership throughout 2011 to steer the movement into openings afforded by the Arab Spring not just politically but in others ways as well, including increased activism in the social and welfare sphere and by using media companies including broadcasting to engage in accelerated *dawa*.

The generation of a post-Mubarak discourse that would delineate the Brotherhood from other Islamist political rivals such as the al-Wasat (Centre) party and the new Salafi al-Nour party was also proving a challenge to the Brotherhood.[33] The ambiguities in which the movement could stay comfortably engaged with while in opposition were now challenged by the discourses of the Brotherhood's opponents and the demand of its youth cadre to invoke clearer positions on the place of *shari'a* in the emergent political dispensation, the challenge of pluralism, and the concept of democracy, freedoms, and human rights. Many scholars noted that to be successful, the Brotherhood would need to 'transform its approach from thinking as an opposition movement to that of a ruling party'.[34] The Brotherhood also went into coalition with other political rivals including the nationalist Wafd party to formalize their assurance, when it came to the constitutional referendum of 2011, that its ambition was to participate in, not dominate, the scripting of a new constitutional framework for the country.[35] Hence, it eschewed alliance with its Islamist brothers in al-Nour, opting for other apparently more political pluralist coalitions.[36] The emergent Democratic Alliance, of which the Brotherhood was a member, attempted to achieve consensus but time and time again fell afoul of tensions and schisms over the role afforded to Islam within the constitutional framework.[37] Salafists meanwhile used such tensions to lobby publicly for a more prominent role for Islam and *shari'a* in constitution making. As Wickham points out,

> The growing assertiveness of Salafi groups placed the Brotherhood in an awkward position. On the one hand, the Brotherhood and the Salafis were part of the same broad ideological current. . . . On the other hand, identifying too closely with the Salafi movement would undermine the credibility of the Brotherhood's democratic commitments and threaten the fragile cross-partisan alliances it had forged with secular groups.[38]

Election is the solution

When the polls for the legislative elections eventually took place in November 2011–January 2012, it was nevertheless inevitable that the Muslim Brotherhood would do well. Irrespective of the difficulties of forming alliances with other political actors or groupings, or the challenge of creating a new constitution when it came to whether the electorate would give them a mandate, the Brotherhood could be confident. Reversing earlier indications and assurances that it would not seek to 'dominate', the Brotherhood fielded candidates in many more than the 50 per cent of the constituencies that it had promised.[39]

The election was the freest and fairest since independence in 1952, and the results would deliver victory to a party that could then control the precarious Democratic Alliance and succour to the wider movement of the Muslim Brotherhood globally. The Democratic Alliance, dominated by the FJP, and the Salafi al-Nour party emerged as the major victors winning 44.9 per cent and 25 per cent of the seats in parliament, respectively. The FJP had come to dominate the Democratic Alliance because it was better organized and fielded so many candidates, being allocated

44 Egypt – Phoenix

70 per cent of the Alliance's seats and 90 per cent of the independent candidates' seats as well. Additionally, many of the original parties in the alliance dropped out, giving the Brotherhood a bigger presence within the Alliance.[40] The promise of victory was irresistible to the leadership, and the potentialities of power were important to the movement not just nationally but regionally and internationally as well.

Once in parliament the Brotherhood then used its proportional weight within the Democratic Alliance and in competition with al-Nour to manoeuvre and secure key positions within this state institution. As a result the newly elected speaker was the FJP secretary general and Brotherhood leader Mohammed Saad al-Katatni. Between the FJP and al-Nour, the Islamists soon came to control the majority of the parliament's legislative committees and set their sights on the constitutional assembly as well. It was not all plain sailing, though. Disquiet at the rapid projection of power by the Muslim Brotherhood led opponents to thwart it in other ways, principally with respect to government formation, as Hamas's opponents had done in 2006 following its legislative victory at the polls.

While in principle SCAF had eschewed the 'political' in terms of attempting to govern the transition through parliament, it was not above using its considerable power to block the Brotherhood in other ways. Specifically, SCAF set about taking away key parliamentary powers from the Brotherhood in order to delimit it. The Brotherhood thus set its sights on the presidency, despite its earlier disavowal, as a way of overcoming the obstacle of SCAF and other opponents. As Wickham highlights, 'Some of the group's top leaders apparently concluded that the Brotherhood had no choice but to run a candidate of its own.'[41] Mahmoud Hussein, secretary general of the Brotherhood, summed up his movement's position:

> We will not demand handover of power to the People's Assembly Speaker, because there is a path approved by referendum, i.e. the election of the President of the Republic. However, if everyone agrees to bring forward the presidential election, we have no objection – if there's commitment to proper procedures.[42]

This decision had its detractors within the movement emphasizing that cohesion was difficult to maintain between elements of the youth and older wing, reformers and conservatives, and the political animals and those who argued for a quietist position. Leaders such as Mohammed el-Beltagy, whose daughter Asmaa would be killed at the Rabaa violence in August 2013, made little secret of their concern that the play for presidential power would leave the Brotherhood in a politically compromising position, but the Old Guard reasoned that SCAF's opposition to them as democratic symbols of the will of the Egyptian people morally bound them to stand for election. Announcing the 'U-turn', FJP leader (and eventual presidential candidate) Mohammed Morsi told media sources,

> We have witnessed obstacles standing in the way of parliament to take decisions to achieve the demands of the revolution. . . . We have therefore chosen

the path of the presidency not because we are greedy for power but because we have a majority in parliament which is unable to fulfil its duties in parliament.[43]

The man initially nominated by the Brotherhood as presidential candidate was Khairat al-Shatir, but he was replaced by Morsi after the Supreme Presidential Election Commission (PEC) declared al-Shatir ineligible on a technicality.[44]

In many respects Mohammed Morsi was the man least likely to win. He was perceived as less compelling than others in the Brotherhood, highly conservative, and a follower rather than a leader. Satirists depicted him as an inarticulate buffoon with a pharaoh complex. Bassam Yousef,[45] in Egypt's version of Jon Stewart's *Daily Show*, continuously poked fun at Morsi, yet the Brotherhood's candidate could count on the backing of the movement which used its organizational resources to build a presidential campaign despite its chosen candidate being disqualified. Morsi's most serious rival was Ahmed Shafiq, whose military career had earned him support from SCAF. Other rivals, however, included a former well-respected Brotherhood reformer, Abdel Moneim Abou el-Fotouh.[46] The presidential run-off came down to two candidates for the final poll. This left Egyptians with Hobson's choice – between Morsi under the Brotherhood-inspired Islamist banner or former ancien régime autocracy epitomized by former air force chief and Mubarak-appointed prime minister Ahmad Shafiq. Indeed, the contest

> began under a rather unpropitious set of circumstances with no parliament, no constitution, and no formal checks on the authority of the PEC, whose capacity to serve as a neutral arbiter of the proceedings was open to dispute, the polls opened on the morning of June 16 under a cloud of heightened tension and uncertainty.[47]

The poll, when it concluded in June 2012, gave the Brotherhood a victory. Morsi became Egypt's first freely elected president after securing 51.7 per cent of the vote, compared to 48.2 per cent for his rival, Ahmed Shafiq. SCAF's reaction was to limit, wherever possible, civilian powers of the president and government. Nevertheless, the installation of Morsi as president on 30 June 2012 signalled a significant victory and watershed in the ability of the Brotherhood, in the wake of the Arab Spring, to marshal popular support to access political power in Egypt. This was unprecedented and had an important demonstration effect on other wings of the movement across the Arab world. Nevertheless, the election had been unbelievably close. Shafiq did much better than predicted, and much of the Morsi vote came from rural Egypt, signs that the victory was perhaps less absolute than the Brotherhood hoped. Fear of 'Ikhwanization' in power galvanized the Brotherhood's opponents, both within and outside Egypt's state institutions, to manoeuvre to restrain and delimit the Islamists. Conflict was inevitable once SCAF and its supporters moved to confine the Brotherhood. Within the Brotherhood itself there were still leaders and activists who opposed the rate of political expansion

46 Egypt – Phoenix

and feared the consequences in terms of the wider social and *dawa*-oriented goals of the movement. It became increasingly apparent that different factions of the Brotherhood reflected a variety of tensions. These tensions were between those leading the movement down a definitive path of governance and politics with its attendant implications for democracy, pluralism, the political and party system, and the compromises necessary for governance and those that sought to maintain the Brotherhood movement steered by the fundamental Islamic impulses formulated by Hassan al-Banna in the 1920s. This would be a state of affairs also exhibited in the differences between Hamas and the Change and Reform government elected in 2006 in the Palestinian Territories and who took complete power in the Gaza Strip in June 2007, as well as in the IAF and the Jordanian Muslim Brotherhood as they sought to navigate a place for themselves in Jordan's political system under narrowing directives of King Abdullah II. In Egypt it became clear that the organizational flexibility demanded by the transition in the wake of the Arab Spring was one which would highlight the multifaceted and dynamic nature of the Brotherhood movement. Within a year the Brotherhood's dream political triumph would turn into a shattering nightmare.

Control

The extent to which the Muslim Brotherhood had the ability and skills to govern and handle the enormity of political power that was placed in their hands by the middle of 2012 must be questioned. The Brotherhood could be deemed to be 'sipping from a poisoned chalice', amidst the high expectations that abounded at the time.[48] It is certainly evident that the weakening internal dynamic within the Brotherhood and tensions over the overall direction that the leadership should drive the movement in the wake of the Arab Spring worked against the group's larger task of steering a large, poor, and populous post-revolutionary state and its citizens through a political transition. This was a transition that was giving rise to attempt to redesign the constitutional architecture of the Leviathan that was the Egyptian state. Indeed the nature of the state itself in Egypt – particularly the bureaucracy and its connections with business interests – was inherently resistant to democracy and its Islamist incarnation in the Muslim Brotherhood. With self-imposed powers, Morsi and the Brotherhood soon pushed through the constitution and, in doing so, alienated those who sought to keep Islamization and the *shari'a* out of politics.

Attempting to govern while still behaving like a besieged, persecuted, and repressed opposition group only seemed to accentuate the Muslim Brotherhood's monopolistic and paranoid practices. It was also challenged to translate the many ideas of power and governance which had shaped narratives within the movement for more than eighty years into reality. This meant that conceptions of rights, economics, social support, education, gender, faith and practice, pluralism and accommodation, consensus, and consultation butted up against the demands of a restive, emancipated, and vocalized populous in Egypt. The silence of acquiescence which had been broken by the Arab Spring and had benefitted the Brotherhood greatly in its wake could also be used against it. The Brotherhood was soon being accused of promoting ideological hegemony over a diverse Egyptian population that had demanded pluralism and inclusion into the political arena.

Yet the Brotherhood and the FJP struggled constantly to effect a rapid organizational and ideological change from opposition to power. The leadership of the Brotherhood and the FJP failed to determine and implement policies that counterbalanced the critique that behind Morsi and the FJP were the conservative Old Guard of the Brotherhood's Shura Council and Guidance Bureau pulling the levers and really determining how Egypt should be governed. President Morsi was seen as more vulnerable to the diktats of the Guidance Bureau than the people, the Egyptian citizens, who had elected him. This national constituency which had elected him and the *shabab* had been the ones taking the risks in Tahrir Square and throughout the many cities, towns, and villages where the Arab Spring broke out. The Old Guard of the Guidance Bureau had barely deigned to lift their voices in defiance of Mubarak while leaving it to the *shabab* to earn its place on its behalf in the new narrative of the Arab Spring.

As its year in power progressed, the Brotherhood seemed unable to craft and communicate a strategic vision for governance of the country, to rebuild its economy, and to continue the march towards freedom and democracy. It became apparent that its conception of democracy, as Brown contends, 'was shallow and often illiberal; further, Egypt had no rules of accepted democratic behaviour', and the Brotherhood had a limited history of its own deeply rooted democratic practices at an organizational level.[49] The Brotherhood made one strategic error and gaffe after another when encouraging the FJP and President Morsi in decision making. In complete reversal of its earlier pledges, the Brotherhood failed to build power slowly, and it eschewed alliance building and pluralism in favour of authority which they all too readily took for themselves alone. A sense of responsiveness to the electorate, the ordinary citizens of Egypt and their discontents, was absent. The Brotherhood instead deployed its energies, its resources, and its newly acquired control to strengthen the political power that had been delivered to them through the electoral mandate of the Egyptian people.

As a result of the Brotherhood's inability to manage Egypt's financial affairs, the economy failed to improve. Six months into power, the budget deficit had rose to 38 per cent, the Egyptian pound had slipped 6 per cent against the US dollar, and GDP growth fell from 5 to 0.5 per cent. Unemployment, an issue pertinent to nearly every Egyptian household, had risen from 8.9 per cent to 12.4 per cent. By July 2013, almost a year into the Morsi presidency, the economy was at the point of collapse.[50] The Brotherhood also began to roll back the newfound freedoms being enjoyed in Egyptian society or failed to implement approaches and policies that supported the rights of minority groups or women. In the face of opposition, the Brotherhood seemed reflexively to increasingly call on and marshal its reservoir of supporters, bringing them out onto the streets. Yet they failed to grasp that democratic governments do not orchestrate a mob; they build a state to offer services and support, identity, and belonging for everyone. The Brotherhood also soon discovered that the Egyptian state was a huge unwieldy dysfunctional mass staffed by ranks of seasoned bureaucrats resistant to the newcomers. There was literally no room in the new ministries that they now oversaw to draw in their own administrators and functionaries, partisans and supporters. The Brotherhood encountered a form of state-based bureaucratic resistance that they were not equipped to deal with.

A form of resistance to the Brotherhood grew within the state and among popular forces outside the state throughout the year that it was in power. The leadership of the Brotherhood grew increasingly oblivious to the external discontents, strongly believing that their popular mandate was a sign of universal approval and universal mandate from the whole of the Egyptian people that could not be challenged before new elections. They had forgotten that they had only won the presidential election by a small margin and had not won an outright majority in parliament either and that the future should lie in alliance building, particularly with the still popular and powerful state military and security forces. Perhaps to expect such an alliance, however, was simply unrealistic. It was one thing for the Brotherhood to attempt to work with other secular, liberal, or Islamist political actors but perhaps quite another to work with the forces which historically had been the chief agent of their repression under successive political leaders since the revolution in 1952. Egypt's armed forces and security services had proved resilient over the decades to attempts by the Brotherhood to Islamize it. Throughout the course of the transition the Egyptian military remained a constant force over politics and society; the Brotherhood attempted to both woo and control it and failed. The military would ultimately determine the nature of the Brotherhood's relationship to the state.

One other factor that the Brotherhood was inclined to overlook was that the military, as a result of its role during the Arab Spring, as well as earlier historical eras, was the alternative populist-supported force in Egypt.[51] Some had considered it a strategic mistake when Morsi, shortly after taking office, abolished SCAF's decrees and empowered himself with full authority and sacked minister of defence and chief of the armed forces and SCAF chairman Mohamed Hussein Tantawi, along with other senior military personnel. Tantawi had been the military figurehead who at the height of the Tahrir Square protest had refused to order Egypt's forces to turn on the people. Morsi replaced him with General Abdel Fattah al-Sisi, a mid-ranking commander of the Egyptian army who has never seen military combat. Amidst growing fears of state-imposed Islamization across government, it was reported that the relationship with Egypt's judiciary and the Brotherhood also deteriorated.[52] The Brotherhood seemed incapable of building alliances with such actors, as, Ennarah argues,

> the Brotherhood seems to have overreached . . . [and] were at loggerheads with the judiciary and the powerful private media conglomerates, and their aggressive, condescending rhetoric alienated the middle and lower classes, leaving them with no real support base outside the Islamist movement.[53]

Requiem for a dream

There are many valuable accounts and analyses of the events that led up to events of July and August 2013 when President Morsi was removed from power and detained and the constitution was suspended.[54] Such analyses differ over the extent to which the Brotherhood, once in power, was governing for all or sacrificing the popular will to meet and even accelerate its own particular Islamist agenda. Pioppi contends that

> the MB-FJP's priority was not to implement a political or economic programme or to give the country a new political . . . imprint . . . but to consolidate its position vis-à-vis state institutions and societal forces,' further arguing that, 'in their battle to control the state, Islamists soon appeared incompetent, arrogant and authoritarian, were fully blamed for the deteriorating living conditions and lost popular consensus outside their inner circle.[55]

It is certainly the case that the Muslim Brotherhood had displayed some incompetence in government or monopolizing tendencies over issues such as the constitution and the place of Islam in it.[56] This had given rise to significant disquiet and concern among the Brotherhood's many opponents both at home and abroad. The fact that the Brotherhood had attempted, on some issues, to govern judiciously particularly in relation to the countervailing demands of other Islamists regionally and locally accounted for little. Whether such incompetency should have been met in the ways it was by SCAF and a number of state powers external to the region has not only angered activists and supporters of the Brotherhood but also caused concern among human rights and democracy groups globally. By early 2013 a belief began to grow between supporters and opponents that an existential battle for the future of Egypt was about to be waged between the Brotherhood and SCAF. Mass rallies calling for Morsi's ouster began to occur, and the anti-Islamist Tamarod group (with important external backing) emerged to play its part in orchestrating the discontent which spilled once again onto Cairo's streets.[57] This external backing from Gulf countries in coordination with the Egyptian military helped propel and raise the threat against Morsi and his regime.[58]

SCAF unilaterally intervened to remove Morsi from power on 3 July 2013, and in response, Brotherhood supporters quickly marshalled mass demonstrations and protests. Pro-Morsi rallies and sit-ins were organized throughout the country and in particular in Cairo at the Rabaa al-Adawiya and al-Nahda Squares.[59] General al-Sisi had inaugurated the new political dispensation with religious mandates from the Grand Sheikh of al-Azhar, Sheikh Ahmed el-Tayeb, and Pope Tawadros II, as well as political support from the National Salvation Front and al-Nour party. He also ensured that Egypt's Islamic institutions, including al-Azhar University, understood where their allegiances must lie.[60] Adly Mansour, head of the Supreme Constitutional Court, was appointed interim president, and new elections to re-establish political power through the ballot box would be held within a nine-month transition. General al-Sisi's crackdown was variously described and regarded as a coup against a freely and fairly democratically elected president and his government by its opponents or an exercise of the populist will against the increasingly authoritarian Muslim Brotherhood by al-Sisi's supporters.

50 Egypt – Phoenix

The Brotherhood knew it could marshal support from its own activists and supporters who were shocked and outraged by the turn of events at General al-Sisi's hands. Thousands descended onto streets to convey conviction for the Brotherhood. Al-Sisi, on the other hand, ordered his security forces to act, and they did so brutally. Human Rights Watch, in its annual summary for 2013, estimated that 'in the months following the ouster of President Morsy, police used excessive lethal force, killing over 1,300 persons at protests, and arrested over 3,500 Brotherhood supporters'.[61] The extent to which repression would replace the hopes and liberties enjoyed by the Muslim Brotherhood in the wake of the Arab Spring was underscored in the analysis offered by the Brookings-based academic Shadi Hamid when he stated,

> The current military government is much more ambitious, with its aim to dismantle the Brotherhood and destroy it as a political force. Unlike Mubarak, the generals have tapped into real, popular anger against the Brotherhood – after its many failures in power – and helped nurture that anger into something ugly and visceral. It's no surprise when armies use force. That's what armies do. But it is scary to see ordinary Egyptians, 'liberal' political parties and much of the country's media class cheering it on so enthusiastically.[62]

It is a fact that when Egyptian security forces were ordered to clear the protestors, the subsequent clashes resulted in the deaths of thousands of Egyptians, the imprisonment of tens of thousands of Brotherhood supporters, and the flight of thousands of others into exile or underground.[63] It also set in motion the radicalization of thousands of members; the prosecution of hundreds of the movement's leaders, resulting in the majority of them also being sentenced to death; and finally the proscription of the movement as a terrorist organization.[64] The scale of violence against the Muslim Brotherhood and the rapid implementation of repressive measures partly paralyzed the movement and immobilized its supporters in fear of their lives.[65] Under General al-Sisi's leadership, the government also targeted the Brotherhood's financial and organizational resources by closing offices, arresting its personnel, and confiscating its assets. Within the year, his government had closed down the organization's important social and charitable support mechanisms, nonprofit business sector, and the FJP. Likewise, the Brotherhood's media was targeted and the Egyptian press was used to mount an unrestrained black propaganda campaign against the movement and its supporters in Egypt and regionally.

General al-Sisi could also count on significant external connivance from some states, as well as the ambiguous support of others. By the spring of 2014, Saudi Arabia, for example, had declared the Brotherhood a terrorist organization,[66] and other Arab states had developed a hostile stance towards the movement. Initially many other state actors, including the United States, had condemned the violence against Morsi and Brotherhood supporters.[67] But the method by which General al-Sisi had obtained and remained in power subsequent to the events of August 2013 were obscured and obfuscated.[68] Important allies of Western states in the

Middle East were complicit in the reaction against the Brotherhood. In June 2014, with the backing of such powers, General al-Sisi took the oath of office to become President al-Sisi, having won the latest electoral contest to take office a week previously, receiving 96.91 per cent of the vote.[69] The Brotherhood dreams were well and truly dead.

Survival mode

By 2016, some three years after the rout of the Brotherhood from power, its future in Egypt, and thus elsewhere across the Middle East and beyond, looked bleak. The events in Egypt, as Brown highlights, had 'also completely reshuffled the country's regional alliances [and] . . . affected thinking throughout Islamist circles everywhere'.[70] The moves orchestrated by al-Sisi, as general and then president, and the Tamarod alliance had a powerful demonstration effect in other contexts where the Muslim Brotherhood had attempted to capitalize on the Arab Spring. The Brotherhood had suffered a major blow to its ambitions, and although it had been suppressed in the past, the scale of the state crackdown was unprecedented. Other Islamist groups in Egypt, such as the Salafist al-Nour party, were either co-opted or declared part of the same terrorist alliance as the Brotherhood, Ansar Bayt al-Maqdis, and other jihadis. The Brotherhood was weakened and struggling to recover from dismantlement and disarray. Mohammed Morsi, the Supreme Guide Mohammed Badie, Deputy Guide Khairat al-Shatir, and the preponderance of the Brotherhood's governing Guidance Bureau, the FJP leaders Mohamed Saad al-Katatni, Essam el-Erian, and Mohamed el-Beltagy, were finished.[71]

In assessing the future of the Brotherhood in Egypt, the optimists pointed to earlier eras in the history of the movement when it had faced repressive sweeps and had survived. The pessimists, on the other hand, pointed out that never before in the history of the movement had it faced the kind of state-orchestrated systemic subjugation combined with a decline in popular support and reactionary temper from other Islamist elements. The Egyptian state had criminalized the movement, declaring it a terrorist organization; its legions of leaders, nationally, regionally, and locally, had been targeted and effectively constrained and internal cohesion strained under the already extant tensions between old and young guard, reformers and conservatives, activists and quietists, radicals and moderates. The energy and dynamic power of the Brotherhood which had animated and galvanized it during the Arab Spring had literally and metaphorically been exhausted.

The pain and memory of the mass killings from the confrontations of the summer of 2013 and the ongoing protests, mobilizations, and campaigns made it almost impossible for Brotherhood to survive. One mode of survival was the noticeable atomization of the organization with localism prevailing over the metropolitan focus of previous years.[72] In many senses this was a case of stripping the organization back to its earliest manifestation and configuration when small groupings of the Brotherhood were organized at neighbourhood and local levels and often clandestinely so. The drawback then, as in the present, of having to work semi-clandestinely or underground was that it gave rise to accusations that the Brotherhood had a secret apparatus with anti-regime and violent tendencies. Yet one advantage that the Brotherhood of the twenty-first century has had over its antecedents, however, is that the Internet and social media (including the Dark Web, Facebook, and Twitter) has allowed it to establish and maintain virtual networks to help the organization survive and reach out to supporters at home and abroad.[73] Such networks, however, were just as vulnerable to security penetration as the human networks or Brotherhood family which had sustained the organization over previous decades. One further difference between past and present in terms of survival tactics was also the role played by women in the Brotherhood as it has been forced to reconstitute and survive.[74] Here the parallel to other 'liberation' and resistance movements where state forces have decimated or repressed and imprisoned male ranks is telling for the activist role that is then played by the women 'left behind' on the home and organizational front.[75] In Egypt the women who mobilized on behalf of the Brotherhood have remained committed to their cause. Such roles, however, are circumscribed by the political and socioeconomic context in which the organization must seek to survive, and this is still a highly hostile one.

In fracturing the organization, the state, under al-Sisi, has also succeeded in undermining internal cohesion of the Brotherhood. The top leadership is inaccessible (in jail or exile), and those lower down the ranks lack experience and capacity to lead and engage in the strategic oversight demanded for survival. Fear has further depleted the energies of the remaining elements of the leadership and driven away many who had clung to the movement in the heady days of the Arab Spring and the post-Mubarak transition. Pre-existing divisions, such as that between the Old Guard and the youth (*shabab*) have been exacerbated, leading to open rifts and defections particularly around issues of resistance against the al-Sisi regime, jihad, and the efficacy of force and violence.[76] The Brotherhood is especially vulnerable to the discourses, in the wake of Rabaa Square violence perpetrated by the state, of Islamists radicalized into defensive arguments which veer towards violence. As Brown and Awad contend, 'Since Morsi's ouster, Brotherhood leaders have insisted that their "strategic" decision was nonviolence, but that they were unable to restrain angry youth, especially those outside the movement, or that their own "counter-violence" is an expected reactionary response.'[77] Nevertheless, the notion that the Brotherhood in Egypt will be totally eradicated because of such internal tensions and atomization can be discounted by present-day survival strategies and the historical precedents. One powerful reason why this is the case is because of the enduring religious rootedness and appeal of the organization. Though commonly viewed through a political lens, the Muslim Brotherhood remains deeply embedded into Egypt's Islamic and Islamized culture. Attempts by the state in Egypt to replace the Brotherhood in this important sphere have always been limited in terms of success. It is true that Sadat was the pious president and that al-Sisi has articulated an agenda for a 'religious revolution' targeted at the Egyptian Islamic establishment, but it has proved impossible for such heads of state – particularly given their backgrounds – to outflank the Brotherhood.[78]

Future face

One can concur with Hamid's argument that 'premature obituaries of the [Muslim] Brotherhood usually turn out to be just that'.[79] Nevertheless, the death knell has been sounded and there are paths that the leadership of the Brotherhood took the organization and the Egyptian people down which proved to be dead ends or even fatal. The Brotherhood in Egypt, as in other examples such as Hamas in the Gaza Strip, failed to truly engage with power sharing and democracy building in parliament or the wider political culture of the country upon winning a majority at the polls. The failure to contribute to the new democratic culture in the transition era appeared to throw a deaf ear to a major call of the Arab Spring protestors who had turned out to oust President Mubarak. President Morsi's and the FJP's manifestation of authoritarianism was not what was expected of a reformist opposition Islamist movement that had critiqued such power when in the hands of the Wafd party, Nasser, Sadat, and Mubarak. The popular movement that swung against Morsi by mobilizing in public squares throughout Egypt in the spring and early summer of 2013 appeared to provide all the political ammunition that SCAF and al-Sisi needed to take him from power through the machinations of their coup.[80] President Morsi was a poor leader for a nation intent on recovering its greatness. He was perceived as obstructive, insular, and lacking in the kind of charisma required of a 'great' Arab leader. Democracy, or rather elections, had not necessarily delivered a democrat to the office of president, and familiar tropes about Islamism and its inherent threat to Arab secular culture abounded. Such binary breakdowns of secularism versus Islamism appeared to veer discourse about the transition in Egypt towards false but highly effective prisms through which politics and power could be ordered for both internal consumption and external support. The notion of an existential battle between such forces where clear lines appear between two sides – one Islamic, the other secular – has begun to steer Egypt and the role of the Muslim Brotherhood away from the Arab Spring protests with their demands for freedom, equality, and prosperity mediated through a democratic political culture.

The Muslim Brotherhood in Egypt has become perceived as a polarizing rather than uniting force. Transition politics, especially in the wake of a move from one dominating political order to a new pluralist era, also should have been supported by external actors in the same way that transitions in eastern Europe or Latin America in the 1990s had been. International actors like the EU, however, privileged security and economy over democracy promotion, leaving Egypt's democracy experiment vulnerable to discourses championed by SCAF.[81] Other actors from the Gulf states opposed the Brotherhood and were willing to channel significant levels of financial and other support to SCAF in order to delimit the Islamist alternative that the Brotherhood presented as a putative model for the region in the wake of the Arab Spring.

The Brotherhood remains integral to the fabric of political Islam in Egypt, but once again its role has been diminished and altered, and the many opportunities open to it in the wake of the Arab Spring have been severely curtailed. Islamism,

54 Egypt – Phoenix

as a result, has become both dynamic and counter-dynamic, and the Brotherhood has been forced to be reactive and to push back as an actor on an increasingly crowded stage. The counter-dynamic is manifest in the jihadification of Islamism epitomized by groups like al-Qaeda and ISIS. The project of Islamism which the Brotherhood has effectively championed since it was founded in 1928 has come to a stuttering halt in the wake of the Arab Spring. Throughout the Egyptian transition, the Brotherhood did itself few favours in terms of securing political longevity. Instead of patiently crafting a constitutional base to scaffold the new political era, it threw caution to the wind and paid a high price as a result. Within a period of three years, the fortunes of the Brotherhood changed dramatically. To paraphrase Victorian novelist Charles Dickens, 'it was the best of times, it was the worst of times,' for the Brotherhood. For the movement it has indeed turned out to be 'the epoch of belief, . . . the epoch of incredulity, . . . the season of Light, . . . the season of Darkness, . . . the spring of hope, . . . the winter of despair,' where they 'had everything before [them], . . . [and after August 2013] had nothing before [them]'.[82] Moreover, the price levied on the Brotherhood in Egypt in terms of its successes and its failures, as we shall see in successive chapters, has also been levied on the Brotherhood movement more widely with catastrophic consequences, both human and political, for future Islamism.

Ultimately the Muslim Brotherhood struggled in the transition from the Arab Spring. Its foray into state politics and governance broke down internal cohesion and exposed fractures within the movement that could not be overcome and were exploited by its opponents and enemies. It also failed to make more concrete its modern democratic credentials and commitment to true social, political, and economic reform which is so badly needed in Egypt and was at the heart of the protests which led to the ouster of Mubarak. The conservative core of the movement embodied in the upper echelons of the Brotherhood remained resilient in the face of the claims and energies of the younger generation which wanted to reach out to and work with a more plural base in Egyptian society and politics. These elements found it difficult to work together within the movement and were then vulnerable to the attacks waged against it by external elements hostile to it. Today the Brotherhood in Egypt has been propelled into an existential crisis. The odds are stacked against its survival. Only its intrinsic sense of endurance and ability to withstand previous repressive waves can turn the odds in its favour.

Notes

1 S. Shehata and J. Stacher, 'Boxing in the Brothers', *Middle East Research and Information Project*, 8 August 2007, http://merip.org/mero/mero080807 (accessed 7 May 2015).

2 C.R. Wickham, *The Muslim Brotherhood: Evolution of an Islamist Movement*, Princeton, NJ: Princeton University Press, 2013, p. 1; L. Noueihed and A. Warren, *The Battle for the Arab Spring: Revolution, Counter-Revolution and the Making of a New Era*, London: Yale University Press, 2012, p. 119.

3 I. Harb, 'The Egyptian Military in Politics: Disengagement or Accommodation', *Middle East Journal*, Vol. 57:2, Spring 2003, p. 269, http://www.jstor.org/stable/4329881 (accessed

20 May 2015); BBC News, 'Egypt Muslim Brotherhood "Quits Election"', *BBC News*, 1 December 2010, http://www.bbc.co.uk/news/world-middle-east-11890726 (accessed 8 May 2015); For Ikhwan statement, see IkhwanOnline, 'The Muslim Brotherhood's Decision of a Run-Off Parliamentary Elections in 2010', *IkhwanOnline*, 1 December 2010, https://www.youtube.com/watch?v=iSpIemEtSts (accessed 8 May 2015).

4 D. Shehata, 'The Fall of the Pharaoh: How Hosni Mubarak's Reign Came to an End', *Foreign Affairs*, Vol. 90:3, May/June 2011, p. 29, https://www.foreignaffairs.com/articles/north-africa/2011-04-14/fall-pharaoh (accessed 20 May 2015).

5 See B. Dehghanpisheh, 'Mohammad Badie on Egypt's Muslim Brotherhood', *Newsweek*, 29 November 2010, http://www.newsweek.com/mohammad-badie-egypts-muslim-brotherhood-70113 (accessed 1 November 2013).

6 See https://www.facebook.com/ikhwanweb.official, https://twitter.com/Ikhwanweb, and http://www.ikhwanwiki.com/ (accessed 20 May 2015).

7 C.R. Wickham, *The Muslim Brotherhood: Evolution of an Islamist Movement*, Princeton: Princeton University Press, 2013, p. 157.

8 See C. Williams, 'How Egypt Shut Down the Internet', *Telegraph*, 28 January 2011, http://www.telegraph.co.uk/news/worldnews/africaandindianocean/egypt/8288163/How-Egypt-shut-down-the-internet.html (accessed 7 May 2015).

9 See K. Fahim and M. El-Naggar, 'Violent Clashes Mark Protests Against Mubarak's Rule', *New York Times*, 25 January 2011, http://www.nytimes.com/2011/01/26/world/middleeast/26egypt.html (accessed 7 May 2015).

10 E.F. Thompson, *Justice Interrupted: The Struggle for Constitutional Government in the Middle East*, Cambridge, MA: Harvard University Press, 2013, p. 318.

11 See M. Lynch, 'Young Brothers in Cyberspace', *Middle East Report*, Vol. 37:245, Winter 2007, pp. 26–33, http://www.merip.org/mer/mer245/young-brothers-cyberspace (accessed 28 April 2015).

12 See K. Al-Anani, 'The Young Brotherhood in Search of a New Path', *Current Trends in Islamist Ideology*, Vol. 9, October 2009, pp. 96–109, http://www.hudson.org/content/researchattachments/attachment/1306/al_anani_vol9.pdf (accessed 28 April 2015).

13 E. El-Din Shahin, 'The Egyptian Revolution: The Power of Mass Mobilization and the Spirit of Tahrir Square', in R.R. Larémont (ed.), *Revolution, Revolt, and Reform in North Africa: The Arab Spring and Beyond*, Abingdon, Oxon and New York: Routledge, 2014, p. 62.

14 C.R. Wickham, *The Muslim Brotherhood: Evolution of an Islamist Movement*, Princeton, NJ: Princeton University Press, 2013, p. 162.

15 M. Awad and H. Dixon, 'Special Report: Inside the Egyptian Revolution', *Reuters*, 13 April 2011, http://www.reuters.com/article/2011/04/13/us-egypt-revolution-idUSTRE73C18E20110413 (accessed 28 April 2015).

16 See M. Hashem, 'A Generational Battle among Brothers', *Carnegie Endowment for International Peace*, 29 January 2015, http://carnegieendowment.org/sada/2015/01/29/generational-battle-among-brothers/i7w0 (accessed 1 February 2015).

17 G. Witte, M.B. Sheridan, and K. DeYoung, 'In Egypt Muslim Brotherhood Reverses Course, Agrees to Talks on Transition', *Washington Post*, 6 February 2011, http://www.washingtonpost.com/wp-dyn/content/article/2011/02/05/AR2011020501707.html (accessed 20 May 2015).

18 See E. El-Din Shahin, 'Sentenced to Death in Egypt', *Atlantic*, 19 May 2015, http://www.theatlantic.com/international/archive/2015/05/death-sentence-egypt-emad-shahin/393590/ (accessed 28 May 2015).

19 E. El-Din Shahin, 'The Egyptian Revolution: The Power of Mass Mobilization and the Spirit of Tahrir Square', in R.R. Larémont (ed.), *Revolution, Revolt, and Reform in North Africa: The Arab Spring and Beyond*, Abingdon, Oxon and New York: Routledge, 2014, p. 63.

20 L. Noueihed and A. Warren, *The Battle for the Arab Spring: Revolution, Counter-Revolution and the Making of a New Era*, London: Yale University Press, 2012, p. 98.

56 Egypt – Phoenix

21 E. El-Errian, 'What the Muslim Brothers Want', *New York Times*, 9 February 2011, http://www.nytimes.com/2011/02/10/opinion/10erian.html (accessed 14 April 2015).

22 A.M. Abou el-Fotouh, 'Democracy Supporters Should Not Fear the Muslim Brotherhood', *Washington Post*, 9 February 2011, http://www.washingtonpost.com/wp-dyn/content/article/2011/02/09/AR2011020905222.html (accessed 14 April 2015).

23 D. Pioppi, 'Playing with Fire: The Muslim Brotherhood and the Egyptian Leviathan', *The International Spectator: Italian Journal of International Affairs*, Vol. 48:4, 2013, p. 54, http://dx.doi.org/10.1080/03932729.2013.847680 (accessed 28 April 2015).

24 C.R. Wickham, *The Muslim Brotherhood: Evolution of an Islamist Movement*, Princeton, NJ: Princeton University Press, 2013, p. 169.

25 See J. Brown, *Salafis and Sufis in Egypt*, Washington, DC: Carnegie Endowment for International Peace, 2011, http://carnegieendowment.org/files/salafis_sufis.pdf (accessed 7 May 2015).

26 On Subhi Salih, see R. Francona, 'Egyptian Military Embracing the Muslim Brotherhood?', *Middle East Perspectives by Rick Francona*, 15 February 2011, http://francona.blogspot.co.uk/2011/02/egyptian-military-embracing-muslim.html (accessed 1 March 2014); and on Qaradawi and his return in February 2011 to lead Friday prayers in Tahrir square, see D. Murphy, 'Egypt Revolution Unfinished, Qaradawi Tells Tahrir Masses', *Christian Science Monitor*, 18 February 2011, http://www.csmonitor.com/World/Middle-East/2011/0218/Egypt-revolution-unfinished-Qaradawi-tells-Tahrir-masses (accessed 1 March 2014).

27 C.R. Wickham, *The Muslim Brotherhood: Evolution of an Islamist Movement*, Princeton, NJ: Princeton University Press, 2013, p. 183.

28 See M. Hashem, 'A Generational Battle among Brothers', *Carnegie Endowment for International Peace*, 29 January 2015, http://carnegieendowment.org/sada/2015/01/29/generational-battle-among-brothers/i7w0 (accessed 1 February 2015).

29 See IkhwanWeb, 'MB Chairman: We Seek to Participate, Not Dominate Elections', *IkhwanWeb*, 20 April 2011, http://www.ikhwanweb.com/article.php?id=28432 (accessed 19 October 2011).

30 See Al Jazeera English, 'Talk to Al Jazeera – Mohamed Saad Katatni: "Not a Religious Party"', *Al Jazeera English*, 27 November 2011, https://www.youtube.com/watch?v=aXVr00yJ420 (accessed 15 April 2015).

31 See S. Shukrallah and Y. Gaber, 'What Was Religion Doing in the Debate on Egypt's Constitutional Amendments?', *Ahram Online*, 22 March 2011, http://english.ahram.org.eg/NewsContent/1/64/8267/Egypt/Politics-/What-was-religion-doing-in-the-debate-on-Egypts-Co.aspx (accessed 19 October 2011).

32 See Al Jazeera English, 'Talk to Al Jazeera – Mohamed Saad Katatni: "Not a Religious Party"', *Al Jazeera English*, 27 November 2011, https://www.youtube.com/watch?v=aXVr00yJ420 (accessed 15 April 2015).

33 See J. Brown, *Salafis and Sufis in Egypt*, Washington, DC: Carnegie Endowment for International Peace, 2011, http://carnegieendowment.org/files/salafis_sufis.pdf (accessed 7 May 2015), pp. 8–9.

34 K. Al-Anani, *The Muslim Brotherhood after Morsi*, Doha: Arab Center for Research and Policy Studies, 2013, http://english.dohainstitute.org/release/eca3b305-1038-473b-a67e-b2a63af9ef21 (accessed 21 February 2015).

35 D. Ezzat, 'Egyptian Islamists, Along with NDP, Campaign Hard for a "Yes" Vote on Constitutional Amendments', *Ahram Online*, 17 March 2011, http://english.ahram.org.eg/NewsContent/1/64/7971/Egypt/Politics-/Egyptian-Islamists,-along-with-NDP,-campaign-hard-.aspx (accessed 14 November 2014).

36 See IkhwanWeb, 'FJP – No Alliance with Salafist al Noor Party', *IkhwanWeb*, 1 December 2011, http://www.ikhwanweb.com/article.php?id=29279 (accessed 15 April 2015).

37 See C. Lombardi and N.J. Brown, 'Islam in Egypt's New Constitution', *Foreign Policy*, 13 December 2012, http://foreignpolicy.com/2012/12/13/islam-in-egypts-new-constitution (accessed 10 April 2013).

38 C.R. Wickham, *The Muslim Brotherhood: Evolution of an Islamist Movement*, Princeton, NJ: Princeton University Press, 2013, pp. 194–5.

39 S. Tadros, 'The Muslim Brotherhood's Shrewd Election Tactics', *National Review*, 31 October 2011, http://www.nationalreview.com/corner/281746/muslim-brotherhoods-shrewd-election-tactics-samuel-tadros (accessed 14 May 2015).

40 See M. Ali, 'Finally, Egypt's Parties Set to Begin the Battle for Post-Mubarak Parliament', *Ahram Online*, 25 October 2011, http://english.ahram.org.eg/News/25030.aspx (accessed 3 March 2015).

41 C.R. Wickham, *The Muslim Brotherhood: Evolution of an Islamist Movement*, Princeton, NJ: Princeton University Press, 2013, p. 254.

42 M. Hussein, 'We Persist in Tahrir Square to Fulfil Demands, Expedite Presidential Elections via Proper Procedures', *IkhwanWeb*, 28 January 2012, http://www.ikhwanweb.com/article.php?id=29606&ref=search.php (accessed 14 January 2013).

43 M. Awad and S. El-Madany, 'In U-turn, Egypt's Brotherhood Names Presidential Candidate', *Reuters*, 31 March 2012, http://uk.reuters.com/article/2012/03/31/uk-egypt-brotherhood-presidency-idUKBRE82U0DQ20120331 (accessed 16 April 2015).

44 B. Smith, 'Egypt's Presidential Election 2012', SNIA/6338, *House of Commons Library*, 23 May 2012, p. 4, http://www.parliament.uk/briefing-papers/SN06338.pdf (accessed 28 April 2015).

45 Bassam Yousef was arrested in April 2013: P. Kingsley, 'Egyptian TV Satirist Bassem Youssef Bailed after Police Questioning', *Guardian*, 1 April 2013, http://www.theguardian.com/world/2013/mar/31/egypt-orders-arrest-tv-satirist (accessed 3 April 2013).

46 D.D. Kirkpatrick, 'Top Challenger in Egypt Vote Is an Islamist, and a Moderate', *New York Times*, 12 March 2012, http://www.nytimes.com/2012/03/14/world/middleeast/top-challenger-in-egypt-vote-is-an-islamist-and-moderate.html?_r=0 (accessed 28 May 2015).

47 C.R. Wickham, *The Muslim Brotherhood: Evolution of an Islamist Movement*, Princeton, NJ: Princeton University Press, 2013, p. 262.

48 L. Noueihed and A. Warren, *The Battle for the Arab Spring: Revolution, Counter-Revolution and the Making of a New Era*, London: Yale University Press, 2012, p. 281.

49 N.J. Brown, 'Egypt's Failed Transition', *Journal of Democracy*, Vol. 24:4, October 2013, p. 50, http://www.journalofdemocracy.org/sites/default/files/Brown-24-4.pdf (accessed 8 January 2015).

50 See M. Davies, 'Egypt Analysts Optimistic for Post-Morsi Economy', *BBC News*, 5 July 2013, http://www.bbc.co.uk/news/business-23183838 (accessed 16 April 2015).

51 See Z. Abul-Magd, 'The Egyptian Military in Politics and the Economy: Recent History and Current Transition Status', *Chr. Michelsen Institute*, Vol. 2013:2, October 2013, http://www.cmi.no/publications/file/4935-the-egyptian-military-in-politics-and-the-economy.pdf (accessed 28 April 2015); H. Albrecht and D. Bishara, 'Back on Horseback: The Military and Political Transformation in Egypt', *Middle East Law and Governance*, Vol. 3:1–2, 2011, pp. 13–23, http://heinonline.org/HOL/Page?handle=hein.journals/measterna3&div=5&g_sent=1&collection=journals#17 (accessed 28 April 2015).

52 See N. El-Behairy and S. Hamed, 'Timeline of Morsi and the Judiciary: One Year in Power', *Daily News Egypt*, 29 June 2013, http://www.dailynewsegypt.com/2013/06/29/timeline-of-morsi-and-the-judiciary-one-year-in-power/ (accessed 15 April 2015).

53 K.M. Ennarah, 'The End of Reciprocity: The Muslim Brotherhood and the Security Sector', *South Atlantic Quarterly*, Vol. 113:2, 2014, p. 416, http://saq.dukejournals.org/content/113/2/407.full.pdf+html (accessed March 24, 2015).

54 See B. Brown, 'Egypt Crowds Cheer Tahrir Square Military Flypast', *BBC News*, 4 July 2013, http://www.bbc.co.uk/news/world-middle-east-23190817 (accessed 16 April 2015); BBC News, 'Egypt Army Arrests Key Muslim Brotherhood Figures', *BBC News*, 4 July 2013, http://www.bbc.co.uk/news/world-middle-east-23189180 (accessed 16 April 2015).

55 D. Pioppi, 'Playing with Fire: The Muslim Brotherhood and the Egyptian Leviathan', *The International Spectator: Italian Journal of International Affairs*, Vol. 48:4, 2013, p. 67, http://dx.doi.org/10.1080/03932729.2013.847680 (accessed 28 April 2015).

56 See S. Hamid and M. Wheeler, 'Was Mohammed Morsi Really an Autocrat?', *Atlantic*, 31 March 2014, http://www.theatlantic.com/international/archive/2014/03/was-mohammed-morsi-really-an-autocrat/359797/ (accessed 28 April 2015).

57 See A. Iskander, 'Tamarod: Egypt's Revolution Hones Its Skill', *Jadiliyya*, 30 June 2013, http://www.jadaliyya.com/pages/index/12516/tamarod_egypts-revolution-hones-its-skills (accessed 20 May 2015).

58 D.D. Kirkpatrick, 'Leaks Gain Credibility and Potential to Embarrass Egypt's Leaders', *New York Times*, 12 May 2015, http://www.nytimes.com/2015/05/13/world/middleeast/leaks-gain-credibility-and-potential-to-embarrass-egypts-leaders.html (accessed 28 May 2015); D.D. Kirkpatrick, 'Recordings Suggest Emirates and Egyptian Military Pushed Ousting of Morsi', *New York Times*, 1 March 2015, http://www.nytimes.com/2015/03/02/world/middleeast/recordings-suggest-emirates-and-egyptian-military-pushed-ousting-of-morsi.html (accessed 28 May 2015).

59 See Human Rights Watch, 'Egypt: Mass Killings by Security Forces', *Human Rights Watch*, 11 August 2014, https://www.youtube.com/watch?v=AUtFM9L6ago (accessed 20 April 2015); M.F. Malmström, 'The Sound of Silence in Cairo: Affects, Politics and Belonging', *Anthropology Now*, Vol. 6:2, September 2014, pp. 23–34, http://www.jstor.org/stable/10.5816/anthropologynow.6.2.0023 (accessed 28 April 2015); K. Solberg, 'Cairo Mourns the Dead after Violent Crackdown', *Lancet*, Vol. 382:9895, 7 September 2013, pp. 847–8, http://dx.doi.org/10.1016/S0140-6736(13)61849-8 (accessed 28 April 2015); M. Mohsen, 'Health Ministry Raises Death Toll of Wednesday's Clashes to 638', *Daily News Egypt*, 16 August 2013, http://www.dailynewsegypt.com/2013/08/16/health-ministry-raises-death-toll-of-wednesdays-clashes-to-638/ (accessed 13 April 2015).

60 A. El-Sherif, *The Muslim Brotherhood and the Future of Political Islam in Egypt*, Washington, DC: Carnegie Endowment for International Peace, 2014, http://carnegieendowment.org/files/mb_future_egypt1.pdf (accessed 28 April 2015), p. 5.

61 Human Rights Watch, *World Report 2014*, New York: Human Rights Watch, 2014, pp. 532–8, http://www.hrw.org/sites/default/files/wr2014_web_0.pdf (accessed 16 April 2015).

62 S. Hamid, 'A Future Worse Than Mubarak's Reign', *New York Times*, August 21, 2013, http://www.nytimes.com/roomfordebate/2013/08/14/is-this-the-end-of-the-arab-spring/a-future-worse-than-mubaraks-reign (accessed 28 April 2015).

63 Human Rights Watch, *All According to Plan: The Rab'a Massacre and Mass Killings of Protesters in Egypt*, New York: Human Rights Watch, 2014, http://www.hrw.org/sites/default/files/reports/egypt0814web_0.pdf (accessed 30 May 2015).

64 Human Rights Watch, 'Egypt: Terrorist Tag Politically Driven', *Human Rights Watch*, 28 December 2013, http://www.hrw.org/news/2013/12/28/egypt-terrorist-tag-politically-driven (accessed 28 May 2015).

65 See K. Abou El Fadl, 'Failure of a Revolution: The Military, Secular Intelligentsia and Religion in Egypt's Pseudo-Secular State', in L. Sadiki (ed.), *Routledge Handbook of the Arab Spring: Rethinking Democratization*, Abingdon, Oxon: Routledge, 2015, pp. 253–70.

66 See BBC News, 'Saudi Arabia Declares Muslim Brotherhood "Terrorist Group"', *BBC News*, 7 March 2014, http://www.bbc.co.uk/news/world-middle-east-26487092 (accessed 9 September 2014).

67 The US initially withheld military aid to demonstrate its displeasure with the deposition of Morsi: 'The Politics of Restoring Egypt's Military Aid', *Washington Post*, 2 April 2015, http://www.washingtonpost.com/blogs/monkey-cage/wp/2015/04/02/the-politics-of-restoring-egypts-military-aid/ (accessed 24 February 2015).

68 See Al Jazeera, 'Global Condemnation of Egypt Crackdown', *Al Jazeera*, 15 August 2013, http://www.aljazeera.com/news/middleeast/2013/08/201381505130985967.

html (accessed 20 April 2015); T. Atlas, 'Obama Caught Between Polarized Allies in Egypt Crisis', *Bloomberg*, 19 August 2013, http://www.bloomberg.com/news/articles/2013-08-18/obama-caught-between-polarized-allies-in-egypt-crisis (accessed 20 April 2015).

69 See P. Kingsley, 'Abdel Fatah al-Sisi Sweeps to Victory in Egyptian Presidential Election', *Guardian*, 29 May 2014, http://www.theguardian.com/world/2014/may/29/abdel-fatah-al-sisi-sweeps-victory-egyptian-election (accessed 20 April 2015); see election results, Ahram Online, 'El-Sisi Wins Egypt's Presidential Race with 96.91%', *Ahram Online*, 3 June 2014, http://english.ahram.org.eg/NewsContent/1/64/102841/Egypt/Politics-/BREAKING-PEC-officially-announces-AbdelFattah-ElSi.aspx (accessed 20 May 2015); Y. Saleh and S. Kalin, 'Sisi Won 96.91 Percent in Egypt's Presidential Vote-Commission', *Reuters*, 3 June 2014, http://www.reuters.com/article/2014/06/03/us-egypt-election-results-idUSKBN0EE1UO20140603 (accessed 20 May 2015).

70 N. J. Brown, 'Political Islam Becomes Less Political', *Immanent Frame*, 11 March 2014, http://blogs.ssrc.org/tif/2014/03/11/political-islam-becomes-less-political/ (accessed 20 May 2015).

71 See Reuters, 'Egyptian Court Sentences Muslim Brotherhood Leader to Death', *Guardian*, 11 April 2015, http://www.theguardian.com/world/2015/apr/11/egyptian-court-muslim-brotherhood-death-sentences-mohammed-badie (accessed 11 April 2015); D.D. Kirkpatrick, 'Prominent Muslim Brotherhood Leader Is Seized in Egypt', *New York Times*, 30 October 2013, http://www.nytimes.com/2013/10/31/world/middleeast/high-ranking-muslim-brotherhood-leader-is-seized-in-egypt.html (accessed 28 April 2015); Jadaliyya and Ahram Online, 'Mohamed Al-Beltagy', *Jadaliyya*, 18 November 2011, http://www.jadaliyya.com/pages/index/3179/mohamed-al-beltagy (accessed 20 April 2015).

72 K. Al-Anani, 'Future Remains Unclear for Egypt's Muslim Brotherhood', *Al-Monitor*, 17 April 2014, http://www.al-monitor.com/pulse/politics/2014/04/egypt-muslim-brotherhood-challenges-future.html (accessed 28 April 2015).

73 See L. Harrera, *Revolution in the Age of Social Media: The Egyptian Popular Insurrection and the Internet*, London: Verso, 2014.

74 A. El-Sherif, *The Muslim Brotherhood and the Future of Political Islam in Egypt*, Washington, DC: Carnegie Endowment for International Peace, 2014, http://carnegieendowment.org/files/mb_future_egypt1.pdf (accessed 28 April 2015), p. 6.

75 See V. Asal, R. Legault, O. Szekely, and J. Wilkenfeld, 'Gender Ideologies and Forms of Contentious Mobilization in the Middle East', *Journal of Peace Research*, Vol. 50:3, May 2013, pp. 305–18, http://jpr.sagepub.com/content/50/3/305.full.pdf+html (accessed 28 April 2015); J. Nagel, 'Masculinity and Nationalism: Gender and Sexuality in the Mmaking of Nations', *Ethnic and Racial Studies*, Vol. 21:2, March 1998, pp. 242–69, http://dx.doi.org/10.1080/014198798330007 (accessed 28 April 2015) .

76 See A. El-Sherif, *The Muslim Brotherhood and the Future of Political Islam in Egypt*, Washington, DC: Carnegie Endowment for International Peace, 2014, http://carnegieendowment.org/files/mb_future_egypt1.pdf (accessed 28 April 2015), p. 14–24.

77 M. Awad and N. J. Brown, 'Mutual Escalation in Egypt', *Washington Post*, 9 February 2015, http://www.washingtonpost.com/blogs/monkey-cage/wp/2015/02/09/mutual-escalation-in-egypt/ (accessed 20 May 2015).

78 See B. Milton-Edwards, *Islamic Fundamentalism since 1945*, 2nd ed., Abingdon: Routledge, 2014; D. Ford, S. Abdelaziz, and I. Lee, 'Egypt's President Calls for a "Religious Rvolution"', *CNN*, 6 January 2015, http://edition.cnn.com/2015/01/06/africa/egypt-president-speech/ (accessed 20 April 2015).

79 S. Hamid, 'The Brotherhood Will Be Back', *New York Times*, 24 May 2014, http://www.nytimes.com/2014/05/24/opinion/more-democratic-less-liberal.html (accessed 28 April 2015).

80 See D.D. Kirkpatrick, 'In Leaked Video, Egyptian Army Officers Debate How to Sway News Media', *New York Times*, 3 October 2013, http://www.nytimes.com/2013/10/04/

world/middleeast/in-leaked-video-egyptian-army-officers-debate-how-to-sway-news-media.html (accessed 28 May 2015); D.D. Kirkpatrick, 'Recordings Suggest Emirates and Egyptian Military Pushed Ousting of Morsi', *New York Times*, 1 March 2015, http://www.nytimes.com/2015/03/02/world/middleeast/recordings-suggest-emirates-and-egyptian-military-pushed-ousting-of-morsi.html (accessed 28 May 2015).

81 See A. Dandashly, 'The EU Response to Regime Change in the Wake of the Arab Revolt: Differential Implementation', *Journal of European Integration*, Vol. 37:1, 2015, pp. 37–56, http://dx.doi.org/10.1080/07036337.2014.975988 (accessed 28 April 2015).

82 C. Dickens, *A Tale of Two Cities*, London: Chapman & Hall, 1898, p. 1.

3

PALESTINE – HAMAS AND THE LINK IN THE CHAIN

> Let me tell you a joke: When the first man landed on the moon do you know what he found? He found a branch of the Muslim Brotherhood and a Hebronite with a shop.
>
> Mahmoud Zahar[1]

Introduction

Hamas[2] is proud to declare itself a 'wing' of the Muslim Brotherhood in Palestine.[3] Founded in 1987 during the outbreak of the first Palestinian uprising (Intifada), Hamas was the outgrowth and reflection of the philosophy, principles, and influences of the Egyptian Muslim Brotherhood. Some of the founders of Hamas were Islamist acolytes of Hassan al-Banna and the ideas promoted by his early Muslim Brotherhood movement. As young students, these individuals were exposed to the activism and ideas of Cairo's political classes and returned to the Gaza Strip changed by such experiences. Through the decades of subsequent repression by the local governing authorities, Israeli occupation, and the resurgence of Islam in the Palestinian Territories, this foundational exposure and experience remained integral to the later expression of political Islam in the form of Hamas. Today, Hamas, having participated in and won elections for the Palestinian Legislative Council in 2006, governs the Gaza Strip, inspired in part by such ideas. At the same time, the group is also regarded by Israel and much of the international community as a terrorist menace infamous for its suicide attacks and rejection of peace. As discussed in the previous chapter, after July 2013 as Egypt grappled with a post-Brotherhood era, the local and regional media speculated about the effects of such seismic political changes in the region, including those in Hamas in the neighbouring Palestinian territory of the Gaza Strip. The intimate ties of Islamism, between Hamas and the Egyptian Muslim Brotherhood, which a year previously had been considered mutually beneficial, was now regarded by Egypt's new leaders in Cairo with suspicion and concern. Would Hamas-governed Gaza become a place of exile for the ousted Brothers from Egypt and a base for reactive violent assault against General al-Sisi and his military leaders?[4]

This chapter outlines and explores the Muslim Brotherhood-inspired roots of Hamas which date back to the period of the British mandate in Palestine. In addition, it examines Hamas's formulations in relation to its historic and enduring relationship with its 'brothers and sisters' in the Egyptian mother organization, as well as within the wider family of the Muslim Brotherhood. The chapter also analyses the case of dispute and violent contest among Palestinians and the state of divide that emerged in 2007 between Hamas and the secular Fatah movement. Moreover, the experience of transitioning from an opposition movement to holding power and the demands of governance and accountability, freedom, and democracy, are analysed with reference to Hamas's control of the Gaza Strip. In progression, the chapter also explains the challenges and opportunities Hamas has faced in the wake of the Arab Spring in relation to a number of issues such as the re-ascendance of the Muslim Brotherhood across the region and its implications for the movement's future and ambitions in the localized context of the Palestinian conflict. This also necessitates consideration of how Hamas dealt with Israel's occupation and as a neighbour to powerful Egypt governed by their Islamist counterparts. Finally, in the wake of the fall of the Muslim Brotherhood regionally, the chapter assesses the future prospects for Hamas.

Roots

Hamas, as indicated above, describes itself as a wing of the Muslim Brotherhood, a relationship which most academic studies and accounts support.[5] These roots commence with an early and almost synonymous relationship which emerged between the Egyptian Muslim Brotherhood and Palestine. Although this relationship would be subject to later disruption and disconnect, as we have explored in earlier chapters of this book, Palestine and the issue of the Palestinians in relation to Zionism and the establishment of Israel in 1948 has always been part of the wider ideological impulses and agendas of the Muslim Brotherhood movement.

The emergence of political Islam in Palestine coincided with that in Egypt and was part of the same series of more general responses to the effects of Western governance, rule, and colonialism on these Arab and identifiably Muslim societies. This was a period of immense change and upheaval in Palestine evidenced by two world wars, the British mandate, Zionism and its objective of statehood for the Jewish people, and the subsequent partition of this land in 1947–8 and further conflict. The attraction of political Islam was reflected in the founding of branches of the Muslim Brotherhood in Palestine and the obvious currency of their ideas as evident among other local Muslim leaders and aspirant Islamists.[6] Hence, the emergent spectrum of Islamism reflected the grip and resonance of the founders of the Egyptian Muslim Brotherhood and their ideas, from radical visions and articulations symbolized by Sheikh Izz ad-Din al-Qassam to the ordinary business of Islamism epitomized by local Palestinian branches of the Muslim Brotherhood. Furthermore, the emergent tension between the governing authorities, the positions of the Muslim Brotherhood, and the role of institutional Islam were also apparent in the Palestinian context. The Mufti of Jerusalem, Haj Amin al-Husseini, a former student at al-Azhar in Cairo who was inspired by Islamist thinker and Brotherhood antecedent Rashid Rida, attempted to reflect this experience in his navigation of ideas and political positioning during this turbulent period.

Indeed, it was as much in Palestine as in Egypt that the early ideas associated with al-Banna and the Brotherhood became reflected in the unfolding political dynamic and contest. The emergence of an indigenous Muslim response and series of demands from and to the governing British authorities and in competition, and increasing conflict, with the Zionists was a portent of things to come. The leadership of the Brotherhood in Egypt and Hassan al-Banna himself were alert and responsive to the emergent political crisis under Britain's mandate in Palestine. The Brotherhood, naturally enough, considered Palestine important because the third most holy site in Islam and other important traditions were associated with Jerusalem, including the Al-Aqsa mosque and the Dome of the Rock. The attempt at state formation by the Zionist movement on land considered holy to all Muslims would always be problematic. The movement instead perceived the majority Muslim population as destined to live, again, under Muslim governance and rule. This was combined with significant mistrust of British motives. The Muslim response, inspired by the Brotherhood and emulated on a local level in Palestine, was also directed in criticism against the incumbent ruling Muslim elite.

The Muslim Brotherhood and those so obviously influenced by it were initially regarded as interlopers. Nevertheless, they would soon be seen to reflect Islamic interests more authentically and with greater support and legitimacy. The ambiguous, self-interested, and sometimes dangerous alliances and relations that local, vested interests had allowed to grow between them and the ruling authorities in the name of Islam were also critiqued. The Muslim Brotherhood and its Palestinian variants captured the popular imagination by employing symbols of Islam in a familiar and common way. Yet they also addressed and offered a critique of such symbols, sometimes declaring them in opposition to the fundamental and pure expression of Islam. Hence, the Muslim Brotherhood attempted to offer an alternative ethos and political agenda for Palestinians. This was often in contention with their nascent nationalist movement as it struggled to meet the challenge posed by manifestations of colonialism and Zionism in Palestine. Moreover, the Brotherhood provided forms of alternate succour to Palestinians as they faced social and economic upheaval in what had for hundreds of years previously been a largely stable, traditional society.

Although it was not until 1945 that the Muslim Brotherhood officially founded branches in Palestine, its influence and contribution was apparent in the previous

64 Palestine – Hamas and the link

decade. This would be a decade during which Zionist immigration and settlement would accelerate, communal violence would break out, and Palestinians would be drawn into a general strike and popular revolt against the British authorities. Indeed there were close ties between the Muslim elites of Jerusalem and Cairo, as well as among the rising ideologues and influential figures of Islamism, including, and in particular, Rashid Rida. The Muslim Brotherhood, Sheikh Izz ad-Din al-Qassam and Haj Amin al-Husseini typified the Islamist response in terms of tensions with respect to both orthodox reformist and emergent radical dimensions of political Islam.

Influence

If radicalism was epitomized in the Egyptian Muslim Brotherhood by Sayyid Qutb, it was apparent too in the impact of Sheikh Izz ad-Din al-Qassam and his short-lived role in the lead up to the Palestinian revolt of 1936–9. Al-Qassam is widely considered to be Palestine's first Brotherhood-inspired leader. Although he was never formally involved in the nascent Brotherhood organization, al-Qassam's ideas and activism shaped the core of the organization's beliefs in its early years and for decades to come. In the early 1900s he left his native Syria to become a student at the al-Azhar mosque in Cairo. During this time, while following the traditional curriculum of the most learned institution in Islam, the young scholar was also exposed to more modern debates and approaches. The approaches which influenced him (whether directly or indirectly) were those advocated by Muslim reformist scholar Mohammad Abduh and the prominent Salafi scholar Rashid Rida. Rashid Rida emerged as a potent influence on Salafi thinking and activism which encouraged the Brotherhood in Egypt and Palestine. Both figures had played a significant role in informing al-Banna's future approach and subsequent formation of the Muslim Brotherhood. Al-Qassam experienced the same kind of powerfully modern imaginings of the role of Islam as al-Banna during this period in Cairo. The critique of traditional, almost dormant Islam espoused by such thinkers informed these two young men. These thinkers were modern in outlook; they eschewed the version of Islam which was popularly presented to them. They viewed traditional Islam as sclerotic and inauthentic and its purity tarnished with needless accretion. They contended that the Islam of folk practice, saint worship, and magic *jinns* (genies) explained, in part, its declining power and political weakness. Rida was a modernist when it came to his faith and its role in defending the Muslim people against the political projects of the West. These Islamist leaders particularly objected to the expansionist nature of European states such as Britain and France which, in the wake of the First World War and the collapse of the Ottoman Empire, appeared to offer only a future of subjugation for Islam in its own lands. The response from these Salafists was also evident in their rejection of local nationalist and national-secularist movements and projects across the Middle East. Rida and his supporters eschewed such trends and instead sought to promote a new Islam.

The future of this particular form of Islamism was not only evident in the high intellectual and religious circles of the day, but activist supporters such as al-Qassam and the Brotherhood also rolled it out to the urban slums and among the rural poor. The support that Izz ad-Din al-Qassam sought to garner increasingly focussed on jihad as emancipation and defence from the invidious effects that Western colonial and nationalist project building was having on their lives. Before coming to Palestine in the early 1920s, al-Qassam had supported other restive Muslim protests and revolts elsewhere in the region. In his homeland of Syria, where he returned after his studies in Cairo to work as a teacher and preacher, he was active in his community. He also attempted to rouse support for his fellow Muslims abroad. For example, in 1911 when Italy invaded Libya, al-Qassam called for a jihad in solidarity with the now subjugated Libyan people. Additionally, during the First World War, al-Qassam served in the Ottoman army and, in the wake of its defeat, raised resistance against the French occupation of his native land.[7]

In Palestine, this proto-Salafist quickly identified himself as an enemy of colonialism and, by extension, Zionism. His impact on Palestinian politics was not only evident in his lifetime but also would endure to the present day. He reflected and articulated the immensely intense political conflict of the time as Palestinian concern grew at Jewish immigration, dispossession, violence, and repressive governance by the British. Palestinian national leaders and incipient nationalists appeared unable to stop the political tide that was moving against them. Leaders vied for power with each other, succumbing to well-worn tropes that allowed the British to 'divide and rule' the native people. Sheikh Izz ad-Din al-Qassam was the antithesis of such preoccupations and concerns. He had no vested interest – no familial ties or bonds in such clannish society – only the spirit of Salafi Islam and a message of jihad. In his adopted city of Haifa and through his job as teacher, preacher, and travelling religious functionary, his message was promoted among the indigent living in shanty homes in the city and the villages and hamlets of the surrounding countryside. He used his positions as an opportunity to promote the Salafi message at the heart of the Brotherhood project and a particular form of jihad that would attract the attention of the governing British.

Indeed Britain's top police officer in Palestine at the time noted that al-Qassam's Islamist interpretation 'sanctions the use of violence . . . bringing together the more religiously minded [to] preach to them the doctrines of Islam, cleverly interpolating such passages from the Qur'an as were calculated to stimulate a spirit of religious fanaticism'.[8] By 1930 al-Qassam had a fatwa (a religio-juridic verdict or counsel issued by a religious scholar) which permitted jihad against the British and the Zionists in Palestine. With this 'call to arms', al-Qassam began to organize small cells of men to prepare the ground to launch attacks. In November 1935, however, in the wake of a Qassamite attack on a British police officer, Izz ad-Din al-Qassam was shot dead by the British. Following his death, thousands mobilized not only to attend his funeral but also to promote his call to jihad. This was evident in the first sparks of the Palestinian general strike and revolt of 1936–9. Lauded as a martyr, al-Qassam epitomized a new form of Islamism. This activism, although different in manifestation from that of traditional Muslim leaders in Palestine at the time, was also apparent in its cause for vexation to the British in the controversial leadership of Haj Amin al-Husseini. Al-Husseini, a Palestinian native of the notable Jerusalem-based classes, would later engage with the same kind of Brotherhood-inspired and Islamist rhetoric as al-Qassam.

The Brotherhood had dispatched emissaries in the mid-1940s to Palestine to establish new branches of the movement in cities and towns such as Jerusalem, Haifa, Nablus, and Gaza. These branches were important loci for burgeoning Muslim political representation and debate that attracted and drew in local Muslim clerics, leaders and other high-profile personalities including those from Palestine's notable families. The appeal of the Brotherhood was wide, as indicated by the thousands of members who joined the Palestinian branches within two years of their founding. Yet the branches in Palestine were significantly beholden to the mother branch in Cairo acting as a satellite rather than an autonomous offshoot. With little actual power in terms of decision making, this vulnerability became apparent in the late 1940s when the UN decided to vote to approve partition of Palestine, which led to the Israeli declaration of independence in May 1948.[9]

Bound

It was not only with the events of 1948 that the fortunes of the Brotherhood in Egypt and Palestine seem tied, but from that period onwards to the late 1960s the successive ruling regimes treated them similarly. If, as was the case under Nasser's rule, the Egyptian Brotherhood was considered problematic, then so too were its supporters and members in Gaza. After the 1948 Arab-Israeli war and the dispossession of hundreds of thousands of Palestinians, the Brotherhood in Gaza tried to organize and respond to the huge influx of dispossessed, stateless Palestinian refugees alongside other local Palestinian political actors. Yet it, like other Palestinian organizations, was subject to the same disruptions attendant to a war and wave of refugees numbering in the hundreds of thousands and now dispersed across the Arab world and beyond. This meant that the leadership rather than the philosophy of the Brotherhood and al-Banna's vision was weakened or had to transform as a new generation of pious yet activist Palestinian Muslims arose. Indeed the ties with Egypt and in particular Cairo created the opportunities for learning and exposure to Brotherhood-inspired Islamism for many nascent Palestinian leaders while they attended colleges and universities to gain training in much-needed professions.

For those Palestinians attracted to the Muslim Brotherhood in particular, the opportunity to be educated in Cairo exposed them to the turbulent yet significant transitions taking place in this leading Arab state. They witnessed first-hand the promise of the Muslim Brotherhood to transform politics from the national to the pan-Islamic (within that lay the prospect of jihad to liberate Palestine), as well as the eventual backlash when in 1952 the Free Officers took power. Following the coup in Egypt, the Muslim Brotherhood, as Chapter 2 highlighted, enjoyed only the briefest of honeymoons with the new regime before the inexorable repression that was to come. The repressive drive against the Brotherhood at home in Egypt had powerful attendant consequences for those associated with the movement residing in Egyptian-administered Gaza. Members of the Brotherhood, including some that would later go on to found political organizations such as Fatah and Hamas, were rounded up in successive purges and thrown into jails in Egypt. Gazan members of the Brotherhood felt so threatened by the Egyptian regime that many fled into exile or abandoned the movement altogether. By the late 1960s and early 1970s, this subjugation also led to its virtual dormancy throughout the Gaza Strip.[10]

In the West Bank the case was slightly different. There the geographic reality of Palestinian territory annexed by the Hashemite Kingdom of Jordan meant that the Brotherhood would be subsumed, from 1952 onwards, to the diktats of King Hussein as he navigated a place for himself and his country in a tumultuous region. Notably the Jordanian Muslim Brotherhood was the only organization to survive the king's decision in 1957 to proscribe and ban all political parties. Yet although they survived the banning, with elections suspended and a government dismissed by the king, the Muslim Brotherhood was politically toothless and perceived as a 'loyal opposition'. This meant that its key relationship with the monarch, King Hussein, would determine the fortunes of the movement in the West Bank and led to its virtual dormancy throughout the 1950s and 1960s. Palestinian members of the Muslim Brotherhood in the West Bank make some small claims that they were active in their own areas but also acknowledge that growing Hashemite antipathy to any form of Palestinian or Palestinian-inspired activism hindered them.[11]

Hamas, the Islamic Resistance Movement

> The Islamic Resistance Movement is one of the wings of Moslem Brotherhood in Palestine. Moslem Brotherhood Movement is a universal organization which constitutes the largest Islamic movement in modern times.
>
> *Hamas Charter, Article 2, August 1988*[12]

The Hamas movement, founded in the Gaza Strip as the first Palestinian uprising (Intifada) erupted, identified itself as part of the Muslim Brotherhood movement. It is important to recognize that an entire article of the Hamas covenant is dedicated to praising the Brotherhood and the ties it claims to it. Hamas declared that the Brotherhood was

> characterised by its deep understanding, accurate comprehension and its complete embrace of all Islamic concepts of all aspects of life, culture, creed, politics, economics, education, society, justice and judgement, the spreading of Islam, education, art, information, science of the occult and conversion to Islam.[13]

And while it is true to argue that Hamas carries features or approaches that typify it as part of the Brotherhood, there are other dimensions of the movement where

68 Palestine – Hamas and the link

it diverges sharply from it. In particular, in the wake of Hamas violence against Israel and particularly its campaign of suicide bombings in both the first and second Intifadas, it became more regularly characterized as a radical, terrorist jihadist movement. Due to their similar tactics against a common enemy of Israel, Hamas also became conjoined with a most un-Brotherhood-like movement: the radical *Shi'a* Lebanese Hizballah (Party of God).[14] Hamas, like Hizballah, is also portrayed as engaged in an absolutist existentialist battle to destroy what it regularly refers to as the Zionist entity.

Hamas is multidimensional in structure if not in terms of ideological orientation.[15] Its political and violence-prone rather than apolitical or social features are usually represented as its major dualist positions.[16] This highlights the dynamic rather than static character of the organization as it has developed over successive decades since it was founded in the Gaza Strip in the late 1980s. Hamas is certainly linked to the Muslim Brotherhood, but it is more of a foundling influenced by the mother organization than its child.

During the first Intifada and the early years of its establishment, Hamas identified objectives and pursued strategies that marked it as very much independent of the Egyptian Muslim Brotherhood. Yet the link between the Brotherhood and Hamas is considered important by authors such as Tamimi.[17] Hamas presented itself as a national Muslim movement defined by its avowed commitment to engage in resistance against Israel. Hamas also sought to embark on a reformist revivalist Muslim project to bring the local population back to the straight path of Islam. Furthermore, Hamas identified itself from the very start as engaged in a competition for forms of political power against a local national-secularist rival – the Palestine Liberation Organization (PLO). At a time of unprecedented national unity that crossed boundaries of social class, religion, rural and urban, gender and generation, the new Islamist movement staked itself outside the Unified National Leadership of the Uprising structure.[18] It was to be a competitor to claim the Palestinian national project in its name, including the confrontation with Israel. Hamas was not a satellite of the Egyptian Muslim Brotherhood or of the Brotherhood movement in Jordan, but its leaders were able to draw inspiration and support knowing that the issues it organized around and the campaigns it led reflected historic concerns of the wider Brotherhood movement over Palestine and, in particular, holy places such as Jerusalem.

In Cairo and Amman, the leadership of the Muslim Brotherhood was able to engender support for Hamas that promoted many of its activities. Indeed Hamas sought to build strong ties and relations with their counterparts in the Muslim Brotherhood in these and other locations across the region. The ties between the Muslim Brotherhood in Jordan and Hamas, for example, were strong particularly until 1999 when Hamas was essentially forced by Jordan to relocate to Damascus in Syria. Up until that point the Jordanian Muslim Brotherhood proved to be powerful supporters for Hamas, and this played an important part in the extent to which King Hussein tolerated the Palestinian movement and its activities in his own kingdom and Hamas's abilities in turn to garner support and resources from the wider

Brotherhood family. Another important venue where the links between Hamas and the Muslim Brotherhood were demonstrably visible was at a conference of Islamists in Khartoum in 1995 attended by Hamas delegates, as well as their colleagues from the Egyptian Muslim Brotherhood.[19] This union of the Brotherhood would sustain Hamas through the ensuing decades as it transitioned from being in the burgeoning Islamist opposition of the Palestinian Territories to the seismic electoral victory of January 2006 when the Palestinian electorate gave them a mandate to govern and victory over their secular rivals in the PLO.

The 2006 election victory for Hamas was considered a watershed moment for the wider Muslim Brotherhood movement and one which the Egyptian Muslim Brotherhood would have been wise to learn from. Hamas soon discovered that even though they enjoyed a democratic mandate there were forces arrayed against them who were unwilling to share power and would also seek to depose them.[20] Hamas, in contesting the elections, had for the first time decided to participate in a system of politics established through the Oslo Accords. This was a reversal of Hamas's previous position of rejecting the accords and the arrangements within them. The Hamas leadership declared that by participating it was merely being responsive to a popular consensus from its supporters that it should contest power and formally enter the Palestinian opposition. It did not expect electoral victory. With victory in 2006, however, a dynamic was established of opposition to Hamas rule and non-cooperation from their opponents in Fatah and Fatah-controlled institutions of governance. This, along with other factors, propelled Hamas from participation to domination and is epitomized in the takeover of Gaza and the rout of Fatah effected by the organization in June 2007. As would be proved in Egypt in the 2011–13 period with the Muslim Brotherhood, the temptation to dominate rather than participate and power share was too difficult for the Hamas leadership to resist.

The Morsi effect in Gaza

There was no Arab Spring in Gaza, but the events taking place in the region would have significant consequences for the Hamas movement. It came as no surprise to anybody that the election of the Muslim Brotherhood's Mohammed Morsi to the presidency in Egypt in the summer of 2012 would have an important impact on Hamas, internal Palestinian political rivalries, and the wider Israeli-Palestinian conflict. Though Morsi's victory was welcomed by all Palestinian political factions, Egypt's choice was also Hamas's and their leadership was delighted that 'their man' and 'their movement' had achieved a convincing popular victory at the ballot box. As in 2006 when Hamas won free and fair Palestinian legislative elections, the opportunity for democracy had resulted in a Muslim Brotherhood victory. In Gaza, the Hamas government organized rallies in which tens of thousands of supporters took part to celebrate the victory of their Egyptian brethren. Amidst the celebratory rifle fire, distribution of sweets, and statements of support from the senior ranks of the leadership, there was a far more palpable sense of achievement than had greeted the Hamas electoral victory in January 2006.[21] One of the few surviving

70 Palestine – Hamas and the link

founders of Hamas, Mahmoud Zahar, termed Morsi's success as a historic victory that had demonstrated that the patience of those in the Muslim Brotherhood movement paid dividends.[22] President Morsi had moved from prison to the presidency, marking the beginning of a period of significant competition between the Muslim Brotherhood and the Supreme Council of the Armed Forces (SCAF) led by General al-Sisi.[23] SCAF was not prepared to tolerate the establishment of a religious state at home or an axis of the Muslim Brotherhood abroad. To this end, Morsi would be considered, as Egyptians said, a 'fat-free' president whose powers with respect to national security and foreign policy would be severely constrained by SCAF.[24] Moreover, Mubarak's authoritarian legacy coupled with a post-revolution society straining under severe economic problems would mean that the primary consideration for the new power holders had to be domestic, not foreign.[25]

Hamas leaders believed that the Morsi triumph would also spell the end of the cosy and problematic relationship which had endured between Cairo and Tel Aviv under Mubarak's leadership. For the wider population of Gaza, there was a hope that the Morsi government would do more than Mubarak had ever done to alleviate them from the hardship wrought by years of Israeli-imposed siege and closure of all of Gaza's borders to the rest of the world except with Egypt. They hoped that the blockade would be eased by President Morsi ordering the continuous opening of the Rafah crossing from Egypt to Gaza for people and trade.[26] Some Hamas leaders even spoke of the possibility of free trade zones opening in North Sinai adjacent to Gaza which would promote hopes of prosperity.[27] In the West Bank, where President Mahmoud Abbas and his Fatah faction of the PLO governed, there were, by way of stark contrast, no celebrations at the Muslim Brotherhood's victory in Cairo, only unease and disquiet.

The Morsi victory appeared to reinforce the long-standing and historic support from Egypt for the Palestinian cause. It was natural that Egypt would feel sympathy for the Palestinians and yet it had to be cognisant of its own national commitments in the Egypt-Israel Peace Treaty. This was a period in which President Morsi had already made clear his intent to maintain the country's treaties and agreements with other states both within the region (including Israel) and outside it. It was essential if Egypt was to play its part in preserving the regional security order and maintain the levels of political and economic support it enjoyed from major state actors such as the United States.

There was also an important and perhaps more urgent national security imperative for Egypt to remain concerned with Gaza in particular. This was a concern shared, in part, by Morsi, the Muslim Brotherhood, SCAF, Hamas, and even Israel: the threat posed by violent radical takfiri-Salafi-jihadist elements and in particular Ansar Bayt al-Maqdis and ISIS.[28] This meant that Hamas would not have everything its own way but would become one, among many, seeking access to the new power holders in Egypt to lobby for support and sympathy. Hamas, though, convinced that the tide of history had finally turned in its favour, would assiduously and continuously associate itself and remind its audience (at home or abroad) of its important linkages with the Muslim Brotherhood. Khaled Meshal, the leader of Hamas's political bureau, was even rumoured to be relinquishing his role as head of the organization to instead stand as the leader of the Palestinian Muslim Brotherhood in alliance with Cairo.[29] It threw its lot firmly in with the new president and Muslim Brotherhood–dominated dispensation, banking that it could capitalize for many years, if not decades to come, on such an alliance. In this respect, Hamas believed the Muslim Brotherhood's transformation would deliver a new political horizon in terms of its competition with its local rivals, chief of which was the PLO's main Fatah faction. It was convinced that under Morsi, even if Palestinian reconciliation were pushed, it would be far more favourable to Hamas than Fatah. The Hamas leadership also believed that the new administration in Cairo would be the key to their wider regional ambitions both as part of the Islamist trend represented by the Muslim Brotherhood, as well as the specific goals and ambitions of Hamas to make alliances with Arab and Muslim state actors and transnational organizations.

There was a sense of limitless possibility for the spread and influence of the Muslim Brotherhood. Hamas had led the way by contesting and winning elections in January 2006, only for the Egyptian Muslim Brotherhood to achieve a similar victory in 2012. These aspirations, however, were severely curtailed in the wake of the fatal attack on Rafah on 5 August 2012 leaving sixteen Egyptian soldiers dead and Hamas leaders worried that they would be in part blamed and punished.[30] 'Hamas never had any involvement in the killings,' asserted one of the founders of Hamas's military wing, Rawhi Mushtaha. 'It's a vicious media rumour that Hamas is involved. We wouldn't have done such a thing during Mubarak's time and certainly not under Morsi.'[31] The leadership was prescient but in reality powerless with respect to its concerns.

Following the attack, both Egypt and Israel alleged that some of the attackers came from Gaza. Hamas had always been under pressure to crack down on Salafi-jihadist elements, and now the impetus to do so accelerated. A Hamas senior leader, Ahmed Yousef, acknowledged this, saying,

> We have an important task to do which is to watch the actions of the jihadi salafis in the Gaza Strip. I think these groups are capable of breaching the security situation here because of the high rate of unemployment among the youth of Gaza. This is a very serious situation and a very big challenge for the government in Gaza to deal with.[32]

The long-standing concern about Salafi-jihadi elements locating to Gaza from northern Sinai in Egypt would be heightened in the wake of the attack and the allegations surrounding militant involvement and support.[33]

Hamas leaders had been trying to urge Egypt's new leaders to help Gaza break out of its isolation. But those efforts suffered a major setback as a result of the Rafah attack. Although its leaders were now travelling regularly for meetings in Cairo and beyond and engaged in positive discussions about trade and border crossings, the attack would mean that the organization would have to readjust its expectations. The myriad of illegal tunnels operated by Hamas from which it derived

72 Palestine – Hamas and the link

much-needed resources and taxation revenue into Gaza were soon identified as a source of the national security problem by Egypt. Hamas would come under significant pressure to close them down. Increasingly, Hamas found it had little choice in the matter when Egypt considered it within its strategic orbit to robustly tackle the Sinai security problem.

Operation pillar of defence: Whose side was Morsi on?

By November 2012, nearly two years after the outbreak of the Arab Spring, the Hamas leadership had grown confident and were coming to believe in the inevitable justness of their cause even if in reality they continued to preside over a war-shattered, besieged, and benighted population in the Gaza Strip; remained in enmity with Fatah; and increasingly engaged in the politics of autocracy rather than democracy in respect of governing Gaza's citizens. In large part this confidence derived not from their power or support in Gaza or the West Bank but the improved status and standing of Hamas regionally. Hamas had been a significant beneficiary of the new geopolitical and diplomatic realities of the Middle East since the Arab Spring and primarily the meteoric successes of the Muslim Brotherhood, which Hamas could hitch on. It had moved adroitly from the Syrian-Iranian axis back into a more natural alliance with the Muslim Brotherhood and particular Sunni states such as Qatar, where it had moved its headquarters after abandoning the regime of Bashar al-Assad in Syria. This led to benefits in terms of Egypt, Qatar, and Turkey and altered relations, as discussed in the following chapter, with Jordan as well.

This confidence, some contend, was evidenced in the wake of the landmark visit paid to Gaza by the emir of Qatar in October 2012,[34] after which Hamas engaged in rocket attacks on Israeli targets and vowed to drive the Zionist enemy out of the region. The rocket attacks were tactical in terms of demonstrating to its own local and new regional constituencies that Hamas remained a resistance movement, as well as a government. Even if Hamas and by extension the Muslim Brotherhood believed that such attacks did not violate the rules of the game with Israel, in reality such an approach overlooked the fact that Israel decided what the rules of the game were too.

Nonetheless, Hamas had not resolved the internal contradiction of being a Palestinian movement that governs and also engages in armed attacks against Israel. Yet it failed to resolve this paradox because to do so would undermine its raison d'être, which in turn was the position it employed to criticize the Fatah leadership in the West Bank and the failure of the peace-through-negotiation option. Additionally, Hamas was under no pressure to resolve this contradiction as a price for inclusion in the wider regional political environment of the Middle East. As Hamas continued to 'look East', the Western-imposed entry price for legitimacy and recognition diminished in Hamas's wider strategic calculations. It felt it could rely on Cairo and the emerging regional Brotherhood axis to provide it legitimacy and cover in Gaza against Israel, but they would be wrong.[35]

The relationship between Morsi-governed Egypt and Hamas was put to the test in November 2012 when Israel assassinated Hamas's top military leader, Ahmad al-Jaabari, and Hamas launched Operation Stones of Shale[36] in retaliation. Israel's response was Operation Pillar of Defence, leading to an eight-day conflict marked by hundreds of air strikes and i over 1,000 rockets launched by Hamas and other Palestinian factions.[37] Hamas Izz ad-Din al-Qassam Brigade leaders, supported by Palestinian resistance factions, launched a previously unmatched barrage of missiles at Israeli targets in southern Israel, as well as Tel Aviv and Jerusalem. The missile attacks on Tel Aviv and Jerusalem were a major psychological victory for Hamas and the factions in Gaza.[38] It indicated, to some extent, that in 2012 Hamas and the Gaza factions were better armed than in 2008.

Israel responded with its own barrage of missiles and air strikes, and as the conflict unfolded, Palestinian civilian casualty numbers grew at an alarming rate to over one hundred. But a ceasefire to end this conflict between Hamas and Israel needed a mediator. In the past that mediator had been Egypt and in particular the powerful state intelligence bureau headed by Omar Suleiman. By November 2012 Suleiman and his General Intelligence Directorate had all but gone and in its place were the Muslim Brotherhood and President Morsi. Under President Morsi, Egypt's new government, now dominated by the Muslim Brotherhood, had been forced to reassess and rebalance state positioning on Israel (and extant peace treaties and protocols), taking popular sentiment into account in ways which preserved preexisting regional and global dependencies yet mediated populist claims instead of ignoring them. This new dimension was apparent in November 2012 when President Morsi supported Gazans and the Hamas government during Israel's Operation Pillar of Defence with public gestures such as keeping the Rafah border between Gaza and Egypt open and sending his prime minister to Gaza. Yet it was the same Morsi government of solidarity and support for Hamas that would step in to act as mediator with Israel and preserve previous Egyptian commitments to peace. President Morsi and his government had to balance Egyptian national interest with responsiveness to Egyptian popular sentiment on the Palestinian issue. In contrast to Morsi, the Brotherhood's Supreme Guide Mohammed Badie certainly presented a different face of the movement to the public.[39] The president and his government, moreover, were bound further by the Muslim Brotherhood's long-standing position on the Palestinian issue in terms of *ummah* and jihad.

Outside of government, the Brotherhood's Supreme Guide Mohammed Badie publicly called for protests to support the Palestinians, and Yusuf al-Qaradawi appeared in Cairo to lead prayers at al-Azhar mosque and demonstrate solidarity with Gaza.[40] But not all in Gaza were overjoyed at the Egyptian effort. As one Hamas blogger wrote, 'We thought he [PM Qandil] would come at the head of an army but he comes to implement the wishes of the Obama designated calm. How can this [path] grant victory to the Muslims?'[41] The ceasefire agreement between Israel and Hamas, brokered by Egypt, that brought hostilities to an end in November 2012 was a victory that Hamas nevertheless claimed.[42] 'Thanks to our resistance and the heroic mujahideen fighters we triumphed and imposed conditions on the

74 Palestine – Hamas and the link

Zionist enemy,' declared Hamas leader Izzat Risheq.[43] 'The truce has entered into execution,' declared a joint statement issued in the name of Khaled Meshal and Palestinian Islamic jihad leader Ramadan Shallah on November 21, 2012. 'Any blast,' the statement warned its fighters, 'is a breach of the *tahdiyah* [calm]. The Gaza war is now over, the occupied is defeated.'[44] By early 2013, however, it was apparent that any victory that Hamas was claiming was a hollow one. Israel's blockade was still maintained on Gaza, and once again its environs, population, and infrastructure were struggling to cope. The Hamas leadership continued to face towards Cairo, but hopes and expectations were thoroughly shattered when, as we discussed in Chapter 2, Morsi and his government were deposed in July that year.[45]

Bereft

The fall of the Morsi regime and ascent of General al-Sisi to the elected office of president in Egypt[46] has had profound consequences for Hamas not only in terms of its control of the Gaza Strip but also in terms of its position as an Islamist organization within the wider Middle East region. It became more than apparent that the loss of Morsi and the moves against the Brotherhood in Egypt would affect Hamas and its ability to govern in Gaza, as well as manoeuvre regionally in alliance with the wider Islamist trend that they represented. One leader was quoted as stating that Hamas,

> particularly at the level of its bases, is in the midst of a setback that has been unprecedented for decades. This came as a result of the closure of the main door in the face of the Hamas movement, which we thought would open other political doors for us and make the Islamic movement a major power in the Arab world.[47]

In the Gaza Strip itself, it was not long before the implications of the changes in power in Egypt became apparent along with the impact on Hamas's ability to govern in Gaza, act as a rival to other political actors, including their foes in Fatah, or mount its operations against Israel. As one Arab columnist noted, 'Hamas' project fell in Egypt before its fall in Gaza.'[48] Things went from bad to worse when the new regime governed by al-Sisi in Cairo moved to not only limit Palestinian access to the wider Arab world through the only land crossing to Egypt at Rafah but also embarked on a systematic push to close down the Hamas-controlled smuggling tunnels which had been Gaza's lifeline.[49] Al-Sisi's decision to close the tunnels would have particular importance for Hamas. Not only were the tunnels a lifeline in terms of smuggled goods, including arms and ammunition to be employed against Israel, but the Hamas government also derived important taxation revenues from the contraband goods that were brought in by Gaza's traders. Evidence of the effectiveness of this campaign by Egypt was apparent by May 2015 when al-Sisi's government announced that 80 per cent of Gaza's tunnels had been closed by it.[50]

In the summer of 2014, Hamas found itself again in violent conflict with Israel. Operation Protective Edge, a fifty-day war, left more than 2,000 Palestinians and 73 Israelis dead.[51] Additionally, 11,000 Palestinians were injured, 500,000 were displaced, and 108,000 ended up homeless.[52] Despite Hamas initially having a 'good war', by August 2014 Israel had succeeded in significantly degrading Hamas's capabilities. Hamas did not succeed in ending the siege on Gaza. Some Palestinians contended that the war only exacerbated the humanitarian crisis in Gaza. They argued that Hamas capitulated on the issue of siege as an expediency of war but there was a high human cost to this long-drawn-out calculation. Moreover, Hamas was unable to achieve rapprochement with Egypt and relations were at an all-time low. Some senior Hamas leaders tried to shift gears to improve the relationship with Egypt as they realized that Morsi and the Muslim Brotherhood would not come back to power anytime soon. Israel had succeeded in pushing Gaza into the lap of General al-Sisi's Egypt – which was not a comfortable place for Hamas's leaders. Egypt, by this point, was interested first and foremost in regime protection and its own internal affairs – not Hamas or Gaza. Conversely, in the wake of the 2014 Gaza war, Palestinian Authority (PA) President Mahmoud Abbas's relations with al-Sisi's regime in Cairo became much more positive. Hamas had a lot to recover from.

Between a rock and a hard place

By February 2015 Hamas found itself embroiled in Egypt's business and once again desperately defending itself amidst a media campaign identifying it as part of a Muslim Brotherhood and jihadi-Salafi conspiracy to challenge not only the government of President al-Sisi but also other powerful states in the Middle East. The Egyptian media carried leaked reports from state security services that alleged that Hamas and the Muslim Brotherhood were in alliance with armed jihadi-Salafi proxies in the region to overthrow state power. In charge sheets against the radical jihadi group Ansar Bayt al-Maqdis, Egyptian state prosecutors also included allegations of collusion with Hamas in acts of terrorism and alliance with the Islamic State (ISIS).[53]

Over a period of eighteen months, the Egyptian state had engaged in a campaign which was inexorably tying the fate of Hamas to the worst excesses and violence of Islamic Salafi-jihadism in the Middle East region in opposition to an arc of cooperation against such forces which had emerged between Egypt, Saudi Arabia, the UAE, and Jordan. If the national security priority for al-Sisi was to root out the Muslim Brotherhood, it was inevitable that Hamas would be targeted. This gave rise to speculation that Egypt wished to break Hamas's control on Gaza and allow other actors, including Fatah or a variant of Fatah led by Mohammed Dahlan, to rule instead.[54]

Hamas was accused of having direct links with attacks on Egypt's security forces, as well as the interests of Egypt in other neighbouring states.[55] As Egypt's coercive grip was challenged in the Sinai, Hamas-controlled Gaza was viewed as a threat

76 Palestine – Hamas and the link

rather than bulwark of the state in its multipronged counter-assaults. Egyptian courts had banned Hamas from organizing in Egypt, confiscated its offices, and designated the armed wing of the movement – the Izz ad-Din al-Qassam Brigades – a terrorist organization amidst claims that it was organizing and perpetrating violence in Egypt.[56] Al-Sisi, after having ordered his security forces to effectively seal Gaza from Egypt (and thus beyond), was creating a buffer zone and bombing Gaza sites suspected of links to militant activities.[57] Hamas-associated media pushed back on claims against them by countering assertions and providing assurances that the group would never attack Egypt.[58] Similarly, its spokespersons described assertions that Egypt would bomb Gaza as part of its wider counter-terrorist efforts to preserve its national security as 'madcap'.[59]

Hamas continued to reject accusations that it was part of an Islamist Salafi-jihadi conspiracy forming an arc of confrontation stretching from Islamic State (ISIS)–controlled Iraq and Syria to the overcrowded refugee camps of the Gaza Strip. Hamas spokespersons took to the media to rebuff such accusations and emphasize the role that it was playing and could play in meeting the challenge posed by such radical Islamist elements. Nevertheless, there was a growing sense that Hamas was imperilled, presenting its enemies and rivals with an opportunity to manoeuvre to predict its downfall or play for the entrance of alternative political and security actors in Gaza.

The organization was not just under pressure from Egypt but was also caught in a wider downward spiral of fortunes for the Muslim Brotherhood in Jordan, Syria, Tunisia, and the waning of support from Gulf states such as Qatar. In Gaza, Hamas was yet to recover from the effects of Operation Protective Edge.[60] Hamas had, as on previous occasions, employed its propaganda machine to declare the war a victory of sorts against Israel, but the absence of a unified government to rebuild and reconstruct Gaza, a salary crisis among tens of thousands of public workers, accompanied by manifold other problems, were challenges to the weakened movement. Debates about its future prospects centre on its position in Gaza relative to its weakened state in other locales such as the Fatah-controlled West Bank. Hamas had emerged from the war of 2014 strengthened, even if the population of Gaza had not. But how could Hamas advance its goals in terms of ideology, resistance, governance, and politics? Working in the group's favour, as opposed to other Islamist movements, Hamas had always been a movement that was not ideologically dogmatic, instead allowing for degrees of pragmatism or flexibility.[61]

Nevertheless, Hamas faced problems. Preoccupied and weighed down by Gaza's economic and reconstruction woes, the energies of the organization that were previously dissipated on a variety of issues and goals became increasingly narrowed. Two years previously, Hamas, along with other Muslim Brotherhood organizations, saw themselves moving forward in terms of strategic calculations about its place in relation to wider issues of governance, resistance, and domination. If conflict with Israel had become rhetorically driven by existential causes and arguments, so too, increasingly, was Hamas's conflict with its rivals in Fatah. The notion of a tunnel with no light at its end was not only a reality in terms of Hamas's links to the rest of the world but also a powerful metaphor for the predicament it found itself in by 2015. The leadership of the movement had to position itself for the future, but given the extent of its regional losses, its options were narrow.

Gaza, and its postwar reconstruction, had come to dominate Hamas's priorities. Its control of the territory was thus more important than ever since Gaza was the only territory where it enjoyed a monopoly of control with respect to political power, coercive force, and military power, as well as a constituency of popular support.[62] It was the combination of these factors which was so significant. This Gaza focus created tensions with respect to its broader-strategic priorities as a Sunni Muslim Brotherhood–inspired resistance movement against Israel. In this respect, Hamas continued to indicate it was not ready for concession on such strategic goals. Until February 2015, the strategic position regarding Israel had, in many respects, remained unchanging. Hamas had other preoccupations but was forced to address such positions in the wake of a visit to the Gaza Strip by Quartet peace envoy Tony Blair. Blair, whose visit was protected by Hamas security forces, promoted a series of public signals and messages focussed on five new conditions[63] which the international community was asserting Hamas should commit to in return for progress in Gaza. The five new conditions on the movement were (1) reconciliation with Fatah, (2) acceptance of the two-state solution to the conflict on 1967 borders, (3) agreement to a two-state solution, (4) desisting from involving itself in the wider Islamist arc or axis in the region, and (5) underwriting security assurances to Egypt that its territory would not be used as a base to undermine or organize attacks from. The undercurrent of Blair's initiative in terms of addressing Hamas was ill-disguised when he told a journalist that Hamas had to progress because the regional situation had changed and was leading to new alliances against ISIS and other Islamist forces. Blair spoke of partnerships between Israel and Saudi Arabia and the 'blockage' of the Palestinian problem.[64]

Hamas responded with a social media broadside[65] led by Musa Abu Marzouk, deputy chairman of the Hamas political leadership, who essentially restated long-held positions and assurances.[66] Calling the Blair terms an attempt to engage in 'displacement tactics as a means to enforce a series of conditions governing the entire process of reconstruction', Hamas condemned the timing and nature of the Quartet position. Abu Marzouk dealt with each one of the five conditions, highlighting that Hamas had already engaged in reconciliation with Fatah and accepted the principle of a Palestinian state on 1967 borders. He also pointed out that as a liberation movement, Hamas would always enjoy support from diverse groups but that it remained committed to a battle with Israel and Israel alone and was not interested in conflict with other states. On the issue of Egypt and the claims that Hamas was making an enemy of its powerful neighbour, the Hamas leader reiterated that Egyptian security and stability were an absolute Palestinian interest.

> For us Egypt is not only a neighbour. Egypt's security, stability and territorial integrity have vital implications for Palestinians. Egypt's strength is ours too . . . The strength of Egypt is the strength of the Palestinian

people, and particularly that of the residents of the Gaza Strip. Hamas will not allow the Gaza Strip to become a base for attacks on Egypt or for causing any damage to the country.[67]

Control of Gaza was, however, also threatening internal cohesion within the Hamas leadership, particularly at the level of the political and military. The centre of gravity moving between and within the political bureau and Izz ad-Din al-Qassam Brigades was unprecedented. In the past the political leadership had enjoyed sole authority over strategic decision making and power within the movement. In the wake of military engagements with Israel – particularly in 2012 and 2014 when the Brigades had been deemed to fight well against Israel – their voice in realms of political and strategic decision taking had been absorbed or reflected in an appetite for prolonged violence and resistance. This has been further evidenced by fears that the military leadership of Hamas has overreached its mandate in terms of operational activities to include political and strategic decisions or influencing of political and strategic decisions. The war of 2014, it has been contended, started because Hamas military cells decided to launch an attack without a green light from the political leadership or at best only sections of it.[68] The prolongation of the war for fifty-one days with the consequences this had in terms of destruction in Gaza and a rising death toll was also allegedly the result of an appetite by the Izz ad-Din al-Qassam Brigades to continue the fight against the wishes of those in the Hamas political leadership in Gaza concerned about the high costs on the local population of Israeli bombardment and destruction. This tension has given rise to concerns that Hamas is undergoing a process of jihadification where, in the absence of political progress on domestic, national, regional and international fronts, the argument for militancy and resistance grows in saliency and impact.[69]

Hamas leadership's internal cohesion has become problematic and thus has affected the broader strategic priorities as they relate to domestic, regional, and international arenas. Domestically such factors were seen in explaining why the leadership, in 2014, entered into another reconciliation agreement with its rivals in the Fatah movement.[70] The movement finds itself in a place it swore that it would avoid. Its leaders said that the movement would always come first and that they would not be seduced by governance or forms of dependency on other actors. The Gaza-based leadership of figures such as Ismail Haniyeh and Mahmoud Zahar had gained at the expense of the external leadership led by Khaled Meshal. Loss of regional support created pressures to return to the so-called Axis of Rejection in alliance with Iran and Syria, which Hamas had previously left in 2011. When the Arab Spring had broken out in Syria later evolving into a sectarian fight, Sunni Islamist forces joined rebel elements against the regime of Bashar al-Assad. The Hamas leadership, including Khaled Meshal, which had been headquartered in Damascus since 1999, embarked on a strategic jettisoning of Assad's patronage and headed to Qatar instead.[71] The orientation to Qatar and the Muslim Brotherhood that Hamas leader Khaled Meshal had spearheaded several years earlier was now weakening. The Muslim Brotherhood was in a state of collapse across the region, and Qatar, bowing to pressure from its Gulf neighbours in Saudi Arabia and the UAE, was turning away from Hamas.[72] Iran had re-emerged as the ally most likely to help Hamas and replenish it in terms of the resources it needed to support the population, especially those on its payroll, as well as Hamas's campaign against Israel.[73] While there was a belief that in the past Iran had not exacted any price from Hamas in return for its support, the new regional environment might change that.[74] Since Hamas had moved from the rejectionist axis in 2011, Iran and its proxy Hizballah in Lebanon had become increasingly embroiled in the raging Islamist and sectarian conflict unfolding in Syria and Iraq, pitting it against Sunni Salafi-jihadist groups and elements including Jabhat al-Nusra, ISIS, and others, including those affiliated with the Syrian Muslim Brotherhood in the Commission of the Shields of the Revolution (*hayat duru al-thawrat*).[75] For Hamas to return into an axis with Hizballah and Iran in a regional climate of dissent with major sectarian overtones could isolate it even further.

Hamas had to balance its priorities and needed to seek external aid even if it meant seeking it from parties who would engender more hostility from its neighbours in Egypt, Israel, and Jordan. The movement had also reentered into a form of relationship for relief and funding purposes with a sworn local foe from the rival Fatah organization.[76] Mohammed Dahlan, a former Fatah leader and PA intelligence chief who had been ousted from the Central Committee of Fatah on charges of corruption, was considered to be a formidable player in terms of support to Gaza through wealthy backers in the UAE and his close relations with the government authorities of al-Sisi in Cairo. Hamas could take small comfort that it had a remaining ally in Turkey governed by President Recep Tayyip Erdogan. In this relationship, Hamas leaders were again dependent on the political and strategic calculations of an Islamist leader known to be keen to prevent rapprochement with Egypt.[77]

By 2015 control of Gaza through governance came first. Hamas was more entrenched than ever in regime preservation rather than political or diplomatic solutions and relations elsewhere. It betrayed an organizational resilience in a Palestinian space that no other actor appeared to be willing to totally occupy. Hamas continued to demand sacrifice from its supporters and the wider Palestinian population in its ongoing challenge to Israel's occupation and blockade. Yet organizational resilience required resources including support from other Islamists under the banner of the Muslim Brotherhood, and these were in very short supply. Indeed in February 2015 Hamas reeled from a further blow against it when an Egyptian court declared that the organization was a terrorist entity, thus ending any hopes that al-Sisi's regime would discriminate between Islamists.[78]

Future face

In the wake of the Arab Spring, and the crushing repression meted out to the Muslim Brotherhood in Egypt, Hamas has experienced unparalleled highs and lows. It sought to ride the Islamist wave on the electoral victory delivered to the Muslim Brotherhood in Egypt, as well as the wider regional amity that was apparent with respect to this form of Islamism in the months that followed the Arab Spring. Clearly the Hamas leadership was strategically adept at attempting to maximize the opportunity with their Brotherhood cohort in power in Cairo and Tunis and with a wider renaissance of their fortunes elsewhere across the region, but such opportunities were short-lived. When that amity soured to enmity against the Brotherhood, Hamas was naturally targeted. In particular the calamity visited upon the Egyptian Brotherhood in July and August 2013 led to fundamental repercussions for Hamas. Since that time it has appeared that Hamas's horizons have narrowed, and its future has become more precarious. Pundits have speculated that the movement may have reached a tipping point or could finally topple.[79]

Domestically the future for Hamas is bound by its monopoly of power in Gaza and an increasing contest to break this monopoly by a variety of its opponents including Salafi-jihadist and takfiri elements.[80] Local popular support for Hamas, however, has remained constant and has not collapsed. There is frustration that Hamas, like the Muslim Brotherhood in Egypt, has effectively failed at alliance building and power sharing with its secular nationalist counterparts in the PLO through the implementation of reconciliation agreements and a unified position on national Palestinian issues.

Regionally it is the case that Hamas is trying to position itself for the future by taking advantage in a reactive manner to opportunities that may come its way. Its regional horizon is presently limited by the loss of patrons, a tightening of the siege of Gaza from Egypt (rather than Israel), the waning influence of ideological allies in the wider Brotherhood movement, and declining saliency of arguments which link Islamism to violent resistance and a seemingly perpetual cycle of conflict with Israel where Hamas enjoys little by way of solidarity to its cause as evidenced in the lack support for post-conflict reconstruction in Gaza. The organization's future, however, will be characterized by continuing endurance. Hamas is a movement that, like the Muslim Brotherhood elsewhere in the Middle East, does not give up. It maintains forms of organizational resilience, though in the wake of the Arab Spring, this resilience has been tested and internal cohesion has strained. In the wake of the Arab Spring and as a wing of the Muslim Brotherhood, Hamas truly thought that it was on the side of the victors. The transition of power, however, to and from the Muslim Brotherhood in Egypt and Tunisia has put it on the losing side. The anticipated ascendency of the Muslim Brotherhood in Jordan spearheading the call for political reform in the kingdom, which would have brought significant benefit to Hamas, broke down under state repression. The emergence of Qatar as an important and new regional patron for Hamas and the Muslim Brotherhood has been circumscribed by its power struggle with Saudi Arabia limiting its capacity to fully champion the Brotherhood trend that had been established in the wake of the Arab Spring. Hamas's future, for the short term at least, is one of dangerous entrenchment in the Gaza Strip.

Notes

1 Mahmoud Zahar, author interview, Gaza City, 8 December 2011.

2 Hamas is an Arabic acronym of the full name of the movement, *Harakat al-Muqāwama al-Islāmiyya*, meaning the Islamic Resistance Movement.

3 See Article 2: Hamas, 'Hamas Covenant 1988', *Yale Law School Lillian Goldman Law Library*, 18 August 1988, http://avalon.law.yale.edu/20th_century/hamas.asp (accessed 10 March 2014).

4 P. Kingsley and P. Beaumont, 'Gaza Wants Back in from the Darkness as Hamas Feels the Isolation', *Guardian*, 25 April 2014, http://www.theguardian.com/world/2014/apr/25/gaza-back-in-hamas-isolation-egypt-unity-palestinian (accessed 30 April 2015).

5 Z. Abu Amr, *Islamic Fundamentalism in the West Bank and Gaza Strip*, Bloomington: University of Indiana Press, 1994; Z. Abu Amr, 'Hamas: A Historical and Political Background', *Journal of Palestine Studies*, Vol. 22:4, Summer 1993, pp. 5–19, http://www.jstor.org/stable/2538077 (accessed 1 May 2015); S. Mishal and A. Sela, *The Palestinian Hamas: Vision, Violence and Coexistence*, New York: Columbia University Press, 2000; B. Milton-Edwards, *Islamic Politics in Palestine*, London: I.B. Tauris, 1996.

6 See B. Milton-Edwards, *Islamic Politics in Palestine*, London: I.B. Tauris, 1996.

7 B. Milton-Edwards and S. Farrell, *Hamas: The Islamic Resistance Movement*, Cambridge: Polity Press, 2010, pp. 20–9.

8 Public Records Office file CO733/257/12, Situation in Palestine 1935, and Tegart Papers, Box 1, File 3c, from report on Terrorism 1936–37, p. 7, Kew, London.

9 See B. Milton-Edwards, *The Israeli-Palestinian Conflict: A People's War*, Abingdon: Routledge, 2009.

10 See B. Milton-Edwards, *Islamic Politics in Palestine*, London: I.B. Tauris, 1996.

11 B. Milton-Edwards, *Islamic Politics in Palestine*, London: I.B. Tauris, 1996, pp. 57–9.

12 See Hamas, 'Hamas Covenant 1988', *Yale Law School Lillian Goldman Law Library*, 18 August 1988, http://avalon.law.yale.edu/20th_century/hamas.asp (accessed 10 March 2014).

13 See Hamas, 'Hamas Covenant 1988', *Yale Law School Lillian Goldman Law Library*, 18 August 1988, http://avalon.law.yale.edu/20th_century/hamas.asp (accessed 10 March 2014).

14 See *Hamas and Hizbollah: The Radical Challenge to Israel in the Occupied Territories*, Carlisle, PA: US Army War College Press, 1994, http://www.strategicstudiesinstitute.army.mil/pubs/download.cfm?q=196 (accessed 1 May 2015); J.L. Gleis and B. Berti, *Hezbollah and Hamas: A Comparative Study*, Baltimore: John Hopkins University Press, 2012.

15 J. Gunning, *Hamas in Politics: Democracy, Religion, Violence*, London: Hurst, 2007; M.I. Jensen, *The Political Ideology of Hamas: A Grassroots Perspective*, London: I.B. Tauris, 2009.

16 Z. Chehab, *Inside Hamas: The Untold Story of Militants, Martyrs and Spies*, London and New York: I.B. Tauris, 2007; S. Roy, *Hamas and Civil Society in Gaza: Engaging the Islamist Social Sector*, Princeton, NJ: Princeton University Press, 2011.

17 A. Tamimi, *Hamas: Unwritten Chapters*, London: Hurst, 2007, pp. 53–5.

18 L. Taraki, 'The Islamic Resistance Movement in the Palestinian Uprising', *Middle East Report*, Vol. 19:156, January–February 1989, pp. 30–2, http://www.jstor.org/stable/3012813 (accessed 28 April 2015).

19 J. Immanuel, 'Hamas Sends Mission to Sudan', *Jerusalem Post*, 8 October 1995.

20 See B. Milton-Edwards and S. Farrell, *Hamas: The Islamic Resistance Movement*, Cambridge: Polity Press, 2010; D. Rose, 'The Gaza Bombshell', *Vanity Fair*, April 2008, http://www.vanityfair.com/news/2008/04/gaza200804 (accessed 4 May 2015); I. Black, 'UN Envoy: Anti-Hamas Rhetoric Undermines Democracy', *Guardian*, 13 June 2007, http://www.theguardian.com/world/2007/jun/13/israel5 (accessed 28 May 2015).

21 B. Milton-Edwards and S. Farrell, *Hamas: The Islamic Resistance Movement*, Cambridge: Polity Press, 2010, pp. 260–2.

22 Agence France-Presse, 'Egypt: Palestinians in Gaza Celebrate Muslim Brotherhood Election Win', *Telegraph*, 24 June 2012, http://www.telegraph.co.uk/news/worldnews/

82 Palestine – Hamas and the link

    africaandindianocean/egypt/9352563/Egypt-Palestinians-in-Gaza-celebrate-Muslim-Brotherhood-election-win.html (accessed 30 April 2015).

23 J. Stacher, 'SCAF and the Muslim Brotherhood', *Middle East Institute*, 14 April 2013, http://www.mei.edu/content/scaf%C2%A0and%C2%A0the%C2%A0muslim-brotherhood (accessed 20 May 2015); N.H. Rashwan, 'Morsi's Coup Against SCAF: The Hows and the Whys', *Ahram Online*, 14 August 2012, http://english.ahram.org.eg/NewsContent/1/140/50324/Egypt/First-days/Morsis-coup-against-SCAF-The-hows-and-the-whys.aspx (accessed 20 May 2015).

24 C.R. Wickham, *The Muslim Brotherhood: Evolution of an Islamist Movement*, Princeton, NJ: Princeton University Press, 2013, pp. 264–5.

25 Ahram Online, 'Morsi's First 100 Days: A Report Card', *Ahram Online*, 9 October 2012, http://english.ahram.org.eg/NewsContent/1/140/55089/Egypt/The-Balance-Sheet/Morsis-first—days-A-report-card.aspx (accessed 20 May 2015); M. Younis, 'Egyptians to Government: Focus on Jobs', *Gallup*, 16 July 2012, http://www.gallup.com/poll/155732/egyptians-government-focus-jobs.aspx (accessed 20 May 2015).

26 S. Claudet and S. Jadallah, 'Will Morsi Offer Change for Gaza?', *Al-Monitor*, 9 September 2012, http://www.al-monitor.com/pulse/originals/2012/al-monitor/do-not-publish-hed-to-come.html (accessed 30 April 2015).

27 Mahmoud Zahar, author interview, Gaza City, 11 February 2013; D. Samak and A. Eleiba, 'Egypt Still Considering Free-Trade Zone with Gaza: Hamas Official', *Ahram Online*, 27 September 2012, http://english.ahram.org.eg/NewsContent/1/64/54018/Egypt/Politics-/Egypt-still-considering-freetrade-zone-with-Gaza-H.aspx (accessed 30 April 2015).

28 B. Milton-Edwards, 'Islamist Versus Islamist: Rising Challenge in Gaza', *Terrorism and Political Violence*, Vol. 26:2, 2014, pp. 259–76, http://dx.doi.org/10.1080/09546553.201 2.690791 (accessed 30 April 2015).

29 Associated Press, 'Head of Hamas, Khaled Mashaal, to Step Down', *Guardian*, 25 September 2012, http://www.theguardian.com/world/2012/sep/25/hamas-khaled-mashaal-step-down (accessed 30 April 2015).

30 Al Jazeera and Agencies, 'Egypt Vows Strong Response to Sinai Attack', *Al Jazeera*, 6 August 2012, http://www.aljazeera.com/news/middleeast/2012/08/20128523429347102.html (accessed 22 February 2015).

31 Rawhi Mushtaha, author interview, Gaza City, 30 April 2013.

32 Ahmad Yousef, author interview, Gaza City, 11 February 2013.

33 Z. Gold, *Sinai Security: Opportunities for Unlikely Cooperation among Egypt, Israel, and Hamas*, Washington, DC: Brookings Institution, 2013, http://www.brookings.edu/~/media/research/files/papers/2013/10/22-sinai-egypt-israel-hamas-gold/22-sinai-hamas-egypt-israel-gold.pdf (accessed 20 May 2015), p. 7; N. Pelham, *Sinai: The Buffer Erodes*, London: Royal Institute of International Affairs (Chatham House), 2012, pp. 13–16, http://www.chathamhouse.org/sites/files/chathamhouse/public/Research/Middle%20 East/pr0912pelham.pdf (accessed 21 May 2015).

34 J. Rudoren, 'Qatar's Emir Visits Gaza, Pledging $400 Million to Hamas', *New York Times*, 23 October 2012, http://www.nytimes.com/2012/10/24/world/middleeast/pledging-400-million-qatari-emir-makes-historic-visit-to-gaza-strip.html (accessed 30 April 2015).

35 International Crisis Group, *Light at the End of their Tunnels? Hamas & the Arab Uprisings – Middle East Report N°129*, Gaza City: International Crisis Group, 2012, http://www.crisisgroup.org/~/media/Files/Middle%20East%20North%20Africa/Israel%20Palestine/129-light-at-the-end-of-their-tunnels-hamas-and-the-arab-uprisings.pdf (accessed 28 May 2015), p. 3.

36 The name of the offensive is derived from the Qur'an, where it is mentioned that Allah sent swarms of birds to smite the 'people of the elephants with stones of baked clay and made them like straw eaten up [by cattle].' The 'people of the elephants' is a reference to the army of the powerful military commander King Abraha, who led an expedition to destroy the Ka'ba in Mecca.

37 B. Hartman, '2012 Story of the Year: Operation Pillar of Defense', *Jerusalem Post*, 2 January 2013, http://www.jpost.com/Features/In-Thespotlight/2012-story-of-the-year-Operation-Pillar-of-Defense (accessed 1 May 2015).

38 Ynet, 'Rockets Fired at Tel Aviv Area for First Time Since Gulf War', *Yedioth Ahronoth*, 15 November 2012, http://www.ynetnews.com/articles/0,7340,L-4306249,00.html (accessed 30 April 2015).

39 See Associated Press, 'Mohammed Badei, Egypt Muslim Brotherhood Leader, Blasts Israel-Gaza Peace Deal', *Huffington Post*, 22 November 2012, http://www.huffingtonpost.com/2012/11/22/mohammed-badei-egypt-muslim-brotherhood-israel-gaza-peace_n_2175371.html (accessed 20 May 2015).

40 H. Kortam, 'Qaradwi's Friday Speech in Al-Azhar', *Daily News Egypt*, 16 November 2012, http://www.dailynewsegypt.com/2012/11/16/qaradwis-friday-speech-in-al-azhar/ (accessed 1 May 2015).

41 Anonymous blogger, n.t., *Al Kotla*, n.d., http://www.alkotla.ps (accessed 19 November 2012).

42 D.D. Kirkpatrick and J. Rudoren, 'Israel and Hamas Agree to a Cease-Fire, After a U.S.-Egypt Push', *New York Times*, 21 November 2012, http://www.nytimes.com/2012/11/22/world/middleeast/israel-gaza-conflict.html (accessed 22 February 2015).

43 Izzat Risheq, statement to the author, 21 November 2012.

44 Joint statement of Hamas and Palestinian Islamic Jihad, 21 November 2012.

45 S. Eldar, 'Hamas Isolated After Coup in Egypt', *Al-Monitor*, 4 July 2013, http://www.al-monitor.com/pulse/originals/2013/07/fall-egyptian-brotherhood-trouble-hamas.html# (accessed 30 April 2015).

46 M. Saleh, 'Political Islam: One Step Backwards Towards a Leap Forward', *Current Trends in Islamist Ideology*, Vol. 16, March 2014, pp. 42–8, http://www.hudson.org/content/researchattachments/attachment/1393/ct_16_posting.pdf (accessed 22 February 2015).

47 H. Balousha, 'Hamas Mitigates Fallout after Muslim Brotherhood Defeat', *Al-Monitor*, 18 July 2013, http://www.al-monitor.com/pulse/originals/2013/07/gaza-hamas-egypt-political-crisis.html#ixzz3YuMeLmXR (accessed 7 May 2015).

48 K. Khayrallah, 'Hamas Fell in Egypt and So Did the MB Project', *al-Rai al-Aam*, 19 September 2014.

49 See N. Pelham, 'Gaza's Tunnel Complex', *Middle East Report*, Vol. 41:261, Winter 2011, pp. 30–5, http://www.jstor.org/stable/41408031 (accessed 3 March 2012).

50 See Middle East Monitor, 'Al-Sisi: "We Destroyed 80% of Tunnels with Gaza"', *Middle East Monitor*, 13 May 2015, https://www.middleeastmonitor.com/news/africa/18593-al-sisi-we-destroyed-80-of-tunnels-with-gaza (accessed 13 May 2015).

51 BBC News, 'Gaza Crisis: Toll of Operations in Gaza', *BBC News*, 1 September 2014, http://www.bbc.co.uk/news/world-middle-east-28439404 (accessed 28 May 2015).

52 United Nations Office for the Coordination of Humanitarian Affairs, *Gaza Initial Rapid Assessment*, Jerusalem: United Nations Office for the Coordination of Humanitarian Affairs occupied Palestinian territory, 2014, http://www.ochaopt.org/documents/gaza_mira_report_9september.pdf (accessed 28 May 2015), pp. 2–4.

53 See Ahram Online, 'Egypt Imposes Media Gag Order on Ansar Beit Al-Maqdis Case', *Ahram Online*, 21 February 2015, http://english.ahram.org.eg/NewsContent/1/64/123586/Egypt/Politics-/Egypt-imposes-media-gag-order-on-Ansar-Beit-AlMaqd.aspx (accessed 23 February 2015); E. Nader, 'Hamas Terrorist Case Postponed to 28 February, Spokesperson Blasts Media "Incitement"', *Daily News Egypt*, 23 February 2015, http://www.dailynewsegypt.com/2015/02/22/hamas-terrorist-case-postponed-28-february-spokesperson-blasts-media-incitement/ (accessed 23 February 2015).

54 S. Eldar, 'Dahlan-Hamas Reconciliation to Open Doors in Egypt', *Al-Monitor*, 7 March 2014, http://www.al-monitor.com/pulse/en/originals/2014/03/mohammed-dahlan-fatah-hamas-reconciliation-meeting-egypt.html (accessed 4 May 2015).

55 M. Salem, 'Hamas Says Media Falsely Implicating It in Egyptian Affairs' *Daily News Egypt*, 5 November 2013, http://www.dailynewsegypt.com/2013/11/05/hamas-says-media-falsely-implicating-it-in-egyptian-affairs/ (accessed 28 May 2015).

84 Palestine – Hamas and the link

56 M. Georgy, 'Egyptian Court Bans Hamas' Armed Wing, Lists as Terrorist Organization', *Reuters*, 31 January 2015, http://www.reuters.com/article/2015/01/31/us-egypt-hamas-idUSKBN0L40BS20150131 (accessed 30 April 2015).

57 See Lafraain Channel, 'Video. Tawfiq Okasha: Sisi Decided an Air Strike on the Gaza Strip', *Klmty.net*, 18 February 2015, http://klmty.net/322285-_توفيق___بديو «عكاشة___السيسي_قرر_توجيه_ضربة_جوية_لقطاع_غزة_بالف».html (accessed 23 February 2015); I. Alexandrani, 'The Politics of the Egypt-Gaza Buffer Zone', *Carnegie Endowment for International Peace*, 25 November 2014, http://carnegieendowment.org/sada/2014/11/25/politics-of-egypt-gaza-buffer-zone/hvdh (accessed 4 May 2015).

58 Al-Resalah, 'Hamas: Rabah's Comments Interference in Egyptian Affairs', *Al-Resalah*, 23 February 2015, http://alresalah.ps/ar/post/110025/-حماس-تصريحات-رباح-تدخل-في-الشأن المصري (accessed 23 February 2015).

59 Al-Resalah, 'Bardawil: Egyptians Rule Out Any Attack Against Gaza', *Al-Resalah*, 23 February 2015, http://alresalah.ps/ar/post/110028/البردويل-نستبعد-أي-هجوم-مصري-ضد-غزة (accessed 23 February 2015).

60 BBC News, 'Gaza Crisis: Toll of Operations in Gaza', *BBC News*, 1 September 2014, http://www.bbc.co.uk/news/world-middle-east-28439404 (accessed 28 May 2015).

61 See J. Wagemakers, 'Legitimizing Pragmatism: Hamas' Framing Efforts from Militancy to Moderation and Back?', *Terrorism and Political Violence*, Vol. 22:3, 2010, pp. 357–77, http://dx.doi.org/10.1080/09546551003765942 (accessed 4 May 2015).

62 Popular support for Hamas in Gaza fluctuates, but still 53 per cent would vote for Haniyeh over Abbas at 42 per cent in a presidential election, and 36 per cent would vote for Hamas compared to 34 per cent for Fatah in PLC elections as reported December 2014: K. Shikaki, and W. Ladadweh, 'Palestinian Public Opinion Poll No 54', *Palestinian Center for Policy and Survey Research*, 15 January 2015, http://www.pcpsr.org/en/node/600 (accessed 31 January 2015).

63 In 2006 the Quartet imposed three conditions on Hamas: cessation of violence, recognition of Israel, and recognition of existing agreements between Israel and the PLO. See B. Milton-Edwards and S. Farrell, *Hamas: The Islamic Resistance Movement*, Cambridge: Polity Press, 2010.

64 See N. Barnea, 'Entire World Is Responsible for Gaza's Fate, Says Blair', *Yedioth Ahronoth*, 21 February 2015, http://www.ynetnews.com/articles/0,7340,L-4629149,00.html (accessed 23 February 2015).

65 See Al-Resalah, 'Blair's Visit to Gaza Is to Test Hamas' Reactions Internationally', *Al-Resalah*, 23 February 2015, http://english.alresalah.ps/en/post.php?id=4532 (accessed 23 February 2015).

66 Al-Resalah, 'Hamas Rejects Blair's Conditions', *Al-Resalah*, 23 February 2015, http://english.alresalah.ps/en/post.php?id=4528 (accessed 23 February 2015).

67 Al-Resalah, 'Hamas Rejects Blair's Conditions', *Al-Resalah*, 23 February 2015, http://english.alresalah.ps/en/post.php?id=4528 (accessed 23 February 2015).

68 Hamas leader Khaled Meshal stated that the organization did not order the kidnappings but later took responsibility for them in the name of the organization. See Jerusalem Post, 'Mashaal Admits Hamas Members Kidnapped and Murdered Naftali, Gilad and Eyal', *Jerusalem Post*, 23 August 2014, http://www.jpost.com/Arab-Israeli-Conflict/Mashaal-admits-Hamas-members-kidnapped-and-murdered-Naftali-Gilad-and-Eyal-371997 (accessed 28 May 2015).

69 See J. Khoury, 'Hamas Rebuilding Gaza Forces as Military Leader Returns to the Helm', *Haaretz*, 29 April 2015, http://www.haaretz.com/news/diplomacy-defense/.premium-1.654029 (accessed 28 May 2015).

70 N. Thrall, 'Whose Palestine?', *New York Review of Books*, 19 June 2014, http://www.nybooks.com/blogs/nyrblog/2014/jun/19/whose-palestine/ (accessed 20 July 2014).

71 See E. Mohns and A. Bank, 'Syrian Revolt Fallout: End of the Resistance Axis?', *Middle East Policy*, Vol. 19:3, Fall 2012, pp. 25–35, http://dx.doi.org/10.1111/j.1475-4967.2012.00545.x (accessed 28 May 2015); A. Abu Amer, 'Hamas Ties to Qatar Have

Cost', *Al-Monitor*, 22 April 2013, http://www.al-monitor.com/pulse/originals/2013/04/hamas-qatar-relationship-independence.html (accessed 23 April 2013).

72 T. Luck, 'In Hamas Leader's Exit from Qatar, Signs of Growing Saudi-Egyptian Influence', *Christian Science Monitor*, 26 January 2015, http://www.csmonitor.com/World/Middle-East/2015/0126/In-Hamas-leader-s-exit-from-Qatar-signs-of-growing-Saudi-Egyptian-influence (accessed 4 May 2015).

73 C. Coughlin, 'Iran Rekindles Relations with Hamas', *Wall Street Journal*, 21 April 2015, http://www.wsj.com/articles/iran-rekindles-relations-with-hamas-1429658562 (accessed 4 May 2015).

74 See Middle East Monitor, 'Iran Severs Ties with Palestinian Islamic Jihad', *Middle East Monitor*, 20 May 2015, https://www.middleeastmonitor.com/news/middle-east/18749-iran-severs-ties-with-palestinian-islamic-jihad (accessed 28 May 2015).

75 See R. Lefèvre, 'The Syrian Brotherhood's Islamic State Challenge', *Project on Middle East Political Science*, 11 February 2015, http://pomeps.org/2015/02/11/the-syrian-brotherhoods-islamic-state-challenge/ (accessed 4 May 2015).

76 On Dahlan and Hamas, see D. Rose, 'The Gaza Bombshell', *Vanity Fair*, April 2008, http://www.vanityfair.com/news/2008/04/gaza200804 (accessed 4 May 2015); B. Milton-Edwards and S. Farrell, *Hamas: The Islamic Resistance Movement*, Cambridge: Polity Press, 2010.

77 G. Lindenstrauss and K. Süfyan, 'Turkish-Hamas Relations: Between Strategic Calculations and Ideological Affinity', *Strategic Assessment*, Vol. 17:2, July 2014, pp. 7–16, http://www.inss.org.il/uploadImages/systemFiles/adkan17_2ENG4_Lindenstrauss%20and%20Kivam.pdf (accessed 28 May 2015).

78 Al Jazeera, 'Egyptian Court Declares Hamas a "Terrorist" Entity', *Al Jazeera*, 28 February 2012, http://www.aljazeera.com/news/2015/02/egyptian-court-declares-hamas-terrorist-group-150228122454458.html (accessed 1 March 2015).

79 See B. Avni, 'Is This the Last Stand for Hamas?', *Newsweek*, 8 July 2014, http://www.newsweek.com/last-stand-hamas-257942 (accessed 28 May 2015); H. Keinon, 'Netanyahu: Toppling Hamas Remains an Option', *Jerusalem Post*, 30 August 2014, http://www.jpost.com/Israel-News/Politics-And-Diplomacy/Netanyahu-Toppling-Hamas-remains-an-option-372828 (accessed 28 May 2015); A. Issacharoff, 'Truce Offer May Signal Hamas Has Reached Breaking Point', *Times of Israel*, 27 July 2014, http://www.timesofisrael.com/ceasefire-offer-may-signal-hamas-has-reached-breaking-point/ (accessed 28 May 2015).

80 See B. Milton-Edwards, 'Islamist Versus Islamist: Rising Challenge in Gaza', *Terrorism and Political Violence*, Vol 26:2, 2014, pp. 259–76, http://dx.doi.org/10.1080/09546553.2012.690791 (accessed 30 April 2015).

4

JORDAN – HASHEMITES AND THE BRETHREN

> What is certain today is that the Muslim Brotherhood in its old form is no longer legal and does not exist.
>
> Abdul Majid Thunaibat[1]

Introduction

As 2014 drew to a close and the new year rang in, the Jordanian Muslim Brotherhood (JMB) found itself repeatedly battered by domestic and foreign events that threatened to upend its place as the dominant opposition group in the country, and possibly even its existence as a legal organization. The JMB's political wing – the Islamic Action Front (IAF) – remained absent from the Jordanian parliament as a result of an election boycott. The Jordanian state was implementing strictures on the content of Friday sermons and believed to be threatening to blacklist pro-JMB preachers. Brotherhood-led protests against Jordan's policy of supporting Western and allied Arab coalition airstrikes on jihadist rebels in Syria and Iraq fell on deaf ears and yet led to more arrests. Fear spread that Jordan's king would succumb to growing popular sentiment to declare the JMB a terrorist organization. It had all been so different three years earlier, when, in the wake of the Arab Spring and the electoral successes of the Muslim Brotherhood in Tunisia and Egypt, the JMB confidently believed that its moment had come as it rose on the apparently advancing wave of regional-wide change in favour of Islamism.

The Muslim Brotherhood has a long history in Jordan, yet it has always been firmly politically constrained by the ruling Hashemite monarchy. In 1957 it was the only movement to survive a ban on political organization, but the price exacted for survival was that it had to act largely as a loyal opposition to the monarchy. It also had to suffer the continuous scrutiny of the regime's infamous secret police, the *mukhabarat*. In 1989, when King Hussein decreed elections for the first time in more than twenty years, the Brotherhood campaigned and won thirty-four out of the eighty seats to the lower house of the Jordanian parliament.[2]

The early promise of democratization and a role for these Islamists in the Jordanian political system, however, was progressively stymied. The Hashemite elite, aware of the powerful external pressures to prevent an Islamist success story in terms of parliamentary power in the region, used successive electoral amendments and general elections to rein in and diminish the translation of popular support for the Brotherhood into a parliamentary majority. In this chapter, this passive-aggressive struggle between monarch and the JMB will be examined. The analysis will incorporate the factors which led the JMB to boycott general elections in 2010, a decision that resulted in the Brotherhood being out of parliament for the first time in twenty-one years. The significance of the Arab Spring within Jordan and the role of the JMB will be examined to draw out domestic effects in terms of the increasingly precarious position of the organization. I will examine Jordan's delicate tribal and Palestinian balances, as well as external factors such as Syria, Hamas, and events in Egypt and the Arab Gulf states to explore the future options for the JMB.

Founding a Hashemite brotherhood

Jordan's Muslim Brotherhood is nearly as well established as the kingdom itself. Indeed, when the Transjordan emirate was formed by the British in 1922 with a Hashemite, King Abdullah I, the importance of Islam, as defined through Hashemite lineage to the Prophet Mohammed, was seen as fundamental to the project at hand.[3] Less than twelve years later, the fledgling state and its king permitted the establishment of a branch of the Muslim Brotherhood founded in Egypt six years earlier by Hassan al-Banna. One early goal of the Egyptian Muslim Brotherhood (EMB) movement (as discussed in Chapter 2) was to grow the movement beyond its borders, and it succeeded in extending branches throughout Palestine, Syria, and Jordan in the 1930s and 1940s. The EMB would become the 'mother' branch of the Muslim Brotherhood with satellite organizations in other countries.[4] Additionally, many young Arabs who had studied in or visited Cairo at the time were exposed to the EMB and sought to assist with founding their own branches back home.

One such individual was 'Abd al-Latif Abu Qura, from the Jordanian town of Salt.[5] Abu Qura came from a wealthy merchant family and had been fortunate enough to go to Egypt for his studies, where he was exposed to the EMB. Upon returning to his native Transjordan, he found like-minded compatriots, and together they formed the Jordanian wing of the movement. The founding committee included Abu Qura, as well as Mohammad Abd al-Rahman Khalifa, Ahmad al-Khatib, Yusuf al-Barqawi, Jamil al-Barqawi, Mamduh al-Sarayira, Muflih al-Sa'd, and Muslim al-Nabulsi.[6] A decade later the new group had grown and enjoyed support from the EMB, expressed in ambassadorial visits to and from Cairo by senior EMB leader Said Ramadan.[7] Governmental approval was clear when the JMB was

88 Jordan – Hashemites and the brethren

permitted to register under Jordanian law in 1945. Further official Hashemite sanction was apparent when King Abdullah I joined Abu Qura to celebrate the opening of the JMB headquarters in Amman. Such mutual support established bonds of loyalty that would emerge from the JMB to the Hashemite monarchy.[8]

The tone of the Brotherhood chimed with the importance attached to Islam by the monarchy in Jordan, as well as more generally among the largely rural and socially conservative burgeoning populous. The Hashemites claimed to be descended from the Prophet Mohammed and had been custodians of the holy sites of Islam in Mecca until their ouster from Saudi Arabia in the 1920s. The Hashemite kings of Jordan employed this important referent to Islam both within the kingdom and later in extension of their power and legitimacy over the Palestinian West Bank and East Jerusalem after the Arab-Israeli war of 1948. The JMB also enjoyed organic and brotherly relations with its counterparts in Palestine until Israel's independence and the outbreak of its conflict with the Arab states in May 1948.[9] The Muslim Brotherhood, including a small contingent of the JMB under the Jordanian Arab Legion commanded by Briton Glubb Pasha, had in fact joined the Arab forces that went to war against Israel.[10]

Indeed the relationship between the JMB and the monarchy was the lynchpin of the group's political survival throughout many turbulent periods not only in the history of the Jordanian kingdom but also more widely when compared to the travails of the Muslim Brotherhood elsewhere in the region.[11] The Arab defeat in the war of 1948 had significant consequences for the Muslim Brotherhood including its Jordanian chapter. Soon after the war, and in the wake of a Palestinian refugee exodus and administrative arrangements for Jordan to govern the Palestinian-populated West Bank and East Jerusalem, there was an unavoidable push for a merger which favoured the Jordanian organization over the Palestinian branches.[12] This was inevitable given the seismic upheaval that affected Palestinian society more widely following the establishment of the state of Israel and the subsequent statelessness of Palestinians.[13] The JMB had also played its part in activities to assist the thousands of Palestinian refugees now existing in tented refugee camps in Jordan. Leaders of the JMB, including Yousef al-Athm, tried to reassure their Palestinian brethren that branches in cities and towns such as Jerusalem and Nablus would assist and help. In reality, as Jordanian annexation of the West Bank and its consequences became apparent amidst the political turbulence of the early 1950s, the JMB emerged dominant over their Palestinian counterpart. Palestinians would remain numerically significant in the JMB, and in later years this would give rise to questions of true fealty to Jordan from its critics. In many respects, the JMB evolved to reflect two dimensions. One was dovish and more exclusively affiliated with the East Bank in terms of membership. The other wing is frequently referred to as the hawks, consisting mostly of Jordanian Palestinians deriving from the Palestinian refugee community which had resided in Jordan since the first Arab-Israeli war of 1948 and was swelled again following the Arab-Israeli Six Day War of 1967.[14] The Palestinian issue and resistance to Israel was a touchstone issue for the JMB that reflected wider community-based concerns about the tumultuous Jordanian-Israeli-Palestinian relationship. As one of the founding members of the JMB put it, 'Palestine is part of our identity as Muslims. Its soil is a *waqf* (religious endowment) held in perpetuity for the *ummah* (community). Its holy places in Jerusalem are as sacred to us as Mecca and Medina.'[15]

In 1951 Jordan's King Abdullah I paid an official visit to Jerusalem's al-Aqsa mosque. The visit came in the wake of several years during which Palestine's future had been increasingly subsumed to his ambition.[16] This ambition, which focussed on increasing Jordan's territoriality around a vision of a Hashemite-led Greater Syria, was unpopular among fellow Arab leaders and nations.[17] On the visit, as the king entered one of the many imposing gates from the Old City into the Haram al-Sharif compound where the mosque was located, a lone gunman shot and killed him. His assassin, a Palestinian tailor from Jerusalem's Old City, however, was alleged to be a member of armed elements supporting the former British-appointed mufti of Jerusalem.[18] Accompanying the king on the visit had been his teenage grandson Hussein, who would, within a matter of years, succeed him on the throne. Abdullah's assassination had major implications for the stability of Jordan which the British authorities tried to compensate for by organizing speedy trials of those allegedly involved in the assassination.[19] The sense of instability increased under Abdullah's initial successor, which was his eldest son, Talal. It soon became apparent that Talal was not fit for the job, and the British clearly hoped to steer Jordan through choppy waters when it supported Talal's son Hussein, then eighteen years old, to the throne in 1953. Hence, while from its very inception the JMB enjoyed the 'favour' of King Abdullah I, his eventual successor, King Hussein, would be compelled to view the movement through a particularly political rather than merely religious lens.[20]

In 1953 a new supreme leader of the organization, East Banker Abd al-Rahman al-Khalifa, also from the town of Salt, succeeded Abu Qura. As outlined above, as a result of a series of divisions within the ranks of the JMB which had led to the emergence of wings which were later described as hawkish and dovish, Abu Qura had been replaced. The doves, like Abu Qura, were in principle reformist, patriotic, and largely content with their status as a charitable religious organization. The hawks, on the other hand, harboured political ambitions in relation to the ideological impulse of Islamism and were inspired by a militancy that was informed by more regional events and their links to counterparts in the Brotherhood in Egypt. Their incipient political ambitions coincided with a time of uncertainty in the kingdom too.

A loyal opposition

It was during this period of the 1950s that the JMB began to outline and articulate its own reactive ideological perspectives and positions. It did so in relation to the rapidly changing and increasingly nationalist-leftist-socialist challenge apparent at the time both in Jordan and elsewhere in the region. In some respect the challenges that the

90 Jordan – Hashemites and the brethren

JMB faced in terms of ideological rivals from Arab nationalist, pan-Arabist, and the popular leftist movements were being similarly experienced by the Brotherhood in Egypt. This identification with the EMB was reflected not only emblematically but in the foundational ideological outlook and goals of the movement as well. The JMB's covenant (*mithhaq*) echoes the fundamental goals of Islamism in terms of the social and religious project it sets with the innate political consequences that this implied for their organization too.[21] Al-Khalifa, despite the important religious significance of Jerusalem in Islam, continued to lead the JMB from and maintain its headquarters in Amman.

Broadly speaking, key goals outlined by the JMB included the call on Muslims to return to Islam through *dawa* and education, an attachment to Palestine, and its liberation as part of wider pan-Islamist ambition and federation. It symbolically offered its resources to Palestine in opposition to Zionist and Western objectives. Focussing on the Hashemite kingdom, the JMB demanded a state that would be supportive of Islam as central to the identity, social norms, and values of its citizens. It identified itself as Jordanian in character but linked to the wider federation of the Muslim Brotherhood movement. Such goals did not present any outward challenge to the Hashemite project in Jordan. The monarchy was not identified as inimical to the JMB's ambitions and nor too were the British – who were intimately involved in Jordan's business – singled out in any anti-imperialist or anti-Western tirade. Objectively speaking, the JMB was limited in its ambitions and clearly aligned them to the fundamental Islamic values on which the Hashemite house of power also rested. The Brotherhood was clearly pro-regime even if this meant ignoring the depth of Western influence over the nature of governance and its structures in the country. The 1952 constitution, for example, incorporating many British concepts of government including equality for all before the eyes of the law, was merely glossed over by the JMB.[22] Instead, it would be popular agitation against the British on the streets that would nearly imperil the JMB's relationship with the king.

In the mid-to late 1950s, the JMB joined other popular elements of the left and Arab national movement in Jordan to protest Hashemite submission to the diktats of British policy and the continuing dominance of the British in the political and military status of the country. In many respects this was a period of instability and crisis for the kingdom. For the JMB, unlike other opposition actors at the time, the watershed in its relations with the monarchy came in 1955 after a period of some twelve months when the regime had decided to put the movement under close scrutiny and attempted to arrest al-Khalifa on suspicion of orchestrating activities considered hostile to the regime. Al-Khalifa was not only inspired by the EMB but also enjoyed close relations with the movement in Cairo through this period. For the EMB, this too was a deeply unstable time which within a matter of months would lead to a major falling out with the new Arab socialist power holders led by Gamal Abdel Nasser and the movement's subsequent persecution and repression. Relations became progressively more problematic between the JMB and the regime following the widespread public protest and rioting that broke out after Jordan

Jordan – Hashemites and the brethren **91**

joined the Western-led Baghdad Pact. The notion that revolution was imminent, that the young king was losing power, and that Jordan would fall from British hands as Egypt did before it in 1952 indicated the seriousness of the crisis. The JMB joined the wave of public protest, and King Hussein appeased his populous by dismissing Glubb Pasha as commander of the Arab Legion. Yet he also began to institute measures that would play a decisive role in limiting the parameters for a political manoeuvre by his enemies and opponents. As part of a major policy of divide and rule and which benefitted the JMB, the king and his advisors identified the Brotherhood as a significant ally against the leftist and Arab nationalist opposition. From this point there emerged an apparent symbiosis between the regime and JMB which would endure for many decades and was designed to shore up the status quo and neutralize all other forms of political agitation.

The JMB emerged from the crisis with the benign support of the Hashemite monarchy and were able to organize and engage in its activities both in Jordan and the West Bank throughout the proceeding period. While the West Bank and its holy places in Jerusalem and Hebron may have been one important spiritual centre of Islam, it was in Amman where the JMB continued to quietly thrive and politically operate in the shadow of emergent professional associations as licensed by the state.[23] The formal political realm was thus essentially denied to the Brotherhood, as the organization was not permitted to register as a political party or contest elections. There were members of the parliament associated with or sympathetic to the JMB, but within the movement the leadership was content to forfeit what would have been seen as a political challenge to the Hashemite throne at a time of great instability in the country and the wider region. As a 'religious' association, the Brotherhood built up a base of support among Jordan's growing Palestinian refugee population, as well as among the East Bank middle and merchant classes who were naturally socially conservative and attracted to the moderate reformist face of the JMB.[24] It was the case, however, that there were individuals or small cliques in the JMB who, from the 1950s until the late 1980s, were attracted to radical perspectives and viewpoints as expressed in the ideological leanings of militant figures including Sayyid Qutb and Abdullah Azzam.[25] Such elements, however, did not gain significant traction within the movement. Only the issue of Palestine elicited sustained and potentially radical or challenging sentiment in relation to the domestic and regional view of the king. As the regime faced mounting challenges from nascent leftist, communist, and radical elements of the Palestine Liberation Organization, the JMB were increasingly supportive of the king and known for their loyalty.

This loyal opposition helped the JMB survive and endure through the 1950s when King Hussein faced the consequences of a coup against the throne of his Hashemite cousins in Iraq, threats at home, and the potentially destabilizing menace of a radical pan-Arabist front led by President Gamal Abdel Nasser of Egypt. This is not to say that the JMB, led by figures such as Abd al-Rahman al-Khalifa or Yousef al-Athm, was always content to remain silent. As al-Athm acknowledged of the period,

92 Jordan – Hashemites and the brethren

> We were shaping our future and this sometimes meant that we were perceived as raising the political temperature of the time. It was not about the King but the policies of his government in steering our people through some rough seas.[26]

In this way the JMB was adroit at evading accusations of treason and treachery against the monarchy but was nevertheless seen by successive governments and their prime ministers as troublesome elements which could be contained, as were other political activists, by arresting them, keeping them under surveillance, closing their presses, and limiting their ability to rouse and agitate among supporters.[27] The regime used such levers to permit or prohibit the Brotherhood's ability to disseminate their ideas through their own newspapers, such as their own version of Egypt's Islamist periodical *Al-Manar* (the Lighthouse), as well as draw supporters to its side. Thus the JMB weathered the decades of unrest, its only apparent Achilles heel being one very close to home: Palestine.

Brotherly ties

As indicated above, the JMB has always been perceived as enjoying important ties to the founding mother organization in Egypt, the Palestinian issue, and the Muslim Brotherhood in neighbouring Syria. When the JMB was licensed in Jordan, it was registered as an organizational branch of the Egyptian movement. Ideological and administrative links were always maintained between the two. The Egyptian movement often rallied in support of the JMB, publicizing its activities and cause, hosting its leaders at conferences and forums, and encouraging parallel approaches on wider debates about issues such as democracy, *shari'a* law, or Jerusalem and the Palestinian issue. The Syrian Muslim Brotherhood (SMB), like the JMB, was considered first and foremost a branch of the mother Egyptian organization even though it remained distinct and autonomous. Relations between the JMB and SMB were complicated by the regime context in which they operated, particularly in the 1980s when Syrian-Jordanian relations were strained. King Hussein was seen as supportive of exiled SMB leaders, but some questioned whether such support was offered only for instrumental purposes.[28] From the 1970s, the Syrian regime under President Hafez al-Assad was operating a murderous policy to repress the SMB, ordering massacres against them in Hama and Homs. In 1980, al-Assad had changed Syrian law to make membership in or association with the SMB a crime punishable by death,[29] and the movement had essentially gone underground. Nevertheless, throughout 1980 to early 1982, the SMB engaged in attacks, such as car bombs, on the Syrian regime. On 2 February 1982, the SMB organized a major revolt in the Syrian city of Hama. The al-Assad regime responded by engaging in a series of attacks on the city to put down the revolt. An estimated 40,000 were killed, and the 'Hama massacre' marked a major turning point in the SMB's fortunes, leaving it broken as an Islamist movement under al-Assad.[30] Syria levied charges against Jordan for harbouring SMB cells in the kingdom. In the wake of the Hama massacre, Jordan, for its part, soon abandoned the SMB exiles it had once supported and was careful to avoid aligning itself so closely to the Syrian Brotherhood movement again.

The link to Palestine, though historic, was always seen as a double-edged sword in terms of its own identity on the Jordanian political scene and its credibility as an independent actor. During Jordanian administration of the West Bank from 1948 to 1967, branches of the Muslim Brotherhood that had been established in Palestine were subsumed to the leadership of the JMB in Amman.[31] Nevertheless, there were always elements within the JMB that did little to hide their strong support for Palestinians and the Palestinian issue. This was bolstered by the demographics of the JMB which succeeded in drawing to its ranks a perceived majority of supporters who were Palestinian rather than Jordanian in origin. However, as academic Jillian Schwedler highlights,

> However, as a general rule the Jordanian Muslim Brotherhood has consistently put it own survival and relations with the monarchy over Palestinian liberation, most notably in supporting the regime during the 1970 events of Black September.[32]

When Hamas was founded in the Palestinian Territories in 1987, elements of the JMB facilitated this offshoot of the Brotherhood both in terms of wider support for Palestinian Islamism and more pragmatic assistance in terms of serving as a nexus for Gulf-based supporters and the new group. While it is difficult to elucidate the links between the JMB and Hamas clearly, there was always evidence that backing was forthcoming from certain leaders of the JMB. Nevertheless, as the fate and fortunes of Hamas waxed and waned, the JMB extended help but only in as much as the regime in Jordan would tolerate. By the early 1990s, for example, Hamas found forms of assistance among the JMB and even located offices in the Jordanian capital. As a US diplomatic cable from the time suggests, public support for Hamas from the JMB was problematic for the regime of King Hussein to deal with:

> The Jordanian regime, cognizant of the widespread public support for the policies of both the MB and Hamas, sees no advantage in openly criticising the MB over its declarations of support for Hamas. In the mind of most Jordanians, to be anti-Hamas is to be anti-Palestinian a moniker the regime seeks to avoid.[33]

This fear of antagonizing popular sentiment over Jordan's Islamists was heightened when in 1997, following a badly bungled assassination attempt by Mossad of Hamas leader Khaled Meshal in Amman, the Hashemite regime quickly moved to publicly endorse Hamas. As journalist Paul McGeough argues, 'In a sense Hamas was always in Jordan – because the Muslim Brotherhood was well established there.'[34] This endorsement was symbolized not only by the personal interventions of King

94 Jordan – Hashemites and the brethren

Hussein to Israel to retrieve a life-saving serum for Meshal but that he ensured the freedom of Hamas founder Sheikh Ahmed Yassin from serving a life sentence in an Israeli prison.[35]

Although Hamas was expelled from Jordan in 1999 by the newly crowned King Abdullah II, the leadership of the JMB and those associated with the pro-Palestinian and pro-Hamas tendency rose to increasing prominence throughout the 2000s. Confirmation of this ascendency occurred in April 2008 with the election of the hawkish and Hamas-leaning Hammam Said to secretary general of the movement. He replaced Salem Falahat, elected to lead in 2006, but who had been plagued by criticism from the hawks of JMB policy which aligned the movement publicly with the government at a time when other state actors, particularly in the General Intelligence Directorate were targeting it.[36] Said was accused of maintaining organizational links with Hamas[37] and widely regarded as representing the Palestinian-rooted and hawkish tendencies of the JMB rather than the reformist pro–East Bank centred doves. Under Said's stewardship, elements within the JMB with pro-Hamas sympathies and strategic ties known as the 'fourth current' also enjoyed increased power in the Brotherhood's *shura* (consultative) council.

Elected faith

The regime's vacillations towards the JMB were evident in the apparently ceaseless cycle of arrest, attacks in the media, and the control of associations directly or indirectly associated with it along with temporary embraces by the king. In this way, a pattern of behaviour evident in state control of the JMB which had started in the 1950s was to continue for decades to come. By the late 1980s, there was a new thaw in relations between the regime and the JMB. Prominent JMB leader Abdullah al-Akayila called for, at the time, 'an end to pressure and hardships' imposed by the regime.[38] In April 1989, following a period of popular protest, riot, and unrest in Jordan, King Hussein announced that parliamentary elections would be held.[39] The JMB participated in a campaign that was the freest ever held in the country and succeeded in winning twenty-two out of the eighty seats in the legislature. Other Islamist independents who had won seats then joined the JMB in forming a thirty-four-seat Islamic bloc in the Jordanian parliament, a serious rival to the traditional tribal parties and loyal 'independents' that had hitherto dominated. The dividend for the JMB was all the more apparent during the 1990–1 period following Saddam Hussein's invasion of Kuwait and the Gulf crisis when King Hussein, as part of a 'bid to accommodate the growing grassroots popularity of the fundamentalists', invited the JMB into the government giving them five[40] cabinet places. Hence, in 1991, seven of the twenty-five members of the government were appointed from the Islamic bloc.[41] The experience in power, however, did not go well; the regime and the public chafed at government directives by JMB ministers ordering schoolgirls to dress modestly for gym when at the same time the kingdom was doing so poorly in addressing International Monetary Fund economic strictures. By June

1991, King Hussein arbitrarily dismissed his government. For the foreseeable future, this was the last time the JMB would ever be as close to enjoying political power of this magnitude in Jordan.

Throughout the early 1990s, King Hussein further manoeuvred and announced changes to the party and electoral system in Jordan which increasingly limited opportunities for the JMB to poll so well again. Nevertheless, despite this change in fortunes, the JMB, unlike their counterparts in Tunisia and Egypt who were severely repressed during this time by Ben Ali and Mubarak, did avoid being outlawed outright by the state. In September 1992, the JMB, along with other Islamists, formed a political wing and successfully registered with the state as the Islamic Action Front (IAF). Five years later, Ishaq Farhan, the head of the IAF, spoke of the extent to which they believed they had established themselves 'with credibility in the political arena', but opined that despite remaining 'loyal citizens', they had not been 'rewarded with political power'.[42] From the start, the JMB tended to dominate this Islamist coalition, and it was soon understood that the IAF was the JMB in all but name. Interestingly the mechanisms for internal democracy within the organizational structure of the IAF strongly reflected the Islamic approach rather than direct democracy. Membership of the *shura* council of the IAF was also dominated by men with little beyond a tokenistic representation of women. The close association which grew between the IAF and the JMB was also apparent in the shared organizational space between the two groups. By 1993 the JMB was struggling to win over the electorate in Jordanian elections, and in the 1997 elections, it boycotted the poll entirely and thus succeeded in absenting themselves from parliament. JMB and IAF founder Abdel Latif Arabiyat, commenting about his movement's situation in 1997, opined that although they had 'appreciated the democratization process since 1989', they had since 'faced difficult subjects, problems and challenges', realizing that limits would definitely be set by the regime as they attempted to immerse themselves in the political system.[43]

When King Hussein was succeeded by his son Abdullah II in 1999,[44] it became increasingly apparent that the young king would not be maintaining a relationship with the kingdom's Islamists. The JMB and the IAF were progressively marginalized. Their attempts to win power were frustrated by further state-imposed ballot box, constituency boundary, and voting changes which were being introduced under the banner of reform but in reality were squeezing democracy in Jordan. Regional events, including a wave of protests in Jordan following the outbreak of the second Intifada in the Palestinian Territories, the rise of al-Qaeda and its bombings in Amman in 2005, and the Western occupation of Iraq following the war of 2003, also served to create a climate of suspicion in the Jordanian regime that was wary of the Islamists and their role. As King Abdullah II deepened alliances with Western countries such as the United States, there was little he was inclined to do to keep Islamists such as the JMB in the parliamentary or political fold. In 2002 the King launched a new 'National Agenda' and 'Jordan First' campaign, but it was also an opportunity to clamp down on dissenting voices, including the Islamists who were unhappy with the regime's policies.

96 Jordan – Hashemites and the brethren

Although the JMB did front IAF candidates in the 2003 elections, they could only succeed in securing seventeen seats, and this declined further in the contest of 2007 where the IAF could secure only 5.5 per cent of the vote for 6 seats in the 110-seat parliament.[45] Hence, the poll of 2007 proved somewhat of a shock for the movement. As Abu Rumman states,

> This result was not only a shock to the leadership, membership and supporters of the Brotherhood, but also to a great majority of observers and analysts. Even the government expected the Brotherhood to get, at the least, 10 to 12 seats.[46]

Part of the explanation for the voting slump of 2007 lay with charges against the regime for gerrymandering but the JMB also had to look inwardly to address a decrease in its popular appeal. This led to rising tensions again between dovish and hawkish elements of the organization and the IAF centring on individual leaders and personalities and the direction the organization should take with respect to the electoral process in Jordan.

The 2007 elections thus proved to be a denouement because as Abu Rumman contends,

> It embodied the escalation of the crisis between the State and the Brotherhood to a new, advanced level, and later led to the emergence of a new, more fierce, political discourse characterized by a 'higher ceiling' of antagonism exhibited by the leaderships of the Muslim Brotherhood, particularly those who were previously considered amongst the 'Doves' trend within the movement. . . . [T]he elections also exposed a growing organizational crisis and a state of polarization.[47]

Leaders of the JMB that were considered to be dovish had included former supreme guides, heads of parliamentary blocs, and founders such as Abdel Latif Arabiyat, Abdel Majid Thunaibat, and Abdullah Akayila. This polarization was evident in the 2008 JMB *shura* council elections which led to the dovish Salem Falahat being replaced by hawk Hammam Said as the new leader of the JMB. It was clear that under the hawkish Hammam the movement would become dominated by people who were hostile to the regime and keen to pursue ties with other Islamist elements, including Hamas, who were considered inimical to the interests of the Jordanian regime.

The IAF boycott of the 2010 elections in Jordan indicated the extent to which the hawks were emerging to dominate not only within the political party but also the JMB itself. As Wickham notes, the decision was also

> in a direct parallel with Egypt, by 2010 the reformist wing of the Brotherhood had concluded that participation by the regime's rules had reached a dead end and that future participation would not be productive unless those rules were fundamentally revised.[48]

It also reflected, more generally, a discontent at the growing marginalization of the JMB in Jordan's electoral process and the struggles it was encountering to establish itself as an autonomous actor. The IAF was supposed to be an umbrella front for Islamism in Jordan, but it had essentially remained a principal of the JMB, only infrequently attempting to defy strictures from them about electoral participation.[49] The question was whether the JMB or the IAF could speak to the same reform agendas as powerfully and effectively as the Jordanian people needed or whether they would continue to be caught up in their own internal power struggles and distracting debates. As Wickham asserts, like the Brotherhood in Egypt, the IAF's 'commitment to democracy continue[d] to be tempered by its opposition to individual freedom and equality' in relation to wider Brotherhood-based interpretations of Islamic law.[50]

Arab Spring: The slippery slope

Jordan's Arab Spring was always more about reform than it was about revolution. Yet the fortunes of the JMB would be changed irrevocably, if not by the Arab Spring itself then by the regional impacts on the wider Brotherhood movement. Ultimately King Abdullah II's regime emerged largely resilient to the discontent expressed by Jordan's citizens. It also remained inured to pressures for substantive political and human rights reform.[51] The JMB and its political counterpart, the IAF, however, found themselves on a slippery slope not only to further political marginalization but also to suppression and possible criminalization.

Jordanian citizens were initially inspired by the Arab Spring. This was apparent as protests erupted in the kingdom throughout 2011. There was a risk to this commonly termed 'pivot' state and 'traditional', 'conservative', pro-Western regime. The Arab Spring had undeniably promoted conditions of instability within the country, exacerbating existing tensions, leaving it vulnerable to powerful external forces on virtually every border. Nevertheless, as the scholar Marc Lynch highlights, a

> long history of Jordanian political turbulence also counter intuitively gave it some resilience in the face of mobilization . . . the Jordanian regime had long experience in dealing with its opponents . . . and maintained pervasive surveillance and monitoring of all groups.[52]

The same broad social and socioeconomic forces which had arisen in Tunisia, Libya, Yemen, Syria, and Egypt also affected Jordan's stability. These social forces were at work in Jordan in respect to the peaceful protests that had broken out throughout 2011. Simply put, the protest movement that coalesced in Jordan could not be reduced to one reflecting *either* the grievances of Palestinian Jordanians or East Bankers, or similarly, one reflecting those of Islamists or leftists and secularists. Instead, protest in Jordan was about a range of different grievances and the alliances of communities that the regime has been used to dividing up in order to rule them. The degree to which all Jordanians suffered from the 2008 economic downturn

98 Jordan – Hashemites and the brethren

coupled with the crisis of the corruption-infested Jordanian economy was significant.[53] There was not the capacity within Abdullah II's regime to buy support or to distract from the situation by way of divide-and-rule strategies. As the fourth poorest Arab country, Jordan's citizens were racked with fears as once again fuel and food prices were rising and subsidies were cut.

Jordan was influenced by the regional dynamic of the Arab Spring. As Hayat al-Missayami, an IAF *shura* council member, said,

> I think what happened in the Arab countries has given us great power in our demands. This is very important. If nothing happened in Egypt and Yemen and so on, I think we would be talking about the election law – a very low-level of demand. Now, we are talking about very high-level demands . . . this is coming from what is happening around us, especially in Egypt.[54]

For demonstrators, a core feature of the change in the region was the willingness to make public that which people had previously been too scared to do so. The choice of slogans in demonstrations and whether they named first the government, then (very often) the wives[55] of the kings or presidents, and finally the ruler had been a core feature of protest across several countries. In Jordan, there was unprecedented open criticism and ridicule of the ruling elite. The protest also came from hitherto unlikely quarters. Military veterans, for example, issued a communiqué challenging Queen Rania by name.[56] Another marked feature of Jordan's protest movement was that it took place with little abatement in the southern tribal areas of the country, which the regime had traditionally relied upon as its basis for support.[57] These were significant events in crossing a boundary of fear and an undeniable change in public culture.

Politically the king appeared to be in crisis-management mode and at times was floundering under the pressure of protest. This was evident in the rampant revolving-door policy towards prime ministers which accelerated in the wake of the Arab Spring with five prime ministers being appointed by the king in the space of a few years. The king appointed and sacked prime ministers depending on how the king sought to manage an increasingly vulnerable situation, something which led him to complain in a candid interview, 'My blood pressure goes highest – my wife knows this – when we have to change governments. . . . Whenever we go through that cycle, nobody is going to be happy.'[58] In the words of Jordan specialist Sean Yom, prime ministers were 'the shock absorbers of the palace'.[59]

It was clear that the popular challenge in Jordan also involved a breakdown in jingoistic tribal nationalism versus urban Palestinianism[60] and notions of the appeal to Hashemite patriotism were temporarily weakened. There was clearly a fear of change in the kingdom, and elements of the political elite recognized this. One group among many in the turbulent wave of protest was the Islamists, but even the JMB was competing on an increasingly crowded stage. The Salafists, for example, were public and prominent in recognizing that the events taking place presented them with political and other religiously inspired opportunities.[61] The extent to which the Islamists were adjusting to the realities of the new situation appeared to be somewhat of an open-ended development.[62] The Islamists that were against any type of accommodation with the regime mingled into the wider protest movement that was calling for reform. There was a perception apparent in the so-called Zarqa trials of 2011 and 2012 that Jordanian security actors were acting to preempt this challenge. Indeed one interpretation of how the Palace intended to deal with protests was to showcase a hard line against Jordan's Islamists, including the JMB, only to be more lenient on others.[63]

Nevertheless, ever aware of the iron fist in the regime's velvet glove, the JMB and the IAF were acknowledged as being 'relatively quiescent' during Jordan's Arab Spring demonstrations and protests.[64] This is not to say that the JMB did not join in protest but rather that they were not significant in terms of mass mobilization. Still, the regime believed the movement was either a dangerous 'Masonic cult' or primary security threat.[65] Such perceptions emerged in 2012 when it became clear that Jordan was increasingly convinced of the strategic threat that the JMB posed. After the successes of the Muslim Brotherhood in Egypt and the election of Morsi to the presidency in 2012, combined with the initial resurgence of the Muslim Brotherhood in the Syrian uprising, there were fears that the JMB would be emboldened to play its hand and agitate against the regime. There was a further concern that the JMB would become handmaiden to the diktat of the mother organization of the Brotherhood headquartered and all-powerful in Cairo.[66] Like the Brotherhood movement elsewhere in the Middle East, the electoral successes of the Egyptian movement, and in particular the ascendance of Mohammed Morsi to the presidency, was bound to encourage the JMB and their ambitions in Jordan. The mother organization in Cairo publicized the role of the JMB and encouraged it to politically challenge the governing authorities.

The JMB was increasingly identified by the regime as part of the problem of the Arab Spring, not its solution. This became more apparent in the latter part of 2014 when the regional swing against the wider Brotherhood movement, which had emanated from Egypt in 2013 and accelerated by the Gulf states of Saudi Arabia and UAE, was manifest in Jordanian policy. Jordan, along with Egypt and the Gulf states, was intent on building a counter-axis to the powerful radical Islamist and Muslim Brotherhood alliances which had emerged in the wake of the Arab Spring.

Alternatives

In some senses, Jordan's Muslim Brotherhood has always enjoyed a form of immunity from state repression in ways which other Brotherhood movements across the region have not.[67] Initially despite the uncertainties and vagaries of a challenging political environment in Jordan as the Arab Spring led to protests and demonstration, the JMB emerged relatively unscathed in terms of state management and response to unprecedented public demands for change and reform.[68] In part this was explicable because the Arab Spring in Jordan did not manifest into a full-scale revolt, rebellion, or revolution where significant mass mobilization proved a

100 Jordan – Hashemites and the brethren

formidable threat to the Hashemite regime. As in the past the Brotherhood proved reluctant to engage in full-scale mobilization of its supporters and remained a partly subjugated actor.[69] In part this is because Jordan's citizens were assuaged by the promises of political reform from their king and a fear of insecurity and instability prompted by the view across Jordan's border in neighbouring Syria.[70]

Attempts by the JMB to mobilize Jordanians and harness their demands under the political banner of the Brotherhood failed in the face of a regime that ran the clock out on them and delayed reforms to the point that other concerns became more pressing. Within a year of the Arab Spring, the organizers and leaders of local protests were mostly in custody or bailed on charges relating to public order or crimes against the good name of the king while the public appetite for street-based marches and rallies had largely abated. Furthermore, attempts by the JMB and IAF to form opposition alliances, notably with a coalition of left and nationalist elements in the National Reform Front (NRF) to promote reform of the Jordanian political system in June 2011, soon foundered and then fell apart.[71] The JMB proved itself unable, in alliance, to curb its explicit Islamist agenda and position itself to lead the opposition representing the true concerns and preoccupations of ordinary Jordanians. Indeed it was a Brotherhood leader's comment about instituting *shari'a* law in Jordan that broke the alliance between them and the NRF. It became clear that 'a growing number of Jordanians became suspicious of the Muslim Brotherhood agenda for Jordan'.[72]

The decision to boycott the 2013 parliamentary elections did nothing to shore up the political position of the IAF or JMB. The king, in the name of reform, had managed to effect changes to an electoral law that was not disposed to the IAF and favoured the more traditional tribal and independent pro-regime forces in the country.[73] Although the IAF had boycotted polls in the past, their absence in 2013 was partially filled by candidates standing for the Islamist al-Wasat (Centre) party. The party had been formed in 2001 drawing on disaffected former members of the IAF as some of their founders. It promoted itself as open to engaging with other political factions in Jordan, and its leaders have consistently opposed violent Islamist extremists.[74] In the 2003 election, the party's candidates failed to win a single seat to the parliament.[75] A decade later it appeared that its moment had come and it won 16 of 150 seats in the parliamentary election, making it the largest bloc in the legislature when its members took their seats. Wickham describes al-Wasat as an 'explicit alternative' to the IAF, and thus the electoral victory for al-Wasat in January 2013 on a political platform of Islamism described as pluralist, centrist, and pro-human rights was a significant blow for the JMB.[76] The mantle of Islamist opposition was now being claimed by al-Wasat, and the JMB looked further marginalized than ever.

In the wake of the Arab Spring, al-Wasat was not the only form of opposition to emerge from IAF ranks to then present a challenge to the JMB. By late 2012, as the momentum of the Arab Spring began to wane in Jordan and after a series of major internal frictions within the JMB over the direction the movement should take, a new breakaway group emerged to form the Jordanian Building Initiative, otherwise known as the Zamzam Initiative. The regime, in permitting its activities, could use Zamzam as an alternative against the JMB. Like al-Wasat, its leaders sought to build support around themes of national consensus and reform (political, social, and economic) which would resonate more widely with Jordanian sentiments at the time. Its founding leaders included prominent JMB members known for their reformist and dovish sentiments, and who declared that their goals were coalition building for reform rather than politics.[77] Zamzam did not put forward candidates in the January 2013 elections and indicated that it had not constituted itself as a formal political party.[78]

The JMB responded to Zamzam with a mixture of reactionary critique and a belief that it was still able to control such renegade elements. By 2014, however, it had become apparent that attempts by the JMB to control the Zamzam group had proved futile and three of its founding members, Ruhayil Gharaibeh, Nabil Kofahi, and Jamal Dheisat, were expelled from the movement by the Brotherhood's 'internal court'.[79] Other dovish elements, however, remained within the JMB and continued to attempt to create a balance or promote forms of internal account-ability in respect of the hawks who by now dominated the leadership, prominently in the form of Secretary General Hammam Said and his deputy Zaki Bani Irsheid. Tensions, speculations, and fissures were apparent again when in July 2014 an Arabic newspaper carried accusations of a 'secret organization' within the JMB controlled by the hawks, and the accusations were confirmed and echoed in the news report by figures from the JMB or its former ranks identified as doves.[80] Such revelations highlighted the ongoing fissures within the JMB and the vulnerabilities that were thus publicly exposed in a largely unprecedented fashion. Column inches in the Jordanian state-controlled media were increasingly devoted to reports of such disputes and the Islamist alternatives to the JMB embodied by al-Wasat and Zamzam.[81]

Throughout 2014 it became increasingly apparent that the regime was ready to pull away and break with the Muslim Brotherhood in an unprecedented broadside against it. Although King Abdullah II had never been very keen on the Islamists, it began to look like his patience was wearing thin, especially with the regional situation. This was tellingly evident as the year drew to a close and news broke of the arrest of JMB leader Zaki Bani Irsheid on charges of treason.[82] Other members of the JMB were arrested and detained to await the state's charges against them.[83] The JMB was identified in pro-regime media, alongside commentaries against the Muslim Brotherhood in general, as inimical to Jordan's pluralistic character.

A bloodless bureaucratic execution

The start of 2015 in Jordan was quite literally a chilling one, as the kingdom of Jordan came to a standstill amidst snow and freezing temperatures. For the leader-ship of the JMB, the chill they were experiencing was also a metaphorical cold blast from the Hashemite palace and security services, leaving them uncertain if they would be frozen out for the foreseeable future. Those who feared that the fortunes

102 Jordan – Hashemites and the brethren

of the JMB were declining further felt certain that the crackdown from the regime in the latter part of 2014 would continue unabated. And they were correct.

Jordan's King Abdullah II had faced growing pressure from his allies to decisively constrain the JMB. In 2014, Egypt, the UAE, and Saudi Arabia had criminalized the Muslim Brotherhood and declared them terrorist organizations.[84] In December 2014, President al-Sisi of Egypt, who had orchestrated the fall of the Muslim Brotherhood and the overthrow of the democratically elected Morsi in Cairo, paid his first state visit to Jordan. Furthermore, King Abdullah II's regime was making no secret of its hostility to the Brotherhood and had joined in a conservative alliance with Egypt and the Arab Gulf states of Saudi Arabia, Bahrain, and the UAE to decisively thwart the project of political Islam post–Arab Spring as envisaged by the Muslim Brotherhood. In this way the king has used the regional conservative alliance to battle against the JMB and increasingly assert authoritarian control over them. The JMB and IAF could certainly be forgiven for thinking that a series of decisive moves to undermine them was afoot in a 'soft divorce', sounding the death knell for its historic and privileged position as Jordan's 'loyal opposition'.[85] The popular constituency of support that the JMB had relied on in the past was also diminished, leaving the movement vulnerable. The internal disputes, power struggles, and decline in the JMB's public support, combined with the new regional environment, were making it difficult for the leadership of the movement to predict the future.

The early months of 2015 would lead to a major implosion of the movement, as well as a backlash from the regime. The first serious indication of the regime being prepared to go on an open offensive was the sentencing by a Jordanian security court of Zaki Bani Irsheid to eighteen months in prison for his Facebook posts against Jordan's ally, the United Arab Emirates. A paltry crowd of angered Islamists turned up to protest the state sentence against the JMB leader. In early February 2015, matters soured further in the wake of the regime's response to the brutal killing of Jordanian air force pilot Muath al-Kasasbeh by the extreme, violent jihadists of ISIS in Syria.[86] As Jordan mourned and the rest of the region united in outrage at the cruel execution, the JMB appeared to be badly out of step. In an appearance on Jordanian television about the Kasasbeh murder, Hamza Mansour, a leading Muslim Brotherhood member and former secretary general of the IAF, failed to give an outright condemnation of ISIS as a terrorist organization.[87] Such a position was perverse, especially as even Jordan's most extremist radical Islamist leaders, including jihadi-Salafi cleric Abu Mohammed al-Maqdisi, had condemned ISIS actions and aligned with the regime and the people in response and condemnation. Internally, the fissures within the movement grew into a major rupture in February of that year following a unilateral decision to expel prominent reformist leaders from the movement.[88] The expelled leaders included former general guide observer Sheikh Abdul Majid Thunaibat; the Zamzam Initiative founder, Sheikh Ruhayil Gharaibeh; Dr. Nabil al-Kofahi; Jamil Duheissat; Nael Zaidan; Khalil Askar; Ibrahim Abu el-Ezz; and Jabr Abu al-Hayja. In public all the leadership of the JMB did was complain that the government was targeting it because of its consistent and unflinching demand for substantial government reform.

In early March 2015, the JMB found itself completely outmanoeuvred and facing a defunct future. Within a matter of days, Hammam Said would be presiding over nothing more than a name rather than an organization which had been officially in existence for more than sixty years. In a series of moves initiated by the regime, in alliance with dissident dovish elements of the JMB who had previously been expelled, forced into exile from the movement, or marginalized, the JMB's legality and legitimacy was reduced to virtually nothing. The Jordanian government sought to 're-designate' the JMB so as to make it officially 'independent' from the mother organization of the Muslim Brotherhood in Egypt. The regime claimed it was acting in response to representations from leaders of the JMB, and in particular Abdel Majid Thunaibat, who had requested a new license to operate independently of the EMB in a new Muslim Brotherhood group called the Muslim Brotherhood Association.[89] The so-called request opened wide the split within the movement under the hawks and a counteroffensive from the doves (powerfully backed by the regime). Thunaibat supporter Ruhayil al-Gharaibeh was quoted declaring,

> The Brotherhood in Jordan does not belong to the current leadership. For that reason, a number of senior members decided to hold a conference to vote on the status of the group so that it becomes a genuine Jordanian organization and independent from the Brotherhood in Egypt.[90]

The JMB's authority, assets, resources, and premises would be threatened if placed under the leadership of former Supreme Guide Abdul Majid Thunaibat.[91]

The Jordanian regime had essentially mounted a powerful, bloodless, bureaucratic execution of the movement. Although Jordanian Prime Minister Abdullah Ensour publicly declared that the new organization should not be considered a replacement but rather a different entity to the JMB, few in Jordan's political scene were convinced and instead believed that the end was actually nigh for the JMB under Said's leadership.[92] JMB head Said was left with little choice. As one newspaper columnist wrote,

> Today, in light of all these developments that must be faced by the Jordanian MB, those insisting on the past and the formulas and facts of the . . . last century, should realize they are rowing and swimming against the current of history. Hence, they must either succumb to the fait accompli and ride the new wagon, or pull out and step down without provoking a lot of commotion, and leave room to the youth and the new generations.[93]

This also prompted new fears about radicalizing tendencies and elements within Jordan and the vulnerability of many within the JMB's youth wing and their sense of belonging within the JMB fold.

Future face

The spring of 2015 would prove far more decisive for the future of the JMB than the Arab Spring of 2011. Yet the moves which the Jordanian state undertook against the movement were a direct result of the new mood within the region following the rise and fall of the Muslim Brotherhood elsewhere and the extent to which Jordan's allies went on to label and criminalize the Muslim Brotherhood as terrorists. The Jordanian regime was aided and abetted in this decisive move against the JMB by its own and the future of the original movement made obsolete. The fait accompli for the JMB led by Hammam Said in Thunaibat's 'new' JMB was apparent as he embarked on a press campaign to bring home the message about the new dispensation for the future of the movement under the banner of the Hashemite regime. He explained to audiences that the JMB under Said's leadership had 'felt ecstatic about the Arab Spring and the arrival of the Muslim Brotherhood to power in Egypt' and that this had emboldened it in Jordan to 'chose the path of extremism . . . [and] become isolated from the state'. Fearing that the JMB were heading for the same fate as those in Egypt, Saudi Arabia, and other Gulf states where they had been 'banned' and declared 'terrorist', Thunaibat parsed his actions in forming and licensing a new movement in Jordan to direct it into a future avoiding the same fate.

A powerful sign of the JMB's emasculation was evident in the spring of 2015, when it attempted to organize a public rally to celebrate its seventieth anniversary and the government forced them to then announce the event indefinitely postponed.[94] In contrast, government support for the new JMB was all too apparent. When it applied for official registration from the Jordanian government, it was quickly approved by the Ministry of Social Development and legalized by the Ministry of Interior. In a final coup de grace, the state also permitted the new JMB to have access to the extensive assets of the old group.[95] The new JMB quickly capitalized on its status and promoted itself as the only movement under the Muslim Brotherhood name in Jordan that was thus deemed legitimate. The old group and its leaders have chafed at the turn of events but ultimately have capitulated in the face of the government's approval of the new group. Hints of defiance from the old leadership though have been indicated in veiled threats about unfettered and angry Muslim youth in both Jordan and the Palestinian Territories. The leadership in provincial districts such as Irbid and Zarqa attempted forms of reconciliation between the old and new, but the outcome of such attempts at worst were likely to lead to capitulation and at best absorption of the old into new.

Decades of loyal opposition from the JMB to the Hashemite regime counted for little in the wake of the Arab Spring. Under King Abduallah II's rule, relations had progressively soured and the willingness of the JMB or the IAF to allow itself to be co-opted into the political system waned. Its opposition increased, and as it accused the government of rigging election results and joined in complaints about corruption, its loyalty was questioned. In part the JMB was increasingly marginalized, and the JMB began to marginalize itself. During the Arab Spring, and clearly inspired by the courageousness and political opportunities that their

Jordan – Hashemites and the brethren **105**

counterparts in Egypt and elsewhere in the Arab world had taken, the movement in Jordan presented itself as a leading opponent of Hashemite rule. This proved intolerable as the king and his supporters rolled back on the Arab Spring and, in alliance with Gulf countries such as Saudi Arabia and the UAE, began to rein the Brotherhood in. At the same time, the internal vulnerabilities of the JMB were exposed as tensions within the movement over determining which future path it should take turned into a major split. As it sets its face to the future, there is small comfort for the old Brotherhood in Jordan that its fate has not yet been sealed and that this fate could now be held in Jordan's new Muslim Brotherhood led by Abdul Majid Thunaibat.

Notes

1 Abdul Majid Thunaibat, as quoted in M. Alvdellat, 'Majeed Thunaibat for "New Arab": "Brotherhood" Ozajua State and Missed the Train', *al-Araby al-Jadid*, 13 May 2015, http://www.alaraby.co.uk/politics/2015/5/12/عبدالمجيد-الذنيبات-ـالـعربي-الجديد-الإخوان- أزعجوا-الدولة-وفاتهم-القطار (accessed 15 May 2015).

2 C.R. Ryan, *Jordan in Transition: From Hussein to Abdullah*, London: Lynne Rienner, 2002, p. 37.

3 Transjordan would gain independence in 1946 to become the Hashemite Kingdom of Jordan.

4 See H. Kandil, *Inside the Brotherhood*, Cambridge: Polity Press, 2014.

5 J. Clark, *Islam, Charity, and Activism: Middle-Class Networks and Social Welfare in Egypt, Jordan, and Yemen*, Bloomington: Indiana University Press, 2004, p. 84.

6 Yousef al-Athm, author interview, Amman, 20 June 1989.

7 R.P. Mitchell, *The Society of the Muslim Brothers*, Oxford: Oxford University Press, 1969, p. 173.

8 M. Boulby, *The Muslim Brotherhood and the Kings of Jordan, 1945–1993*, Atlanta: Scholars Press, 1999, pp. 54–5.

9 B. Milton-Edwards, *Islamic Politics in Palestine*, London: I.B. Tauris, 1999.

10 E.L. Rogan, 'Jordan and 1948: The Persistence of an Official History', in E.L. Rogan and A. Shlaim (eds), *The War for Palestine*, 2nd ed., New York: Cambridge University Press, 2007.

11 M. Abu Rumman and H. Abu Hanieh, *The 'Islamic Solution' in Jordan: Islamists, the State, and the Ventures of Democracy and Security*, Amman: Friedruch-Ebert-Stiftung, 2013, http://library.fes.de/pdf-files/bueros/amman/10360.pdf (accessed 3 March 2015), p. 13.

12 S. Bar, *The Muslim Brotherhood in Jordan*, Tel Aviv: Moshe Dayan Center for Middle Eastern and African Studies, 1998, pp. 12–3.

13 See B. Milton-Edwards, *The Israeli-Palestinian Conflict: A People's War*, Abingdon: Routledge, 2009.

14 See B. Milton-Edwards and P. Hinchliffe, *Jordan: A Hashemite Legacy*, 2nd ed., Abington: Routledge, 2009.

15 Yousef al-Athm, author interview, Amman, 20 June 1989.

16 M. Wilson, *King Abdullah, Britain and the Making of Jordan*, New York: Cambridge University Press, 1987.

17 See A. Shlaim, *Collusion across the Jordan: King Abdullah, the Zionist Movement, and the Partition of Palestine*, New York: Columbia University Press, 1988.

18 Guardian, 'Assassination of King Abdullah', *Guardian*, 21 July 1951, http://www.theguardian.com/theguardian/1951/jul/21/fromthearchive (accessed 29 November 2014).

19 B. Milton-Edwards and P. Hinchliffe, *Jordan: A Hashemite Legacy*, 2nd ed., Abington: Routledge, 2009, p. 32.

106 Jordan – Hashemites and the brethren

20 A.H. Abidi, *Jordan: A Political Study, 1948–1957*, London: Asia Publishing House, 1965, p. 147.
21 Jordan Muslim Brotherhood, Covenant, Jordan Muslim Brotherhood, Amman, 1993.
22 M. Abu Nowar, *The History of the Hashemite Kingdom of Jordan*, Vol. 1 of *The Creation and Development of Transjordan, 1920–29*, Reading: Ithaca Press, 1989, p. 207.
23 H. Amirah-Fernandez, 'Jordan: A Delicate Domestic and Regional Equilibrium', in F. Brichs (ed.), *Political Regimes in the Arab World: Society and the Exercise of Power*, Abingdon, Oxon: Routledge, 2013, p. 263; P. Larzillière, 'Political Commitment under an Authoritarian Regime: Professional Associations and the Islamist Movement as Alternative Arenas in Jordan', *International Journal of Conflict and Violence*, Vol. 6:1, 2012, pp. 11–25, http://www.ijcv.org/index.php/ijcv/article/view/186/pdf_47 (accessed 12 May 2015).
24 J. Schwedler, *Faith in Moderation: Islamist Parties in Jordan and Yemen*, New York: Cambridge University Press, 2006, p. 131.
25 Palestinian-born Abdullah Azzam had been a member of the Jordanian branch of the Muslim Brotherhood and later inspired elements of the mujahideen movement in Afghanistan including Usama Bin Laden.
26 Yousef al-Athm, author interview, Amman, 20 June 1989.
27 See Q. Wiktorowicz, *The Management of Islamic Activism: Salafis, the Muslim Brotherhood, and State Power in Jordan*, Albany: State University of New York Press, 2001.
28 See New York Times, 'Syria Reports Killing Nine in Raid on Moslem Brotherhood Hideout', *New York Times*, 21 December 1980, n.p.; P.B. Gupte, 'A Look into the Muslim Brotherhood: Antipathy for Syria, Praise for Jordan', *New York Times*, 7 December 1980, p. 14; R. Lefèvre, *Ashes of Hama: The Muslim Brotherhood in Syria*, London: Hurst, 2013, p. 132.
29 R.H. Dekmejian, *Islam in Revolution: Fundamentalism in the Arab World*, Syracuse, NY: Syracuse University Press, 1995, p. 109.
30 See R. Lefèvre, *Ashes of Hama: The Muslim Brotherhood in Syria*, London: Hurst, 2013.
31 See B. Milton-Edwards, *Islamic Politics in Palestine*, London: I.B. Tauris, 1996.
32 J. Schwedler, *Faith in Moderation: Islamist Parties in Jordan and Yemen*, New York: Cambridge University Press, 2006, p. 200; and for an account of 1970 Black September, see B. Milton-Edwards and P. Hinchliffe, *Jordan: A Hashemite Legacy*, 2nd ed., Abington: Routledge, 2009. See also See L. Tal, 'Dealing with Radical Islam: The Case of Jordan', *Survival: Global Politics and Strategy*, Vol. 37:3, pp. 139–56, 1995, http://dx.doi.org/10.1080/00396339508442807 (accessed 12 May 2015).
33 US Embassy Amman, 'Jordanian Islamists' Relationship with Hamas', *Wikileaks*, 21 September 1998, https://wikileaks.org/plusd/cables/98AMMAN8578_a.html (accessed 12 May 2015).
34 P. McGeough, *Kill Khalid: The Failed Mossad Assassination of Khalid Mishal and the Rise of Hamas*, London: Quartet Books, 2009, p. 72.
35 See P. McGeogh, *Kill Khalid: The Failed Mossad Assassination of Khalid Mishal and the Rise of Hamas*, London: Quartet Books, 2009.
36 See statement from the office of the Jordanian Prime Minister on 31 May 2007 following a meeting with JMB leadership: Prime Ministry, the Hashemite Kingdom of Jordan, 'Prime Minister Meets Leaders of Islamic Movement', *Prime Ministry, The Hashemite Kingdom of Jordan*, 31 May 2007, http://www.pm.gov.jo/english/index.php?page_type=news&part=1&id=3081 (accessed 2 February 2015).
37 See S. Hattar, 'Jordan's Brotherhood Schism Presents a Mirror of Society', *Bitter Lemons*, Vol. 8:36, September 17, 2009, http://www.bitterlemons-international.org/previous.php?opt=1&id=290 (accessed 5 January 2015).
38 Dr Abdullah al-Akayila, author interview, Amman, 22 June 1989.
39 See B. Milton-Edwards, 'A Temporary Alliance with the Crown: The Islamic Response in Jordan', J. Piscatori (ed.), *Islamic Fundamentalisms and the Gulf Crisis*, Chicago: AAAS, 1991, pp. 91–2.
40 Mideast Mirror, 'Muslim Brotherhood Joins Cabinet in Long-Awaited Reshuffle, *Mideast Mirror*, 2 January 1991, p. 10.

41 See B. Milton-Edwards, 'Climate of Change in Jordan's Islamist Movement', in A.S. Sidahemed and A. Etshesami (eds), *Islamic fundamentalism*, Boulder, CO: Westview Press, 1996, pp. 123–42.

42 Ishaq Farham, author interview, Amman, 5 April 1997.

43 Abdel Latif Arabiyat, author interview, Amman, 5 April 1997.

44 B. Milton-Edwards and P. Hinchcliffe, 'Abdullah's Jordan: New King, Old Problems', *Middle East Report*, Vol. 29:213, Winter 1999, pp. 28–31, http://www.jstor.org/stable/3013387 (accessed 12 May 2015).

45 M. Lynch, 'Spoilt Ballots,' *National UAE*, 30 October 2009, http://www.ikhwanweb.com/article.php?id=21399 (accessed 2 February 2015).

46 M. Abu Rumman, *The Muslim Brotherhood in the 2007 Jordanian Parliamentary Elections: A Passing 'Political Setback' or Diminished Popularity?*, Amman: Friedrich-Ebert-Stiftung, 2007, http://library.fes.de/pdf-files/bueros/amman/05320/05320-eng.pdf (accessed 3 March 2015).

47 M. Abu Rumman and H. Abu Hanieh, *The 'Islamic Solution' in Jordan: Islamists, the State, and the Ventures of Democracy and Security*, Amman: Friedruch-Ebert-Stiftung, 2013, http://library.fes.de/pdf-files/bueros/amman/10360.pdf (accessed 3 March 2015), p. 76.

48 C.R. Wickham, *The Muslim Brotherhood: Evolution of an Islamist Movement*, Princeton, NJ: Princeton University Press, 2013, p. 208.

49 See J. Schwedler, *Faith in Moderation: Islamist Parties in Jordan and Yemen*, New York: Cambridge University Press, 2006, pp. 88, 95.

50 C.R. Wickham, *The Muslim Brotherhood: Evolution of an Islamist Movement*, Princeton, NJ: Princeton University Press, 2013, p. 209.

51 See Human Rights Watch, 'Jordan: Arrest Wave Signals Growing Intolerance for Dissent', *Human Rights Watch*, 14 September 2012, http://www.hrw.org/news/2012/09/14/jordan-arrest-wave-signals-growing-intolerance-dissent (accessed 15 September 2012); C. Wilke, 'Flaws in Jordan's Largest Terrorism Trial', *Human Rights Watch*, 21 November 2011, http://www.hrw.org/news/2011/11/21/flaws-jordan-s-largest-terrorism-trial (accessed 29 May 2015).

52 M. Lynch, *The Arab Uprising: The Unfinished Revolutions of the New Middle East*, New York: PublicAffairs, 2012, p. 120.

53 See Z. Abu-Rish, 'Jordan's Current Political Opposition Movements and the Need for Further Research: An Interview with Tariq Tell (Part 2)', *Jadaliyya*, 24 August 2012, http://www.jadaliyya.com/pages/index/7007/jordans-current-political-opposition-movements-and (accessed 3 March 2015).

54 Hayat al-Missayami, as quoted in J. Amis, 'The Jordanian Brotherhood in the Arab Spring', *Current Trends in Islamist Ideology*, Vol. 14, January 2013, p. 43, http://www.hudson.org/content/researchattachments/attachment/1145/20130124_ct14final.pdf (accessed 24 February 2015).

55 This was the case with corruption allegations against Leila Trabelsi in Tunisia, Suzanne Mubarak in Egypt, Asma al-Assad in Syria, and Queen Rania in Jordan. Right or wrong, in this unprecedented opening out of public debate in authoritarian states of different kinds, attacking the wives of regime leaders became a closer-than-usual proxy for attacking their husbands.

56 See A. David, 'The Revolt of Jordan's Military Veterans', *Foreign Policy*, 16 June 2010, http://mideast.foreignpolicy.com/articles/2010/06/15/the_revolt_of_jordans_military_veterans (accessed 12 November 2013).

57 International Crisis Group, *Popular Protest in North Africa and the Middle East (IX): Dallying with Reform in a Divided Jordan*, Amman/Brussels: International Crisis Group, 2012, http://www.crisisgroup.org/~/media/Files/Middle%20East%20North%20Africa/Iran%20Gulf/Jordan/118-popular-protest-in-north-africa-and-the-middle-east-ix-dallying-with-reform-in-a-divided-jordan.pdf (accessed 3 March 2015); see also the range of articles by S. Yom, L.A. Brand, F.Y. Hammad, C.R. Ryan, N. Seeley, M. Abu Rumman, J. Schwedler, M. Valbjørn, A. David, J. Sowalsky, A. Barwig, and C. Satkowski in *Arab Uprisings – Jordan: Forever on the Brink*, Washington, DC: Project on Middle East

108 Jordan – Hashemites and the brethren

Political Science, 2012, http://pomeps.org/wp-content/uploads/2012/05/POMEPS_BriefBooklet11_Jordan_Web.pdf (accessed 3 March 2015).

58 J. Goldberg, 'The Modern King in the Arab Spring', *Atlantic*, 18 March 2013, http://www.theatlantic.com/magazine/archive/2013/04/monarch-in-the-middle/309270/?single_page=true (accessed 5 January 2015).

59 S. Yom, 'Don't Forget about Jordan: A Regime Caught between Contagion and Consent', *Foreign Policy*, February 2, 2011, http://foreignpolicy.com/2011/02/02/dont-forget-about-jordan-a-regime-caught-between-contagion-and-consent/ (accessed 3 March 2015).

60 See B. Milton-Edwards and P. Hinchliffe, *Jordan: A Hashemite Legacy*, 2nd ed., Abington: Routledge, 2009.

61 B. Milton-Edwards, 'Revolt and Revolution: The Place of Islamism', *Critical Studies in Terrorism*, Vol. 5:2, August 2012, pp. 219–36, http://dx.doi.org/10.1080/17539153.2012.686658 (accessed 7 May 2015); as to the notable absence of Islamism within the first wave of the uprisings, see also F. Gerges, *The Rise and Fall of Al Qaeda*, New York: Oxford University Press, 2011.

62 B. Milton-Edwards, 'Revolt and Revolution: The Place of Islamism', *Critical Studies in Terrorism*, Vol. 5:2, August 2012, pp. 219–36, http://dx.doi.org/10.1080/17539153.2012.686658 (accessed 7 May 2015).

63 For one account of how things are playing out, see J. Davis, 'The Re-emergence of the Jihadist Salafis in Jordan', *Jadaliyya*, 28 July 2011, http://arabic.jadaliyya.com/pages/index/2256/the-reemergence-of-the-jihadist-salafis-in-jordan (accessed 3 March 2015).

64 J. Schwedler, 'Jordan: The Quiescent Opposition', in R. Wright (ed.), *The Islamists Are Coming: Who They Really Are*, Herndon, VA: United States Institute of Peace Press, 2012, http://theislamistsarecoming.wilsoncenter.org/islamists/node/23188 (accessed 5 January 2015).

65 J. Goldberg, 'The Modern King in the Arab Spring', *Atlantic*, 18 March 2013, http://www.theatlantic.com/magazine/archive/2013/04/monarch-in-the-middle/309270/?single_page=true (accessed 5 January 2015).

66 D. Schenker, 'Down and Out in Amman: The Rise and Fall of the Jordanian Muslim Brotherhood', *Foreign Affairs*, 3 October 2013, http://www.foreignaffairs.com/articles/139982/david-schenker/down-and-out-in-amman (accessed 24 February 2015).

67 See J. Schwedler, *Faith in Moderation: Islamist Parties in Jordan and Yemen*, New York: Cambridge University Press, 2006, pp. 68–9; L. Guazzone (ed.), *The Islamist Dilemma*, London: Ithaca Press, 1995, p. 143.

68 See International Crisis Group, *Popular Protest in North Africa and the Middle East (IX): Dallying with Reform in a Divided Jordan*, Amman/Brussels: International Crisis Group, 2012, http://www.crisisgroup.org/~/media/Files/Middle%20East%20North%20Africa/Iran%20Gulf/Jordan/118-popular-protest-in-north-africa-and-the-middle-east-ix-dallying-with-reform-in-a-divided-jordan.pdf (accessed 3 March 2015).

69 Q. Wiktorowicz, *The Management of Islamic Activism: Salafis, the Muslim Brotherhood, and State Power in Jordan*, Albany: State University of New York Press, 2001, pp. 5, 95.

70 See P. Moore, 'Why Not Jordan?', *Middle East Research and Information Project*, 13 November 2012, http://www.merip.org/why-not-jordan (accessed 13 December 2014); J. Schwedler, 'The Politics of Protest in Jordan', *Foreign Policy Research Institute*, March 2012, http://www.fpri.org/footnotes/1701.201203.schwedler.politicsprotestjordan.html (accessed 14 December 2014).

71 See IkhwanWeb, 'Jordanian MB Forms Political Alliance to Fight Corruption', *IkhwanWeb*, 2 June 2011, http://www.ikhwanweb.com/article.php?id=28664 (accessed 12 December 2014); O. Al Sharif, 'Is Jordan's "Arab Spring" Over?', *Al-Monitor*, 15 September 2013, http://www.al-monitor.com/pulse/originals/2013/09/jordan-arab-spring-over.html (accessed 24 February 2015).

72 See O. Al Sharif, 'Is Jordan's "Arab Spring" Over?', *Al-Monitor*, 15 September 2013, http://www.al-monitor.com/pulse/originals/2013/09/jordan-arab-spring-over.html (accessed 24 February 2015).

Jordan – Hashemites and the brethren **109**

73 J. Amis, 'The Jordanian Brotherhood in the Arab Spring', *Current Trends in Islamist Ideology*, Vol. 14, January 2013, p. 51, http://www.hudson.org/content/researchattachments/attachment/1145/20130124_ct14final.pdf (accessed 24 February 2015).

74 See US Embassy Amman, 'Credible Muslim Voices in Jordan', *Wikileaks*, 12 September 2007, https://cablegatesearch.wikileaks.org/cable.php?id=07AMMAN3797 (accessed 6 January 2015).

75 See Berkley Center for Religion, Peace & World Affairs, 'Al-Wasat Islamic Party', *Georgetown University*, 2014, http://berkleycenter.georgetown.edu/organizations/al-wasat-islamic-party (accessed 12 May 2015).

76 C.R. Wickham, *The Muslim Brotherhood: Evolution of an Islamist Movement*, Princeton, NJ: Princeton University Press, 2013, p. 214.

77 O. Al Sharif, 'Zamzam Rattles Jordan's Muslim Brothers', *Al-Monitor*, 6 October 2013, http://www.al-monitor.com/pulse/originals/2013/10/zamzam-jordan-brotherhood-sharif.html (accessed 24 February 2015).

78 See T. Al-Naimat, 'Zamzam and the Jordanian Brotherhood', *Carnegie Endowment for International Peace*, 4 February 2014, http://carnegieendowment.org/sada/2014/02/04/zamzam-and-jordanian-brotherhood/h03b (accessed 24 February 2015).

79 T. Luck, 'Muslim Brotherhood Expels Three over "Zamzam" Initiative', *Jordan Times*, 21 April 2014, http://jordantimes.com/muslim-brotherhood-expels-three-over-zamzam-initiative (accessed 6 January 2015).

80 See T. Al-Smadi, 'JMB Investigate Existence of Secret Organization', *al-Hayat*, 1 July 2014, http://alhayat.com/Articles/3322248/تنظيم-سري-بوجود-يحققون-إخوان-الأردن داخل-الجماعة (accessed 9 December 2014).

81 T. Al-Naimat, 'Zamzam and the Jordanian Brotherhood', *Carnegie Endowment for International Peace*, 4 February 2014, http://carnegieendowment.org/sada/2014/02/04/zamzam-and-jordanian-brotherhood/h03b (accessed 24 February 2015).

82 R. Sweis, 'Brotherhood Leader's Arrest in Jordan Is Seen as Warning from Monarchy', *New York Times*, 7 December 2014, http://www.nytimes.com/2014/12/08/world/brotherhood-leaders-arrest-in-jordan-is-seen-as-warning-from-monarchy.html (accessed 24 February 2015).

83 See Islamic Movement Ajloun, 'The Islamic Movement of Ajloun Calls to Stop the Policy of Arrests', *Muslim Brotherhood (Jordan)*, 14 December 2014, http://www.ikhwan-jor.com/Portals/Content/?info=YVdROU5UVTJPU1p6YjNWeVkyVTlVM1ZpY0d GblpTWjBlWEJsUFRFbSt1 (accessed 12 May 2015).

84 See Associated Press, 'Egypt Declares Muslim Brotherhood a Terrorist Group', *Guardian*, 25 December 2013, http://www.theguardian.com/world/2013/dec/25/egypt-declares-muslim-brotherhood-terrorist-group (accessed 4 March 2015); D.D. Kirkpatrick, 'Saudis Put Terrorist Label on Muslim Brotherhood', *New York Times*, 7 March 2014, http://www.nytimes.com/2014/03/08/world/middleeast/saudis-put-terrorist-label-on-muslim-brotherhood.html (accessed 12 May 2015); R. El Gamal, 'UAE Lists Muslim Brotherhood as Terrorist Group', *Reuters*, 15 November 2014, http://www.reuters.com/article/2014/11/15/us-emirates-politics-brotherhood-idUSKCN0IZ0OM20141115 (accessed 4 March 2015).

85 See R. Al-Jabari, 'Jordan and the Brotherhood: A Soft Divorce?', *As-Safir*, 28 November 2014, http://assafir.com/Article/1/386832 (accessed 4 March 2015).

86 See F. Van Tets, 'After the Death of Mu'ath al-Kasasbeh the Tide May Be Turning Against Isis in Jordan', *Independent*, 6 February 2015, http://www.independent.co.uk/news/world/middle-east/after-the-death-of-muath-alkasaesbeh-the-tide-may-be-turning-against-isis-in-jordan-10030151.html (accessed 17 February 2015).

87 JoSat TV, 'MEMRI: Jordanian Muslim Brotherhood Leader Hamza Mansour Refuses to Acknowledge That ISIS Are Terrorists', *Middle East Media Research Institute*, 2 February 2015, http://www.memritv.org/clip/en/4765.htm (accessed 25 February 2015).

88 See B. Al-Badarin, 'Split in Jordan's "Brothers" as 7 Leaders Are Expelled', *Al-Quds Al-Arabi*, 15 February 2015, http://www.alquds.co.uk/?p=296147 (accessed 17 February 2015).

89 See M. Hattar, 'Tensions Brew in Jordan over Muslim Brotherhood Rift', *Agence France-Presse*, 2 May 2015, http://news.yahoo.com/tensions-brew-jordan-over-muslim-brotherhood-rift-134051523.html (accessed 29 May 2015).

90 M. Al-Amir, 'Jordanian Muslim Brotherhood to Split from Egypt Parent: Sources', *Asharq al-Awsat*, 2 March 2015, http://www.aawsat.net/2015/03/article55341956/jordanian-muslim-brotherhood-to-split-from-egypt-parent-sources (accessed 12 May 2015).

91 See D. Schenker, 'Down and Out in Amman: The Rise and Fall of the Jordanian Muslim Brotherhood', *Foreign Affairs*, 3 October 2013, http://www.foreignaffairs.com/articles/139982/david-schenker/down-and-out-in-amman (accessed 24 February 2015).

92 M. Al-Daameh, 'No Change in Jordan Muslim Brotherhood Status: PM', *Asharq al-Awsat*, 7 March 2015, http://www.aawsat.net/2015/03/article55342099/no-change-in-jordan-muslim-brotherhood-status-pm (accessed 7 March 2015).

93 See S. Kallab, 'The Expected End of the Muslim Brothers', *al-Jarida*, 4 March 2015, http://www.aljarida.com/news/index/2012721563/ (accessed 4 March 2015).

94 See O. Al-Sharif, 'Jordan Takes Sides in Islamist Rift', *Al-Monitor*, 12 May 2015, http://www.al-monitor.com/pulse/originals/2015/05/jordan-government-side-muslim-brotherhood-society-split.html# (accessed 29 May 2015).

95 See K. Malkawi, 'Legislation Bureau Says Newly Licensed Brotherhood Entitled to Manage Group's Assets', *Jordan Times*, 28 May 2015, http://jordantimes.com/legislation-bureau-says-newly-licensed-brotherhood-entitled-to-manage-groups-assets (accessed 29 May 2015).

5

TUNISIA – RENAISSANCE

The cure for a failed democracy is more democracy, [. . .] dictatorship disguised in religion is the worst kind of dictatorship.

Rachid Ghannouchi[1]

Introduction

In December 2010, few could have imagined that the death of an ordinary street vendor would launch a sweeping revolt across the Middle East and reignite the hopes of Islamists in the largely secular country of Tunisia. Yet for the local Tunisian Muslim Brotherhood movement known as Ennahda (Renaissance), this is exactly what occurred. Ten months later, the party, inspired by and based on the principles of the Muslim Brotherhood, won the majority of seats in the country's first ever free and fair elections[2] and prepared itself for power sharing in government with the country's secularist politicians. The precariousness of power sharing and the power of the ballot box was writ large for Ennahda when, in the wake of further national elections in 2014, the party's popularity among the Tunisian electorate slumped and it faced defeat at the hands of their electoral rivals in the secularist Nidaa Tounes party. By February 2015, Nidaa Tounes had invited Ennahda into another power-sharing government but one that would be dominated by secularists and not Islamists.

In this chapter, the history of Ennahda and the decades of severe regime repression will be outlined from the point of independence in 1956 when a secular Arab state was established, to the group's founding in 1981 as the Mouvement de la Tendance Islamique (MTI), the contest of elections in 1989, and the group's banning in 1992. The chapter will also examine the subsequent exile of its leaders by then president Ben Ali to it regaining legal status and the return from exile of its leader

112 Tunisia – Renaissance

Rachid Ghannouchi in 2011 and the import of the 2014 presidential and legislative elections when Ennahda fell from power.

The chapter will also analyze the extent to which Ennahda can pursue its Islamist agenda in a state traditionally recognized as one of the most secular in the Middle East. Hence, the challenge that has faced the organization and its potential for emulation, in terms of the role of the Muslim Brotherhood in other political transitions within the region and power holding, will be examined in the wake of the Arab Spring, known locally as the Jasmine Revolution. There has been much speculation that it is the Ennahda 'model' which offers the best hope for Islamism and Islamist movements in the transition dispensation in countries such as Tunisia, Egypt, Libya, and Yemen where dictators fell from power.[3] The experience of Tunisia differentiates the experiences of the Muslim Brotherhood across the Middle East where the ruling regimes have been more resilient and enduring in the face of revolt, protest, rebellion, and revolution. The contribution to Islamist discourse on moderate Islamism and democracy epitomized by Ennahda leader Rachid Ghannouchi will be explored in this chapter, as he has steered his movement into governmental power and power-sharing arrangements and was compelled to address social justice and equality issues such as Personal Status Codes, women's rights, radical jihadi and Salafi contestations, and separation of state and Islam. The subsequent ballot box rejection of Ennahda's discourse of moderate Islamism in Tunisia in 2014 is all the more worthy of analysis when combined with the debate about the inevitable impact on Tunisian Islamist discourses and the place of the Muslim Brotherhood within them as thousands of Tunisians were reportedly flocking to Syria and Iraq to join extreme jihadi-Salafi groups while others mounted attacks at home.

Islam and independence: Losing faith in Tunisia

Tunisia has long been cited as a 'modern' Arab state. Nevertheless, in its battle for independence from France, Tunisia perversely has always appeared to retain the key characteristics of the secular French state and a unique attachment to interpretations of the concept of *laicite* (separation of church and state). In the Tunisian case, however, this actually led to recognition of the place of Islam in relation to the state[4] but was, as we shall see, heavily circumscribed by the leaders of the post-independence dispensation. This also naturally set the post-independent state in opposition to Islam. Leaders of the independent state, such as its first president, Habib Bourguiba, sought to delimit or even eliminate a role for Islam in the state- and nation-building process. Indeed early on within the Tunisian independence movement (1952–6), the Bourguiba-led cohort was able to subordinate leaders such as Salah Ben Youssef who had competing visions of independence which were more inclusive of Islam. In post-independence Tunisia, as well as other newly independent states such as Egypt, the mobilizing power of Islamist discourse would be usurped by the wider nationalist discourse of state building, modernization, and emancipation. Islam would only be operationalized as part of such discourse, not in opposition to it.

Bourguiba, as president of the new state, led the march to redirect society and culture and the religious norms and customs of Islam associated with it which, as Hermassi describes, demanded the penetration of 'the domestic circle, which from time immemorial had been left to itself, even by the colonial state. The national state was going to project its action into the circle of family relations, the cornerstone or weltanschauung of Islam.'[5] For Bourguiba's party, Parti Socialiste Destourien, to shape the state 'one-party style', it had to dominate, whether over its political rivals, the labour unions, or wider supporters of a role for Islamists. Autonomy of other actors was not part of the rigid vision of Bourguiba and the state he began to build, shape, and consolidate throughout the 1960s and 1970s. This was a state which was hostile to Islam because it was seen as the antithesis of the secular modern system that lay at the heart of Bourguiba's project. To this end, Bourguiba pushed Islam to the margins in terms of the role it might play post-independence in shaping the public political arena or the institutions of the new state. Even Ramadan, the holy month of fasting for Muslims, was not sacred. Bourguiba declared that although a 'beautiful custom', it contributed to the 'stagnation, weakness and decadence' of the country and was used as a pretext to 'paralyze' productivity in a modern and developing economy. 'Break the fast,' Bourguiba told *TIME Magazine* in 1960, 'and you will be stronger to confront the enemy.'[6] Bourguiba's concept of the 'enemy' was sold to the populous as a new form of jihad, thus inverting the breaking of a faithful observance into a form of higher nationalist obligation. Echoing this perspective and repudiation of Islam and its strictures over public life, Moore cites Bourguiba declaring to his people, 'I do not believe that religion should be able to impose such a sacrifice. . . . This is an abusive interpretation of the religion.'[7] Such declarations by no means fooled everyone and inevitably drew criticism and opposition from some members of the *ulema* (religious scholars of Islam), as well as others who would have preferred for Islam to be properly integrated into Tunisia's modernizing project. Such opposition was inevitably manifest in clashes that erupted over the Ramadan strictures and the legitimacy of those that ruled on them, leaving Bourguiba and the *ulema*, including the Grand Mufti, in opposition to each other.

Islam was subjected to deeply privatizing processes, and previous state-led or state-based associations with Islam were severely circumscribed or terminated. The role of Islam in the legal system of the state, for example, was abolished with the announcement that *shari'a* courts would be closed and changes would be made to the Personal Status Codes as they pertained to women that had hitherto been shaped by Muslim codes and practice.[8] Traditional colleges and schools of Muslim learning such as Zaytuna were downgraded and incorporated into the secularized state system for higher education and the cadres of Muslim *ulema* left to decline in status and relevancy.[9] *Waqfs* (religious endowments made in perpetuity such as mosques), which had been administered autonomously and included educational institutions and charitable associations, were also placed under the control of the new state and its secular political elite. As such, those in the *waqf* system lost their autonomy and were obliged to fall behind state conceptions and prescriptions regarding the place of Islam.

114 Tunisia – Renaissance

As indicated above, Bourguiba, like many other state leaders in the Middle East and the wider political milieu, also established women as an issue of contest in relation to wider Muslim and Islamist norms and values.[10] In 1956, for example, he instituted Personal Status Codes which had specific implications for Tunisian women.[11] The new laws centred on unprecedented and increased legal rights for women in respect to their individual status. For example, the Personal Status Codes banned the 'traditional' practice of taking more than one wife (polygamy as permissible in Islam) and extrajudicial divorce (*talq*). As Zartman contends, the new laws were

> frontally assaulting . . . old [religiously inspired] principles. . . . But more important than the emancipation of woman and her admission to legal access were the spirit of the reform and its willingness to confront tradition. In effect, the political elites had arrogated to themselves legislative authority in the most traditional sensitive area. For once, sovereign reason and man's ability to elaborate law were affirmed with force over the traditional law of *shari'a*.[12]

Bourguiba used his power to make the woman part of the modern project in opposition to Islam, which for him represented the past.[13] By the early 1980s, Tunisian women were integral to the country's workforce and women's organizations were important to civic life and activity. Some of these organizations were also key opponents to the Islamist movement.

Interestingly, this representation and understanding of Islam that Bourguiba opposed in favour of his modernity project was similar to the ways in which other Arab national leaders, such as Gamal Abdel Nasser and those of the Free Officer movement, perceived the faith system and its political role. The politics of independence and the politics of nation building in this period of the late 1950s and 1960s across the Arab world conceived of Islamism, particularly as it was epitomized by the Muslim Brotherhood, as backward and antimodern. The lens of many nationalist leaders for understanding Islam linked it to traditional modes of production, social mores and values, and power structures where Islam in service of the state reinforced obedience to forms of despotic rule. The impulse of Muslim reformers and modernists who had inspired the Muslim Brotherhood in opposition to such structures was marginal to the discourses promoted by leaders such as Habib Bourguiba. The common ground as epitomized by the Muslim Brotherhood and nationalist leaders such as Bourguiba or Nasser against colonial subjugation was effectively lost when the battle for independence in such states was won.

Bourguiba's opposition to Islam would be preserved with little flexibility throughout the decades of his rule. By depriving Islamic leaders of a role in the political and institutional milieu of the state, he sought to circumscribe and dictate the expression of Islam. This pushed Islam back into the mosque and the home to the realm of personal piety and social functioning. Muslim preachers and clerics were diminished, and the importance of their institutions, including Zaytuna, was diminished with them. In its place Bourguiba sought to create a society and, in particular, a political elite that was modern, secular, Arab, and inspired by the division of faith and state inherited from the French project in the Maghreb. To create such a society, Bourguiba had to educate it and task it to the modern national project. To this end the hitherto intimate relationship between state and Islam in the realm of education was an obstacle to reform that had to be removed. Education reforms thus began to undermine the place of Islam as a societal binding force in the curriculum and the dispensation of the state to those, including the *ulema*, for using school classes as a location to transmit the faith. As Boulby highlights, within a decade of establishing the post-independent state, Bourguiba had largely succeeded in weakening Islam as a force with a political or independent voice:

> Islam lost much of its vitality in the decade following independence. It was largely an Islam stripped of its institutional basis, challenged in almost the totality of its tradition and deprived by the state of any autonomy in the classroom or even the mosque.[14]

Throughout the 1970s, when Bourguiba cemented power by having himself declared 'president for life', there were indications that Islamic opposition might grow. Addressing and appearing to be sympathetic to growing undercurrents of socioeconomic discontent, incipient Islamism was evident in the events that followed the state's brutal suppression of the general strike of 1978.[15] This nascent Islamism was apparent in the more populist revival of Islam evident in the increasing rates of mosque attendance and other public acts of piety during Ramadan and religious feasts such as Eid al-Fitr and Eid al-Adha. Like the revivalist surge led by the Muslim Brotherhood in the 1970s in other Arab states such as Egypt, this revivalism led to the increased public appearance of forms of Islamic dress in both men and women but particularly with respect to women wearing the hijab. The alternative offered by Islamist groups encouraged Muslims to engage with the literatures and commentaries of the faith in pamphlets, books, and widely distributed cassette recordings across the country and the wider region. Compelled by domestic pressure to open the political system, Bourguiba offered to hold the first multiparty elections since independence but kept Islamists out of the running by refusing to register their parties or candidates. Even in the 1980s when Bourguiba was in his last years in office, he continued with his relentless campaign to keep Islamism out and to break it as a nascent opposition movement. This resulted in a state-led drive to crack down on Islamist movements that included imprisoning their leaders.

Renaissance

Like other movements of political Islam, which grew out of or were inspired by the Muslim Brotherhood, the inception of Ennahda in the late 1970s and early 1980s occurred as a response to a wider regional impulse that saw the Muslim Brotherhood insert itself in the political arena and in contest with the state.[16] This contest with the state and the authoritarian elite at its helm also gave a voice to the many hundreds of thousands in Tunisia and millions more generally across the Arab world who chafed against the socioeconomic stasis of state-orchestrated modernization which benefited the few rather than the many.[17] It was no coincidence that it was during this period of the 1980s when severe socioeconomic crisis led to food riots and protest against authoritarian state systems in the region which had retreated in terms of service provision in fields of education, health, and welfare support to the majority of the population, including the well-educated middle class.[18] This middle class, which would prove so important to the mobilization of new Islamist movements, was increasingly alienated from the authoritarian state.[19] People were drawn to the new Islamic movements because the sense of authenticity and identity that they offered was familiar as part of an ancient and traditional faith structure. The Islamist movement served as symbolic riposte to the increasing antipathy and sense of alienation that many Muslims experienced in reference to the Westernization of the modernity project and inherent attachment to a value system which sat uneasily with Islam.

The founders of Ennahda's predecessor, the MTI, were Rachid Ghannouchi and Abdelfattah Mourou.[20] They represented a wider grouping of clerics who had organized and centred on activities at Zaytuna University throughout the Islamic revival of the 1970s to offer a counternarrative to the dominance of the Bourguiba-envisioned state. They had encouraged forms of revivalism that had led to increased piety and observance in terms of the societal presence of Islam, as well as a newly articulated narrative that resonated with and among those that chafed under the one-party state system to which the modernity project was so firmly tied and one which had begun to falter. The MTI had the potential to capture an opposition that could agitate for reform or change but which would always be viewed by the incumbent regime as a threat to its monopoly of power and coercive force over society. The leaders of the new movement did not shy away from mounting what they considered to be a legitimate criticism of the state, though they refrained from publicly expressing political ambition for control of the state and sought to reassure their opponents that they would not advocate violence. Much like the Muslim Brotherhood elsewhere, the political ambitions of the group were firmly kept in check, and instead, the social, cultural, and broadly religious reformist agenda was outlined in its programme and activities. Political Islam, through the expression of the MTI, was thus perceived as a radical challenge to the state. Islamism would not be conceived of as part of the opposition or part of the debate about reform because neither was to be countenanced as being legitimate or salient by an incumbent one-party regime effectively presided over by an autocrat.

Rachid Ghannouchi was an unlikely candidate to lead Tunisia's Islamist movement. Unlike Hassan al-Banna, the founder of the Muslim Brotherhood in Egypt, Ghannouchi had not grown up in a religiously scholarly family but instead one that was rural and working class in origin. Education, however, was the route to Islamist emancipation for Ghannouchi, and like so many of his contemporaries, it was the opportunity to study at the university level and particularly in the Arab world and beyond that inspired this new leader. This education included studies at Zaytuna

University, the University of Cairo, the University of Damascus, and later at the Sorbonne in Paris. Ghannouchi was an intellectual and powerfully eloquent advocate for his cause. Careful to draw attention to the social project inherent to contemporary Islamic revivalism, he declared that the objectives of the new movement were to

> contribute to laying the cultural and social bases of a civil society which assumes its most important functions, one which the state serves and which constitutes the only source of legitimacy . . . There is no place for dominating society in the name of any legitimacy – historic, religious, proletarian, or pseudo-democratic.[21]

Abdelfattah Mourou, on the other hand, came from an urban, religiously educated background that was more similar to other leaders of the new Islamist revival trend across the Middle East. He followed in the religious footsteps of his family members by becoming an imam but also trained as a lawyer. The divergent backgrounds of the founding leaders of the MTI were important in generating the wide appeal the movement always enjoyed. The MTI, like the Muslim Brotherhood, could draw on such individuals to inspire a populist movement, and throughout the early 1980s, an increasing number of young Tunisians emerged to engage with the new movement on university campuses, and in the cities and towns of the country. This put the group on a collision course with the secular champion Bourguiba, and it was inevitable that antagonism would define the relationship between the young leaders of the nascent Islamist movement and the ageing president of the post-independent state.

In the early 1980s, the university campus was an ideal ground for breaking new territory for a variety of opposition groups, including the Islamists, who helped orchestrate or joined in forms of student activism and protest. At this point the regime was content to keep this new threat under surveillance and repression by targeting individual leaders. But when further social and economic unrest broke out in towns and cities and was directed at tourist resorts in the ensuing years, the state organized mass arrests and imprisonments which also targeted the MTI. Following bread riots in 1984, however, Prime Minister Mzali appeared to give opposition elements a voice in the state-controlled national debate.[22] As with Jordan and the Muslim Brotherhood there, it became apparent that such openings would be short-lived and would be resisted by other, more powerful elements of the ruling regime that were firmly opposed to giving Islamists any ground at all. Such members of the regime remained convinced that the MTI was inspired by foreign elements (Libyan, Iranian, or Egyptian) to topple it from power in a radical, revolutionary project to collapse the one-party state.

Repression was inevitable, and the state soon targeted the leaders of the MTI, accusing them of being complicit in violent rebel elements in Tunisia and in conspiracy with foreign elements from Libya. This resulted in periods of imprisonment throughout the 1980s for the nascent movement. President Bourguiba was

118 Tunisia – Renaissance

'increasing obsessed with the MTI in his last year in office', but the bloodless coup against him in November 1987 and advent of Zine el-Abidine Ben Ali as president had only a marginally ameliorating effect on the movement.[23] Ben Ali's regime declared the old president senile and incapable of governing the country, and he was placed under house arrest until his death in 2000.[24] Ben Ali had commenced his presidency by declaring a new era which, he hoped, would be seen as drawing a line under the collapsed legitimacy of Bourguiba. This new era would incorporate elements of public reconciliation which would include a well-managed place for Islam rather than Islamism. It is true that the new incumbent did reach out the hand to all his opponents in the spirit of national reconciliation when he came to power in 1987 and sought to couple Islam with an official state-based role for it in the public arena. To this end, there was a process of rehabilitation that meant that institutions such as Zaytuna were partially revived and other public measures of state-imposed piety were apparent in state broadcasting of the call to prayer, religious programming, and amnesties for many imprisoned for membership of the MTI. Ramadan also assumed more public religious importance compared to the zealous secularization of the Bourguiba era. By 1989, as a measure of his benevolence, President Ben Ali permitted the release of Ghannouchi from prison as part of his Ramadan amnesty.[25]After his release from prison, Ghannouchi publicly criticized the former president's project arguing,

> Bourguiba put forward the slogan of the state's prestige, but its real content was the monopoly of the party, of the capitalist interests within which power in the country was located, and the monopoly which Bourguiba exercised over this state. The time has come to raise the slogan of the prestige of society, of the citizen, and of the power which serves both.[26]

However, this tolerance did not extend politically for the MTI. For its part, the MTI during this period was in a process of dynamic political change and increasingly ambitious, evident in the formation of its own political party, the Ennahda.

By 1989 the party had tried to register officially but was prevented by the governing regime. It had believed, perhaps naively, that by changing its name to one that did not include any reference to Islam it would be better accepted by the regime.[27] However, in common with laws in other Arab states such as Jordan and Egypt where there was a decision to ban the formation of religious political parties, Ennahda was thus forbidden from competing in the elections that Ben Ali called for on 2 April 1989. The MTI had hoped that, like the Muslim Brotherhood in Jordan, it could constitute itself as a political party and meet government approval to contest the elections. The hurdle it encountered was that in Tunisia religious parties were prohibited from contesting elections. As in Egypt, however, the group circumvented the formal ban by contesting the election as 'independents' for seats in the 141-member legislature. Again a useful parallel can be drawn with the Muslim Brotherhood in Egypt, which in 1989 also stood individual candidates for legislative elections due to a state ban on the group organizing and being registered as a political party. In this way, the Egyptian movement was able to get some representatives elected to the legislature. Like Egypt and Jordan, Ennahda was not the only opposition element though and had to mount a challenge against not only the ruling state party of the Rassemblement Constitutionnel Démocratique (RCD) but the socialist opposition Mouvement des Démocrates Socialistes as well. The state ensured that the media was used to express a sense of widespread fear that an Islamist victory at the polls would inevitably lead to a significant rollback on the constitutional protections, especially for women, that lay at the heart of the secular Tunisian post-independence project. This was cause for genuine concern for many social and political actors, including women's rights activists.

Nevertheless, Ennahda fronted independent candidates in the first post-Bourguiba legislative poll that year, winning 17 per cent of the votes, which gave rise to further alarm among Ben Ali's ruling party elite. Although the RCD won the majority of votes, Islamists came second and the socialists, in turn, polled very poorly, deepening concern that the opposition would essentially represent a growing, radicalized Islamist monolith. It became increasingly apparent that Tunisia was caught between the leviathan of a secular, one-party state little disrupted by the internal coup mounted by Ben Ali against Bourguiba and a dynamic, energetic Islamist opposition that was growing in size and inspiration, influenced as it was by the wider Islamist trend in the Middle East at the time.

The prospect that the Islamists would accede to power through the ballot box was of significant concern to the regime especially given the regional tensions in the wake of ballot box challenges from the Muslim Brotherhood and their Islamist ilk mounted in other countries. To this end, the regime engaged in another round of repressive measures to meet the challenge posed to it. The Islamists were once again thrown into prison or forced into exile. Charged with being part of a wider Islamist insurgency that promoted the violent overthrow of the state, the regime of Ben Ali was able to effectively push the Islamists once again from the public arena. Ennahda's moderate reformist agenda did nothing to shield it from the charge that it would overthrow the state, and it was condemned by the regime and its Western supporters. Ghannouchi was frequently accused of being a radical for espousing a position which placed Islam at the heart of the governance project in the contemporary Middle East. Notwithstanding the fact that by most standards Ghannouchi's vision was no more radical than most reformist Islamists at the time, the moderates, critics opined, were always in danger of being swallowed by the radicals whose ambitions for power would not be contained to peaceful processes of reform.[28] Ben Ali's 'reconciliation turned out in the end' to be what Ghannouchi referred to as a 'short wedding party' and 'the hopes in democracy introduced by Tunisia's new ruler were quickly dispersed'.[29] One outworking of the election as a contest for power was the subsequent self-exile of Ennahda leader Rachid Ghannouchi in 1989 to London. Dunn contentiously argues that this move left the movement vulnerable to 'increasing radicalization', 'growing confrontation with the state', and 'destruction of the movement as an above-ground organization'.[30] Viewed from another dimension, the plural vision of Islam and politics envisioned by leaders like

120 Tunisia – Renaissance

Ghannouchi which could have been accommodated within the Tunisian system if it were truly democratic would, in reality and under Ben Ali's leadership, prove redundant. Moreover, Ben Ali, from this perspective, was aided and abetted by the West in truly thwarting democracy in the name of the plural Islamist vision espoused by Ennahda. Ghannouchi highlighted the contradiction of the many Western governments of the time which criticized Islam for being anti-democratic while at the same time supporting Arab states in the Middle East which were authoritarian and keeping democracy at bay by parsing it as an Islamist conspiracy.[31] Yet the strains within Ennahda were inevitable, and in the early 1990s, the movement underwent a significant split, following episodes of violence which Ennahda was charged with organizing, with Mourou leading his wing of the movement away from Ghannouchi.[32]

Hence, although Ben Ali had appeared to encourage Ennahda, when it proved through the ballot box that it could emerge as a true competitor to the hitherto unchallenged hegemony of the RCD, he engaged in repressive measures to beat it back down and all but destroyed it over the coming years and decades of his rule. In turn, Ennahda was excoriated and accused of employing violence and appearing to call for the overthrow of Ben Ali's secular, liberalizing, Western-facing regime. Indeed throughout the 1990s and 2000s Ben Ali's regime was increasing lauded as a progressive, liberalizing state even if such a state gave nothing more than the illusion or facade of democracy.[33] Indeed, as Gelvin highlights, in the decades preceding the Arab Spring, 'the Tunisian government expanded and intensified repression to such an extent that Human Rights Watch declared Tunisia to be one of the most repressive states in the world – a world that, it should be remembered, includes Myanmar and Syria.'[34] The Islamist movement had been effectively dismembered by the regime and its leadership imprisoned or exiled.

In exile, Ennahda leaders encountered and became part of a variety of changing currents of Islamism that emerged in the wake of the crackdowns of the 1990s. Figures such as Ghannouchi continued to act as a standard bearer for the debate about the new Islamism and its role in the twenty-first century, but this was a debate that in the wake of 9/11 was harder to advance as so many articulations of political Islam were treated with deep-seated scepticism and mistrust. Nevertheless, within the Arab world Ennahda joined with others in the ideological fold of the Muslim Brotherhood to debate and continue to direct discourse about future political trends and directions, as well as major issues of concern such as the situation for the Palestinians, the wars in Iraq and Afghanistan, the election victory of Hamas in the Palestinian Territories in 2006, and the radical Islamist trend epitomized by al-Qaeda.[35] At a conference in Beirut in 2000, for example, Ennahda joined other Islamists from the Palestinian Territories, Algeria, and beyond to debate Muslim action over Jerusalem. The delegates used the breaks in the conference to explore the political landscape of the Middle East and the prospects for the Muslim Brotherhood. In Europe, Ennahda was also exposed to new dimensions of Muslim identity and accommodation within liberal democratic political systems and secular cultures manifest in countries such as the UK, France, and Germany.

Ignition

Socioeconomic crisis and political discontent had clearly characterized the Middle East region in the first decade of the twenty-first century, but there was a widespread assumption that Arab regimes, irrespective of their political makeup, were good at suppressing restive populations who occasionally rioted or demonstrated.[36] Authoritarian resilience was the main game in terms of regime preservation and in turn was powerfully aligned to wider international and particularly Western government priorities to fight the radical Islamist threat epitomized by al-Qaeda. While corrupt, nepotistic, authoritarian regimes and their supporters in the West allied to counter Islamism, it was demonstrations fuelled by frustration at widespread poverty, high unemployment, food inflation, and lack of freedoms and rights that led to the greatest period of sustained rebellion and instability in the Middle East for decades. The Arab Spring unfolded when protests broke out in Tunisia in December 2010 following the self-immolation of an impoverished vegetable vendor after his sense of powerlessness in the face of Tunisian government authority propelled him to his fatal act. The death of Mohammed Bouazizi in the Tunisian provincial town of Sidi Bouzid quickly led to a wave of demonstrations and protests as people mobilized throughout the country.[37] The state, under President Ben Ali's orders, deployed its police forces to put the rebellion down, killing and injuring those who had taken to the streets. However, Ben Ali's place in power became increasingly untenable when his own military forces refused to deploy against protestors and, in a shocking move, he fled the country into exile to Saudi Arabia on 14 January 2011.[38] One of the most well-established post-independent states in the Middle East appeared to crumble before the eyes of the protestors. The region had not given rise to such a significant collapse of power in the face of popular protest since 1979 when the Shah of Iran left his Peacock throne. Ben Ali's flight marked a watershed as it proved possible once again that autocratic and repressive regimes in the Middle East could be brought to their knees as a direct result of the people.

The tens of thousands of people who took to the streets and began to mobilize to lead, direct, support, and participate in the Tunisian revolt were demanding change. The people constituted many interests and reasons for protest and reflected the wider tradition of activism in the country. The social profiles of the protestors included men and women, youth, the employed and unemployed, and successful professionals including lawyers, engineers, and doctors, as well as students and many from Tunisia's labour movement. The revolt had a spatial and virtual role as blogs, Facebook posts, attacks on government websites by anonymous writers, and tweets allowed people to communicate quickly to organize protests.[39] Thus there were generational, gendered, and class-based dimensions to the protest that was directed against Ben Ali's regime, and no major town or city in the country was left untouched by the rapidly unfolding events. The labour movement, and in particular the main Union Générale des Travailleurs Tunisiens, began to direct the mobilization that was taking place. State violence and the regime response in general against the protestors united people in their determination to continue their demonstrations. Support for President Ben Ali quickly diminished, and the ruling party, the RCD, distanced itself from Ben Ali and his cohorts. The popular revolt was stimulated by trends which helped transform people's energies to demand the ouster of Ben Ali. This diverse mobilization made it difficult for the regime to suppress, as there was no one source for discontent that they could close down.

Contest and power

Even though Ennahda had played no part in igniting the Arab Spring in Tunisia, there was a certainty that it would be well placed to position itself in the new political space created by the fall of Ben Ali's regime. In one powerful sense, the absence of Ennahda in the events themselves was explicable as a result of the decades of severe repression that the movement had endured under Ben Ali's regime. Yet, as with elsewhere in the Middle East, the Arab Spring created a form of opening by which the Muslim Brotherhood movement and its local variants such as Ennahda could be willingly tested when it came to constitution making and elections for newly reconstituted legislatures and parliaments. The enduring appeal of the type of Islamism that Ennahda represented in Tunisia in terms of fundamental debates about Islam and democracy, as well as governance and the faith system in the public space, would assume particular importance. As the first country to hold elections after the Arab Spring, this would prove to be a test of contemporary Islamism in a new era to see if it could live up to its own promise or whether, as some predicted, the Arab Spring would lead to an Islamist winter where one form of authoritarian state control would be replaced by another.[40] And although Ennahda did not ignite the rebellion that spread across the region in 2010–11, it was part of the post–Ben Ali populist swell that would steer and shape the transition period where the demand was for a new political dispensation and a greater break with the figures of the ancien régime.

Ennahda was able to quickly organize a campaign to contest the elections and successfully registered as a political party in March 2011. In Ben Ali's wake, Ennahda had almost 'immediately reached out to the tens of thousands of former activists. . . . They established offices in every Tunisian province, quickly setting up sections for youth, women, social services and politics.'[41] There were indications and expectations, which leader Rachid Ghannouchi articulated, that the party would do well. Addressing fears that the party, if successful, would usher in a theocratic state, Ennahda attempted to provide reassurances. 'We believe in a civic state, based on equality between all citizens, regardless of faith, gender or race. We believe that the right to political and social association and organisation should be guaranteed for every citizen,' declared Ghannouchi on the day of the election.[42] Indeed Ennahda won 89 seats in the 217-seat legislature, capturing 37 per cent of the vote and dominating all the other parties in the election, the next largest receiving less than 10 per cent.[43] This was more than enough to accede to power, but Ennahda would have to share it with the secular Le Congrès pour la République (CPR) with 29 seats and Forum Démocratique pour le Travail et les Libertés (Ettakatol) with 20 seats.[44] From whatever perspective one chose to view it, the victory was important in terms of the portents for change heralded in the wake of the Arab Spring, not just in Tunisia, but the region as a whole.

Coalition government would prove to be a major test of the Islamist project in the transition that would be considerably more different than the experiences of the Muslim Brotherhood in Egypt during the transition period from 2011–13. Ennahda would have to lead a government through a momentous period of upheaval and transition that was affecting not only Tunisia's political system but its tourist-dependent economy and social milieu too. In power, Ennahda had to lead the national debate about the shape, character, and power of the political institutions of the Tunisian state in the transition. The functions and powers of the presidency, the government, and the assembly would need to be reshaped to ensure a progressive move from patterns of authoritarian governance to a more liberal, democratic one that could also accommodate Islam. There were many fears that with Ennahda leading the debate, democracy, and secularism would be easily sacrificed or relinquished in favour of an attempt to at last realize the utopian Islamist vision of leaders such as Rachid Ghannouchi. Yet this was the bind because Ennahda's vision of governance now had to be accommodated with the realities of sharing power and competitive politics. Indeed Guazzone highlights that under Ennahda's leadership the Jebali and Larayedh governments can be described as 'mostly reactive, relatively inefficient and lacking a generally innovative program'.[45] Guazzone does acknowledge that there were, as was the case elsewhere in the region at the time, 'structural and conjunctural' factors associated with the politics of the post-authoritarian Middle East which went some way in explaining Ennahda's inability to govern. Indeed any analysis of the impact of the Arab Spring and the populist revolts on disrupting authoritarian power in the region at the time highlighted similar factors as they pertained to debates about constitutions, democracy, government formation, the economy, and the role of state forces including the military. Such analysis also included the demand to change the nature of state institutions, the security sector reform, and the challenge of overturning a system which for decades had been characterized by deep-seated and highly unpopular practices of corruption and nepotism.[46]

The challenge, as Ghannouchi would later acknowledge, was formidable,

> Our experience in ruling occurred at a very delicate moment that Tunisia had been witnessing. We inherited a heavy burden from the previous regime, on one hand, and a people thirsty for freedom, development, and a higher standard of living, who face difficulties in confronting obstacles, on the other.[47]

Governance and power was a challenge for Ennahda that was unprecedented in its experience, and its initial run had proved wrought with difficulties.

Ennahda also had to contend with their own Islamist challenge as the Brotherhood in Egypt and Islamists elsewhere had in other electoral contests. This was particularly pertinent for Ennahda and its leadership because of the particular type

124 Tunisia – Renaissance

of Islamism that it had long championed. Since its early foundation, the Islamist position which Ennahda had sought to promote was one that accommodated the modernist project in terms of the intimate tie to conceptions of democracy and the place of Islam within and as part of it. Furthermore, as part of Ennahda, and in particular Rachid Ghannouchi's conceptions of the part and place of Islam in the modern state, the pan-Islamic dynamic of other Islamist thinkers was replaced with conceptions of citizenship tied more structurally to the modern Tunisian nation-state. Such conceptualizations were apparent in the electoral platform outlined by Ennahda as it sought to contest the 2011 elections.[48] The movement made public its commitment to a set of values that embraced more than just Islam, and described

> a holistic value system based on the realisation of values stemming from the cultural and civilisational heritage and Arab Islamic identity of Tunisian society . . . [including] social justice and solidarity, combating corruption, rational consumption, avoiding the wasteful use of resources, and consider-ing work a fundamental component of human dignity.[49]

In this vision, the state would be a 'political civil entity' that 'oversees public matters, protects social peace, works for economic development, respects individual and public liberties, upholds democratic practices, and ensures equality between citizens in rights and in obligations'.[50]

As was becoming evident, Ennahda was establishing a hitherto untested approach to power that could somehow marry its particular conception of Islam and democracy in a state-based form that remained cognizant of the secular heri-tage now at the heart of the Tunisian model. This would be an approach, therefore, that acknowledged the Tunisian state as embodying the legacies of Bourguiba in terms of a construct reflecting a nuanced Tunisian identity which over the decades had accommodated itself to the notion that Islam did not need to be integral to governance nor *shari'a* to the laws underpinning the functions of the state in its relationship to the people. This approach could not simply venture to replicate the Muslim Brotherhood 'model' attempted by Hamas or the Muslim Brotherhood in Egypt, but had to be anchored in the Tunisian context. Governing also had the impact of beginning to weaken the wider ideological impulse of Islamism espoused in the past by Ennahda. While for many years its leadership had had time to ponder and develop a discourse that mediated a role between Islam and democracy, plural-ism and the place of Islam in the modernity project, once in power more pressing issues such as the challenge of the economy and national security refocused their energies.

Despite the best of intentions, governance by Ennahda was beset with problems and crises which it seemed ill-equipped or ill-prepared to overcome. Adding to the sense of instability were the assassinations in 2013 of Chokri Belaid and Mohamed Brahmi, who were both outspoken critics of Ennahda and other Islamists. Their deaths at the hands of those suspected to have links to radical Islamist jihadist groups such as the Libyan Islamic Fighting Group and Ansar al-Shari'a led to the eruption of popular protest in their wake which were a compelling reminder to Ennahda of the precariousness of power.[51] Critics of Ennahda believed that their electoral victory and governance in Tunisia was also benign encouragement to radical Islamists including Salafist parties and groups, as well as jihadist elements linked to others in the Maghreb and beyond.[52] Hence, the rise of the Salafis affected Ennahda's prospects residing alongside them as they did on the Islamist spectrum. As a leader, Rachid Ghannouchi appeared unable to reassure the citizens of Tunisia that he was indeed a national, rather than narrowly Islamist, representative of the nation and state over which his Ennahda party led the government. He tried to shift blame for the assassinations of Brahmi and Belaid on radical Salafi-jihadist elements which were also responsible for other outbreaks of violence, protest, and attempts to enforce Islamic codes or customs such as for women to wear the hijab or niqab.[53]

But the assassinations brought to the fore fears about rising violent jihadism in Tunisia as evidenced by such attacks, as well as growing anger at perceived Islamization by Ennahda and others, including the Salafists within the Tunisia. Salafism and Ennahda were increasingly perceived as sharing the same Islamist agenda. In the wake of Ennahda's triumphant endorsement at the polls, it appeared that Salafists were increasingly emboldened to promote their agenda and sometimes violently so.[54] Salafism had been evident under President Ben Ali filling a vacuum in Ennahda's absence, but in the wake of the Arab Spring, they became increasingly active in voicing their agenda and lobbying Ennahda to institute Islamic law as part of the new constitution. The Salafists had made important inroads into many poverty-stricken districts of Tunisia's towns and cities recruiting young, unemployed men at the margins of society and denied opportunity by Ben Ali's state. Salafi-jihadi elements were also apparent as they enjoined supporters to engage in and recruit for the unfolding conflict in Syria and staged attacks in Tunisia itself, such as the September 2012 attack on the US Embassy in Tunis, the violence of insurgent cells near the border with Libya, and the attack on tourists at the Bardo museum in March 2015. In an important demonstration of national unity, which involved Ennahda, there were attempts by the transitional government to push back on the acceptability of such violence from jihadist quarters. Ennahda Prime Minister Ali Larayedh had in the past warned of an 'inevitable confrontation' with Salafists, but following Belaid's assassination and these other high-profile incidents, he told Le Monde, 'It has already taken place and will continue to occur.'[55] Indeed it was argued that Ennahda leaders 'played no small part, helping to avert the worst thanks to its prudent management of radical religious groups through a mix of dialogue, persuasion and co-optation'.[56] Ennahda, however, like other groups within the family of the Muslim Brotherhood, also found itself at the receiving end of Salafi and Salafi-jihadi critiques and pronouncements that its agenda for Islamization was either un-Islamic or not Islamic enough.[57] Many radical elements had indeed denounced the role of groups such as Ennahda and the Muslim Brotherhood for promoting change and access to power through the ballot box.[58]

Nevertheless, many of Tunisia's secular-leaning citizens remained unconvinced by such explanations. Increasingly Ennahda was regarded as complicit in attempts

126 Tunisia – Renaissance

to enforce Islamization or policies of Islamic compliance on the people.[59] Tunisians were seeing Ennahda's apparent control of governance and the Islamist hue it was attempting to impose as threats to the creation of secular democratic norms in the wake of the Arab Spring. Many were frustrated that Ennahda simply did not seem to understand the rules of the new 'democracy' game and that even if the ancien régime was deposed, many of the secular values – particularly as they related to women and their status – remained at the bedrock of Tunisian identity and the concept of state and rights. The violent overspill of jihadist elements, from elsewhere in the Maghreb, also made Tunisians wary of their own homegrown Islamists, fearing that Ennahda might turn out to be wolves in sheep's clothing.

Tunisians were irked that Ennahda even considered it likely that the new constitution could be Islamist-inspired or that, for example, women's rights could be rolled back through legislative proposals that would chip away at the rights accorded to women through the Personal Status Codes.[60] The concerns of women and groups supporting the rights of women were apparent in a series of protests on social media sites by Tunisian feminists and women's rights activists against the socially conservative agenda of Ennahda.[61] Ghannouchi was also criticized for 'paying lip service' to equality of rights while presiding over a government that was proposing constitutional reform that would have undermined basic principles as they related to the rights of Tunisian women.[62] Such women have attempted to situate the debate about Tunisia's political future and democracy around their role in society and the rights they enjoy while pushing back against Ennahda.[63] It is around issues such as women or other forms of constitutional reform that Tunisians have also come to understand that Ennahda is a movement and a political party of Islamism that is actually dynamic, not static, and one that embraces a variety of views and positions.[64] Ghannouchi, for example, can best be understood as a moderate within the party, while others took a less liberal position on issues as they related to social or secular political discourses in Tunisian society.

Nevertheless, for some there was cause for optimism that Tunisia under the Ennahda-led coalition reflected a post-Islamist realization of state and governance. Nader Hashemi argued, for example, that the country was a 'harbinger of what an Islamist-led "civil state" might look like. . . . In many ways Tunisia represents a bright spot in the Arab Spring, particularly in terms of reconciling the tensions between Islam, secularism, and democracy.'[65] But such tensions threw up violent crisis and obstacles to governance, continuing economic stagnation that no matter how powerfully charismatic and eloquently equipped Rachid Ghannouchi was could not be easily overcome. By January 2014 the party had 'turned its back' on the incorporation of the *shari'a* into the constitution.[66] In attempting to institute constitutional reform, it was as if the leadership of Ennahda had forgotten the very slogans that the demonstrators had shouted and sung in the casbah, on the streets and town squares across the country in the days of protest leading to Ben Ali's fall. Time and time again, those slogans of the revolution demanded the preservation of citizen's rights and constitutional reform but not in the name of Islam.

Loss

The uncertainties of power for Ennahda were put to the test again when it competed in legislative elections in October 2014, just three years after the initial poll that put them into power with their secular rivals in the CPR and Ettakatol. Tunisia had experienced unprecedented changes since 2011, and in the wider region the era of transition wrought by the events that unfolded in Tunisia in December 2010 had morphed into a complex sectarian and civil war in Syria, a military coup against the Brotherhood-led Morsi regime in Egypt at the hands of General al-Sisi's SCAF, the fragmentation of Libya and Yemen, and the further rise of jihadist forces bent on violent confrontation with its enemies.[67] Against this wider anti-Islamist trend in the region, Ennahda stuck with Tunisia's democracy project and put itself in the hands of the voters once again. This time, however, the Tunisian electorate handed a victory at the ballot box to Ennahda's new secular rivals in Nidaa Tounes, who won 86 out of the 217 seats compared to Ennahda's 69 in the legislature.[68] Nonetheless, Ennahda emerged from the contest as the second-biggest party in parliament, and its vote percentage only dropped by 10 per cent despite the rhetoric suggesting its demise.[69] It thus contended that the electoral loss was still a 'win' in terms of the wider accommodation of the democracy project in Tunisia to Islam and vice versa. But it was still believed that voters had turned away from the party because it had failed to institute forms of governance that centred on the economic recovery of the country and the growing national security threat of violent jihadism. Indeed some were concerned that the Ennahda's ambiguous position on the latter had given tacit encouragement to acts of violence that had severe consequences for the safety of the country's citizens and its tourism-dependent economy. Ennahda's leaders conceded that the task they had faced was formidable. They had effectively retreated from power when they had withdrawn from the government earlier that year and Ghannouchi had acknowledged that their task had involved the 'challenging work of building institutions, healing old wounds and forging compromise around shared values'.[70] In contrast to the 2011 poll, secular parties had managed to coalesce and overcome many of the internal tensions which had lost them votes and also had united under the leadership of Beji Caid Essebsi, who had taken the reins of power when Ennahda had handed them over during their withdrawal from government earlier that year. Essebsi had government experience, and Ennahda had calculated that by stepping down it could perhaps survive to stay in the tent of democratic politics in Tunisia to better avoid the fate of their fellow Islamist brethren in Cairo who had been deposed the previous year.

Ennahda hoped to survive and remain in the legislature at a time when other Islamists were toppled and collapsed under the weight of an anti–Muslim Brotherhood axis that had powerfully emerged in the region throughout 2013. The party's leaders believed that they could enjoin their electoral rivals to share power with them. While in power, they had avoided the temptation of constitutional reshaping that had elicited such a powerful, violent, and populist backlash as it did in Cairo.[71] The movement remained on message: Islam and democracy and not imposition of presidential or governmental fiat. In contrast, the challenge for Nidaa Tounes was how to manage forms of Islamism represented by Ennahda at a time when Tunisia had been faced with a mounting challenge from Salafi-jihadism.[72] Ennahda wanted to be partners in a coalition government again but understood that this time it would not only be the junior partner but that the stain of failure from the previous administration which it had led would persist. Nidaa elements blamed Ennahda for failing to rebuild the economy and a constant preoccupation with the place of Islam in the state that was undermining national unity in the post–Ben Ali dispensation. Ennahda was also criticized for failing to be unambiguous in their dismissal of the radical Islamist threat within Tunisia and elsewhere in the region. Instead, there were many occasions, its critics contended, when it was either seen to permit Salafists or jihadists to take a form of public platform without first preventing such displays of Islamism. There was a fear that the mosques, Islamist student societies, and Islamic community associations would be permitted to become breeding grounds for radical and violent Salafi-jihadists. In some respects, Ennahda's opponents concluded that the large number of Tunisians who had joined the ranks of radical jihadists in Syria and Iraq such as Islamic State (ISIS) and Jabhat al-Nusra was a worrying indication of the consequences of such ambiguity and the undermining of national security at home. Leftists, in particular, from the Popular Front led by Hamma Hammami, also continued to blame Ennahda for the assassination of Chokri Belaid and Mohamed Brahmi in 2013.[73] Hoping to diffuse further tension, Ennahda announced in 2014 that it would not present a candidate for forthcoming presidential elections.[74] Nevertheless, it was accused of meddling from afar in the contest between Moncef Marzouki and Beji Caid Essebsi in favour of the former as a 'friend' of political Islam.[75] The second runoff of the polls in December 2014, however, delivered a victory for Essebsi and was considered yet another indication of the limits of power for Ennahda.

By early February 2015, Nidaa had finally, and after much wrangling, formed a new coalition government (Nidaa Tounes, Ennahda, and the smaller Afek Tounes and Free Patriotic Union) which included rather than kept out Ennahda.[76] In part the decision was forced upon Nidaa's leadership, given indications that Ennahda would not give a vote of confidence if they were not accorded a place at the governmental table. This had given rise to protest from Nidaa and Popular Front party members who continued to oppose any form of inclusion for the Islamist rivals whom they blamed for the perilous state of the economy and threats to national security including the assassinations of leftist politicians by jihadists in 2013. Nidaa Tounes leader Abdelaziz Kotti, for example, made public his objections to any role for Ennahda in the new government, urging the Islamists to support it but 'without being a part' of it, echoing concerns again about investigations into their role in the assassinations of 2013.[77]

Winning a vote of confidence from the legislature, the Nidaa-led government was explicit about its commitment to the economic recovery of the country and continuing the difficult transition to democracy by promoting a pluralist political system. The support for the latter worked against Nidaa's initial assumption that it would manage to form a government in a narrowly based coalition with fellow Tunisian secularists in the Free Patriotic Union. Ennahda, along with other smaller legislative factions, essentially strong-armed Nidaa into the compromise coalition approved in February 2015 and led by Habib Essid, the newly appointed prime minister. But by including Ennahda in the coalition, Nidaa could help underwrite responsibility for the task of governance and security during a period of ongoing instability and economic crisis nationally, as well as regionally, by placing some accountability on the shoulders of its Islamist rivals. It was also a strategic calculation to keep Tunisia's Islamists within the political tent as a useful foil to legitimate any future efforts and actions against the Salafi-jihadist trends and threats. Such a calculation was particularly important to the newly formed and essentially nascent Nidaa Tounes party emerging as it had done on the Tunisian landscape in 2012 to oppose the insertion of Ennahda into government by popular vote. As Wolf points out,

> When [it was formed] it positioned itself as a 'modern' alternative to the Islamist Ennahda party . . . [It] drew a wide range of people, including supporters of Tunisia's Destourian ('Constitution') movement, trade unionists, leftists, and independents, as well as former members of Ben Ali's Constitutional Democratic Rally (RCD) party. Despite the members' ideological differences, they agreed to unite to counterbalance the Islamists in light of the challenges facing the country: religiously-motivated violence, economic stagnation, and delays in drafting the Constitution.[78]

Nidaa may well have pacified its supporters and critics with the compromise it reached with Ennahda permitting it only one ministerial post (the Ministry of Vocational Training and Employment) in return for its support of the new government. For its part, Ennahda remained wary of the Nidaa coalition particularly given its many links to Ben Ali's old regime and ties also to the interests of Tunisia's powerful trade union and competing business interests. Yet it has the benefit of ameliorating fears that Nidaa will crack down on the movement along lines similar to the criminalization of the Muslim Brotherhood in Egypt and elsewhere across the Middle East following the events of July 2013. '"We learned a lesson from Egypt,"' said a senior Ennahda leader. '"We decided that at this stage of the democratic process we need to unite the country and not to polarize the political scene."'[79]

Future face

On 14 January 2015 the people of Tunisia celebrated the fourth anniversary of their revolution and the ousting of their former president. Four years later, Tunisians could congratulate themselves for having steered through the first phase of their transition from autocracy to democracy by successfully holding two free and fair legislative elections of which the outcomes had been respected by all contesting

130 Tunisia – Renaissance

parties. Furthermore, Tunisia was evolving into a multiparty state for the first time in its history and arguably the most democratic state in the history of the Arab world. And while it was the case that the country's Islamists had not exactly steered the people to or through the revolution that tripped a wave of popular protest across the Middle East, they had been fundamental to this first phase of transition. In contrast to everywhere else in the Middle East, Tunisia, the birthplace of the Arab Spring, has been the only place to realize its ideals. It has emerged relatively unscathed from the vicious cycle of violent conflict and repression that now characterizes those other countries where change also happened, notably its neighbour Libya. Amidst the regional turmoil, Tunisia still gives hope to those believing in the transformative impulse of the people's revolt against authoritarian rule in the Middle East. Tunisia has overcome hurdles which others in the region have stumbled or fallen over such as toppling a corrupt repressive leader, negotiating a new constitution acceptable to the majority of citizens, and holding successive elections for the national assembly and president where outcomes have been respected and new forms of political discourse and culture have emerged.

The future for the Muslim Brotherhood in Tunisia as envisioned by Ennahda, however, is far from assured in terms of driving through the type of inclusion of Islam into state and politics that leaders such as Rachid Ghannouchi had long envisioned. Nevertheless, Ennahda could seek solace in the fact that after Ben Ali's departure it had been able to rapidly rebuild itself in demonstration that many of its ideas and approaches appealed to particular pious elements of the Tunisian population even if so many more were tied to a sense of national identity that sought to repel Islam from the corridors of power and the secularized public space. The hopes and aspirations expressed by many that Ennahda would serve as a successful model for 'democratic consolidation' by 'political Islamic actors in all Arab countries', however, was circumscribed by the challenges of governing which Ennahda encountered and the exceptional departure from the emerging norm that it seemed to portend.[80] Ennahda had failed to capture the majority of Tunisians in either the elections of 2011 or 2014, always encountering resistance from their secular and leftist rivals so much so that Ennahda's concept of the Muslim civil state (*dawla madaniyah*) was successively emptied of its Muslim content beyond a passing nod to the place of Islam as the 'religion' of the country.[81] By 2015 Tunisia was the only place in the Middle East which could be thought of as any kind of model of transition from revolt and rebellion to democracy in the wake of the Arab Spring. In explaining this phenomenon of progress and in overcoming challenges, the Tunisian people have been ascribed with managing to maintain their strong secular tradition with the embrace of Islamism epitomized by Ennahda. Like other groups within the family of the Muslim Brotherhood, Ennahda gained power peacefully and democratically, but unlike its counterparts, it shared power and then relinquished power peacefully, respecting new constitutional norms and the emergent democracy. In this way Ennahda can enjoin other Islamists in the Muslim Brotherhood family to follow their path, but what it cannot alter is the specific context of conflict in which their brethren across the Arab world are now embroiled in. In the country where the seeds of the Jasmine Revolution had been planted, it had come to blossom fully, giving hope that the upheavals of the region had not totally been in vain.

Notes

1 As quoted in D.D. Kirkpatrick, 'As Moderate Islamists Retreat, Extremists Surge Unchecked', *New York Times*, 18 June 2014, http://www.nytimes.com/2014/06/19/world/middleeast/as-moderate-islamists-retreat-extremists-surge-unchecked.html (accessed 26 February 2015).
2 BBC News, 'Tunisia's Islamist Ennahda Party Wins Historic Poll', *BBC News*, 27 October 2011, http://www.bbc.co.uk/news/world-africa-15487647 (accessed 5 May 2015).
3 I. Bel Aiba, 'Ennahda Leader Says "Tunisia Model" Way to Defeat Islamic State', *Agence France-Presse*, 23 October 2014, http://news.yahoo.com/ennahda-leader-says-tunisia-model-way-defeat-islamic-000837755.html (accessed 7 May 2015); F. El-Issawi, 'Islamists of Tunisia: Reconciling National Contradictions', *London School of Economics*, 13 April 2012, http://blogs.lse.ac.uk/ideas/2012/04/islamists-of-tunisia-reconciling-national-contradictions/ (accessed 7 May 2015).
4 Article 1 of the 1956 Tunisian constitution describes the state as 'faithful to the teachings of Islam'. See J.P. Jones, 'The Constitution of Tunisia', *University of Richmond School of Law*, 2014, http://confinder.richmond.edu/admin/docs/Tunisiaconstitution.pdf (accessed 26 February 2015).
5 A. Hermassi, 'The Political and the Religious in the Modern History of the Maghrib', in J. Ruedy (ed.), *Islamism and Secularism in North Africa*, Houndmills and London: Macmillan and the Center for Contemporary Arab Studies, 1994, p. 92.
6 Time, 'TUNISIA: Breaking the Fast', *Time*, 22 February 1960, p. 28, http://content.time.com/time/magazine/article/0,9171,939596,00.html (accessed 14 November 2014).
7 C.H. Moore, *Tunisia Since Independence: The Dynamics of One-Party Government*, Berkeley and Los Angeles: University of California Press, 1965, p. 56.
8 K. Perkins, *A History of Modern Tunisia*, New York: Cambridge University Press, 2005, pp. 140–2.
9 L.C. Brown, 'The Islamic Reformist Movement in North Africa', *Journal of Modern African Studies*, Vol. 2:1, March 1964, p. 61, http://dx.doi.org/10.1017/S0022278X00003669 (accessed 7 May 2015).
10 B. Milton-Edwards, *Islamic Fundamentalism since 1945*, 2nd ed., Abingdon: Routledge, 2014, pp. 34–5.
11 See M.M. Charrad, 'Cultural Diversity within Islam: Veils and Laws in Tunisia', in H.L. Bodman and N. Tohidi (eds), *Women in Muslim Societies: Diversity within Unity*, Boulder, CO: Lynne Rienner, 1998, pp. 63–79.
12 A. Hermassi, 'The Political and the Religious in the Modern History of the Maghrib', in J. Ruedy (ed.), *Islamism and Secularism in North Africa*, Houndmills and London: Macmillan and the Center for Contemporary Arab Studies, 1994, p. 92.
13 J.L. Esposito, *The Islamic Threat: Myth or Reality?*, 3rd ed., New York: Oxford University Press, 1999, p. 161.
14 M. Boulby, 'The Islamic Challenge: Tunisia Since Independence', *Third World Quarterly*, Vol. 10:2, April 1988, p. 595, http://www.jstor.org/stable/3992658 (accessed 7 May 2015).
15 J.L. Esposito, *The Islamic Threat: Myth or Reality?*, 3rd ed., New York: Oxford University Press, 1999, pp. 164–5.
16 M.C. Dunn, 'The Political and the Religious in the Modern History of the Maghrib', in J. Ruedy (ed.), *Islamism and Secularism in North Africa*, Houndmills and London: Macmillan and the Center for Contemporary Arab Studies, 1994, p. 151.
17 N. Pratt, *Democracy and Authoritarianism in the Arab World*, Boulder, CO: Lynne Rienner, 2007.

132 Tunisia – Renaissance

18 See J.L. Esposito, *The Islamic Threat: Myth or Reality?*, 3rd ed., New York: Oxford University Press, 1999.

19 See S. Heydemann, *Upgrading Authoritarianism in the Arab World*, Washington, DC: Brookings Institution, 2007, http://www.brookings.edu/~/media/research/files/papers/2007/10/arabworld/10arabworld.pdf (accessed 7 May 2015).

20 M. Willis, *Politics and Power in the Maghreb: Algeria, Tunisia and Morocco from Independence to the Arab Spring*, London: Hurst, 2012, pp. 175–7.

21 As quoted in F. Halliday, 'Tunisia's Uncertain Future', *Middle East Report*, Vol. 20:163, March–April 1990, p. 26, http://www.jstor.org/stable/3012554 (accessed 7 May 2015).

22 See M.C. Dunn, 'The Political and the Religious in the Modern History of the Maghrib', in J. Ruedy (ed.), *Islamism and Secularism in North Africa*, Houndmills and London: Macmillan and the Center for Contemporary Arab Studies, 1994, pp. 153–6.

23 M.C. Dunn, 'The Political and the Religious in the Modern History of the Maghrib', in J. Ruedy (ed.), *Islamism and Secularism in North Africa*, Houndmills and London: Macmillan and the Center for Contemporary Arab Studies, 1994, p. 155.

24 See L.B. Ware, 'Ben Ali's Constitutional Coup in Tunisia', *Middle East Journal*, Vol. 42:4, Autumn 1988, pp. 587–601, http://www.jstor.org.queens.ezp1.qub.ac.uk/stable/4327834 (accessed 28 May 2015).

25 Ramadan amnesties releasing prisoners is a common practice in ruling regimes across the Arab states of the Middle East.

26 As quoted in F. Halliday, 'Tunisia's Uncertain Future', *Middle East Report*, Vol. 20:163, March–April 1990, p. 26, http://www.jstor.org/stable/3012554 (accessed 7 May 2015).

27 M.C. Dunn, 'The Political and the Religious in the Modern History of the Maghrib', in J. Ruedy (ed.), *Islamism and Secularism in North Africa*, Houndmills and London: Macmillan and the Center for Contemporary Arab Studies, 1994, p. 157.

28 See M.C. Dunn, 'The Political and the Religious in the Modern History of the Maghrib', in J. Ruedy (ed.), *Islamism and Secularism in North Africa*, Houndmills and London: Macmillan and the Center for Contemporary Arab Studies, 1994, p. 149.

29 A.S. Tamimi, *Rachid Ghannouchi: A Democrat within Islamism*, New York: Oxford University Press, 2001, p. 73.

30 See M.C. Dunn, 'The Political and the Religious in the Modern History of the Maghrib', in J. Ruedy (ed.), *Islamism and Secularism in North Africa*, Houndmills and London: Macmillan and the Center for Contemporary Arab Studies, 1994, p. 149.

31 See R. Ghannouchi, 'The Battle Against Islam', *Middle East Affairs Journal*, Vol. 1:2, Winter 1992, p. 5; J. Brownlee, *Democracy Prevention: The Politics of the U.S.-Egyptian Alliance*, New York: Cambridge University Press, 2012.

32 See F. Burgat, 'Les islamistes au révélateur de la crise', *Annuaire de l'Afrique du Nord*, Vol. 31, 1992, pp. 201–13, http://aan.mmsh.univ-aix.fr/Pdf/AAN-1992-31_45.pdf (accessed 28 May 2015).

33 See E. Lust-Okar and S. Zerhouni (eds), *Political Participation in the Middle East*, Boulder, CO: Lynne Rienner, 2008.

34 J.L. Gelvin, *The Arab Uprisings: What Everyone Needs to Know*, New York: Oxford University Press, 2012, pp. 57–8.

35 M.P. Angrist, 'Understanding the Success of Mass Civic Protest in Tunisia', *Middle East Journal*, Vol. 67:4, Autumn 2013, pp. 547–64, http://muse.jhu.edu.queens.ezp1.qub.ac.uk/journals/the_middle_east_journal/v067/67.4.angrist.html (accessed 28 May 2015).

36 See R. Owen, *The Rise and Fall of Arab Presidents for Life*, Cambridge, MA: Harvard University Press, 2012.

37 See C. Alexander, 'Tunisia's Protest Wave: Where It Comes From and What It Means for Ben Ali', *Foreign Policy*, 3 January 2011, http://foreignpolicy.com/2011/01/03/tunisias-protest-wave-where-it-comes-from-and-what-it-means/ (accessed 28 May 2015); J. Borger, 'Tunisian President Vows to Punish Rioters after Worst Unrest in a Decade', *Guardian*, 29 December 2010, http://www.theguardian.com/world/2010/dec/29/tunisian-president-vows-punish-rioters (accessed 28 May 2015); W. Davies, 'Tunisia:

President Zine al-Abidine Ben Ali Forced Out', *BBC News*, 15 January 2011, http://www.bbc.co.uk/news/world-africa-12195025 (accessed 23 May 2015).

38 See Z. Barany, 'Comparing the Arab Revolts: The Role of the Military', *Journal of Democracy*, Vol. 22:4, Oct. 2011, pp. 28–39; E. Bellin, 'Reconsidering the Robustness of Authoritarianism in the Middle East: Lessons from the Arab Spring', *Comparative Politics*, Vol. 44:2, January 2012, pp. 127–49, http://dx.doi.org/10.5129/001041512798838021 (accessed 29 May 2015); R. Brooks, 'Abandoned at the Palace: Why the Tunisian Military Defected from the Ben Ali Regime in January 2011', *Journal of Strategic Studies*, Vol. 36:2, April 2013, pp. 205–20; P. Droz-Vincent, 'From Fighting Formal Wars to Maintaining Civil Peace?', *International Journal of Middle East Studies*, Vol. 43, 2011, pp. 392–4; D. Lutterbeck, 'Arab Uprising, Armed Forces, and Civil-Military Relations', *Armed Forces and Society*, 13 April 2012, pp. 1–25; S. Nepstead, 'Nonviolent Resistance in the Arab Spring: The Critical Role of Military-Opposition Alliances', *Swiss Political Science Review*, Vol. 17:4, 2011, pp. 485–91.

39 See P. Shakarian, J. Shakarian, and A. Ruef, *Introduction to Cyber-Warfare: A Multidisciplinary Approach*, Waltham, MA: Elsevier, 2013, p. 90.

40 R. Spencer, 'Middle East Review of 2012: The Arab Winter', *Telegraph*, 31 December 2012, http://www.telegraph.co.uk/news/worldnews/middleeast/9753123/Middle-East-review-of-2012-the-Arab-Winter.html (accessed 7 May 2015); J. Phillips, 'The Arab Spring Descends into Islamist Winter: Implications for U.S. Policy', *Heritage Foundation*, 20 December 2012, http://www.heritage.org/research/reports/2012/12/the-arab-spring-descends-into-islamist-winter-implications-for-us-policy (accessed 7 May 2015); Washington Times Editorial Board, 'From Arab Spring to Islamist Winter', *Washington Times*, 25 October 2011, http://www.washingtontimes.com/news/2011/oct/25/from-arab-spring-to-islamist-winter/ (accessed 7 May 2015).

41 M. Lynch, 'Tunisia's New al-Nahda', *Foreign Policy*, 29 June 2011, http://foreignpolicy.com/2011/06/29/tunisias-new-al-nahda/ (accessed 3 March 2015).

42 R. Ghannouchi, 'A Day to Inspire All Tunisians – Whether Islamic or Secular', *Guardian*, 17 October 2011, http://www.theguardian.com/commentisfree/2011/oct/17/tunisians-islamic-secular-ennahda-election (accessed 3 March 2015).

43 National Democratic Institute, *Final Report on the Tunisian National Constituent Assembly Elections*, Washington, DC: National Democratic Institute, 2011, https://www.ndi.org/files/tunisia-final-election-report-021712_v2.pdf (accessed 28 May 2015), p. 19.

44 See T. El-Amrani and U. Lindsey, 'Tunisia Moves to the Next Stage', *Middle East Research and Information Project*, 8 November 2011, http://www.merip.org/mero/mero110811 (accessed 20 May 2015).

45 L. Guazzone, 'Ennahda Islamists and the Test of Government in Tunisia', *The International Spectator: Italian Journal of International Affairs*, Vol. 48:4, December 2013, p. 36, http://dx.doi.org/10.1080/03932729.2013.847677 (accessed 5 May 2015).

46 See S. Heydemann and R. Leenders, 'Authoritarian Learning and Authoritarian Resilience: Regime Responses to the "Arab Awakening"', *Globalizations*, Vol. 8:5, 2011, pp. 647–53, http://dx.doi.org/10.1080/14747731.2011.621274 (accessed 31 May 2015); R. Hinnebusch, 'A Historical Sociology Approach to Authoritarian Resilience in Post-Arab Uprising MENA', *Project on Middle East Political Science*, 19 December 2014, http://pomeps.org/2014/12/19/a-historical-sociology-approach-to-authoritarian-resilience/#sthash.F73yNrUs.dpuf (accessed 29 May 2015); E. Bellin, 'Reconsidering the Robustness of Authoritarianism in the Middle East: Lessons from the Arab Spring', *Comparative Politics*, Vol. 44:2, January 2012, pp. 127–49, http://dx.doi.org/10.5129/001041512798838021 (accessed 29 May 2015).

47 A. Al-Sabiri, 'Al-Nahda Leader Ghannouchi: Tunisia Heading Towards "Muslim democratic state"', *Al-Akhbar English*, 29 September 2014, http://english.al-akhbar.com/node/21749 (accessed 7 May 2015).

48 See R. Ghannouchi, 'A Day to Inspire All Tunisians – Whether Islamic or Secular', *Guardian*, 17 October 2011, http://www.theguardian.com/commentisfree/2011/oct/17/tunisians-islamic-secular-ennahda-election (accessed 3 March 2015).

49 C. Kurzman, Ennahda Movement Programme: For Freedom, Justice and Development in Tunisia, Ennahda Electoral Programme 2011, University of North Carolina at Chapel Hill, 30 April 2015, http://kurzman.unc.edu/files/2011/06/Nahda_2011_summary_in_English.pdf (accessed 7 May 2015), p. 11.

50 C. Kurzman, Ennahda Movement Programme: For Freedom, Justice and Development in Tunisia, Ennahda Electoral Programme 2011, University of North Carolina at Chapel Hill, 30 April 2015, http://kurzman.unc.edu/files/2011/06/Nahda_2011_summary_in_English.pdf (accessed 7 May 2015), p. 12.

51 See Al Jazeera, 'Ansar al-Sharia Blamed for Tunisia Killings', *Al Jazeera*, 27 August 2013, http://www.aljazeera.com/news/africa/2013/08/2013827131811488516.html (accessed 2 September 2013); T. Joscelyn, 'Ansar al-Sharia Responds to Tunisian Government', *Long War Journal*, 3 September 2013, http://www.longwarjournal.org/archives/2013/09/ansar_al_sharia_tuni_6.php (accessed 4 September 2013).

52 See D. Gartenstein-Ross, B. Moreng, and K. Soucy, *Raising the Stakes: Ansar al-Sharia in Tunisia's Shift to Jihad*, ICCT Research Paper, International Centre for Counter-Terrorism, The Hague, February 2014, http://www. icct.nl/download/file/ICCT-Gartenstein-Ross-Moreng-Soucy-Raising-the-Stakes-ASTs-Shift-to-Jihad-Feb-2014 (accessed 20 May 2015).

53 See B. Ben Bouazza, 'Tunisia Manouba University Students Face Off Over Islamic Veil on Campus', *Associated Press*, 1 April 2012, http://www.huffingtonpost.com/2012/01/04/tunisia-manouba-university-veil_n_1184117.html (accessed 7 May 2015).

54 See T. Amara, 'Two Dead as Protesters Attack U.S. Embassy in Tunisia', *Reuters*, 14 September 2012, http://uk.reuters.com/article/2012/09/14/us-protests-tunisia-school-idUSBRE88D18020120914 (accessed 18 May 2015); B. Ben Bouazza, 'Tunisia: Attackers Set Fire to Muslim Saint Shrine', *Associated Press*, 16 October 2012, http://news.yahoo.com/tunisia-attackers-set-fire-muslim-saint-shrine-174125155.html (accessed 18 May 2015); F. Merone, 'Salafism in Tunisia: An Interview with a Member of Ansar al-Sharia', *Jadaliyya*, 11 April 2013, http://www.jadaliyya.com/pages/index/11166/salafism-in-tunisia_an-interview-with-a-member-of- (accessed 28 May 2015).

55 T. Joscelyn, 'War of Words Escalates in Tunisia', *Long War Journal*, 27 March 2013, http://www.longwarjournal.org/archives/2013/03/war_of_words_escalat.php (accessed 29 May 2015).

56 International Crisis Group, *Tunisia: Violence and the Salafi Challenge – Middle East and North Africa Report N°137*, Tunis/Brussels: International Crisis Group, 2013, http://www.crisisgroup.org/en/regions/middle-east-north-africa/north-africa/tunisia/137-tunisia-violence-and-the-salafi-challenge.aspx (accessed 19 May 2015).

57 See L. Jacinto, 'Tunisia's Islamist Ennahda Party Turns on Salafists', *France 24*, 22 May 2013, http://www.france24.com/en/20130522-tunisia-islamist-ennahda-party-salafist-ansar-sharia (accessed 29 May 2015).

58 See B. Milton-Edwards, 'Revolt and Revolution: The Place of Islamism', *Critical Studies in Terrorism*, Vol. 5:2, August 2012, pp. 219–36, http://dx.doi.org/10.1080/17539153.2012.686658 (accessed 7 May 2015).

59 See Reuters, 'Protests Erupt in Tunis after Opposition Leader Shot Dead', *France 24*, 26 July 2013, http://www.france24.com/en/20130725-tunisia-thousands-protest-after-tunisian-opposition-leader-brahmi-shot-dead/ (accessed 7 May 2015).

60 See F. Al Yafai, 'A Losing Battle as Ennahda Tries to Define Tunisian Women's Role', *National UAE*, 21 August 2012, http://www.thenational.ae/thenationalconversation/comment/a-losing-battle-as-ennahda-tries-to-define-tunisian-womens-role (accessed 3 March 2015).

61 See E. Greenhouse, 'How to Provoke National Unrest with a Facebook Photo', *New Yorker*, 8 April 2013, http://www.newyorker.com/tech/elements/how-to-provoke-national-unrest-with-a-facebook-photo (accessed 22 February 2015); A. Alami, 'Women Face Fight to Keep Their Rights in Tunisia', *New York Times*, 20 February 2013, http://www.nytimes.com/2013/02/21/world/middleeast/women-face-fight-to-keep-their-rights-in-tunisia.html (accessed 3 March 2015).

62 See E. Melkonian, 'Women's Rights in Tunisia: Promising Future or Religio-political Game?',*OpenDemocracy*,16 January 2015,https://www.opendemocracy.net/openglobalrights/ elsy-melkonian/women%E2%80%99s-rights-in-tunisia-promising-future-or-religiopolitical-game (accessed 28 May 2015).

63 Z. Touati and S. Zlitni, 'Social Networks and Women's Rights Activism in Post-Revolutionary Tunisia', in M.S. Olimat (ed.), *Arab Spring and Arab Women: Challenges and Opportunities*, Abingdon, Oxon and New York: Routledge, 2014, pp. 162–75.

64 See F. Cavatorta and F. Merone, 'Moderation through Exclusion? The Journey of the Tunisian Ennahda from Fundamentalist to Conservative Party', *Democratization*, Vol. 20:5, 2013, pp. 857–75, http://dx.doi.org/10.1080/13510347.2013.801255 (accessed 28 May 2015).

65 N. Hashemi, 'The Arab Spring Two Years On: Reflections on Dignity, Democracy, and Devotion', *Ethics & International Affairs*, Vol. 27:2, Summer 2013, p. 217, http://dx.doi. org/10.1017/S0892679413000099 (accessed 7 May 2015); O. Roy, 'The Myth of the Islamist Winter', *New Statesman*, 13 December 2013, http://www.newstatesman.com/ world-affairs/world-affairs/2012/12/myth-islamist-winter (accessed 20 May 2015).

66 See I. Mandraud,'La Tunisie tourne le dos à la charia',*Le Monde*,7 January 2014,http://www. lemonde.fr/international/article/2014/01/07/la-tunisie-officialise-le-renoncement-a-la-charia_4343892_3210.html (accessed 3 March 2015).

67 See B. Milton-Edwards,'Revolt and Revolution: The Place of Islamism', *Critical Studies in Terrorism*, Vol. 5:2, August 2012, pp. 219–36, http://dx.doi.org/10.1080/17539153.2012 .686658 (accessed 7 May 2015).

68 See A. Wolf,'Can Nidaa Tounes Lead Tunisia?', *Middle East Institute*, 21 November 2014, http://www.mei.edu/content/article/can-nidaa-tounes-lead-tunisia (accessed 20 May 2015).

69 See Economist, 'The Secularist Comeback', *Economist*, 29 October 2014, http://www. economist.com/news/middle-east-and-africa/21628920-surprising-defeat-islamist-nahda-party-secularists-comeback (accessed 26 May 2015).

70 R. Ghannouchi, 'Tunisia Shows There Is No Contradiction between Democracy and Islam', *Washington Post*, 24 October 2014, http://www.washingtonpost.com/opinions/ tunisia-shows-there-is-no-contradiction-between-democracy-and-islam/2014/10/24/ 2655e552-5a16-11e4-bd61-346aee66ba29_story.html (accessed 7 May 2014).

71 See M. Marks, *Convince, Coerce, or Compromise? Ennahda's Approach to Tunisia's Constitution*, Doha: Brookings Doha Center, 2014, http://www.brookings.edu/~/media/research/files/ papers/2014/02/10-ennahda-tunisia-constitution-marks/ennahda-approach-tunisia-constitution-english.pdf (accessed 6 May 2015).

72 M. Marks, 'Youth Politics and Tunisian Salafism: Understanding the Jihadi Current', *Mediterranean Politics*, Vol. 18:1, 2013, pp. 104–11, http://dx.doi.org/10.1080/136293 95.2013.764657 (accessed 28 May 2015); G. Ben Khalifa, 'The Secret of the Salafists' Appeal in Tunisia', *Al-Monitor*, 1 May 2013, http://www.al-monitor.com/pulse/culture/ 2013/05/disadvantaged-tunisian-youth-embrace-salafism.html#ixzz3bTpwvZm0 (accessed 28 May 2015).

73 See J. Legge,'Tunisia Shocked by Assassinations: Opposition Leaders Mohamed Brahmi and Chokri Belaid Killed with the Same Gun', *Independent*, 26 July 2013, http://www. independent.co.uk/news/world/africa/tunisia-shocked-by-assassinations-opposition-leaders-mohamed-brahmi-and-chokri-belaid-killed-with-the-same-gun-8733972.html (accessed 20 September 2013).

74 Middle East Monitor,'Tunisia's Ennahda Party Will Not Run a Candidate in the Presidential Election', *Middle East Monitor*, 8 September 2014, https://www.middleeastmonitor.com/ news/africa/13979-tunisias-ennahda-party-will-not-run-a-candidate-in-the-presidential-election (accessed 29 May 2015).

75 See H. Al-Fathali, 'Ennahda's Ghannouchi Plays Mediator in Tunisia', *Al-Monitor*, 1 December 2014, http://www.al-monitor.com/pulse/politics/2014/12/ennahda-mediator-tunisia-president-elections-nidaa-tunis.html (accessed 2 February 2015).

76 T. Amara, 'Tunisia's Islamist Party Agrees to Join Coalition Government', *Reuters*, 1 February 2015, http://www.reuters.com/article/2015/02/01/us-tunisia-politics-idUSKBN0L51OB20150201 (accessed 29 May 2015).

77 See Noozz.com, 'A. Kotti "Ennahda Does Not Go Out the Window . . . "', *Noozz*, 13 January 2015, http://noozz.com/Tunisia/Articles/ViewNews/364851 (accessed 7 May 2015).

78 See A. Wolf, 'The Future of Tunisia's Nidaa Tounes Party', *Middle East Institute*, 25 July 2014, http://www.mei.edu/content/at/future-tunisias-nidaa-tounes-party (accessed 12 December 2014).

79 J. Diehl, 'Tunisia Boldly Embraces Democracy', *Washington Post*, 26 October 2014, http://www.washingtonpost.com/opinions/jackson-diehl-tunisia-boldly-embraces-democracy/2014/10/26/8d86b19a-5adc-11e4-b812-38518ae74c67_story.html (accessed 26 May 2015).

80 L. Guazzone, 'Ennahda Islamists and the Test of Government in Tunisia', *The International Spectator: Italian Journal of International Affairs*, Vol. 48:4, December 2013, p. 49, http://dx.doi.org/10.1080/03932729.2013.847677 (accessed 5 May 2015).

81 See D. Pickard, *Lessons from Constitution-Making in Tunisia*, Washington, DC: Atlantic Council of the United States, 2012, http://www.atlanticcouncil.org/images/files/publication_pdfs/403/mec121213tunisia.pdf (accessed 26 May 2015).

6

YEMEN – THE MUSLIM BROTHERHOOD AND THE TIES OF TRIBE

While we confirm our respect for the experience of the Muslim Brotherhood emanating from moderation as a method of life and Da'wah (Call), we emphasize that Islah is an official Yemeni political party, and we do not care about any other names named by others.

Islah Party Yemen[1]

Introduction

The diversity of Yemenis protesting during the Arab Spring was surprising given the extent to which this poorest of Arab states in the Middle East is usually depicted: tribal and gradually bowing to the influence of al-Qaeda in the Arab Peninsula (AQAP) and Houthi rebels. Among the groups that congregated in Taghir (Change) Square in the Yemeni capital of Sanaa in January 2011 were artists, theatre performers, youth groups, women, tribesmen, and the Deaf and Dumb Youth Revolution Alliance, as well as a spectrum of Yemen's Islamist elements including the most influential organization, the Yemeni Muslim Brotherhood's Yemeni Congregation for Reform (Islah party). As tens of thousands of Yemenis began to demonstrate and call on President Ali Abdullah Salih to step down, Islah was marshalling its supporters onto the streets and playing a leading role. On Sanaa's university campus, students chanting 'Time for Change' and anti-government slogans were led by popular Islah leader and women's activist Tawakkul Karman while her counterpart Abdulmalik al-Qasuss addressed protestors, declaring, 'We gather today to demand the departure of President Salih and his corrupt government.'[2]

Motivated to action by complaints of economic crisis, hardship, social injustice, and a fear that President Salih's constitution meddling would all but assure him more years in power, the protests took on a momentum that was hard to ignore.

Nevertheless, as dissent and revolt erupted, Islah, like the Muslim Brotherhood elsewhere in the Arab world, was initially slow to understand the import of change unfolding before its very eyes. Its initial actions were designed to facilitate a negotiated departure for Salih rather than an undignified departure and exile coup of the kind that had befallen Ben Ali in Tunisia and Mubarak in Egypt.[3] In this respect, it played an increasingly important role in the transition from power as Islah leader Mohammed al-Yadoumi commenced negotiations with the ruling regime to relinquish power. Yet the organization was hampered by the growing toll of death and injury inflicted by the regime against protesters which included many from its own ranks. The months of revolt and revolution wore on throughout 2011. The regime ordered the military and police to continue to respond with violence, and President Salih engaged in stalling tactics. The leadership of Islah, compelled as much by growing populist pressure as its own conviction, joined with other opposition groups to pressure for a faster pace of change. In July 2011, as the Yemen uprising continued, al-Yadoumi was targeted for assassination in an attack widely condemned by Yemeni coalition members in the Joint Meeting Parties (JMP) and blamed on pro-Salih forces or government elements.[4] Increasingly Islah became invested in the project for change. As German diplomat Philip Holzapfel highlighted, 'As the best organized opposition party across the country, Islah considered itself the natural leader of the revolution and entitled to harvest the fruits of regime change as much as its peers in Egypt and Tunisia.'[5]

When, in November 2011, President Salih finally handed over power to his vice president, Abd Rabbo Mansour Hadi, in a face-saving deal brokered by the Gulf Cooperation Council (GCC) known as the Gulf Initiative,[6] fears abounded among the protestors that the transition of power would reinforce three prime elements of Yemeni society: the Islamists, the tribe, and the military.[7] Salih's formal dominance over Yemen which had lasted for decades was, however, finally brought to an end. His control of the Yemeni state, since reunification in 1990, had been ended not as a result of the vitriolic jihadist fervour of al-Qaeda or the power of the tribes or even the Houthi rebellion but as a result of populist pressure and protest. President Salih had hoped that US patronage would save him from the fate of President Mubarak of Egypt and President Ben Ali in Tunisia, contending that he was the only one who could save Yemen from falling to al-Qaeda and other rebel elements. Somewhat surprisingly, the US government did not step in to prop up this particular ailing president.

In the wake of President Salih's departure, the interim leader, former vice president Abd Rabbo Mansour Hadi, formed a transitional unity government and called for presidential elections. This presented an opportunity for Yemen's political opposition to ascend to power.[8] The main alliance of opposition parties (JMP) included among its number the most prominent Islamist actor in Yemen: the Muslim Brotherhood–inspired Islah (a.k.a., the Yemeni Congregation for Reform) party. However, this was not the first time that the Muslim Brotherhood in Yemen had shared power in government with the nationalist General People's Congress (GPC) between 1994 and 1997, but it was the first time that a ruling transitional coalition was being built outside of President Salih's hegemonic grip over the GPC.

The challenge of explaining and analyzing the role of the Muslim Brotherhood movement and its manifestation in Yemen is intricately tied to the challenge of explaining Yemen's complex political environment. One dimension of Islah that distinguishes it from other manifestations of the Muslim Brotherhood across the Arab world, however, is that it commenced its political life in power as part of an alliance with the ruling GPC. Its leaders explain the motive for its alliance with Salih's governing party power claiming that in this way Islah was always present on the national stage. 'We were characterised by not excluding society and not taking a hostile stance towards government,' claimed Mohammed Qahtan, a senior Islah leader. 'When political plurality was introduced,' he continued, 'we shared power with the Socialist Party and we entered a tripartite coalition.'[9] It was only later in its development that Islah left power and became an opposition party, hence inverting the usual political position of the Muslim Brotherhood elsewhere in the Arab world where opposition is the norm and power incumbency rare. Yet unlike other Brotherhood-affiliated groups elsewhere, Islah has also been beset with internal ideological schism. This has made it more difficult for the party to transcend such differences and to present itself as unified and coherent in its positions to the constituencies it seeks to represent. And it is these constituencies themselves which are largely tribal and fractious in terms of a unitary Islamist agenda that have also undermined Islah's political ambitions to fashion Yemen as a state governing in the name of Islam. As Yemen expert Stephen Day explains,

> The primary axis of Yemeni politics in the twenty-first century is not religious or ideological, partisan or class-based. Earlier struggles between Arabists and tribal traditionalists, Islamists and socialists have faded. Today Yemen is returning to a much older pattern of regionalism. . . . Yemen remains a fragmented country, where politics is largely defined by the competing interests of groups in multiple regions across a topographically complex landscape.[10]

Thus the task in this chapter is to analyze the extent to which the Muslim Brotherhood (as represented by Islah) can employ Islam as a societal and political unifier to transcend tribal ties and powerful competing regional pressures in a weak and failing state. The transition currently underway in Yemen, which will be examined in the chapter, presents Islah with a formidable challenge. This challenge comes from the tribal structure of the country; the huge issue of unemployment and youth unemployment in particular; and the legacy of secularism between North and South Yemen, as well as the conflict presented by other Islamist competitors, including AQAP and Shi'a-supported Houthi rebels who took over power in February 2015, forcing President Abd Rabbo Mansour Hadi to flee the capital Sanaa. The presence of Houthi rebels in power also led to Saudi military intervention and escalating tensions in their rivalry with Iran apparent in the Yemeni arena. The chapter will also examine the extent to which parliamentary participation for the Muslim Brotherhood and its affiliates in Yemen have presented the opportunities for power rather than co-optation and what lies ahead for the Muslim Brotherhood's Islah squeezed by the dual forces of Houthi political control and a Saudi military campaign to oust them.

Tribe trumps

The most significant factor that any political party or group must contend with in Yemen is the tribe and its place in society and politics. 'As the history of Yemen has repeatedly demonstrated, tribes have been central players – if not the central player – in the politics of the country,' writes eminent anthropologist of Yemen Steven C. Caton.[11] In some respects then it is difficult to overstate the influence of the tribes in Yemen. Writing in 1974, Fred Halliday had declared that the Yemeni civil war of the 1960s served to reinforce and exacerbate existing tribal stratification; tribal leaders presided over internal disputes and oversaw dealings with external powers. Tribes were still ranked by a hierarchy of 'power, wealth and ownership of the means of production'.[12] Likewise, the tribe has always explained the fragmentation of Yemen and the difficulties which the state has had in acting as a national unifier of the people; this was apparent in the 'lack of influence of the central government outside the major cities and the widespread distribution of arms in society'.[13] There remains the contradiction of 'tribal practice affecting contemporary affairs quite deeply and yet belonging, in the view of many, to a previous age'.[14]

Thus, tribalism has worked against the fundamental principles of the modern nation-state in Yemen by competing against the state in respect of the monopoly of legitimate coercive force, rule of law, loyalty of citizens, and the protection of rights (particularly individual). Yemen's state actors and politicians reinforce the power and influence of the tribes by being in constant negotiation and competition with each other for patronage and support of the most powerful tribal heads. Without tribal support, no leader of Yemen has been able to maintain power. As O'Neill highlights, 'Tribes wield incredible power and influence, a state of affairs inevitably portrayed as both archaic and dangerous. . . . The tribes have their own laws and customs, and their own rules of interaction.'[15]

Such a context inevitably has impacted Yemen's Muslim Brotherhood movement – Islah – as it has sought to achieve its political objectives. Islah has attempted to operate in recognition that tribe can transcend Islam even if that is a fundamental contradiction to its position as an Islamist party. Internally it has sought to win influence or draw on the powerful leadership roles within tribes that certain of its leaders, such as Sheikh Abdullah Ibn Husayn al-Ahmar of the Hashid federation, can bring. In playing by the rules of the tribal game, however, replicating tribal factionalism, diffusion, and difference, Islah again leads itself in the opposite direction of the unitary position that otherwise has distinguished the Muslim Brotherhood. Islah replicates and reinforces the values of tribalism in the political realm and thus has undermined its capacity for ideological cohesiveness in relation to issues including the development of modern Yemen, the role of women, the place of *shari'a*, the role of the state, plurality of politics, and citizenship and rights.

So long as the tribe has remained prominent in Yemen, so too has its influence on Islah remained apparent. In particular, the Hashid confederation, headed until 2007 by Sheikh Abdullah Ibn Husayn al-Ahmar, saw no contradiction in using Islah (which he helped found) also as a vehicle in pursuit of its own interests and power in relation to its own attempts to subsume the state or tame it. The Hashid federation, located north of Sanaa, is regarded as 'typically . . . the most dominant . . . in terms of their influence in the [Government of Yemen] institutions and Yemeni tribal society'.[16] The Hashid confederation was content to reflect its tribal interests in Islah as one among other political parties in Yemen (including the ruling GPC) in order to enhance its position in relation to the state. This fact has always made Islah vulnerable to the shifts in allegiance dictated by the Hashid leaders. Its only protection from the vagaries of such decision making was the leadership of prominent Hashid leaders such as Sheikh Abdullah Ibn Husayn al-Ahmar, who was then supported and succeeded upon his death by many of his sons, including Sheikh Sadiq bin Abdullah al-Ahmar.[17] The confederation's constituents in the northern regions of Yemen such as Sanaa and Amran ensured a strong electoral showing for Islah in securing seats at municipal and national legislative levels.[18]

Roots

The Muslim Brotherhood draws its support from Yemen's majority Sunni community, which accounts for about 60 per cent of the population. The group was founded in North Yemen between the 1940s and the 1960s and was inspired by the Egyptian Muslim Brotherhood. This inspiration came as a direct result of the experiences of the founding members of the Yemeni Muslim Brotherhood who had studied in Egyptian universities where they were exposed to the Brotherhood's presence on campuses and in student councils and societies. Their experiences of the ideological platform of the Egyptian Muslim Brotherhood, the solidarity they enjoyed by sharing their university experiences with other students drawn from across the Arab world, and the context of political change in the region at the time influenced the men who would return to Sanaa, Taiz, and Ibb. They would seek to create a reformist Islamist organization that would call on their fellow Yeminis to return to the fundamental principles and teachings of Islam. But the ideals of the Brotherhood in Sunni-dominated urban cities such as Cairo or Alexandria would be challenged by the reality of their tribally dominant, sectarian, diverse, and largely rural home country. Prominent founders and leaders of the Muslim Brotherhood in Yemen, who would later found Islah, including individuals such as Sheikh Abdul Majid al-Zindani, had thus studied in the same Egyptian universities and joined Brotherhood-influenced student organizations at the same time as their Arab compatriots from other parts of the region who would also go on to found branches of the Muslim Brotherhood in their home countries. Sheikh al-Zindani and others like him were able to establish the same primary structures and decision-making forums as the Egyptian Brotherhood, including mechanisms for consensus reaching such as the Shura Council of the Yemeni Brotherhood.

The Islah party in Yemen, like some of its counterparts in the Muslim Brotherhood across the Arab world, enjoys a history where it has been both in opposition and co-opted by a ruling regime into temporary governance pacts. This has led Islah's leadership to be considered shrewd political actors prepared to enjoin power if it provides an opportunity for its ultimate survival. Its survival, mainly as an opposition force, has always depended on its ability to portray itself as nodding to tribal power while being capable of mediating a role for itself with other political parties in Yemen. Islah reflects a broad Sunni Wahhabi-inspired Islamism in a society where other Muslim sects, and particularly the Zaydi, have also flourished. While Sunni Muslims account for 60 per cent of the population, the Zaydi are close to 35 per cent.[19] The Houthis are Zaydi Shi'a Muslims, who are relatively unknown in the West, yet, as discussed above, they constitute an estimated 35 per cent of Yemen's population. They derive from North Yemen, and their predecessors were the monarchs of the Mutawakkilite imamate overthrown in 1962.[20] North Yemen was effectively self-constituted and separate from the south until reunification in 1990. Houthi political fortunes were revived in the 1990s when they founded the Ansar Allah (Partisans of God) movement, which today is led by Abdul Malik al-Houthi. Over the last decade the government in Sanaa has consistently identified Houthi rebels as an enemy that must be repulsed. The Houthis for their part did not hide their antipathy against Sanaa or its allies such as the United States, particularly with respect to the controversial drone strike policy in the country. This means that as an Islamist party, Islah has always had to mediate other contending Islamist factions, elements, and influences whether from socially conservative Zaydis attracted to the message of Islah, the Salafi represented by al-Zindani, AQAP, or the Houthi, among others.[21]

Stephen Day asserts that the roots of the Muslim Brotherhood in Yemen were planted in the country shortly after the 'mother' organization in Egypt was also founded to 'slowly' grow in membership throughout the 1940s and the 1960s.[22] Its proto-leadership, like others across the Arab world who also founded local branches of the Muslim Brotherhood, had been educated in the same Egyptian educational institutions that had spawned the Islamic revivalist movement and a reevaluation of the struggle for Islam and its impact on the political system. The Brotherhood in Yemen drew encouragement and inspiration from the Brotherhood in Egypt and its ideologues. By the late 1960s, the Yemeni Brotherhood had also emerged as a political and social response to the flourishing parties of the Arab national and leftist movements such as the Ba'athists and socialists. The Brotherhood in Yemen concentrated this initial organization of activity and ideological proselytizing in the important tribal areas of Yemen including Taiz. During this period Sheikh Yassin Abdelaziz was the main leader of the Brotherhood in these tribal highlands where he was regarded as an important Muslim scholar and later a spiritual founder of Islah.

By the 1970s, a further manifestation of the Brotherhood was apparent in the Islamist movement that was led in North Yemen by a sheikh named Abdul Majid al-Zindani. Al-Zindani has been described as a 'political chameleon and opportunist' who in his career has been both a fervent 'royalist' and then later a 'Wahhabi' fundamentalist and 'spiritual advisor to Osama Bin Laden at the start of the anti-Soviet jihad in Afghanistan'.[23] On his return to Yemen in 1970, al-Zindani became a founder of the Muslim Brotherhood but stayed tied to neighbouring Saudi Arabia

Yemen – The Brotherhood and the tribe **143**

and turned to Saudi-based institutions such as the Muslim World League to support the establishment in 1984 of the Commission on Scientific Signs in the Quran and Sunnah. The Brotherhood came to serve as a broad Sunni repository for Islamists in Yemen. It was capable of representing a spectrum of Islamist belief and ideological positioning encompassing the moderate reformist roots of the Muslim Brotherhood but reflecting or also allowing for Salafi fundamentalist positioning, echoing neighbouring Salafi-Wahhabi Saudi Arabia.

Sheikh al-Zindani became notable through the establishment of his 'Scientific' schooling system (similar to the *madrassa* model of Afghanistan and Pakistan) with a mission of educating the many illiterate child boys of Yemen in Salafi-Wahhabi pedagogy. This pedagogy was, in turn, derived from neighbouring Saudi Arabia and the close relationship that had sprung up between Wahhabi sponsors and so-called Yemeni-Salafi converts.[24] The schools were called scientific institutes, and in peripheral regions of North Yemen, they soon rivalled state education provision and even began to overtake it in terms of the range and depth of support offered to the children enrolled in such institutions.

A further dimension of Islamist politics in the north of Yemen centres on sectarian schisms between Sunni elements and the Shi'a Houthis of the Zaydi tribal areas in Saada province. The province served as centre of power for both Yemen's first imamate and Zaydi Shi'a Islam. In the wake of the overthrow of the imamate in 1962, the Zaydi remained staunchly royalist and hostile to any extension of power into the region by the new republican government.[25] Houthi family power emanates from this Zaydi community and its sense of grievance which grew in the wake of the collapse of the imamate in the 1960s. Under their leadership, including influential Zaydi scholar Badr al-Din al-Houthi and many of his sons, such as Husayn al-Houthi (a former Yemeni parliamentarian), Mohammad Badr al-Din al-Houthi (one of the founders of the Believing Youth), Yahya Badr al-Din al-Houthi (another Yemeni parliamentarian and Houthi spokesman), and Abdulmalek Badr al-Din al-Houthi (a commander of Houthi rebels), there emerged a new Islamist force.[26] As Freeman explains, the Houthis thus represent both a family and a set of wider Zaydi Islamist interests which challenge forms of power holding in the country.[27]

Before the reunification of Yemen in 1990, Islamism flourished to a greater extent in the north than it did in the populist Marxist state of the south. Yemeni veterans of the mujahideen movement in Afghanistan which had fought and achieved victory over Soviet forces had, by this point, also returned to Yemen. They were soon part of the 'shock forces' used by President Salih to target the communist south in a post-unification civil war which did not end until 1994.[28] 'Arab Afghan' Salafis, as the former mujahideen fighters were known, not only attacked the regime and its security forces but also led violent campaigns for control of Aden in order to impose Islamic rule. Links with other mujahideen elements in Afghanistan including radical Islamist terror elements such as Usama Bin Laden's al-Qaeda were also maintained leading Western intelligence sources to concern when in 2000 the *USS Cole* was attacked in the port of Aden.[29]

144 Yemen – The Brotherhood and the tribe

Yemeni unification and the foundation block for Islah

The unification of North and South Yemen in May 1990 created an opportunity for a new pan-Yemen political party. Thus on 13 September 1990 the establishment of Islah took place in the Yemeni capital of Sanaa. Those that had formed the core of the Muslim Brotherhood including Sheikh Abdullah Ibn Husayn al-Ahmar, Sheikh Abdul Majid al-Zindani, Sheikh Yassin Abdelaziz, and Abdulmalek Mansour, along with other Brotherhood founders from Taiz, now formed the backbone of Islah. The first secretary general of the party was Abdelwahab al-Ansi (1990–4), who was generally regarded as a moderate and pro-establishment figure. Al-Ansi was viewed as an important conduit for inter-party negotiations among Yemen's post-unification governing elite. Indeed, he even served as deputy prime minister in the coalition government of the GPC and Islah in the 1990s.

But to describe Islah as a purely Islamist vehicle for politics in the newly reunified state would be a mischaracterization. Categorizing Islah has proven to be somewhat of a challenge to scholars, as they represent a form of Islamist outlier. It simultaneously represents moderate Islamists, social conservatives, and radical Salafi elements. As Dresch and Hayel contended, 'Islah contained members of several differentiated groups holding many shades of opinion, from rejection of all parliamentary forms to nothing less than constitutional pluralism. If the phrase be allowed, Islah formed a broad church.'[30] Islah has argued for the implementation of *shari'a*. Islah was founded as a conservative reformist Islamist party that inevitably also reflected degrees of Yemeni tribalism and radical Islamism. Despite being headed by moderate Islamists tribal leaders such as Sheikh Abdullah Ibn Husayn al-Ahmar, radical elements in the party have played a part at its core, including Sheikh al-Zindani, who was later put on the UN Sanctions List of individuals associated with al-Qaeda.[31]

The Brotherhood represented a third way within Islah – neither radical Salafi like al-Zindani nor tribally tied to the Hashid like al-Ahmar – leaving it to mobilize for power from within the relatively comforting confines of a state-registered and approved political party. Hence, from its foundation, Islah was a flag of convenience for a diverse grouping of Yemeni Islamists. The Brotherhood's influence was apparent in Islah's stance as a moderate, pro-state, and nonviolent political organization. The Brotherhood component of Islah was never able to dominate for long and the Islah alliance was under continual pressure from internal contesting forces and differing ideological viewpoints which made it a challenge for the party to present itself as unified and consistent. In the 1990s, for example, it could not agree on major issues pertaining to the role that any Islamist party might play in the Arab world or Yemen specifically. With respect to democratization, for example, there were apparent tensions within Islah which betrayed the varied sectional interests lobbying for influence from within. It was only in time and after Islah had moved into opposition that it debated the issue further and developed a new position in favour of democracy in relation to its compatibility with Brotherhood principles of consensus (*shura*).[32] Such fissures were also evident in the 2006 local elections in

Yemen – The Brotherhood and the tribe **145**

Yemen when President Salih helped the GPC defeat Islah as a result of divide-and-rule tactics which led him to build alliances with al-Zindani while excluding other leading elements in Islah. As Longley notes,

> At the same time the President was labelling Islah 'terrorists'. . . he was coaxing members of these groups into his own camp. . . . The primary target of Salih's divide and conquer campaign was Islah. In a brilliant political move, the President courted the Salafi component of Islah by winning the tacit support of . . . Zindani.[33]

Additionally, other Islamist trends have accounted for the varied nature of Islah since it was founded in 1990. It has, for example, drawn in Salafi Wahhabi, as well as Zaydi Shi'a elements to its programme and activities. As Yemen scholars Stacey Philbrick Yadav and Sheila Carapico explain, some Zaydi joined Islah and 'adopted or converted to a "Sunni" identity inspired by Saudi Wahhabism and/or the Egyptian Society of Muslim Brothers'.[34] This does not mean that Islah cannot be considered a majority Sunni party but rather that it is not exclusively so, particularly when compared, for example, to the Muslim Brotherhood in Egypt or Jordan where no such sectarian Shi'a element could be accommodated. In this respect, one can contend that Islah reflects a surprising syncretism that also incorporates other important dimensions of Yemeni identity such as tribe.[35] By the time the first election in the newly reunified Yemen was held in 1993, Islah was recognized as a 'Saudi-backed' political party which was 'a marriage of convenience between Sheikh 'Abdallah al-Ahmar, the head of the powerful Hasid confederation, and the urban-based Muslim Brothers'.[36] The Brotherhood, however, has had a core role in determining the political and wider ideological orientation of the party. This is evident in the founding principles of the party: to strive for social reform of Yemeni society on the basis of Islam and to do so by legitimate means. Additionally, the ability to maximize and draw on tribal links within the newly reunited state created important opportunities for Islah and its Brotherhood backers to manoeuvre the new party into later alliances with Salih's GPC. The tribal affiliations of Islah remained varied and coloured it as heterogeneous with blurred lines attending not only to its support bases in Yemen but also among the senior leadership of the party. The founder and first leader of Islah, Sheikh Abdullah Ibn Husayn al-Ahmar, who was also the 'Sheikh of Sheikhs' of the Hashid tribal confederation, best epitomised the layered political repository that the party had become. In 1991, an article in the French newspaper *Le Monde* styled Sheikh al-Ahmar as a medieval throwback, the typical tribal leader forcibly binding his followers to him through networks of customary code and patronage. Continuing the colourful description, the newspaper continued,

> Right in the centre of the Yemeni capital, Shaykh Abdullah reigns as master, dispensing justice by traditional law and not hesitating to imprison in the cells in the basement of his dwelling, with their feet in irons, those of his subjects reckoned guilty. A member of the General Popular Congress . . . Shaykh

> Abdullah has for a long time played at two tables: power [within Yemen] and Saudi Arabia. He seems finally to have opted for opposition to the regime by creating . . . the People's Reform Party (Islah).[37]

Absent even from this account was the role played by Sheikh al-Ahmar in deposing the former imamate and his allegiance (and that of his followers) to President Salih even when in opposition to him politically. Sheikh al-Ahmar, had, for example, joined in government coalition with President Salih (1993–7) and in 2006 came out in favour of him as candidate for the presidential elections. To this end, al-Ahmar also served as the Speaker of the Yemeni legislature until his death in 2007 and had continued to lead his tribe and his party domestically, as well as within the region.

Ali Abdullah Salih, who had ascended to power in Yemen through the military to become president of North Yemen from 1978 to 1990, wanted to draw Islamists into his ruling GPC block as a way of consolidating power in the newly expanded state. Aware of his leftist rivals in the Yemeni Socialist Party (YSP) from the south, he sought to build an alliance with the socially conservative, tribally based Islamists. He also did this as part of his wider legitimacy building and political programme of consolidation. Thus President Salih saw the formation of Islah as an opportunity to broaden his support base beyond the ruling GPC to reach out to important tribal-Islamist constituencies reliant on patronage networks. Salih envisaged the Islah party and his own links to Sheikh al-Ahmar as an opportunity to augment his own grasp on the newly reunified country and create a 'loyal opposition' much as King Hussein had done with the Muslim Brotherhood in Jordan. With Sheikh al-Ahmar, Islah could count on important tribal support from the northern pro-Saudi Hashid, while the radical al-Zindani captured the growing Salafi trend within Islamism which would become apparent throughout the Arab world during the following decades. The Muslim Brotherhood stayed within the Islah fold as the party presented it with an opportunity to contest for political power within the Yemeni arena. However, Salih was also compelled to recognize that,

> as paramount tribal leader, Ahmar had special standing, with more natural authority than a modern president. He was also chairman of Islah and speaker of parliament. . . . Indeed, because the state's actions often reflected tribal preferences, Saleh had to seek the sheikh's concurrence on any major endeavour. Saleh also did not dare directly confront Islah while the grand sheikh was alive. The president needed Ahmar's continued support when other Islah factions opposed him.[38]

Contest

When Islah first contested elections in 1993, it was relatively successful, winning 62 out of 301 seats in the Yemen legislature and electing Sheikh al-Ahmar as Speaker of the House. Three years later there was a shift in power within the party and the Muslim Brotherhood was able to gain influence over the ruling secretariat of

Islah. Among the leaders of the Brotherhood within Islah were Abdelwahab al-Ansi, Mohammed Qahtan, Mohammed al-Saadi, and Mohammed al-Yadoumi, who would become secretary general and later succeed Sheikh al-Ahmar as leader following al-Ahmar's death in 2007. Nevertheless, under the leadership of the Muslim Brotherhood faction, it became apparent that there would be an attempt to steer the party away from the alliance with President Salih's governing GPC and hence autonomy from the governance project.

When a reunified Yemen presented the opportunity for electoral contest, reformist elements in Islah (mostly under the banner of the Muslim Brotherhood) indicated that they were generally supportive of the opportunity to participate in elections and thus take seats in the Yemeni legislature. In this respect they differed little from their brethren in Egypt or Jordan, who at the time had also taken similar positions with respect to such opportunities. This was, in part, an instrumental approach adopted by the Brotherhood to such political openings and which led many opponents and sceptics to question the extent to which such Islamist elements could be truly democratic.[39] And even though at the time not every movement associated with the Brotherhood across the Middle East and North Africa was contesting elections, there were enough to encourage those within Islah who supported this trend. In distinction, however, the radicals within Islah opposed such positions because they perceived them as both an ideological and practical inhibitor on their ambitions to pursue their objective for the creation of a Yemeni state governed by *shari'a* law.[40]

In the electoral contest of 1997, a GPC majority victory compelled Islah away from power sharing, and by the end of the decade, Islah was moving away from the orbit of President Salih and the GPC and into opposition. This was evident in 2001 when Islah rejected any carve-up or electoral pact with the ruling GPC ahead of municipal polls. During this election, Islah presented itself as a more credible opposition party autonomous of the ruling GPC and President Salih and closer, in this respect, in its demands for democracy, to Yemen's leftists in the YSP. The association of an Islamist party with a secular leftist party such as the YSP was to some extent unprecedented in the context of Yemen, but where Islah led, others would follow. In terms of the Brotherhood's broader operational approach of pragmatism and expediency for the sake of political survival against a common political foe, the Brotherhood in Egypt had, in 2005, played a leading role in forming the National Coalition for Reform and Change (*al-Tahaluf al-watani min ajl Islah wa al-Taghir*) alongside the Revolutionary Socialists, communists, and individual Marxists and Nasserists with the aim of creating a united national opposition front.[41] Likewise, in Tunisia the post–Ben Ali elections in 2011 led to a governing troika which included the Islamists of Ennahda, the secular centre-left CPR, and the Ettakatol.[42]

Nevertheless, there were some within the Brotherhood in Yemen who considered the association with YSP as problematic and contradictory to the core foundation of the movement and its Islamist agenda. The leadership of Islah, however, perceived the alignment as the only possibility in terms of advancing their agenda in the face of an increasingly authoritarian and intransigent ruling regime headed by

148 Yemen – The Brotherhood and the tribe

Salih. In alliance with the socialists, who in turn brought elements of representation from the south and incorporated other tribal-leaning elements, Islah could pressure from the outside. The status of Islah as a core element of the opposition was cemented in 2002 when along with the YSP it joined with other parties to form a broad coalition, the JMP.[43] This autonomy provided the opportunity for Yemen's Brotherhood movement to create distance from the GPC which would later pay dividends. Yet this rise created a split within Islah between pro and anti-Salih elements and a sense of unease at participating in alliances with socialists, Marxists, and the Zaydi Hizb al-Haqq against the regime presided over by President Salih. In the 2006 presidential election, the JMP fielded a candidate against the incumbent Salih, winning a decent 21.8 per cent of the vote.[44] This was significant given the challenge of running against a candidate who was incumbent and able to marshal more significant finances and resources for a 'winning' presidential campaign. Within Islah, this experience with the JMP encouraged pragmatists and allowed them to keep radical Salafi elements on the margins in terms of representing the party to the rest of society. This increasingly allowed for Islah to emerge as an Islamist party that recognized that its contribution lay in relating Islam to the state and governance through democracy rather than an Islamist theocracy where a central state authority governed. This may have been an unconscious recognition that a strong central state in Yemen proved elusive for any type of ruler in this ultimately tribal society. Moreover, it was the case that Salih's form of democracy was poorly manifest in an inherently weak state where central state authority was either frequently absent or contested by other societal forces.

The death of Sheikh al-Ahmar in 2007 was tied to a period of flux and uncertainty within Islah. Certainly al-Ahmar's authority and his leadership of the Hashid were important in guiding Islah for nearly two decades. The sheikh was viewed as a figure that was able to unite disparate elements within Islah, as well as provide important support to Salih in the early 1990s as he sought to consolidate his rule over the newly reunified country. Al-Ahmar's authority as a tribal leader fused with his political role created significant legitimacy that his opponents did not dare contest. The fact that al-Ahmar could also rely on his own standing tribal armed forces added to his almost invincible public stature, and the patronage that others sought from him became all the more understandable. With this force removed from Islah, there were elements in the party that felt that an opportunity to truly undertake a contest for power against the incumbent Salih could be mounted – but only in alliance with the JMP.

This was clear when a National Salvation Plan was unveiled by the JMP in 2009 as a response to mounting crisis and instability across Yemen. By this point, al-Qaeda infiltration into Yemen was substantive and a Houthi rebellion had been brewing since 2004. A secret US government diplomatic cable described the plan as representing a 'first real effort at drafting national party polices', but one that did not 'contain new or different proposals for solving Yemen's myriad problems'.[45] President Salih appeared to agree to some reforms as proposed by Islah and other JMP members but bargained for postponement of legislative elections. In reality,

Salih used the opportunity to shore up his relations with the United States in a war against al-Qaeda and to embark on public campaigns attacking Islah and its Islamist credentials. By turns, in meetings in 2009 with US diplomatic officials, Hamid al-Ahmar, who was described as 'Islah Party leader, prominent businessman, and de facto leader of Yemen's largest tribal confederation', warned that he would organize popular demonstrations to oust an 'isolated' President Salih from power if he did not ensure that the forthcoming legislative elections would be fair.[46] Before the Arab Spring in Yemen, the al-Ahmar family's loyalty to Salih also included that of General Ali Mohsen al-Ahmar, a man variously described as Salih's 'distant cousin' or 'step-brother'. General Ali Mohsen was an influential military figure, businessman, and Islah supporter. A secret US embassy cable from Yemen in 2005 had described General Ali Mohsen as 'the second most powerful man in Yemen'.[47] Nevertheless, General Ali Mohsen had been in dispute with President Salih over issues of succession in Yemen, and during the long-drawn-out violence before Salih's departure, General Ali Mohsen would use his considerable military authority to turn the regime's guns on its very own president.[48]

Time for change (*Taghir*)

Challenge, revolt, and the prospect of change had always been a reality in Yemen and one that President Salih had assiduously sought to head off. Whether the challenge was domestic or external, the president engaged in measures and employed the state and its forces to this end. The outbreak of protest in early 2011, however, coming as it did on the historical tide of popular force that had ousted Ben Ali and Mubarak in Tunisia and Egypt, respectively, would prove, formally speaking, to be Salih's last stand. After pro-Salih supporters had preempted protesters by occupying the city's main Tahrir square, small protest events in Sanaa gained momentum and grew in size and representativeness, in front of Sanaa University, which was renamed Taghir (Change) Square, in the Yemeni capital.[49] Yet the depth of complaint and the demand for change was evident as protests broke out across the country including the southern towns and cities of Aden, Taiz, and Al Mukalla. One of the protest leaders warned, 'The situation in Yemen is a lot more dangerous than in any other Arab country. It would be foolish for the regime to ignore our demands.'[50]

The pro-statist elements of the GPC were noticeably absent from the popular mobilization taking place, and although the protesters were calling directly for the removal of President Salih, their complaints were also levelled against the deeply ingrained culture of corruption and clientelism that had characterized the political system in Yemen for so long. In the spring of 2011, the protest elements had established a more formal umbrella grouping calling themselves the Civil Coalition of Revolutionary Youth (CCRY). With more than 50 per cent of the population in the country under the age of fifteen and youth unemployment rates of 40 per cent, it was hardly surprising that the youth of Yemen would take the lead. CCRY drew support from a broad range of Yemeni citizens, including students, civil rights activists, the business community, lawyers, and disgruntled

150 Yemen – The Brotherhood and the tribe

legislators. More importantly, however, their success hinged on their ability to coordinate with other disparate groups such as the tribes and their leaders, clerics, leftists, and others with a set of demands to oust Salih, reform the constitution, and create a more transparent and democratic state. These common goals were an important factor in uniting such elements, as the chairman of CCRY declared, 'These groups have each expressed their aspirations, in one way or another, for freedom, democracy and justice in Yemen. They reject tyranny and the monopolization of power and wealth.'[51] Given the significance attached to tribe in society and politics in Yemen, it was inevitable that the protest movement would have to entail tribal support to succeed in its stated goals. This was evident in both the north and the south of the country. In the north, the Houthi mobilized quicker than some other opposition elements, such as Islah, to support the movement for change and played a role in organizing against the government and pro-state GPC elements in areas such as their Saada stronghold. In Sanaa, their student supporters were dispatched to set up a large presence with the CCRY in Taghir Square.[52] While elements like the Houthi would remain focussed on any territorial control issue in their northern stronghold it was also the case that in the early days of the revolt there was cooperation between north and south.[53]

It was the violence of the regime including the 'massacre of March 18' otherwise known as 'Bloody Friday', which marked a turning point in the extent to which other major political and tribal elements of Yemeni society, including the Hashid confederation led by Sheikh al-Ahmar's sons (Sadiq, Hamid, Hussein, and Himyar), as well as the Hirak movement of the south of the country, united against Salih.[54] While much attention was paid to the protests in Sanaa, the demonstrations had been most fervent from the beginning in the south of the country, adding yet another complex dimension to the uprising.[55] The regime response to protest was based on a predictable policy of suppression and limited concession aimed at partially addressing protest demands but not enough to imperil the grip of President Salih and his family. As protest grew, so did state violence, in echo of the way in which other authoritarian regimes across the region attempted to 'manage' their citizens. After Ben Ali and Mubarak fell, it seemed like change was possible everywhere. But suddenly in Syria, Bahrain, and also Yemen, the regimes fought back, bloodily.

> The change of momentum from the more inspiring and hopeful events in Tunisian and Egypt on the one hand, to the more cynical events in Libya and Bahrain on the other hand, left Salih to conclude mistakenly that he, too, might be able to repress protesters in the streets, and survive as Yemen's ruler.[56]

When General Ali Mohsen al-Ahmar ordered his forces to protect protestors in Taghir Square, processes of negotiation and dialogue between the regime and the protest movement became increasingly stunted as more and more elements of society defected from Salih and joined the protestors. This was exacerbated by the conflict which arose between President Salih and the al-Ahmar family, culminating in a week of violence in May 2011 in which the death toll mounted.[57] This bloodshed was the final straw that led the Hashid confederation to throw its weight behind the opposition.[58] Sheikh Sadiq al-Ahmar promised to send the president 'barefoot' from Yemen in a definitive statement ending all previous alliances with Salih's power base.[59]

The participation of competing elements of the political elite in the revolt against Salih changed the dynamics of social and youth protest which had initially inspired the campaign for reform and challenge to the status quo. The youth protest movement was being outmanoeuvred as more and more 'official' opposition elements joined the fold.[60] As Philip Holzapfel contends,

> Once they realized what was happening, the parties representing the three centers of gravity opposed to the regime – Sunni Islamists, Houthi (Ansâr Allah) rebels, and al-Hiraak in the South – joined, and subsequently sought to dominate, Change Square in Sanaa. What had begun as a small youth protest was taking the shape of a multipartisan uprising against the regime – and would soon stir up the deeper divisions of the Yemeni political arena.[61]

The JMP, for example, mobilized its supporters to participate in the broad calls for change and reform with the implications it had for President Salih's attempts to stay in power. The coalition tried to hedge its bets by avoiding any early and definitive call to oust President Salih, much like the Brotherhood had done in Egypt and Jordan. As the tide began to move against President Salih, however, the JMP sided with those calling for the expedited ouster. Few in Yemen were fooled into thinking that the JMP along with other opposition elements such as Islah were genuinely in tune with and seeking to transform Yemen according to the democratic social and economic demands of the protestors. Instead, it was clear that such political elites were positioning themselves to mobilize to command power in the wake of Salih's departure. The JMP were soon part of the GCC initiative to transition Salih from power, leaving the youth opposition movement which was leading the revolt excluded.[62] Many leading the youth revolt were sceptical of the involvement of established political elites who, over the years, had played their own part in sustaining and supporting Salih. They predicted that the involvement of such elements would not guarantee the democratic shift that they were demanding of the incumbent political regime. Moreover, these protest leaders were concerned that any change of power was now merely going to perpetuate a system of governance that had long kept the people of Yemen impoverished and under deeply fractious and fragmented authoritarian-tribal rule.

The Islamists, and in particular Islah, along with the military, were soon to mobilize and turn against Salih and his shrinking circle of supporters, most of whom were family members. Regime violence and the response from the protest elements were drawing in the most powerful elements of society who perceived the revolt as an opportunity for change at the top. These elements, in an important triumvirate of Islamism, the tribe, and the military, would steer and eventually play an important part in determining the point at which the country would accept the terms of the deal offered to secure the future of Yemen through mediation by external GCC states. Islah, after years of opposition politics but with an intimate knowledge of the processes of governing, was able to mobilize and employ available resources far more effectively than the newly formed youth groups to gain the advantage when power was changing. The group was increasingly able to steer or dominate the youth-led movement and drive the change agenda of the protest movement.

In April 2011 President Salih appeared to capitulate to demands for his removal but then engaged in a series of foot-dragging exercises which he believed would prolong his stay in power.[63] After his presidential compound was bombed and he was forced to flee Yemen and seek medical treatment in Saudi Arabia, hopes were raised that at last the time for change had come. Yet it would not be until February 2012 that President Salih would formally quit Yemen and the post of president after signing a GCC agreement the previous November in which power was handed to Vice President Abd Rabbo Mansour Hadi. A national unity government of ministers drawn from the GPC and JMP had already taken office in December 2012, so it was no surprise when they swung their weight behind Hadi as the single candidate in the presidential election of February 2012. The youth opposition, moderates, and reformists were all but excluded from power. President Hadi divided Yemen's cabinet government between the partisan forces of the GPC and the Islah-dominated JMP. The legislature remained in stalemate, and the party system, which, along with President Salih, had characterized the enduring weakness of the Yemeni political system, was incorporated into the post-revolt solution. The revolutionary ideals of reform, democracy, and freedom were sidelined in the post-Salih power arrangements.

Nevertheless, Islah, and thus the Yemeni Muslim Brotherhood, committed itself to remain in the governing coalition under President Hadi. This made it complicit in both the anticipated successes of being in power again and the inevitable failures that would beset any Yemeni transition. Having worked in an alliance against Salih with Hadi, the GPC, and the YSP and sided (along with the powerful al-Ahmar family) with those supporting the Arab Spring, Islah would experience intense pressures and retribution in the wake of the regional swing against the Muslim Brotherhood and the Houthi rising at home. The moves against Morsi and the Freedom and Justice Party in Egypt led by General al-Sisi supported by Saudi Arabia and the UAE had significant consequences for Islah in Yemen.[64] The decision to declare the Muslim Brotherhood a terrorist organization included Islah, drawing them further into the web of regional politics, with some contending that Saudi Arabia was targeting them while encouraging local Houthis as a countervailing force to their power.[65]

Houthi challenge

While many were accurate in their predictions that the post-Salih transition in Yemen would be a formidable one for the ruling coalition, few predicted that the greatest challenge of all would come from Houthi rebels led by Abdulmalek

Yemen – The Brotherhood and the tribe **153**

al-Houthi. Indeed, amidst the global headlines from the Arab Gulf after the death of King Abdullah bin Abdulaziz in late January 2015, the news of the resignation of the government in Yemen to Houthi rebels passed virtually unnoticed. Fears that a fierce competition would break out to fill the power vacuum left by the departure of the Hadi government would be founded two months later with an intervention led by Saudi Arabia.

The competition is multilayered, fluid, tribal, and supported in part by elements outside Yemen as well. It includes, of course, the Houthi rebels; former President Ali Salih, himself from the Zaydi sect who, it is alleged, has also supported the Houthis; and the government formerly led by Abd Rabbo Mansour Hadi. There are also elements of AQAP poised to move from its zones of control in Yemen to expand its power. Additionally, there are allegations that ISIS, sometimes in competition with fellow jihadi-Salafists AQAP, are active in at least three of Yemen's six provinces, including the mostly Sunni south of the country. Additionally, the secessionist tendencies of the southern-based al-Hirak movement have now grown with the proclamation of 'independence' by some states in recent days and a call to boycott the governing authorities in Sanaa. Any of these factors could promote a further crisis or collapse of state or state failure in Yemen.

As the country appeared to be literally splitting apart with no one actor able to single-handedly keep the country unified, a Saudi-led military coalition began air strikes and an intervention to restore the government of former President Hadi and oust the Houthi leadership.

This can only be achieved with real power sharing, and this is something that has long been in short supply in Yemen. The question here is the extent to which Saudi Arabia may tolerate a Somali-type failed state on its doorstep while at the same time it faces the threat of ISIS to its northern border with Iraq. Hence, the challenge is not only for Yemen internally but also for the new power holders in Riyadh and strategists in many Western state capitals seeking to diminish the threat of another Paris-style attack.

The rebels sought to exploit the rising discontent and protest in Sanaa throughout the summer and autumn of 2014 when their supporters took to the streets to call for the government to step down. Houthi leaders had been agitating for change in the transitional arrangement for Yemen, demanding greater representation in power as part of the National Dialogue Conference. Additionally, the Houthi forces publicly complained that Hadi's government was being propped up by the United States as part of its wider strategic goal to control the Arabian Gulf. Moving their forces into Sanaa and a number of government institutions, it appeared that Abdulmalek al-Houthi was prepared to take power without further delay or negotiation with President Hadi. Despite attempts by the UN to mediate, Houthi conflict with the ruling elite ignited again in January 2015 when the first draft of the new Yemeni constitution was about to be presented. When President Hadi refused any further concession to Houthi demands, rebel elements moved decisively against him and within the month he had been deposed from power.[66]

154 Yemen – The Brotherhood and the tribe

There is also little love lost between the Houthis and Islah, and hence the Muslim Brotherhood were now firmly in their sights and as they sought to consolidate their power over the south of the country. Since the Arab Spring, this mutual enmity between Islah and the Houthis had increased and was evident during the eruption of violent conflict in northern Houthi-dominated governorate of Sa'dah in and around the town of Dammaj in 2013–14. Clashes began when Houthi combatants blamed Salafi elements based at a centre for Islamic studies (Dar al-Hadith) of infiltrating armed foreign elements intent on launching a jihad against them. The subsequent violence further heightened tensions throughout the country, ceasefires were short-lived, and the Houthi fighters then laid siege to the Dar al-Hadith.[67] Al Qaeda weighed in against the Houthis, and then Islah were involved as they joined in actions undertaken by local tribal and Sunni elements in Jawf setting up blockades on roads into Sa'dah Governorate to stop food and fuel from reaching Dammaj.

Certainly Hadi's ouster and collapse of the coalition was bad news for Islah. The Houthis accused Islah of colluding with AQAP in attacks against them, and by May 2015 the rebels sought to clear them out of their positions across the country.[68]

Islah's role in the coalition was significantly underpowered in terms of rising to the challenge of economic crisis, Houthi rebellion, and growing regional hostilities. Its leaders soon realized how little protection there was in being part of this broad alliance of social, tribal, and political forces when faced with a foe like the Houthis from the north. The exemplar of this realization came in July 2014 when the Houthi rebels turned their attention on the Islah and Al-Ahmar tribal stronghold of Amran, located some fifty kilometres north of the Yemeni capital. In a fierce battle between Al-Ahmar and Islah loyal forces against Houthi rebels, it was reported that President Abdel Hadi's government remained silent and failed to offer mediation. Following the decisive rout of the Al-Ahmar and Islah in the town and after many Al-Ahmar leaders fled into exile, Islah party offices and the homes of Al-Ahmar leaders were seized or blown up in a move described as 'eliminating the historical influence and domination' of al-Ahmar.[69] Islah's lack of influence was underscored in 2015 in the wake of the Saudi-launched offensive against the Houthis named Operation Decisive Storm when it was relegated to symbolic flag-waving on the sidelines of a powerful military mobilization.[70]

Future face

In 2011, encouraged by the signs of change around them, the Muslim Brotherhood did eventually get drawn into the people's revolution and their demands to oust Salih from power. In doing so, the Brotherhood found encouragement from potentially new allies in the Gulf, principally Qatar, but would end up losing favour in the process from their traditional backers in Saudi Arabia and elsewhere in the Middle East region. When Salih finally relinquished his hold on the state to the JMP, of which the Brotherhood was an important component, the group participated in the ensuing alliance with the GPC in the national unity government led

Yemen – The Brotherhood and the tribe **155**

by Hadi. Within the unity government, the Brotherhood tried to ensure that it could dominate in a transitional arrangement which Yadav and Carapico described as a Saudi–GCC sanctified 'elite pact' which resurrected the 'insufferable status quo ante'.[71] Islah leaders publicly recognized that they – like any other political or tribal element in Yemen – could not govern alone, but instead they sought to build alliances within the new governing order led by President Hadi in which their agenda could increasingly prevail.[72] First, Islah ensured that these alliances were built into and sustained through the political system at the level of government. Second, it employed its leverage to ensure that they enjoyed support within the military and the tribes, as evidenced by the maintenance of the close tie they enjoyed with General Ali Mohsen al-Ahmar in soliciting support from within the Yemeni military and security institutions, as well as other tribal elements.[73]

The increasing dominance of Islah on the domestic front led to the strengthening of Brotherhood-inspired regional alliances on the external front. The implications of this for Yemen initially led to tension with Saudi Arabia and Iran and a warming of relations with Qatar, Turkey, and of course Egypt until President Morsi was ousted from power in July 2013. The tension with Tehran, though, further exacerbated relations between Islah and the Houthis, who, as described above, then emerged as a major opponent of the transitional regime.[74] The National Dialogue process with its promise of elections in February 2014 failed to deliver on many fronts. As Schimtz highlighted, 'the two-year transition period ended without a new constitution or elections,' and the Houthi advance on Sanaa soon created new facts on the ground.[75]

The turn of events since the high days of the Arab Spring in 2011 could not have been more stark for Islah and the wider forms of Muslim Brotherhood identity which they represented just four years later. In this case, however, the fortunes of the movement were far more deeply affected by the outworking of Yemen's highly complex balance of power relations between tribal, religious, and political forces internally than the regional tilt away from the Muslim Brotherhood in the wake of events in Egypt in July to August 2013. In siding with Yemen's popular masses against Salih, they cut their ties with significant political forces which would soon be apparent in the reconfiguration of power in the transition and the backing given to the Houthi rebellion.[76] While it was true that Islah were secondary casualties of the blacklisting initiatives against the Muslim Brotherhood led by Saudi Arabia and the UAE, they were able to reorient and work towards a rapprochement with Riyadh following the rise of the Houthis and the ascension of new King Salman to the al-Saud throne. There was also speculation that Islah leaders such as Abdel Rahman Fadil, Abdelwahab al-Anasi, and Abdul Majid al-Zindani would continue to build further alliance with Gulf state actors such as Qatar to increase resilience in the movement regionally.

By late 2015, although the future for Islah looked quite bleak, the star in its firmament, Nobel Peace Prize winner Tawakkul Karman refused to be pessimistic about the role it might once again play in determining Yemen's future. Asked about the arrest, persecution, and exile of Islah members, Karman drew common parallel to that of her party and other Yemeni political activists: 'It is true that Islah is being

156 Yemen – The Brotherhood and the tribe

subjected to persecution at the hands of the Houthis but so too are the youth of the peaceful revolution of all inclinations and parties. They are subjected to kidnapping and murder.' She then said,

> However, such persecution and oppressive measures cannot destroy a large political party that has long experience and huge popularity. What applies to Islah applies to the others too. They will not be brought to their knees by the persecution exacted on them by the Houthi militias. When the political process is resumed soon, everyone will return including the Islah Party.[77]

Notes

1 Yemeni Congregation for Reform, 'Islah Refutes the Allegations of the Former President', *AlIslah.net*, 31 October 2013, http://al-islah.net/new/EN/view_en.aspx?id=3669 (accessed 30 May 2015).

2 M. Haidar, 'Thousands of Yemenis Stage Rallies Against President', *Al-Manar*, 27 January 2011, http://31.24.33.46/english/adetails.php?fromval=3&cid=20&frid=23&seccatid=31&eid=651 (accessed 30 May 2015).

3 L. Campbell, 'Yemen: The Tribal Islamists', in R. Wright (ed.), *The Islamists Are Coming: Who They Really Are*, Herndon, VA: United States Institute of Peace Press, 2012, http://theislamistsarecoming.wilsoncenter.org/islamists/node/23190 (accessed 27 May 2015).

4 The JMP coalition was founded in 2005 and includes the following Yemeni political factions: Islah, the Yemeni Socialist Party (YSP), Hizb Al-Haq (a semireligious party), the Unionist party, and the Popular Forces Union party. See Al Jazeera, 'Who's Who in Yemen's Opposition?', *Al Jazeera*, 10 March 2014, http://www.aljazeera.com/indepth/spotlight/yemen/2011/02/2011228141453986337.html (accessed 29 May 2015).

5 P.B. Holzapfel, *Yemen's Transition Process: Between Fragmentation and Transformation*, Washington, DC: United States Institute of Peace, 2014, http://www.usip.org/sites/default/files/PW95-Yemen%20in%20Transition-Between%20Fragmentation%20and%20Transformation.pdf (accessed 27 May 2015), p. 8.

6 F. Al-Muslimi, 'A New Deal in Yemen?', *Carnegie Endowment for International Peace*, 31 October 2014, http://carnegieendowment.org/syriaincrisis/?fa=57091 (accessed 31 May 2015).

7 T. Thiel, *Yemen's Arab Spring: From Youth Revolution to Fragile Political Transition*, London: London School of Economics IDEAS, 2012, http://www.lse.ac.uk/IDEAS/publications/reports/pdf/SR011/FINAL_LSE_IDEAS__YemensArabSpring_Thiel.pdf (accessed 9 June 2014).

8 See A.A.H. Al-Yemeni, *The Dynamic of Democratisation – Political Parties in Yemen*, Bonn: Friedrich-Ebert-Stiftung, 2003, http://library.fes.de/pdf-files/iez/01459.pdf (accessed 21 April 2015).

9 A. Eleiba, 'Interview: Mohammed Qahtan, Senior Member of Yemen's Islah', *Ahram Online*, 27 November 2014, http://english.ahram.org.eg/NewsContent/2/8/116588/World/Region/Interview-Mohammed-Qahtan,-senior-member-of-Yemens.aspx (accessed 27 May 2015).

10 S.W. Day, *Regionalism and Rebellion in Yemen: A Troubled National Union*, Cambridge: Cambridge University Press, 2012, p. 309.

11 S.C. Caton (ed.), *Yemen*, Santa Barbara, CA: ABC-CLIO, 2013, p. 165.

12 F. Halliday, *Arabia Without Sultans*, Harmondsworth: Penguin, 1974, p. 37.

13 F. Halliday, *Nation and Religion in the Middle East*, London: Saqi Books, 2000, p. 68.

14 P. Dresch, *Tribes, Government, and History in Yemen*, New York: Oxford University Press, 1989, p. 394.

Yemen – The Brotherhood and the tribe **157**

15 B. O'Neill, 'Yemen, a Prisoner of Its Own History', *National UAE*, 7 May 2010, http://www.thenational.ae/arts-culture/yemen-a-prisoner-of-its-own-history#full (accessed 21 April 2015).

16 B.A. Salmoni, B. Loidolt, and M. Wells, *Regime and Periphery in Northern Yemen: The Huthi Phenomenon*, Santa Monica, CA: RAND Corporation, 2010, http://www.rand.org/content/dam/rand/pubs/monographs/2010/RAND_MG962.pdf (accessed 8 May 2015), p. 45.

17 See Al Jazeera, 'Profile:Sheikh Sadiq al-Ahmar', *Al Jazeera*, 26 May 2011, http://www.aljazeera.com/indepth/features/2011/05/2011526112624960404.html (accessed 19 May 2015).

18 R.D. Burrowes and C.M. Kasper, 'The Salih Regime and the Need for a Credible Opposition', *Middle East Journal*, Vol. 61:2, Summer 2007, p. 272, http://www.jstor.org/stable/4330388 (accessed 8 May 2015).

19 See US Department of State, *Yemen 2012 International Religious Freedom Report*, Washington, DC: US Department of State, Bureau of Democracy, Human Rights and Labor, 2013, http://www.state.gov/documents/organization/208632.pdf (accessed 27 May 2015), p. 2.

20 F. Halliday, *Arabia Without Sultans*, Harmondsworth: Penguin, 1974, p. 101.

21 See S.P. Yadav and S. Carapico, 'The Breakdown of the GCC Initiative', *Middle East Report*, Vol. 44:273, Winter 2014, http://www.merip.org/mer/mer273/breakdown-gcc-initiative (accessed 29 May 2015); A.L. Alley, 'Yemen Changes Everything . . . and Nothing', *Journal of Democracy*, Vol. 24:4, October 2013, pp. 74–85, http://muse.jhu.edu/journals/journal_of_democracy/v024/24.4.alley.html (accessed 30 May 2015).

22 S.W. Day, *Regionalism and Rebellion in Yemen: A Troubled National Union*, Cambridge: Cambridge University Press, 2012, p. 102.

23 S.W. Day, *Regionalism and Rebellion in Yemen: A Troubled National Union*, Cambridge: Cambridge University Press, 2012, p. 102.

24 B.A. Salmoni, B. Loidolt, and M. Wells, *Regime and Periphery in Northern Yemen: The Huthi Phenomenon*, Santa Monica, CA: RAND Corporation, 2010, http://www.rand.org/content/dam/rand/pubs/monographs/2010/RAND_MG962.pdf (accessed 8 May 2015), p. 91.

25 F. Halliday, *Arabia Without Sultans*, Harmondsworth: Penguin, 1974, p. 83.

26 See L. Winter, 'Conflict in Yemen:Simple People, Complicated Circumstances', *Middle East Policy*, Vol. 18:1, Spring 2011, pp. 102–20, http://dx.doi.org/10.1111/j.1475-4967.2011.00476.x (accessed 27 May 2015).

27 J. Freeman, 'The al Houthi Insurgency in the North of Yemen: An Analysis of the Shabab al Moumineen', *Studies in Conflict and Terrorism*, Vol. 32:11, 2009, pp. 1008–19, http://dx.doi.org/10.1080/10576100903262716 (accessed 30 May 2015).

28 S. Carapico, 'No Exit: Yemen's Existential Crisis', in D. McMurray and A. Ufheil-Somers (eds), *The Arab Revolts: Dispatches on Militant Democracy in the Middle East*, Bloomington: Indiana University Press, 2013, p. 123.

29 S.W. Day, *Regionalism and Rebellion in Yemen: A Troubled National Union*, Cambridge: Cambridge University Press, 2012, p. 196; Q. Wiktorowicz, 'The New Global Threat: Transnational Salafis and Jihad', *Middle East Policy*, Vol. 8:4, December 2001, pp. 18–38, http://dx.doi.org/10.1111/j.1475-4967.2001.tb00006.x (accessed 27 May 2015).

30 P. Dresch and B. Haykel, 'Stereotypes and Political Styles: Islamists and Tribesfolk in Yemen', *International Journal of Middle East Studies*, Vol. 27:4, November 1995, p. 406, http://journals.cambridge.org/article_S0020743800062486 (accessed 8 May 2015).

31 See United Nations, 'QDi.156 ABD-AL-MAJID AZIZ AL-ZINDANI', *United Nations Al-Qaida Sanctions Committee*, 10 June 2013, http://www.un.org/sc/committees/1267/NSQDi156E.shtml (accessed 21 April 2015).

32 A. Hamzawy, 'Islamist Participation in Arab Politics: The Case of the Yemeni Congregation for Reform', *Taiwan Journal of Democracy*, Vol. 6:1, July 2010, p. 32, http://www.tfd.org.tw/export/sites/tfd/files/publication/journal/dj0601/002.pdf (accessed 8 May 2015).

33 A. Longley, 'The High Water Mark of Islamist Politics? The Case of Yemen', *Middle East Journal*, Vol. 61:2, Spring 2007, p. 246 http://www.jstor.org/stable/4330387 (accessed 8 May 2015).

34 S.P. Yadav and S. Carapico, 'The Breakdown of the GCC Initiative', *Middle East Report*, Vol. 44:273, Winter 2014, http://www.merip.org/mer/mer273/breakdown-gcc-initiative (accessed 29 May 2015).

35 J. Schwedler, *Faith in Moderation: Islamist Parties in Jordan and Yemen*, New York: Cambridge University Press, 2006, pp. 178–9; A.L. Alley, 'The Rules of the Game: Unpacking Patronage Politics in Yemen', *Middle East Journal*, Vol. 64:3, Summer 2010, pp. 385–409, http://www.jstor.org/stable/40783106 (accessed 8 May 2015).

36 S. Carapico, 'Elections and Mass Politics in Yemen', *Middle East Report*, Vol. 23:185, November/December 1993, p. 3, http://www.merip.org/mer/mer185/elections-mass-politics-yemen (accessed 28 April 2015).

37 As quoted in P. Dresch and B. Haykel, 'Stereotypes and Political Styles: Islamists and Tribesfolk in Yemen', *International Journal of Middle East Studies*, Vol. 27:4, November 1995, p. 406, http://journals.cambridge.org/article_S0020743800062486 (accessed 8 May 2015).

38 L. Campbell, 'Yemen: The Tribal Islamists', in R. Wright (ed.), *The Islamists Are Coming: Who They Really Are*, Herndon, VA: United States Institute of Peace Press, 2012, http://theislamistsarecoming.wilsoncenter.org/islamists/node/23190 (accessed 27 May 2015).

39 See S. Huntington, *The Clash of Civilizations and the Remaking of World Order*, New York: Simon & Schuster, 1996; B. Lewis, 'Islam and Liberal Democracy', *Atlantic*, February 1993, http://www.theatlantic.com/magazine/archive/1993/02/islam-and-liberal-democracy/308509/ (accessed 22 April 2015); R. Wright, 'Islam, Democracy and the West, *Foreign Affairs*, Vol. 71:3, Summer 1992, pp. 131–45.

40 J. Schwedler, *Faith in Moderation: Islamist Parties in Jordan and Yemen*, New York: Cambridge University Press, 2006, pp. 178–9.

41 C.R. Wickham, *The Muslim Brotherhood: Evolution of an Islamist Movement*, Princeton, NJ: Princeton University Press, 2013, p. 114.

42 V.M. Moghadam, 'What Is Democracy? Promises and Perils of the Arab Spring', *Current Sociology*, Vol. 61:4, July 2013, pp. 393–408, http://csi.sagepub.com/content/early/2013/04/16/001139211347973 (accessed 8 May 2015).

43 See V. Durac, 'The Joint Meeting Parties and the Politics of Opposition in Yemen', *British Journal of Middle Eastern Studies*, Vol. 38:3, December 2011, pp. 343–65, http://dx.doi.org/10.1080/13530194.2011.621697 (accessed 27 May 2015).

44 New York Times, 'Yemeni President Wins Re-election', *New York Times*, 24 September 2006, http://www.nytimes.com/2006/09/24/world/middleeast/24yemen.html (accessed 30 May 2015).

45 See US Embassy Sanaa, 'JMP's "National Salvation Plan" Just Another Detour on the Road to the 2011 Elections', *Wikileaks*, 19 September 2009, http://www.wikileaks.org/plusd/cables/09SANAA1687_a.html (accessed 20 October 2014).

46 See US Embassy Sanaa, 'Yemen: Hamid Al-Ahmar Sees Saleh as Weak and Isolated, Plans Next Steps', *Wikileaks*, 31 August 2009 https://search.wikileaks.org/plusd/cables/09SANAA1617_a.html (accessed 20 October 2014).

47 See US Embassy Sanaa, 'US Embassy Cables: Who Will Succeed Salih in Yemen?', *Guardian*, 21 March 2011, http://www.theguardian.com/world/us-embassy-cables-documents/40815 (accessed 16 June 2014).

48 BBC News, 'Top Yemeni General, Ali Mohsen, Backs Opposition', *BBC News*, 21 March 2011, http://www.bbc.co.uk/news/world-middle-east-12804552 (accessed 29 May 2015).

49 See S. Al-Ariqi, 'How Change Square Became the Birthplace of an Uprising', *Yemen Times*, 11 February 2014, http://www.yementimes.com/en/1754/report/3465/How-Change-Square-became-the-birthplace-of-an-uprising.htm (accessed 27 May 2015); Agence France-Press, 'Saleh Supporters Take Over Yemen Protest Site', *Hindustan Times*, 3 February 2011, http://www.hindustantimes.com/world-news/saleh-supporters-take-over-yemen-protest-site/article1-658245.aspx (accessed 27 May 2015).

50 A. Shadid, N. Bakri, and K. Fahim, 'Waves of Unrest Spread to Yemen, Shaking a Region, *New York Times*, 27 January 2011, http://www.nytimes.com/2011/01/28/world/middleeast/28unrest.html (accessed 3 May 2014).

51 Husam Al-Sharjabi as quoted in T. Finn, 'With Democracy in Mind Yemen's Youth Are Revolting', *Global Post*, 13 May 2011, http://www.globalpost.com/dispatch/news/regions/middle-east/110512/yemen-protests-youth-revolution-Salih (accessed 2 February 2014).

52 M. Wells,'Yemen's Houthi Movement and the Revolution',*Foreign Policy*,27 February 2012, http://foreignpolicy.com/2012/02/27/yemens-houthi-movement-and-the-revolution/ (accessed 21 April 2015).

53 See Yemen Post Staff,'Houthi Militants Clash with Armed Forces in Amran', *Yemen Post*, 27 May 2014, http://www.yemenpost.net/Detail123456789.aspx?ID=3&SubID=7876 (accessed 16 June 2014).

54 T. Thiel, *Yemen's Arab Spring: From Youth Revolution to Fragile Political Transition*, London: London School of Economics IDEAS, 2012, http://www.lse.ac.uk/IDEAS/publications/reports/pdf/SR011/FINAL_LSE_IDEAS__YemensArabSpring_Thiel.pdf (accessed 9 June 2014); S.W. Day, *Regionalism and Rebellion in Yemen: A Troubled National Union*, Cambridge: Cambridge University Press, 2012, p. 281.

55 N. Bakri and J.D. Goodman,'Thousands in Yemen Protest Against the Government',*New York Times*,27 January 2011,http://www.nytimes.com/2011/01/28/world/middleeast/28yemen.html (accessed 30 May 2015).

56 S.W. Day, *Regionalism and Rebellion in Yemen: A Troubled National Union*, Cambridge: Cambridge University Press, 2012, p. 5.

57 See L. Esparza,'Sheik Hashim Al Ahmar: One Year after Hasaba.English.', YouTube video, posted 2 June 2012, https://www.youtube.com/watch?v=1TajuCbSJYA (accessed 19 May 2015).

58 K. Fattah, 'Yemen: A Social Intifada in the Republic of Sheikhs', *Middle East Policy*, Vol. 18:3, Fall 2011, pp. 79–85, http://www.mepc.org/journal/middle-east-policy-archives/yemen-social-intifada-republic-sheikhs (accessed 27 May 2015).

59 See Reuters,'Tribal Leader Says Salih Will Leave Yemen Barefoot', *Reuters*, 26 May 2011 http://www.reuters.com/article/2011/05/26/yemen-tribe-idUSLDE74P0VJ20110526 (accessed 21 April 2015).

60 S.W. Day, *Regionalism and Rebellion in Yemen: A Troubled National Union*, Cambridge: Cambridge University Press, 2012, p. 284.

61 P.B. Holzapfel, *Yemen's Transition Process: Between Fragmentation and Transformation*, Washington, DC: United States Institute of Peace, 2014, http://www.usip.org/sites/default/files/PW95-Yemen%20in%20Transition-Between%20Fragmentation%20and%20Transformation.pdf (accessed 27 May 2015), p. 13.

62 N. Al-Sakkaf, 'The Politicization of Yemen's Youth Revolution', *Carnegie Endowment for International Peace*,27 April 2011,http://carnegieendowment.org/2011/04/27/politicization-of-yemen-s-youth-revolution/6b7t (accessed 21 April 2015).

63 See T. Manwire (ed.), *The Arab Spring: Rebellion, Revolution, and a New World Order*, London: Guardian Books, 2012.

64 A.I. Al-Moshki, 'Saudi Arabia Blacklists Yemeni Groups', *Yemen Times*, 13 March 2014, http://www.yementimes.com/en/1763/news/3590/Saudi-Arabia-blacklists-Yemeni-groups.htm (accessed 27 May 2015).

65 See D. Hearst,'Saudi Crapshoot in Yemen', *Huffington Post*, 28 September 2014, http://www.huffingtonpost.com/david-hearst/saudi-high-risk-bet-in-ye_b_5895984.html (accessed 19 May 2015).

66 See Al Jazeera,'The Houthis Reject the Appointment of bin Mabarak as Prime Minster', *Al Jazeera*, 8 October 2014, http://goo.gl/D0s8dw (accessed 30 May 2015).

67 See A. Madabish, 'Yemen: National Dialogue Calls for Immediate End to Dammaj Conflict', *al-Sharq al-Awsat*, 14 November 2013, http://www.aawsat.net/2013/11/article55322399/yemen-national-dialogue-calls-for-immediate-end-to-dammaj-conflict (accessed 30 May 2015).

68 See A.M. Al-Shrhabi, 'Houthi Victory Is Defeat for Yemen's Islah', *Al Monitor*, 29 September 2014, http://www.al-monitor.com/pulse/politics/2014/09/yemen-coup-agreement-political-shift-houthi-saleh-end-wars.html# (accessed 29 May 2015).

69 Al-Hayat, 'The Fall of Amran Robs "Brotherhood" and Puts Huthi Stronghold at the Gates of Sana', *Al-Hayat*, 20 July 2014, http://alhayat.com/Articles/3683172 (accessed 14 August 2014).

70 See Yemeni Congregation for Reform, 'Islah Party Announces Decisive Storm Support', *IkhwanWeb*, 4 April 2015, http://www.ikhwanweb.com/article.php?id=32080 (accessed 29 April 2015).

71 See S.P. Yadav and S. Carapico, 'The Breakdown of the GCC Initiative', *Middle East Report*, Vol. 44:273, Winter 2014, http://www.merip.org/mer/mer273/breakdown-gcc-initiative (accessed 29 May 2015).

72 See Yemen Post Staff, 'Islah Leader Calls for Unity', *Yemen Post*, 4 December 2013, http://www.yemenpost.net/Detail123456789.aspx?ID=3&SubID=7405 (accessed 2 March 2014).

73 See K. Fahim, 'Yemen's Opposition May Be Caught by Its Own Double Game,' *New York Times*, 2 December 2011, http://www.nytimes.com/2011/12/03/world/middleeast/yemens-opposition-party-islah-faces-credibility-gap.html?_r=1 (accessed 30 May 2015).

74 See W. Al-Jalil, 'Yemen's Political Stalemate Persists, as Houthis Gain Influence', *Al-Monitor*, 25 May 2014, http://www.al-monitor.com/pulse/politics/2014/05/yemen-political-stalemate-houthis-gain-influence.html (accessed 21 April 2015); ES Press, 'The Houthi-Islahi Conflict and Its Danger for the Future of Yemen,' *Wefaq Press*, 8 September 2014, http://wefaqpress.net/news_details.php?sid=19125 (accessed 30 May 2015).

75 C. Schmitz, 'Yemen's National Dialogue', *Middle East Institute*, 10 March 2014, http://www.mei.edu/content/yemens-national-dialogue (accessed 9 March 2015).

76 See Al Jazeera, 'Yemen's Saleh Declares an Alliance with Houthis, *Al Jazeera*, 11 May 2015, http://www.aljazeera.com/news/2015/05/cloneofcloneofcloneofstrikes-yemen-saada-breach-150510143647004.html (accessed 30 May 2015).

77 MEE Staff, 'MEE INTERVIE:Yemen's "Mother of the Revolution"on the Way Forward', *Middle East Eye*, 8 May 2015, http://www.middleeasteye.net/news/mee-interview-yemens-mother-revolution-speaks-exile-about-way-forward-558001274#sthash.aWX9pTfj.dpuf (accessed 30 May 2015).

7

TRANSNATIONAL BROTHERHOOD

What I propose is [a] systematic and coordinated fight against the bases of Islamic terrorism. I was informed that cover organization is Muslim Brotherhood. The chief of Al Qaeda is [a] member of the Muslim Brotherhood. The chief of [the] Taliban is a member of the Muslim Brotherhood. The same with Hamas, the same with Hezbollah, the same with Al Nusra, and so on.

President Zeman[1]

Introduction

In March 2015 in an editorial in the *Financial Times* titled 'Cameron Acts Clumsily on the Muslim Brothers', a variety of links were drawn between 'the threat of Islamist terrorism on Britain's streets', the need to 'keep a watchful eye on extremist Muslim groups', and British foreign policy in relation to a 'desire to propitiate the Gulf States' and the 'lure of contracts big and small'. The editorial, like the British government, acknowledged the Muslim Brotherhood as 'the most important Pan-Islamic organisation in the world with millions of followers' and that in Britain the Brotherhood proved to be the 'intellectual inheritance for a lot of UK-based groups', including the Muslim Association of Britain.[2] The editorial thus placed the Muslim Brotherhood at the centre of concerns linking international trade, contracts, and foreign policy between the West and the Middle East. The transnational influence and apparent tensions that the Muslim Brotherhood's global reach evinced was apparent in the extent to which Western governments have been compelled to try to understand what the group represented in relation to a number of globalized concerns, as well as specific national interests. Despite its recent political setbacks across the region that have been documented in this book, the Brotherhood is still understood as a global movement that remains relevant to discourses about political Islam, extremism, jihad, the Middle East, Islam, and the West.

162 Transnational Brotherhood

This final chapter of the book will look at both past and present attempts by the Muslim Brotherhood to address the more existential issue of Muslim unity (*ummah*) under its own organizational banner regionally and globally. It will examine past founding of regional branches and regional relations in the 1940s and 1950s, as well as commitment to universal Islamist causes such as the Palestinian issue. It will also examine the ways in which, in the twenty-first century, the Muslim Brotherhood has embraced transnational technologies in pursuit of a global Brotherhood enjoined in the same ideological goals. The import of this global ambition will be examined through reference to fears of the Muslim Brotherhood transforming the Arab Spring into an 'Islamist Winter' where the outcome of revolt and revolution is the inauguration of Islamist regimes across the Middle East. Conversely, the limits of the Ikhwan project, historically bounded by the nation-state in the Middle East and the distinct national manifestations of the Brotherhood, will be explored as a counteranalysis to the fear and threat of a region increasingly dominated and governed by the Islamists of the Brotherhood. The global consequences of this resurgence in terms of strategic and security policy and counterterrorism agendas will be explored. The questions posed about the Muslim Brotherhood in relation to contemporary security policies has proved particularly vexatious for Western governments who seek to counter the threat of radical Islam and decide whether, where, and when the Muslim Brotherhood merits approaches to proscription and labelling as terrorist or not. In making such assessments, Western governments are in turn increasingly cognizant of the criminalization of the Muslim Brotherhood by Gulf states such as Saudi Arabia and the UAE which since the Arab Spring have seen the rise of the Brotherhood as distinctly inimical to their own strategic goals.[3]

Brotherhood and *ummah*

The notion of transnationalism is a cornerstone of contemporary Islamism theologically entwined with wider concepts of Muslim belonging and community (*ummah*). Today, Muslims are a transnational 'population' numbering some 1.6 billion living across the globe.[4] This establishes a sense of transcending identity which Muslims can collectively claim. For Muslims, the expression of community is primarily apparent in major rites such as Ramadan or the Hajj, but there is a secondary dimension to this collective sense of identity that has also been apparent for many in the expression of the political project of Islam. Early extensions of pan-Islamism as imagined by contemporary Muslim political thinkers such as Jamal al-Din al-Afghani and Rashid Rida always incorporated pan-Islamic ambition into the basic project of Islamic reform and revivalism. Pan-Islamism envisioned in this way could unify the Muslim community of the Middle East as a form of resistance against the imposition of Western political, socioeconomic, and military control. In this respect, the conception was an articulation of anti-Westernism and anti-imperialism by the nascent Islamist reformist movement and its leaders.[5] Pan-Islamism was, however, always to be actualized by a 'series of local, territorially defined, Muslim nationalisms with anti-colonial agendas', which became intimately tied to groups like the Muslim Brotherhood and movements such as global jihadism.[6] Al-Afghani is regarded as one of the most prominent architects of pan-Islamism in terms of allying the religious doctrine of Islam to the emergent political aspirations of contemporary Muslim groups and organizations.[7] There can be little doubt that the end of the Ottoman Empire and the collapse of the caliphate by 1924 gave impetus to Muslim thinkers and activists to accelerate the quest for new forms and forums for the expression of a transcending Muslim political identity.

Such events and aspirations of a transnational Islamism came as a contribution to the establishment of a lasting infrastructure for contemporary Muslim politics for which organizations and movements such as the Muslim Brotherhood would be responsible. It was a reaction to the increasingly large-scale and globally connected mobilization of Muslims within the Middle East, and between the region and South Asia and beyond. Muslim Brotherhood founder Hassan al-Banna, for example, always ensured that the universal notion of the transcendent Muslim state project and Muslim belonging remained a key aspiration of the movement he founded. Indeed, the Muslim Brotherhood in Egypt and in its later iterations across the Middle East and beyond were in the habit of expounding on the evils of nationalism and the virtues of a Muslim project that went beyond the artificially imposed borders of the colonial construct that was the modern national state. This pan-Islamic project was one the movement took to heart in establishing chapters throughout the region in the ensuing years. In this respect, the Muslim Brotherhood epitomized the reactionary character of the Muslim revivalist project of the late nineteenth and early twentieth centuries to the impositions of the colonial period. This was mainly a reaction to Western domination, yet at the same time this particular emergent organizational response was also a riposte to Ottoman Islamism as a form of control over Arab provinces of the Middle East.

Al-Banna played a pivotal role in articulating a vision of transnational Islamism while at the same time establishing an organization that was very much rooted in the Egyptian context and as a response to its colonial condition. The reactionary anti-Western outlook which he expressed through the Muslim Brotherhood was thus dualist in terms of its both nationalist and transnational visions. The elaboration of Islam as a system or way of life with political content included spoke to a discourse that transcended the Western notion of the nation-state in the Middle East.[8] Hence, the local coexisted alongside the transnational as an early activity of the Muslim Brotherhood was to reach out across the borders of the Egyptian state to contribute to the articulation of other nascent Islamist discourses and appeals at the time. The Muslim Brotherhood's political themes resonated with wider audiences of Muslims concerned with the place of Islam in the modern age, reaction to secularization, and the receding of Muslim faith from the political public space. The values and symbols of nation and belonging were incorporated by al-Banna into a tiered process in which Muslims would

164 Transnational Brotherhood

become connected to each other again. As al-Banna, writing to Egyptian rulers in 1947, declared:

> According to the Islamic understanding, the Homeland comprises of (1) the country itself. (2) the other Islamic countries, for all of them are seen as a home nation and an abode for the Muslim. (3) This extends to the first Islamic Empire which the Pious Ancestors built with their dear and precious blood, and over which they raised the banner of Allah. The impression that they left still calls out to their past glory and excellence. The Muslim will be asked before Allah (SWT) why he did not work to restore its lands. (4) Then the Homeland of the Muslim expands to encompass the entire world.[9]

Thus Hassan al-Banna and other ideologues of the movement such as Sayyid Qutb always envisioned their project as having a transcending or transnational dimension existing alongside the nationally based projections and activities. Additionally, as we shall we in the coming sections, this was manifested where the Brotherhood sought to champion symbolic leading causes or issues. Such universal causes included and continue to include support for the Palestinians which led it to assume and lead wider Muslim mobilization not only in Egypt but also across the Muslim world on this issue.[10] This, in turn, established a form of competition at a transnational level with other political actors, including other Islamists, as well as opponents among secularists and leftists, most notably Arab nationalists and pan-Arabists until 1967. The point here is not to detract from the Muslim Brotherhood's focus on the particular localized context but to acknowledge that alongside it stood an ideological formulation of Islamism that was designed to transcend borders and appeal to wider audiences for the purposes of unity and mobilization. Territoriality, as constructed through the Western prism and articulated by local Arab nationalist leaders, challenged the incipient discourses of Islamism.

The Brotherhood was thus hostile to local nationalism manifest in Egypt and beyond at the time, preferring to articulate more universal notions of nation and belonging. As Kepel highlights, the Brotherhood 'was from the first opposed to the other indigenous anti-colonialist or nationalist movements that wanted to build an independent state on the model of European democracies'.[11] Nationalism, particularly as inspired by secularism, was perceived as hostile to Islam because it narrowed the vision of state and faith (*dawla wa din*) to unacceptable boundaries. As Mura highlights, al-Banna intended for the Brotherhood to capture wider appeal of Muslim values:

> It is the Islamic brotherhood, in light of its intrinsic 'humanitarianism', that forms the expansion of Islam into a movement for justice and equality, legitimizing such expansion and distinguishing it from those forms of conquest and aggression based on mere 'ethnic' or 'racial' factors such as 'nationalism' and 'patriotism.'[12]

Further, Al-Banna frames the Brotherhood within the larger the Muslim project, declaring,

> He [the Muslim conqueror] did not fight for the sake of such loyalties, nor did he conquer for the sake of nationalism, and he did not win victories for the sake of racial sentiment; but rather acted only for the sake of Allah and Allah alone, who has no partner.[13]

This interpretation, while inspiring almost limitless possibilities in terms of the ambitions of the movement in its Islamizing mission, simultaneously challenged and threatened ruling powers across the Muslim world. This notion of its international aspirations and power has always animated its critics and rivals and has remained a perception it has found difficult to shake off.

Opponents of the Muslim Brotherhood, even at this early stage, would point to these ambitions as dangerous, threatening to constructed orders and projects of nation and state. It was for this reason that the Brotherhood usually remained secretive about the existence of an international organization directed from Cairo. In an article carried in the French *Le Monde* newspaper in 2000, there was an acknowledgement – at least from some in the movement – that the organization had not only long harboured international ambitions as evidenced through the early establishment of branches of the Muslim Brotherhood across the Arab world but, as part of a long-term strategy for survival, had also always attempted to maintain a *tanzim al-dawli* (international movement).[14] There was always an acknowledgement, however, that irrespective of its ambitions it was much more difficult for the Brotherhood to actually maintain this international dimension of the movement. Within the wider Middle East region, attempts by exiled members of the Brotherhood to establish 'international' organizations and headquarters outside of Egypt left them vulnerable to the vagaries of the political tastes of the host state in which they organized. As we shall see, this vulnerability was apparent in states such as Saudi Arabia and Kuwait in the early 1990s when the Brotherhood sided with Saddam Hussein following his invasion of Kuwait. Such Gulf state actors had previously provided refuge to the Muslim Brotherhood when they had been persecuted by the Egyptian regime under President Nasser in the mid-1950s and 1960s and the Ba'athist regime in Syria in the late 1970s and early 1980s. Many in the Brotherhood had used the refuge of their sojourn in Gulf countries such as Saudi Arabia to continue to support the Brotherhood back in their native lands, as well as attempt to build, often with benign patrons from Saudi Arabia and Kuwait, an international Brotherhood organization. Many of them were also employed by the state in their religious institutions, schools, universities, and civil service, allowing them the freedom to build well-resourced networks of supporters, activists, and even secret members. These links and activities, however, were severed and halted in 1990 and a new and enduring narrative began to emerge about the Muslim Brotherhood from such regimes, one of hostility and blame for radicalizing and inciting a young

166 Transnational Brotherhood

generation that would provide the ideological ammunition and manpower to radical jihadist groups such as al-Qaeda.

Strength in numbers

Throughout its history, the Brotherhood has attempted to forge a sense of international ambition and transnational presence reflecting both an ideological and practical desire to flourish and survive periodic crackdowns ordered against the movement by the regime in Cairo. In the 1950s and late 1960s, for example, following President Nasser's brutal campaigns of repression against the movement there was evidence of a flight of Egyptian members of the movement to take refuge in relatively safer countries, as well as an attempt to galvanize branches of the movement across the region to take more leading roles. In this way the Brotherhood outside of Egypt could marshal support and resources as their counterparts were subject to Nasser's repressive measures. Nevertheless, the centre of gravity within the movement remained in Cairo. This is where the Guidance Office of the whole movement was located and from which other branches across the region radiated out. And while it is true that within each country in the Middle East the Brotherhood developed its own organizational structures, engaged in licensing or other relationships with the governing regimes, and held their elections to governing *shura* councils, the designation of ultimate leadership remained with the Egyptian mother organization.

It was from this point that in the 1970s elements of the leadership in Cairo began to flex their muscles and articulate an ambition to raise the international reach of the movement. This led to tensions within the movement between those in the leadership who sought to preserve the group through quiet perseverance and those, such as future Supreme Guide Mustafa Mashour (1996–2002), who believed that the Brotherhood's future survival depended on it evolving as a dynamic organization with an international front. This international front, aligned to supportive and influential state actors, could, it was argued, help the Brotherhood preserve itself.[15] When the Egyptian Brotherhood was targeted in the late 1960s and its leadership and members were imprisoned or forced into exile, they could at least take comfort knowing they had external supporters and backers in exile and internationally who would continue to work for the wider Islamist project. This did, however, serve to make the group vulnerable to the political and strategic agendas of others and could backfire as one regime would utilize patronage of the Brotherhood as a tool of conflict against another.[16] Moreover, it undermined the oft-repeated claims of the Brotherhood's leaders that the movement maintained an independence that transcended national borders and allegiances.

During the Arab Cold War (1958–70), inter-Arab politics centred on a regional contest for supremacy between the radical republics led by Egypt's President Gamal Abdel Nasser and the pro-Western states led by monarchies in countries such as Saudi Arabia.[17] The post-independence radical states posed a challenge to the regional order both in terms of their revolutionary nationalist, socialist aspirations at a state level but also in terms of their unification tendencies at a pan-Arab level. Such unification efforts were evident in the formation of the United Arab Republic in 1958 between Egypt and Syria. This form of unification Arabism also encouraged these states to interfere in the politics of other Arab states in the region and clash, in a form of proxy war, with the pro-Western conservative states in countries such as Jordan, Yemen, and elsewhere in the region. Inevitably these power struggles and proxy wars drew in and depended on having support from a variety of other actors, including the Muslim Brotherhood, within the region, as well as internationally as the Arab Cold War echoed the wider axis of conflict in the Cold War era.

In countries such as Jordan and Gulf states such as Saudi Arabia and Kuwait, many 'exiled' members of the Brotherhood established places within the nascent educational and professional structures of the state. This created a new and largely unfettered space for them to address aspects of Sunni revivalism and their role in it which could later be utilized by said host states in their own domestic and foreign battles. As discussed in Chapter 4, in the 1970s, for example, the Brotherhood in Jordan remained loyal to the Hashemite regime as it fought off both local nationalist challenges from the Palestine Liberation Organization and other Arab socialist, leftist, and nationalist elements. It also stood shoulder to shoulder with King Hussein when Jordan ended up in conflict with Syria in 1970–1 and again in the early 1980s. The Brotherhood, for its part, was always circumspect about its 'role' in such contexts and conflicts. Nevertheless, in states such as Kuwait, the Brotherhood used its position to draw in new and more regionally and globally networked supporters that were attracted to their populist Islamist message and agenda. This initially chimed with the wider resonances of the Islamist revival of the 1970s evident in a variety of Islamic fundamentalist movements across the Middle East and allowed for reservoirs of support (rather than active membership) to develop. Furthermore, there was an important ideological flowering of thought from important Brotherhood ideologues during this period, particularly as it related to fundamentalism more generally across the Muslim world, as well as conceptualizing jihad which by the early 1980s found support in new arenas such as Afghanistan. Indeed, in the context of Afghanistan, scholars such as Olivier Roy have pointed to ideological influences of the Muslim Brotherhood, particularly in relation to the pivotal discourses of Sayyid Qutb and Abdullah Azzam in inspiring and directing the mujahideen movement against Soviet occupation: 'An international support network was established, challenged mainly through the Muslim Brotherhood.'[18]

Europe also became an important locus of the internationalizing currents of the Muslim Brotherhood. The presence of the Muslim Brotherhood in Europe was a product of repressive waves against the movement in the Middle East from the 1960s onwards.[19] Over the decades, as Muslim Brotherhood leaders from countries such as Egypt, Algeria, Tunisia, and Syria sought refuge in Europe, there emerged new discourses and developments. Former leaders and adherents of the Brotherhood initially organized in support of each other providing communal help and solidarity for a number of decades. In the 1980s, however, the Brotherhood began

168 Transnational Brotherhood

to establish itself in relation to the wider Muslim communities in which they were situated. As Islamist scholar Brigitte Maréchal explains,

> The Muslim Brotherhood was slow in taking the significance of permanent implantation in Europe into account. But, progressively their priorities changed and they became more interested in diffusing their ideas among local populations . . . [and] were able to take advantage of a greater freedom of expression than that which had been available to them when their activities were confined to the interior of mosques.[20]

To this end, the Brotherhood was associated with or founded particular mosques, student groups, charities, and community activities, as well as national and regional networks. These networks grew in sustaining the movement in exile, as well as helped establish its representative role in European contexts. The networks where the Brotherhood was able to establish itself included the European Council for Fatwa and Research and the Federation of Islamic Organizations in Europe (FIOE). Such networks have proved robust but have not succeeded in allowing the Brotherhood to become the sole representative voice or force for Islamism in the European context. Their influence has thus been limited by the diverse character and manifestation of Islamism within individual European states, as well as regionally.

With a sense of presence in Europe established, a parallel discourse of fear emerged that such a presence could constitute a network across Europe and beyond for violent terrorist threats in association with the movement.[21] Those suspicious of the Brotherhood in Europe and who saw it as a wider manifestation of Islamic radicalism and violence highlighted jihadist threats which they believed were inherent to the movement. Hence, wherever the Brotherhood was to be found, there was an assertion that it represented a plot to engage in a form of Muslim conquest of Europe.[22] Such assertions fed into wider fears and obsessions with the Muslim presence in Europe, and its diverse and multiple forms were instead presented as a monolithic menace which transcended ethnic, national, and political identities. The Muslim Brotherhood, in countries such as the UK and Germany, were represented as being headquarters for a global jihadist trend intimately linked to terrorism. Others maintained that in Europe the Brotherhood and its leaders have experienced and responded positively to the challenge of reconciling their beliefs and identity with plural, secular, and liberal-democratic societies and political contexts.[23] There is evidence that the Muslim Brotherhood's leaders and foremost intellectuals have been at the forefront of a new Muslim politics where discourse about rights, personal status, democracy, consensus, alliance, plurality, and citizenship has led to new iterations of Islamism.[24] The transnational power of this new iteration of Islamism, however, was largely treated with scepticism. Pro-democratic, consensual, and plural iterations of the Brotherhood in Europe, it was contended, were unlikely to be manifest in the Middle East where the prospect of monopolizing power and running Islamic states would be too strong to resist.[25] The Brotherhood then, for better or worse, has contributed to transnational Islamist debates in Europe and from Europe about their wider roles and connections in the Middle East.

The Muslim Brotherhood in Europe certainly had hoped to positively influence representations of Muslim and Islamist identity among the migrant, and particularly Arab migrant, communities which were established in countries such as France, Germany, the UK, and Belgium. As advocates of a universal approach to Islam where faith and politics were seen as inextricably linked, however, it was inevitable that the message of the Brotherhood was seen as problematic in European contexts where faith and politics are not so inextricably tied. Their ambition was represented as a core threat to European values and security debates and frequently conflated with other discourses about Islamism, jihad, and terrorism. Maréchal highlights how this link was later apparent in wider representations of Islam through the Brotherhood's influence in organizations such as the FIOE and the Muslim Charter with its presentation of a ' "universal dimension" of their understanding of Islam despite the potential tensions and even incompatibilities, both political and legal, that this concept might have on a discourse on integration and citizenship'.[26]

The 'Cyberhood'

While the transnational dimension of the Muslim Brotherhood hitherto discussed has been focussed on its physical presence, whether in the Muslim world or Europe, the Brotherhood's dissemination of its ideas through various media has been equally important to the organization. This has been especially true in the past few decades as new technologies, mostly notably the Internet, have allowed Brotherhood members worldwide to remain engaged in the Ikhwan project. The Brotherhood has always emphasized propagation of its ideas and the concept of the call of Islam which it has always enjoined Muslims to return to. Since its founding in 1928, the Brotherhood has produced its own books and pamphlets and attempted to circulate its own publications, each of which have always been promoted by its media savvy activists.[27] Over the decades this media has extended to include magazines and journals associated with the movement, such as the Egyptian-published *Jaridat al-Ikhwan al-Muslimin* (the Muslim Brotherhood newspaper), *Majallat al-Da'wa* (Outreach magazine) in the 1950s, publishing houses which produced and distributed the writings of major leaders such as Hassan al-Banna or Sayyid Qutb, and recordings of sermons and speeches sold first in cassette and later disk form. The extent to which such media and dissemination activities were permitted by state authorities depended on both the content which the Brotherhood was attempting to share with the wider society and the legal status of the group at the time. By the late 1990s there was evidence that the Brotherhood, keen as ever to embrace technology to spread its message, had incorporated the Internet and nascent social media platforms into its activities. With the advent of Internet communication technologies and social media, the Brotherhood used these new platforms to address a number of audiences locally, regionally, and transnationally. In many ways this amplified not

170 Transnational Brotherhood

only the message of the movement but succeeded in signifying it in other ways to wider yet globally disparate audiences too.

The audiences that the Brotherhood addressed were, initially, circumscribed by the new medium that they were utilizing and the context they were utilizing it in. While in the late 1980s and 1990s the Brotherhood had relied on the limited (and frequently clandestine) publication and distribution of magazines, booklets, newspapers, and periodicals, its adoption of the Internet allowed it to transcend strictures put on its underground publication and distribution. The application of the Brotherhood to the virtual sphere was first evident in those that resided outside the Middle East in the European and North American diaspora. These early 'Cyberhood' members initiated and led virtual debates which allowed them to transcend national boundaries. Through these online relationships the Brotherhood could literally circumvent the bureaucracy of Arab states who were sure to be hostile to their cause. In cyberspace these young members of the Brotherhood did not need to worry themselves about passport control or visa permit regimes which in real life would have prevented them from interacting with each other. On new Islamist-leaning websites such as IslamOnline, which was founded in 1997, Brotherhood members established their own vigorously debated presence in a variety of user forums. Hence, the initial audience was limited by geography in terms of where the Internet could flourish (or was permitted) and also by rates of Internet literacy which were higher in Europe and North America among the Brotherhood's exiles and supporters than in the Middle East. On virtual forums the Brotherhood took the opportunity to promote their position to self-selecting audiences but that nevertheless were now newly connected with each other.

By the turn of the century, growing Internet literacy around the world meant the Brotherhood had the potential to attract new followers in the Arab world and use this new media to thwart the Egyptian regime's prohibition on Brotherhood-owned print or broadcast media. The group sought to realize this ambition in setting up Ikhwanonline, the Arabic-language website that served as a hub for all Brotherhood activities and news.[28] Prior to the Arab Spring, one reporter noted that over the past decade the Brotherhood had

> transformed from a shadowy social organization with power bases in mosques and charities, to a media and tech-savvy machine. In Egypt's political wasteland, the strongest opposition to the secular regime not only owns the street — today, they dominate the Web.[29]

In 2005, the Brotherhood also started an official English-language website on Ikhwan-Web which soon functioned as a mouthpiece for the organization directed at Western audiences in Europe and North America.[30] The Brotherhood's intention for the portal was made clear in a statement from IkhwanWeb's editor, who described it as 'the MB ideological platform for the Western world, and . . . primarily directed to the public, academics, researchers, media, think tanks and decision making centers in the West'. The editor continued by asserting that the 'basic mission' of IkhwanWeb was to 'bridge the knowledge gap between the MB and Western intellectuals so that they get to know its ideology without distortion, and understand our political, cultural, and moderate religious message'.[31]

Other audiences and the importance attached to them became apparent with evidence of the Brotherhood's accelerating embrace of social media and virtual platforms throughout the first decade of the twenty-first century.[32] Even in countries where the Brotherhood was banned by the government, their online presence was apparent and facilitated by virtual hosting in other domains. The 'audience' which the Brotherhood was reaching out to through wiki sites, Facebook, YouTube, Twitter, and other social media was increasingly transnational and multilingual. This gave the Brotherhood a powerful opportunity to use the medium to literally translate its own message and to make that message in its own form. The Twitter feed @ikhwanweb, for example, which was set up in 2009 by the Brotherhood, has become a significant forum for the Brotherhood's global publicity machine. Hundreds of thousands of people from across the globe follow the Twitter account, outrivalling other Sunni Islamists such as Hamas or even ISIS.[33] Its tweets have ranged from the banal (updates on weather) to the profound in terms of global debates about freedom of speech, democracy, state and anti-state violence, and the future of the movement.[34] The account's followers were exposed to rapidly devised content frequently authored by Gehad El-Haddad, who, before being arrested by Egyptian authorities in 2013 as part of their crackdown on the Brotherhood, had his own Twitter account with more than 70,000 local and international followers.[35] Tweets from young activists and figures such as El-Haddad were important in what Bohn refers to as the Brotherhood's mission transnationally to 'engage with an English-speaking audience and liberals who wouldn't otherwise interact with them'. Quoting one Brotherhood Twitter administrator, the echo of mastering the message by the movement was once more apparent: '"We're tweeting to humanize the Brotherhood and correct misconceptions," . . . "We're not this big, scary terrorist organization."'[36] This command of the Internet has distinguished the Muslim Brotherhood and many of its branches across the Middle East in relation to their opponents, as Shadi Hamid notes, 'The Brotherhood has always been paranoid about how people view it. It's an organization that's very sensitive to outside criticism . . . And they'll use any means possible to try to shift public opinion more in their direction.'[37]

Hence, the Brotherhood could serve to its audiences its own account of what it was, who it represented, and its credentials to call on others to join it; it was not reliant on the mediation of others to project its message. Brotherhood activists could design and create content that they believed optimized their appeal and transcended traditional boundaries. On Ikhwanonline, the Brotherhood uploads and shares its own propaganda in the form of press statements, documents, photos, campaign buttons, and video content. The Brotherhood's wiki site, Ikhwanwiki, links in thousands of articles and documents connecting the movement globally and regionally. Such websites form an important repository of information establishing a new form of imagined community to which supporters and activists for

172 Transnational Brotherhood

the Brotherhood across the globe can access and in turn utilize. The Brotherhood wiki page, for example, is a portal which offers thousands of access points to articles, biographies, opinions and ideas, historical events pertaining to the Brotherhood, documents, a library, and a photo gallery, as well as audio and video content.[38] One section of the page is devoted to the 'Brotherhood around the world' and links to pages which detail the Brotherhood in or in relation to twenty-eight countries including Morocco, Yemen, Kuwait, the United States, Somalia, Chechnya, Senegal, and Germany.[39] Such portals allowed the Brotherhood to represent themselves to transnational audiences and bypass the repressive state contexts in which they were forced to operate. They could also appeal to a key demographic constituency of support among young (mostly male) tech-savvy Muslims keen to join the borderless virtual universe of the Cyberhood. In the Middle East, for example, in states like Yemen, Egypt, Jordan, Tunisia, Libya, and the Palestinian Territories, the majority of the population are young people who enjoy good rates of literacy and whose engagement with new technologies has been facilitated by relatively easy access to cell phones and the Internet. As Howard asserts, while there are 'roughly 140 literate Muslim adults for every new book published in countries with large Muslim communities [there are] almost 6,000 Muslim internet users for every internet host maintained'.[40]

The subversive potential of the Internet and the limits of the Brotherhood's control of it in terms of 'managing the message' did, however, also become increasingly apparent. As Richter notes, the Brotherhood 'made consistent use of the new media to reappear as an autonomous and potent political actor' and developed a public relations strategy that was elaborated globally through its Internet presence and other pro-Brotherhood-friendly media.[41] This also led to new contests with their opponents and enemies in virtual space such as hacktivists like one anonymous poster who, in November 2011, declared, 'Operation Muslim Brotherhood Takedown' and attacked Muslim Brotherhood websites.[42] Since the Egyptian military's overthrow of President Morsi in Egypt and the regional backlash against the Muslim Brotherhood in its wake, the movement's media outlets have played an increasingly important role in maintaining group solidarity and identity as the regime has sought to crush the movement. While it is important not to downplay the extensive and disciplined network by which the Muslim Brotherhood operates, the Internet, social media, and other new technologies have played a key role in maintaining communication links and thus the movement's hierarchy and operation. Following the takeover, the Supreme Council of the Armed Forces under al-Sisi moved quickly to close down Brotherhood-affiliated broadcast and print media which had been set up after Mubarak's ouster.[43] Brotherhood members and leadership have also used the Internet and social media to maintain communication links between the leadership, some of which in exile, and supporters in Egypt to help organize rallies and carry out other operations. Social media in particular has proven to be decisive in misleading security forces about plans for large demonstrations and thus allowed the Brotherhood to continue to hold them in Egypt.[44] Other scholars have attributed the importance of social media and other pro-Brotherhood media in organizing and documenting low-profile violence by Brotherhood-affiliated groups and the difficulty Egyptian authorities have had in stemming their proliferation online.[45] Perhaps the most notable example of the Brotherhood's use of Internet activism occurred after the Rabaa massacre in August 2013, in which over 1,150 Brotherhood demonstrators were killed.[46] Brotherhood online activists and supporters propagated an image of a yellow four-fingered hand with the phrase 'R4BIA' on social media to protest the killings. The symbol went viral and reached Muslim and non-Muslim audiences alike so successfully that one report noted it had 'turn[ed] Facebook yellow'.[47]

In contrast with previous bouts of repression by regime forces throughout the Muslim Brotherhood's history, since 2013 the Brotherhood has been able to leverage these new technologies to continue to engage supporters in order to maintain pressure on the regime. It has done so using its own websites (Ikwanonline, Ikhwanweb, etc.) and social media accounts which Egyptian authorities have been unable to shut down unlike the printing presses and cassette recorders of the past. Importantly, this has also kept the Brotherhood relevant to Western and English-speaking audiences and policymakers who during previous crackdowns had essentially no access to information on the movement. The rapid technological advancement of the past decade has also meant that unlike the past, Brotherhood supporters now have access to relatively inexpensive and easy-to-use video cameras to document various Brotherhood events from demonstrations and speeches to human rights abuses by the ruling regime.[48] A more critical side to this new media paradigm was the creation of foreign-based pro-Brotherhood satellite channels. While some Islamist and pro-Brotherhood television channels existed in Egypt prior to the uprisings, such as Al-Nas, whose motto was 'a channel that will take you to heaven', and Al Jazeera Mubasher Misr, they, along with the group's official Misr 25 channel, were shut down days after Morsi was overthrown.[49] In their place, a number of pro-Brotherhood channels based in Turkey and broadcast using French satellites have continued to report to audiences globally on their broadcast networks with names such as Rabaa (the square where Brotherhood protesters were massacred), Misr al-An (Egypt Now), Mekameleen (We are continuing), and al-Sharq (the East).[50] While the channels 'act more as vocal and aggressive mouthpieces of the MB than as news organizations offering professional, independent and impartial reporting', they have largely succeeded at maintaining group solidarity despite attempts by the Egyptian government to pressure Europe and Turkey to close them.[51] And in fact, these channels were the source of leaked recordings alleging massive military corruption, Gulf support and coordination with the military during the protests against Morsi, and severe media censorship and propaganda that have been described as 'Egypt's version of the Watergate scandal' and were widely reported in the Western press.[52] The Brotherhood and its supporters embrace of the Internet and new technologies have played significant roles in organizing and maintaining the group's supporters, reaching out to new followers, and resisting the regime's narrative, all while the Muslim Brotherhood remains officially banned in a number of countries throughout the Middle East. YouTube is also utilized by Brotherhood members

174 Transnational Brotherhood

and supporters to upload videos that allow them to circumvent the state and produce their own propaganda. One such example is a 'music video' uploaded by the Jordanian Brotherhood in 2012 drawing attention to lack of freedoms and gerrymandering of elections in the Hashemite Kingdom. To the beat of a traditional Arab *tabla* drum, lyrics proclaim,

> Tell all Jordanians that we want to leave in peace This corrupted government is not a legal government They sold out all companies and Arab Jordanians Let us not forget the intelligence and secret services . . . they 'confiscated' our freedom They falsified the election results with the municipal council What can one say about this tragic situation? We just want to live in peace We want to reform our system, our demands are legal we only want social justice, reform and peace.[53]

Losing

There is a clear consensus that the Arab Spring was not an Islamist-inspired or Islamist-led revolt. Instead, the major mobilization of a multiplicity of communities, of which Islamists of many varieties were a part, was apparent in understandings of the events that unfolded following the self-immolation of Mohammed Bouazizi in Tunisia in December 2010. The elation and hopes of the Arab Spring, however, soon gave way in the ensuing transitions to what was increasingly referred to as an 'Islamist Winter' and fears for the stability of the wider region under the stewardship of the Muslim Brotherhood. The Brotherhood's enemies were quick to claim that in its rise to power in the individual states of the Middle East and North Africa, the movement would quickly marshal its supporters in a wider ambition to promote an international Islamist threat of takeover. The prospect of a new Middle East governed by the Brotherhood and assisted by its sympathizers and supporters internationally was one that a number of political actors across the region sought to halt.

As a movement with transnational ambitions, there was little by way of overarching direction in advancing the Brotherhood agenda on a region-wide level. The Brotherhood and its variants across the Middle East when faced with the challenge of making the Arab Spring an opportunity to unite and articulate a set of political goals that aligned with the reality which protesters had articulated failed to produce slogans which promoted solidarity that could endure. Their lexicon of 'Islam is the solution' and slogans of change and reform coupled with religious injunctions against the mixing of the sexes, the prohibition of alcohol, or the imperative for *shari'a* proved woefully insufficient in meeting the demands of protestors who were motivated by concerns at the realities of unemployment, high food and utility prices, frustration at government bureaucracy, inadequate state services, and a general lack of liberties. Furthermore, the various Brotherhood branches failed to utilize their decades in opposition to restructure their movements internally to make them more plural, more representative beyond the patriarchal archetype of the Brotherhood, and more democratic.[54] Consensus was always secured through the function of the *shura* council. Women, though encouraged into the Muslim Brotherhood and organizationally catered for with their own sections and forums and activities, were never truly incorporated into decision-making structures for the movement. Similarly, youth wings had their energies literally clipped by the higher echelons of the movement, particularly in Syria, Egypt, and Jordan, where they again were excluded from real decision making, strategy setting, or power through control of resources. Hamid claims that the Muslim Brotherhood did democratize their internal structures, but the evidence of the extent to which this was achieved in a transparent and truly plural manner is absent, even in the case of Ennahda in Tunisia.[55]

The Brotherhood was caught out by the reality of governance and politics which consisted of demands from an electorate, as well as an empowered population. This was a population that had discovered it could topple state leaders by going to the public square and occupying it. In part, the Brotherhood was also so significantly habituated to opposition that many of its leaders were simply incapable of believing that electoral context would establish victory and free governance. In this respect, power through victory at the ballot box became a double-edged sword that hung over the head of the Brotherhood and was then used by its opponents to cut it down to size. Indeed within the Muslim Brotherhood organization it became apparent that the pace of events which had taken everyone by surprise and the resources that were being mobilized for the transition and the political project of election therein left little inclination or opportunity for the movement to address fundamental issues in relation to the governance project and its long-standing yet dualist commitments to democracy and an Islamic project. The religious guidance that might have been duly apparent for the reconciliation of such dualist commitments was glaringly absent and functioned to highlight the difference between a revolution harnessed by theocrats as opposed to pious, believing activists with political ambitions. It became very clear that the promotion of an overarching regional or international vision in relation to a set of compelling and guiding narratives from Islamists about the Arab Spring and the forms of governance that might be possible in the transition were few and far between. This left an opportunity for other Islamist actors to provide meaning, interpretation, and validation to earlier claims and ambitions that were transnational in nature. The Brotherhood, meanwhile, was increasingly left to grapple with the challenges of national governance and socioeconomic crisis, leaving it depleted on wider ideological and transnational fronts. Opposition to the Brotherhood soon grew.

Such opponents not only resided in the corridors of power, the presidential palaces, and fortified intelligence compounds of the Arab state but also emerged among the people that had mobilized to call for change and reform and actually succeeded in toppling presidents from power. Of the latter they were disappointed that the modern and seemingly incorruptible Brotherhood which they believed had been manifest in their midst had proved to be something different on assuming forms of power. Its positions of compromise which the leadership believed it was making with respect to transitioning politics and realizing the demands of the Arab Spring protest were received negatively. The stance of the Brotherhood on issues

176 Transnational Brotherhood

relating to democracy, economic reform, women's rights, freedom of assembly, the rise of jihadi-takfiris, pluralism, or constitutional safeguards was proving inadequate in terms of the claims and expectations manifest in the Arab Spring and the transitional era. Although the Brotherhood's activists had stood shoulder to shoulder with liberals, as well as secularists, workers, labour union activists, feminists, and others in the public space to protest and call for change, in the wake of the Arab Spring notions of coalition and alliance dissipated. Instead, central issues about the role of Islam in the Arab state came to the fore and dominated public debate within the Middle East, as well as the West. The Brotherhood parried demands for it to take a position on national interest and principled international issues, because as Hamid notes, it 'instinctively knew that details could be dangerous and would do little but frighten an array of domestic and international actors, who were all to ready to assume the worst about Islamist intentions'.[56]

Backlash

In September 2013 the Egyptian state issued orders through a court edict to prohibit and further circumscribe the Muslim Brotherhood.[57] The assets of the organization were to be seized and all its activities were to be closed down. Such drastic action, the state argued, was to prevent the Brotherhood and its associated bodies, such as the Freedom and Justice Party (FJP), from further violation of Egypt's laws.[58] The state and its government, led by General al-Sisi, determined that there was no place in the political arena for the Muslim Brotherhood and that if it were to survive it would have to confine itself to a role as a nongovernmental organization forbidden to organize politically or align itself in any way with militia or paramilitary groups. In essence the state had ordered the disbanding of the Muslim Brotherhood deploying judicial measures to declare it unconstitutional, terroristic, and therefore illegal.[59] As highlighted in Chapter 2, the Egyptian decision was soon followed by similar measures in Gulf states such as Saudi Arabia and the UAE to declare the organization a terrorist entity and to scrutinize and review the Muslim Brotherhood in other realms internationally through frames of enmity. The depiction just two years earlier of the Muslim Brotherhood as a torchbearer for a new wave of democracy in the Middle East was abruptly terminated as evidenced in the backlash that was now rapidly unfolding.

From Egypt the backlash against the Muslim Brotherhood and the agenda it represented in terms of transnational Islamism spread across the region, decimating the fortunes of the movement and its adherents in countries from North Africa to the Gulf. The Muslim Brotherhood was being portrayed as a terroristic threat, frequently allied to radical and violent jihadi-takfiri tendencies. Only in Tunisia, where Ennahda had assiduously worked to build an alliance with secularists after having been voted out of government, did it look like the Brotherhood had anything other than denigration and decimation ahead of it. In Yemen, though, Islah was caught between the poles of Houthi vengeance and Saudi capriciousness as this fragile state descended even further into the mire of conflict. In Jordan, the Brotherhood was all but outlawed as the Hashemite monarch failed to demur when a new Muslim Brotherhood was registered and presented as a benign religious movement.[60] In Syria, the Brotherhood remained banned by Hafez al-Assad's regime and designated a terrorist threat, brutalized and effectively ousted by radical jihadi groups such as Jabhat al-Nusra and ISIS. Much of the standing it had enjoyed in the early years of the Syrian uprising was diminished as it became clear that it was no longer relevant to the post-ISIS dispensation.[61] By 2015, the majority of its leadership remained in exile and marginal to the wider regional power plays, peace talks, and proxy wars, only casually engaged by Turkey as a useful 'front' for its own strategic ambitions in Syria. In the Palestinian Territories of the West Bank, Hamas had been forced underground, and in the Gaza Strip, its fortunes had been tied to the Egyptian Brotherhood in a Gordian knot by Egypt's military regime led by President al-Sisi. The support for the Brotherhood movement which after 2011 it had hoped to capitalize on to restore its fortunes and win back populist support against its secular rivals in Fatah was at an end. So too were the aspirations and dreams that a Muslim vanguard across the Middle East led by the Brotherhood would finally compel Israel to rethink its strategic interest in occupying Palestine. In Libya, the Muslim Brotherhood and their Islamist bloc allies refused to relinquish power even after it failed to win more than 12 per cent of the vote in elections to the parliament in 2014. Strategically it became apparent in the West there were some that believed that the Brotherhood could act as a bulwark against the advance of ISIS. This left some in the West reluctant to encourage their ouster by other Libyan forces. Within the region, however, the Brotherhood's opponents in Saudi Arabia made no secret of their contempt for the Brotherhood as it ruled from Tripoli leaving the democratically elected government forced to try and govern the country from the eastern city of Tobruk. One Saudi editorial opined that Tripoli was thus 'controlled by a violent Muslim Brotherhood gang called the Nawasi Brigade, which,' it claimed, 'has been infiltrated by the local offshoot of Daesh (the self-proclaimed ISIS)'.[62]

By 2015, it was evident that the repercussions of events in Egypt against Mohammed Morsi and the Muslim Brotherhood in July and August 2013 following the military takeover was having a seismic impact on the strategic environment of the wider region and its links to the international system.[63] The Brotherhood was being dealt successive blows at the behest of Arab leaders allied to defeat them. At almost every turn it appeared that the Brotherhood was being squeezed, on one hand, by authoritarian regimes at home with support from those in the Gulf, and by its Islamic and Islamist opponents on the other. More widely, as Samer Shehata argues, 'Political Islam in Egypt has suffered a tremendous blow, its biggest setback since its emergence as a formidable ideology and political movement in the early 20th century.'[64] The new enemies of the Brotherhood were from within the same Sunni Islamic and Islamist camp for which they had long acted as a vanguard. It appeared that whether they were Wahhabi-inspired Saudi Arabians, takfiri jihadists from ISIS or al-Qaeda, or Salafi fundamentalists, there existed a form of consensus to establish enmity against the Brotherhood's Islamist vision and to variously deem them apostate, not Islamic enough, or too terroristic. The Brotherhood and its national

178 Transnational Brotherhood

iterations apparent in Hamas, Islah, and Ennahda were frequently denounced for their embrace of democracy, for seeking power through the ballot box and for using their power to order security operations against jihadi-takfiris, Salafis, and other fundamentalist opponents.

It proved difficult for the Brotherhood to work in power or opposition with its Islamist brethren. In Egypt, for example, although the Salafi al-Nour party contested the 2011–12 elections alongside the FJP and won 121 seats to the parliament, it chafed under the Brotherhood's leadership and its domination of governance project.[65] Indeed, despite the apparent similarities in Islamist ideology, the notion of an Islamist alliance was never a reality as both sides remained suspicious of each other despite their cooperation on a narrow set of issues including attempts to Islamicize the new 2012 Egyptian constitution. What goodwill was left quickly fell apart in January 2013 in Egypt when al-Nour party members were sacked from a presidential commission and others resigned in protest.[66] El-Dine contends that in the wake of the coup against the Brotherhood in Egypt,

> The Salafist al-Nour party can be considered as the one benefiting from the Brotherhood's demise. Its leaders supported Morsi's ouster, adopted the military-led transitional roadmap, and participated in the drafting of the 2014 constitution. Their contribution has been seen as providing 'Islamic legitimacy' to the new political order. Al-Nour's leaders justified their pragmatic stance as an effort to preserve national unity, to keep Islamists represented in the government, and to escape the Brotherhood's fate.[67]

In total distinction to the Brotherhood, the Salafists have benefitted from important forms of patronage and protection from Gulf states such as Saudi Arabia as it has sought to ward off the possibility of transnational Brotherhood power. Hence, in Egypt

> the Saudis have given financial aid to . . . those Egyptian Salafis who have become the military's tacit allies against the Brotherhood. . . . The Saudis [also] purportedly channeled money to the Salafist al-Nour party during Egypt's 2011–12 parliamentary elections.[68]

In siding with al-Sisi's bid for power and the reinstitution of military rule in Egypt, the Salafists have benefitted from the backlash against the Brotherhood and inserted their particular formulation of Saudi-approved Salafism into state power structures, though it remains to be seen to what extent al-Sisi's regime will tolerate their presence.[69]

Ejection

In addition to Egypt, regimes around the Arab world have also been challenged to confront the Salafi trend. In Jordan, the Muslim Brotherhood continued to distance itself from a resurgent Salafist trend in the country in the hope that it would protect its sense of alliance with the ruling regime. The Hashemite regime, meanwhile, has co-opted some elements of the Salafist trend in its wider conflict with ISIS in Syria and Iraq while at the same time moved to repress further the Muslim Brotherhood.[70] In the Palestinian Territories of the Gaza Strip, Hamas has repeatedly found itself in contention and violent conflict with some Salafi elements and found it impossible to build alliances with them in common cause against Israel or local secular opponents.[71] In Tunisia, Ennahda was compelled to take the Salafi threat in hand following violent attacks and threats on secular politicians and tourists since its ascent to power. In Yemen, the Brotherhood is vulnerable to the implication of the machinations of the Salafists, led by Sheikh Zindani, in Islah particularly in relation to the balance of power within Islah as it is represented at Saudi-hosted peace talks.

Radical jihadi groups blamed the Brotherhood for their acts of 'apostasy' in embracing elections, engaging with democracy, and participating in governance. For example, Sinai jihadists Ansar Bayt al-Maqdis, who in November 2014 declared an oath of allegiance to ISIS, also accused the Brotherhood of taking the 'shameful path of peace and democracy'.[72]

The Brotherhood also appeared to be ejected from the newly reshaping and narrowing Islamist spectrum which had become increasingly dominated by takfiri jihadism and its attendant violence. Present-day jihadists no longer appear to be inspired by the Brotherhood of Tahrir or Rabaa or the governments of Morsi and Ghannouchi. The Brotherhood also failed to build accord among Islamists and has emerged from the Arab Spring weakened in its transnational standing. It simply could not command the kind of regional and thus transnational coalescence of Islamism that it anticipated in the wake of the Arab Spring. In derailing the Brotherhood, its opponents also succeeded in significantly undermining the transition to democracy which the Arab Spring had heralded as jihadification. Instead, as former CIA deputy director was quoted as saying,, 'The Arab Spring was a boon to Islamic extremists across both the Middle East and North Africa . . . from a counter-terrorism perspective, the Arab Spring had turned to winter.'[73]

The Brotherhood has also failed to work successfully at building alliances with secularists, and the collapse of support for the Brotherhood across the Middle East has reignited the pre–Arab Spring polarity of Arab politics. The possibilities of a new politics of consensus, power sharing, and plurality are increasingly delimited as Islamists return to reactionary positions and the inevitably of religious determinism while secularists reassert their national anti-Islamist agendas. Only in Tunisia is there hope that a new politics of consensus and power sharing between secularists and Islamists can remain and that the binaries of secular and Islamist can slowly be broken down.[74] In reality, it appears that

> Tunisians were 'the only people who won something out of what happened in Egypt.' . . . The ripple effects of the Egyptian coup initially exacerbated tensions between Islamists and secularists in Tunisia but then helped persuade Islamists to compromise to prevent the failure of the country's democratic experiment.[75]

180 Transnational Brotherhood

In other contexts the Brotherhood finds itself increasingly isolated and marginalized in debates about the post-Islamist order or the place of Islamism in secularizing and democratic orders. In the regional reordering since Morsi and his government were deposed in July 2013, the Brotherhood has been vilified as one of the worst forms of Islamism and tied in violent symbiosis with virulent, violent iterations of jihadi terrorism as practiced by ISIS and other al-Qaeda offshoots.

Future face

In the wake of the Arab Spring, the Muslim Brotherhood stood at a significant crossroad as it faced the opportunity to be part of the challenge to and transition of authoritarian power in the Middle East. The moment appeared, at last, to be ripe for the Muslim Brotherhood to capitalize on the popular support it enjoyed, the reformist democracy-embracing political agenda it espoused, and its position as one of the most well-organized opposition groups in the region to have power. For decades since its founding as a pan-Islamic movement, the Brotherhood had struggled to realize its vision, and the Arab Spring appeared to present a perfect moment of synchronism when constituent movements in different countries could act in unison to claim power and work together towards unified Brotherhood goals such as the Palestinian issue. But with the opportunity came drawbacks which exposed schisms and differences within the constituent Brotherhood movements at a national and regional level. The Brotherhood was soon struggling with highly repressive counterrevolutionary forces determined to delimit and circumscribe it. Additionally, it was not the only Islamist actor assuming domination and was soon rivalled by other Islamist forces and elements including Salafists and jihadi takfiris that reviled the Brotherhood and its reformist ways.

The moderates and reformists of the Muslim Brotherhood who had wanted to enjoin activists and supporters in a new political project found themselves thwarted and challenged by hostile elements internally and externally. Their goal to use the opportunity of the Arab Spring and calls for reform and democracy to progress Islam into the political framework of unifying Islamism were quickly delimited. New regional alliances emerged that were united in thwarting the Muslim Brotherhood in its goal of creating an arc of unity across the region and beyond to the capitals of Europe. The regional alliance spearheaded by Saudi Arabia and other Gulf states such as the UAE has directly sought to delimit and severely circumscribed the regional and international ambitions of the Muslim Brotherhood. They have effectively criminalized the movement and also used their influence with other state actors to establish an arc of hostility to their activities regionally and internationally. This reflects a form of Islamist cold war where the mantle of leadership is claimed in the name of Wahhabi/Salafi-inspired Islamism by Saudi Arabia. It is perhaps surprising to outside observers that within the house of Sunni Islam there should be such a significant schism between the discourse of Islamism as envisaged by the Brotherhood and that of Saudi-supported Wahhabi/Salafism, but in reality the conflict arose over the Brotherhood's popular mandate and success in claiming state power in the wake of the Arab Spring. Furthermore, the regional network of Salafi-jihadism epitomized by the rapid rise and manifestation of ISIS, al-Qaeda, and the Ansar Shari'a-supporting brigades of the Maghreb, Levant, and Gulf has further eroded the regional support which the Brotherhood had once drawn as it set the limits of jihadism in a contemporary age. In the West, the Brotherhood survives but its leaders remain under constant surveillance and suspicion, their future uncertain. In sum, the dream of uniting Muslims under the banner of the Brotherhood lives on, but the realization of such a goal is severely limited by the repercussions of regional and international realignment in the wake of the Arab Spring and the Brotherhood's role in it.

Notes

1 J. Schachtel, 'Czech President at AIPAC: World Must Unite to Destroy Muslim Brotherhood', *Breitbart*, 2 March 2015, http://www.breitbart.com/national-security/2015/03/02/czech-president-at-aipac-world-must-unite-to-destroy-muslim-brotherhood/ (accessed 3 March 2015).
2 Financial Times, 'Cameron Acts Clumsily on the Muslim Brothers', *Financial Times*, 17 March 2015, http://www.ft.com/cms/s/0/5dbeaf8e-cc9d-11e4-b5a5-00144feab7de. html#axzz3bbhguuTv (accessed 30 May 2015).
3 Associated Press, 'UAE Backs Saudis with Muslim Brotherhood Blacklist', *Fox News*, 9 March 2014, http://www.foxnews.com/world/2014/03/09/united-arab-emirates-backs-saudi-arabia-move-to-label-muslim-brotherhood/ (accessed 30 May 2015).
4 Pew Research Center, *The Future of World Religions: Population Growth Projections, 2010–2050*, Washington, DC: Pew Research Center, 2015, http://www.pewforum.org/files/2015/03/PF_15.04.02_ProjectionsFullReport.pdf (accessed 30 May 2015), p.7.
5 See N.R. Keddie, *An Islamic Response to Imperialism: Political and Religious Writings of Sayyid Jamāl Ad-Dīn 'al-Afghānī'*, Berkeley: University of California Press, 1983.
6 A. Khalid, 'Pan-Islamism in Practice: The Rhetoric of Muslim Unity and Its Uses', in Elizabeth Özdalga (ed.), *Late Ottoman Society: The Intellectual Legacy*, Abingdon: RoutledgeCurzon, 2005, p. 202.
7 N.R. Keddie, 'The Origins of the Religious-Radical Alliance in Iran', *Past and Present*, Vol. 34:1, July 1966, p. 75, http://www.jstor.org/stable/650055 (accessed 30 May 2015).
8 See B. Lia, *The Society of the Muslim Brothers in Egypt: The Rise of an Islamic Mass Movement, 1928–1982*, Reading: Ithaca Press, 1998.
9 H. al-Banna, 'Toward the Light', BDIslam, May–June 1947, pp. 3–4, http://bdislam.com/manhaj/books/Towards%20the%20Light.pdf (accessed 26 March 2015).
10 See B. Milton-Edwards, 'Perpetual Struggle: The Significance of the Arab-Israeli Conflict for Islamists', in S. Akbarzadeh (ed.), *Routledge Handbook of Political Islam*, London: Routledge, 2012, pp. 236–50.
11 G. Kepel, *Muslim Extremism in Egypt: The Prophet and the Pharaoh*, London: Saqi Books, 1985, p. 12.
12 A. Mura, 'A Genealogical Inquiry into Early Islamism: The Discourse of Hasan al-Banna', *Journal of Political Ideologies*, Vol. 17:1, February 2012, p. 72, http://dx.doi.org/10.1080/13569317.2012.644986 (accessed 30 May 2015).
13 H. al-Banna, 'To What Do We Invite Humanity?', *The Quran Blog*, p. 20, https://thequranblog.files.wordpress.com/2008/06/_2_-to-what-do-we-invite-humanity.pdf (accessed 26 March 2015).
14 See W. Kristianasen, 'Muslim Brotherhood, a Row in the Family', *Le Monde diplomatique*, April 2000, http://mondediplo.com/2000/04/03tanzim (accessed 30 May 2015).
15 See M. El-Ghobashy, 'The Metamorphosis of the Egyptian Muslim Brothers', *International Journal of Middle East Studies*, Vol. 37:3, August 2005, pp. 373–95, http://dx.doi.org/10.1017/S0020743805052128 (accessed 30 May 2015).

16 See R. Lefèvre, *Ashes of Hama: The Muslim Brotherhood in Syria*, London: Hurst, 2013, p. 132.

17 See M. Kerr, The Arab Cold War: Gamal 'Abd al-Nasir and His Rivals, 1958–1970, 3rd ed., Oxford: Oxford University Press, 1971.

18 O. Roy, 'Has Islamism a Future in Afghanistan?', in W. Maley (ed.), *Fundamentalism Reborn? Afghanistan and the Taliban*, London: Hurst, 2001, p. 201.

19 B. Maréchal, *The Muslim Brothers in Europe: Roots and Discourse*, Boston: Brill, 2008, p. 57.

20 B. Maréchal, *The Muslim Brothers in Europe: Roots and Discourse*, Boston: Brill, 2008, p. 62.

21 See R.D. Edwards, 'Dreaming of an Islamist Ireland', *Standpoint*, 25 May 2010, http://standpointmag.co.uk/node/2937/full (accessed 30 May 2015); A. Gilligan, 'How the Muslim Brotherhood Fits into a Network of Extremism', *Telegraph*, 8 February 2015, http://www.telegraph.co.uk/news/worldnews/middleeast/11398538/How-the-Muslim-Brotherhood-fits-into-a-network-of-extremism.html (accessed 31 May 2015).

22 See L. Vidino, 'The Muslim Brotherhood's Conquest of Europe', *Middle East Quarterly*, Vol. 12:1, Winter 2005, pp. 25–34, http://www.meforum.org/687/the-muslim-brotherhoods-conquest-of-europe (accessed 26 May 2015).

23 See A.S. Tamimi, *Rachid Ghannouchi: A Democrat within Islamism*, New York: Oxford University Press, 2001, pp. 71–5.

24 See E. Bakker and R. Meijer (eds.), *The Muslim Brotherhood in Europe*, London: Hurst, 2012.

25 L. Vidino, *The New Muslim Brotherhood in the West*, New York: Columbia University Press, 2010.

26 B. Maréchal, 'Universal Aspirations the Muslim Brotherhood in Europe', *ISIM Review*, Vol. 22, Autumn 2008, p. 36, https://openaccess.leidenuniv.nl/bitstream/handle/1887/17269/ISIM_22_Universal_Aspirations_The_Muslim_Brotherhood_in_Europe.pdf?sequence=1 (accessed 30 May 2015); see also Federation of Islamic Organisations in Europe, 'Muslims of Europe Charter', *Federation of Islamic Organisations in Europe*, 2008, http://www.cie.ugent.be/documenten/muslim_charter.pdf (accessed 26 May 2015).

27 R.P. Mitchell, *The Society of the Muslim Brothers*, Oxford: Oxford University Press, 1969, pp. 42, 88–90.

28 C. Richter, 'Media Strategies of the Major Social Movement in Egypt: The Muslim Brothers' Website ikhwanonline.net', in N. Schneider and B. Gräf (eds), *Social Dynamics 2.0: Researching Change in Times of Media Convergence: Case Studies from the Middle East and Asia*, Berlin: Frank & Timme, 2011, p. 92.

29 S.A. Topol, 'Meet Radical Islam's Tech Guru', *Daily Beast*, 26 December 2010, http://www.thedailybeast.com/articles/2010/12/26/meet-radical-islams-tech-guru-the-muslim-brotherhood-creates-a-media-savvy-machine.html (accessed 30 May 2015).

30 See S. Bardhan, 'Egypt, Islamists, and the Internet: The Case of the Muslim Brotherhood and Its Rhetoric of Dialectics in Ikhwanweb', *Digest of Middle East Studies*, Vol. 23:2, Fall 2014, pp. 235–61, http://dx.doi.org/10.1111/dome.12049 (accessed 30 May 2015).

31 K. Hamza, 'Faith and Media: Muslim Brotherhood's Media, from the Missionary to the Political Discourse: Ikhwanweb as an Example', *IkhwanWeb*, 16 June 2009, http://www.ikhwanweb.com/article.php?id=20546 (accessed 27 May 2015).

32 K. Hamza, 'Faith and Media: Muslim Brotherhood's Media, from the Missionary to the Political Discourse: Ikhwanweb as an Example', *IkhwanWeb*, 16 June 2009, http://www.ikhwanweb.com/article.php?id=20546 (accessed 27 May 2015).

33 See C. Alfred, 'Who's Behind the Islamic State's Propaganda on Twitter?', *Huffington Post*, 6 March 2015, http://www.huffingtonpost.com/2015/03/06/isis-twitter-census_n_6817308.html (accessed 28 May 2015).

34 See J.D. Stuster, 'Rick Sanchez Wages Flame War Against Muslim Brotherhood Twitter Feed', *Foreign Policy*, 4 April 2013, http://foreignpolicy.com/2013/04/04/rick-sanchez-wages-flame-war-against-muslim-brotherhood-twitter-feed/ (accessed 27 May 2015).

35 See 'Gehad El-Haddad', Twitter post, 12 September 2013, https://twitter.com/gelhaddad (accessed 27 May 2015).

Transnational Brotherhood **183**

36 L.E. Bohn, 'The Muslim Brotherhood Takes Twitter', *Foreign Policy*, 18 November 2011, http://mideast.foreignpolicy.com/posts/2011/11/18/the_muslim_brotherhood_takes_twitter (accessed 27 May 2015).

37 S.A. Topol, 'Meet Radical Islam's Tech Guru', *Daily Beast*, 26 December 2010, http://www.thedailybeast.com/articles/2010/12/26/meet-radical-islams-tech-guru-the-muslim-brotherhood-creates-a-media-savvy-machine.html (accessed 30 May 2015).

38 See Muslim Brotherhood, 'Ikhwan Wiki', *Muslim Brotherhood*, 2015, http://ikhwanwiki.com/index.php (accessed 27 May 2015).

39 See Muslim Brotherhood, 'Brotherhood around the World', *Muslim Brotherhood*, 2015, http://ikhwanwiki.com/index.php?title=تصنيف:الإخوان_حول_العالم (accessed 27 May 2015).

40 P.N. Howard, *The Digital Origins of Dictatorship and Democracy: Information Technology and Political Islam*, New York: Oxford University Press, 2011, pp. 162–3.

41 C. Richter, 'The Egyptian Muslim Brotherhood Movement and Its Media Strategies: The Mobilising Effect of Religion in Contentious Politics', in J. Haynes and A. Hennig (eds), *Religious Actors in the Public Sphere, Means, Objectives and Effects*, Abingdon: Routledge, 2011, p. 173.

42 See Anonymous, 'Operation Brotherhood Takedown Is Engaged', *Anonymous DGAF*, 7 November 2011, https://www.youtube.com/watch?v=s6MWJ2YYitc (accessed 1 June 2015); S. Allers, '[CT] MORE EGYPT/CT/CYBER – Anonymous to Target Egypt's Muslim Brotherhood', *Wikileaks*, 9 November 2011, https://wikileaks.org/gifiles/docs/12/1276191_-ct-more-egypt-ct-cyber-anonymous-to-target-egypt-s-muslim.html (accessed 1 June 2014).

43 Committee to Protect Journalists, 'Al-Jazeera Station Raided, 3 Others Shut in Egypt', *Committee to Protect Journalists*, 3 July 2013, http://www.cpj.org/2013/07/al-jazeera-raided-3-others-shut-egypt.php (accessed 30 May 2015); Associated Press, 'Egypt Shuts Down Muslim Brotherhood Newspaper', *Huffington Post*, 25 September 2013, http://www.huffingtonpost.com/2013/09/25/egypt-shuts-down-muslim-brotherhood-newspaper_n_3987152.html (accessed 30 May 2015); Al Jazeera and Agencies, 'Egypt's Military Shuts Down News Channels', *Al Jazeera*, 4 July 2013, http://www.aljazeera.com/news/middleeast/2013/07/2013740531685326.html (accessed 31 May 2015).

44 A. El-Sherif, *The Muslim Brotherhood and the Future of Political Islam in Egypt*, Washington, DC: Carnegie Endowment for International Peace, 2014, http://carnegieendowment.org/files/mb_future_egypt1.pdf (accessed 28 April 2015), p. 6.

45 E. Trager, 'Egypt's Invisible Insurgency', *New Republic*, 19 March 2014, http://www.newrepublic.com/article/117072/egypts-young-islamists-use-facebook-organize-violence (accessed 31 May 2014); M. Awad and N.J. Brown, 'Mutual Escalation in Egypt', *Washington Post*, 9 February 2015, http://www.washingtonpost.com/blogs/monkey-cage/wp/2015/02/09/mutual-escalation-in-egypt/ (accessed 20 May 2015); S. Samir, 'Pro-MB Turkish Channel Incites Attack on Police Forces', *Cairo Post*, 25 January 2015, http://www.thecairopost.com/news/134794/inside_egypt/pro-mb-turkish-channel-incites-attack-on-police-forces (accessed 31 May 2015).

46 Human Rights Watch, *All According to Plan: The Rab'a Massacre and Mass Killings of Protesters in Egypt*, New York: Human Rights Watch, 2014, http://www.hrw.org/sites/default/files/reports/egypt0814web_0.pdf (accessed 30 May 2015), p. 2.

47 E. El-Shenawi, 'Four-Finger Salute: Egypt Rivals Use 'Rabaa Hand' to Turn Facebook Yellow', *Al Arabiya*, 22 August 2013, http://english.alarabiya.net/en/media/2013/08/21/Four-finger-salute-Egypt-rivals-use-Rabaa-symbol-to-turn-Facebook-yellow.html (accessed 30 May 2015).

48 See Human Rights Watch, 'Egypt: Mass Killings by Security Forces', *Human Rights Watch*, 11 August 2014, https://www.youtube.com/watch?v=AUtFM9L6ago (accessed 20 April 2015).

49 H. Kortam, 'Complaint Brought Against Al-Nas Channel', *Daily News Egypt*, 9 September 2012, http://thedailynewsegypt.com/2012/09/09/complaint-brought-against-al-nas-channel/

184 Transnational Brotherhood

(accessed 31 May 2015); Al Jazeera and Agencies, 'Egypt's Military Shuts Down News Channels', *Al Jazeera*, 4 July 2013, http://www.aljazeera.com/news/middleeast/2013/07/2013740531685326.html (accessed 31 May 2015).

50 BBC News, 'Egypt's Brotherhood Expands Media Machine', *BBC Monitoring International Reports*, 8 December 2014, http://www.bbc.co.uk/monitoring/egypts-brotherhood-expands-media-machine (accessed 31 May 2015); Middle East Monitor, 'Egypt Urges European Ambassadors to Close Pro-Muslim Brotherhood Satellite Channels', *Middle East Monitor*, 4 February 2015, https://www.middleeastmonitor.com/news/africa/16780-egypt-urges-european-ambassadors-to-close-pro-muslim-brotherhood-satellite-channels (accessed 31 May 2015).

51 BBC News, 'Egypt's Brotherhood Expands Media Machine', *BBC Monitoring International Reports*, 8 December 2014, http://www.bbc.co.uk/monitoring/egypts-brotherhood-expands-media-machine (accessed 31 May 2015); Middle East Monitor, 'Egypt Urges European Ambassadors to Close Pro-Muslim Brotherhood Satellite Channels', *Middle East Monitor*, 4 February 2015, https://www.middleeastmonitor.com/news/africa/16780-egypt-urges-european-ambassadors-to-close-pro-muslim-brotherhood-satellite-channels (accessed 31 May 2015).

52 P. Kingsley, 'Will #SisiLeaks Be Egypt's Watergate for Abdel Fatah al-Sisi?', *Guardian*, 5 March 2015, http://www.theguardian.com/world/2015/mar/05/sisileaks-egypt-watergate-abdel-fatah-al-sisi (accessed 31 May 2015).

53 Ikhwan Jordan, 'Audio Jordan Friday Rescue', *Ikhwan Jordan*, 13 October 2012, https://www.youtube.com/watch?v=sPEvAVVgC0E (accessed 1 June 2015).

54 The one exception to this statement is Ennahda in Tunisia, which was unique for its internal democratic institutions. See A.S. Tamimi, *Rachid Ghannouchi: A Democrat within Islamism*, New York: Oxford University Press, 2001, p. 72.

55 S. Hamid, *Temptations of Power: Islamists and Illiberal Democracy in a New Middle East*, New York: Oxford University Press, 2014, p. 4.

56 S. Hamid, 'Islamists Struggle to Match Religious Values to Politics', *Woodrow Wilson International Center for Scholars*, 28 May 2014, http://www.wilsoncenter.org/islamists/article/islamists-struggle-to-match-religious-values-to-politics (accessed 28 May 2015).

57 BBC News, 'Egypt Court Bans Muslim Brotherhood "Activities"', *BBC News*, 23 September 2013, http://www.bbc.co.uk/news/world-middle-east-24208933 (accessed 30 May 2015).

58 BBC News, 'Egyptian State TV Explains Court Verdict Banning Brotherhood Activities,' *BBC Monitoring International Reports*, 23 September 2013.

59 See E. Cunningham, 'Egypt's Military Backed Government Declares Muslim Brotherhood a Terrorist Organization', *Washington Post*, 25 December 2013, http://www.washingtonpost.com/world/middle_east/egypts-military-backed-government-declares-muslim-brotherhood-a-terrorist-organization/2013/12/25/7cf075ca-6da0-11e3-aecc-85cb037b7236_story.html (accessed 30 May 2015).

60 See Agence France-Presse, 'Tensions Brew in Jordan over Muslim Brotherhood Rift', *Gulf News*, 2 May 2015, http://gulfnews.com/news/mena/jordan/tensions-brew-in-jordan-over-muslim-brotherhood-rift-1.1502999 (accessed 30 May 2015).

61 See R. Lefèvre, 'The Syrian Brotherhood's Islamic State Challenge', *Project on Middle East Political Science*, 11 February 2015, http://pomeps.org/2015/02/11/the-syrian-brotherhoods-islamic-state-challenge/ (accessed 4 May 2015).

62 See Saudi Gazette Editorial Board, 'Libyan Conflict Nearing the Endgame?', *Saudi Gazette*, 21 May 2015, http://www.saudigazette.com.sa/index.cfm?method=home.regcon&contentid=20150522244604 (accessed 26 May 2015).

63 See A. Boukhars, N.J. Brown, M. Dunne, R. Lefèvre, M. Muasher, F. Wehrey, K. Wilkens, and S. Williamson, 'The Egypt Effect: Sharpened Tensions, Reshuffled Alliances', *Carnegie Endowment for International Peace*, 13 February 2014, http://carnegieendowment.org/2014/02/13/egypt-effect-sharpened-tensions-reshuffled-alliances# (accessed 30 May 2015).

64 S. Shehata, 'The Military vs. the Islamists', *Woodrow Wilson International Center for Scholars*, 4 November 2013, http://www.wilsoncenter.org/islamists/article/the-military-vs-the-islamists (accessed 28 May 2015).

65 BBC News, 'Egypt's Islamist Parties Win Elections to Parliament', *BBC News*, 21 January 2012, http://www.bbc.co.uk/news/world-middle-east-16665748 (accessed 30 May 2015).

66 K. Al-Anani, 'The Salafi-Brotherhood Feud in Egypt', *Al-Monitor*, 21 February 2013, http://www.al-monitor.com/pulse/originals/2013/02/muslim-brotherhood-salafist-feud-in-egypt.html# (accessed 31 May 2015).

67 C.C. El-Dine, *Fragile Alliances in Egypt's Post Revolutionary Order: The Military and Its Partners*, Berlin: Stiftung Wissenschaft und Politik (German Institute for International and Security Affairs), 2014, http://www.swp-berlin.org/fileadmin/contents/products/comments/2014C46_chams_el_dine.pdf (accessed 30 May 2015), p. 4.

68 F. Wehrey, 'The Authoritarian Resurgence: Saudi Arabia's Anxious Autocrats', *Journal of Democracy*, Vol. 26:2, April 2015, p. 76, http://muse.jhu.edu/journals/journal_of_democracy/v026/26.2.wehrey.pdf (accessed 27 May 2015).

69 See A. Bayoumi, 'Egypt's Salafi Party Faces Growing Isolation', *Al Jazeera*, 18 May 2014, http://www.aljazeera.com/news/middleeast/2014/05/egypt-salafi-party-faces-growing-isolation-2014514111139164795.html (accessed 31 May 2015).

70 See A. Abuqudairi, 'Jordan Releases Anti-ISIL Salafi Leader', *Al Jazeera*, 17 June 2014, http://www.aljazeera.com/news/middleeast/2014/06/jordan-releases-anti-isil-salafi-leader-2014617121457552506.html (accessed 31 May 2015); J. Reed, 'Jordan Tackles Homegrown Islamists as It Joins Attacks on Isis', *Financial Times*, 5 October 2014, http://www.ft.com/cms/s/0/08fc027c-4a29-11e4-bc07-00144feab7de.html#axzz3bbhguuTv (accessed 31 May 2015).

71 B. Milton-Edwards, 'Islamist Versus Islamist: Rising Challenge in Gaza', *Terrorism and Political Violence*, Vol. 26:2, 2014, pp. 259–76, http://dx.doi.org/10.1080/09546553.2012.690791 (accessed 30 April 2015).

72 M. Bassiouni, 'Ansar Bayt Maqdis Joins Islamic State', *al-Safir*, 11 November 2014, http://assafir.com/Article/1/383372 (accessed 27 May 2015).

73 G. Miller, 'Former CIA Official Cites Agency's Failure to See al-Qaeda's Rebound', *Washington Post*, 3 May 2015, http://www.washingtonpost.com/world/national-security/former-cia-official-cites-agencys-failure-to-see-al-qaedas-rebound/2015/05/03/d68e7292-f028-11e4-8abc-d6aa3bad79dd_story.html (accessed 1 June 2015).

74 T. Amara, 'Tunisia Approves Secular-Islamist Coalition Government', *Reuters*, 5 February 2015, http://www.reuters.com/article/2015/02/05/us-tunisia-government-idUSKBN0L91KB20150205 (accessed 14 May 2015).

75 A. Boukhars, N.J. Brown, M. Dunne, R. Lefèvre, M. Muasher, F. Wehrey, K. Wilkens, and S. Williamson, 'The Egypt Effect: Sharpened Tensions, Reshuffled Alliances', *Carnegie Endowment for International Peace*, 13 February 2014, http://carnegieendowment.org/2014/02/13/egypt-effect-sharpened-tensions-reshuffled-alliances# (accessed 30 May 2015).

EPILOGUE

> Islam is concerned with the question of Jihad and the drafting and mobilisation of the entire Ummah into one body to defend the right cause with all its strength than any other ancient or modern system of living, whether religious or civil.
>
> Hassan al-Banna[1]

In the wake of 9/11, the world, and in particular the Western world, appeared to engage in a quest to know more about Islam. Presidents and prime ministers were reported to be placing copies of the Koran on their bedside tables as they sought to acquaint themselves with the faith that had inspired the deadly bombers of Usama Bin Laden's al-Qaeda movement. And yet, in many respects, this quest for knowledge tended to focus all but exclusively on forms of Salafi-jihadist Islamism associated with al-Qaeda and its offshoots. In the initial volleys of the newly termed 'Global War on Terrorism', the United States and Western states targeted al-Qaeda and the Taliban in Afghanistan, only soon to be followed by its violent and fanatic offshoots such as al-Qaeda in Iraq and al-Qaeda in the Arab Peninsula (AQAP). Muslims were regarded as being in possession of choices about who represented them and who claimed their faith in expression of political acts contesting power and legitimacy on a global scale. The political choice they were perceived by the West to be making was symbolized by the lethal violence of the suicide bombers of al-Qaeda. The political future that al-Qaeda offered was of a triumphant, dominant Islam with a blueprint for power. The challenges within poor, under-developed, corrupt failed states and broken societies were to be surmounted by the programmatic vision of al-Qaeda. The group's dystopian vision and violence was treated in much of the West as if it represented the Muslim mainstream, particularly in the Middle East.

Oppressed and overled

The Muslim Brotherhood, despite being the singular largest and most significant manifestation of contemporary Islamism, was frequently overlooked in this period. Its transnational dimensions of Islamism appeared not to merit the attention or resources in terms of understanding and strategic response. Western governments and policymakers were content for the leaders of those states in which the Muslim Brotherhood was manifest to conflate them with the violent radical fundamentalism of al-Qaeda. Yet the Muslim Brotherhood, as this volume has illustrated, is a complex, far-reaching, and dynamic expression of contemporary Islamism that speaks to the politics and identity of many Muslims across the Middle East and beyond.

In the wake of the Arab Spring, the movement has been battered and beaten but remains largely resilient due to a vanguard that continues to engage in diverse forms of activism that, although may appear sometimes contradictory, is rationalized in terms of the end goal. In Egypt the Muslim Brotherhood emerged phoenixlike in the wake of the Arab revolution that toppled President Mubarak only to descend into the flames again when General al-Sisi mounted a putsch in July 2013. The strength of the state and its resilience as located within the institutions of the military were too much for the Brotherhood or, as argued, any other political group outside the powerful nexus between business and the military in Egypt.

Nevertheless, for nearly ninety years the Muslim Brotherhood and its affiliate branches and organizations in countries such as Egypt, Yemen, Syria, Jordan, Libya, and Tunisia have undertaken a comprehensive attempt to translate the philosophy of its leadership into a series of social, economic, and political activities in service of their societies. They have sought to represent the wide appeal of Islam as a contemporary solution to modern-day problems and travails. The Muslim Brotherhood, however, has always struggled to portray its moderation and win others over. Secularists often revile its programmes of Islamization and treat it as a significant threat to the modern order arguing that the Brotherhood is bent on an agenda that is old-fashioned and restricting. The Left understand that in the Islamist parlance of the Brotherhood there is no place for their liberal, democratic worldview or political programmes. Other Islamists, such as radical Salafi-jihadis, excoriate the Brotherhood for appearing to embrace Western-imposed constructs such as democracy and elections, declaring them apostate as a result. Thus the Brotherhood's agenda has been treated with deep-seated mistrust and suspicion as a thinly veiled attempt to take over the levers of political power not only in Arab states across the Middle East but also across the globe.

The Muslim Brotherhood has attempted to grow itself as a true mass-based Muslim movement representing a modern political force for Islam. In the West, the debate about the Muslim Brotherhood, however, has been received in a variety of ways. There are those that vehemently object to it and regard its mission and ambitions as a significant threat to democracy and the secular state, equality, and feminism. In this way, the leitmotif of the Arab Spring protests clashes against the vision of the Muslim Brotherhood and thus cannot be supported. The struggle of ideas which had characterized the movement for many decades amounted to tense and sometimes increasingly tenuous commitments to non-violence, pluralism, democracy, and power sharing. This was how the Muslim Brotherhood came to understand that it could reach a middle ground and appeal to a wider base. This was how the leadership of the movement steadily came to understand the reality of its existence and survival in authoritarian states and fragile transitions and revival. This was not, however, how everyone, particularly among the younger generations of the movement, sought to impact state or society. This 'discourse of generalities' has inevitably blurred the line between a Brotherhood movement typified by peaceful transformation and the sometimes violent events and advocacy of change which some elements have always suggested or advocated through jihad.[2]

Killing the spirit of a revolution

In the wake of the Arab Spring, unprecedented levels of violence were waged, once again, against the Muslim Brotherhood and its supporters. This is evidenced, for example, by the graphic images of the hundreds bludgeoned or shot to death during peaceful public protests or the revered elders of the movement dressed in the red death row outfits imposed by state courts.[3] Moreover, as conservative reactionary states have sought to push back on the spirit and momentum of the Arab Spring, the Muslim Brotherhood and its branches have been blamed for inspiring or organizing terrorist plots to disrupt power in states across the globe. Increasingly the Brotherhood has been proscribed and its leaders blacklisted and imprisoned. Few are willing to defend the Muslim Brotherhood in relation to its commitment to democracy and nonviolence, and important governmental reports which may conclude that the organization is not a terrorist menace have been quashed.[4]

The Muslim Brotherhood has also been found wanting in respect to important debates about governance and the principle of inclusivity internally and externally. In this sense, the middle ground is still up for debate with the Brotherhood across the region trying to create a space for itself in the middle ground of Arab political life with attendant consequences in terms of alliance building, power sharing, and cooperation. Within the Muslim Brotherhood there have been debates and arguments that the middle ground is diminished in the wake of the Arab Spring with radicals perceiving the events as an opportunity to push out or marginalize the advocates within their own movements who have called for cooperation. In Egypt the Brotherhood has differing views coexisting within the movement, but Mohammed Morsi represented the inward-looking and deeply conservative strand of the movement which alienated many reformists and other sectoral groups which had been the key movers and shakers of the popular groundswell during the Arab Spring. Ennahda, or perhaps more correctly Ghannouchi himself, appeared to exemplify an alternative route for the Brotherhood as an inclusive modern movement capable of working with other parties with disparate views. Inevitably, though, this has led to the question of whether Tunisia or Ghannouchi himself is simply the exception

190 Epilogue

to the rule. The younger generation of the Muslim Brotherhood across the region has emerged, partly emboldened by the events of the Arab Spring, to argue that the movement lost important ground because it simply was not inclusive enough.

Certainly there is evidence from opinion polls and ballot boxes that after the initial peaks of popular support for the Muslim Brotherhood, its approval has now declined.[5] The populous has found the Brotherhood wanting, and support for the movement has declined but not totally collapsed.[6] Likewise, the Brotherhood's base, which it considered secure and under monopolistic grasp, has weakened.[7] The expectations that the Brotherhood had created through many years of Islamist rhetoric and simplified oppositional representation could not be met once the movement was in power or sought to mobilize the street behind it to capitalize on the calls of protestors as they echoed around the Arab world. The context in which the Brotherhood has had to work during and since the Arab Spring has begun to turn resolutely and implacably against them whether in terms of a hostile media; hostile state institutions including their bureaucrats and their police, intelligence services, and armed forces; or other hostile political actors whom it must contend with. Indeed, other political actors have also proved to be less than willing to join in sharing power or building alliances with the Brotherhood.[8] The spirit of solidarity so apparent during the heady days and early months of the Arab Spring have quickly dissipated into antagonism and acute mistrust of the Brotherhood.

Fictions and facades

The Brotherhood's spirit and philosophy of authentic political change and a new Muslim identity accommodating democracy and the politics of participation became problematic when measured against the reality of power and governance through extant state structures and institutions. The ingrained political norms and culture of Arab politics in its authoritarianism have proved resilient to Islamism fragmenting it through challenge and conflict.[9] The discourse which the movement had employed to win supporters from the middle classes and students which attempted to portray it as both authentically modern and Muslim appeared to be failing and collapsed when, in 2013, the Brotherhood was once against criminalized by the state. The language of reformism so evident in the Brotherhood's doctrine, however, was tested and found wanting when it came to governance at state level and did not, after all, translate well in the transition from authoritarian power to transitional governance. The hope that after decades of providing communities with well-organized social and welfare support, education projects, and programmes of Islamization, the Brotherhood was equipped to steer millions of citizens through a major political transition proved vain. And as the movement's energies were absorbed by trying to run a state machinery that was resistant to change, it did not see the challenges to its power and authority or its consequences coming. The leadership of the Brotherhood, its newly elected representatives and government ministers, fell into the trap, like their predecessors in Jordan in 1990 and in the Palestinian Territories in 2006, of thinking and more importantly believing that they were equipped to handle the

Epilogue **191**

challenges of governance and of managing state institutions and their personnel without accommodation of other perspectives and agendas.

Now the Brotherhood is mostly beleaguered and embattled and firmly back on the margins of the political arena. It is increasingly viewed with distrust and cynicism by a greater number of ordinary people who in the past would have supported or aligned with its agenda. The Brotherhood's reactive and reactionary viewpoints began to chime badly with public sentiment about democracy, freedom of expression, secularism, and human rights. The headlong rush to claim power through elections and the decision to rescind earlier commitments to allow others to contest for power have proved, in some part, to have sown the seeds of its own destruction. Again, it is as if the Brotherhood convinced itself that amidst the calls of the Arab Spring it alone was hearing a demand for it to be elected. The Brotherhood of the past imagined by its founder in 1928 has become outmoded, and in its place something more instrumental, reactive, and less reformist has emerged. Similarly, the truly international structure of the Brotherhood as imagined by its founder and promoted in the early decades of the movement by its leaders and supporters has also changed. Under the leadership of the General Guide of the Egyptian Brotherhood, there were always constraints on such international ambitions which drew the energies of constituent Brotherhood organizations inward rather than outward.

Global limits

The notion of the Brotherhood as a wide network of mutually supporting and mutually connected leaders and followers was certainly powerfully absent in the wake of the Arab Spring. Power was first and foremost domestically harnessed and even in areas where the Brotherhood had traditionally held a unified position, such as on Israel and supporting Palestinian rights, left much to be desired. Hamas leaders in the Gaza Strip, for example, had firmly believed that a Muslim Brotherhood president and parliament in Egypt would have actively championed their cause and taken a much harder stance against Israel than it did. Although in public Hamas leaders glossed over the glaring inadequacies of the Morsi government to aid and support them, in private they expressed dismay and concern that their belief in the powerful and strong informal links with Egypt that they had always enjoyed counted for so little when it came to public power, national security, and governance.[10] Under President Morsi, Egypt's peace treaty with Israel remained totally intact. As analyst Abdel Monem Said Aly notes,

> Morsi failed to dominate the basic tools of foreign policymaking. The Army maintained its independence; the intelligence organs opposed the Muslim Brotherhood's pursuit of hegemony; and the Ministry of Foreign Affairs bureaucracy stealthily resisted the efforts of Egypt's new rulers to penetrate its ranks.[11]

This means that little went the Brotherhood's way when it came to foreign policy.

192 Epilogue

While it was true that some individual-inspired links flourished with Cairo's hospitality open to the Brotherhood from across the globe and that the Brotherhood's use of social media and the Internet attempted to portray a globally connected and unified movement, this was short-lived and betrayed the difficulties presented to the Brotherhood in terms of transforming itself for power domestically while at the same time harnessing this power to promote the movement transnationally. The part played by the Brotherhood in Egypt came as a significant litmus test of regional and international opinion about the power and reach of the organization and some concluded that if curtailed in Cairo, then the rest would follow. Certainly the muted response from other Brotherhood organizations to the events of July to August 2013 and the rout from power of the Brotherhood in the face of widespread popular dissent and dissatisfaction exploited by Egypt's military elite and its backers was telling. It was telling both in terms of the inward-looking preoccupations with survival in regimes which in the wake of the Arab Spring were targeting the Brotherhood with major repressive measures but also because it exposed the myth of networked interconnectedness that many presupposed existed in the Muslim Brotherhood as a global entity.

Ultimately nationalism and nationalist elements, which were long the nemesis of the Brotherhood, have triumphed. Even in terms of the Brotherhood's own internally directed orientations and manifestations, the movement reflected an acculturated preoccupation or concern with national concerns. Furthermore, the connected networks which had grown and flourished in the past among exiled members of the Brotherhood in Gulf states such as Saudi Arabia and Kuwait in the 1960s and early 1970s or among Muslim Brotherhood student societies in Europe in the 1980s and early 1990s had been broken up. Such exiled Brotherhood networks had either been dismantled by incumbent regimes in which they were 'hosted', transformed through indigenization processes in Europe of original Muslim migrant communities, or voluntarily disbanded in the wake of the Arab Spring upon the triumphal re-entry of the Brotherhood back to the liberated capitals of the region. In the era which now equates the Muslim Brotherhood with terrorism, there has been a radical rethink about the Brotherhood's networks. The 'hospitality' that their leaders and supporters can now enjoy is limited to destinations such as Doha and Istanbul. The hospitality of Europe which exiles had come to enjoy is also altered and circumscribed by domestic national security agendas, as well as strategic alliances with state actors in the region – and especially the Gulf states – who are hostile to the Brotherhood and any 'protection' afforded to them in European capitals.

Opposition to the Muslim Brotherhood is palpable in such European capitals, and at best European governments are ambivalent about the movement, its leaders, and its experiences in the wake of the Arab Spring. While it is unlikely that Western governments will go as far as their Arab allies in Saudi Arabia and the UAE and proscribe the Muslim Brotherhood for its part in the democratic transitions wrought in the Middle East by the Arab Spring, there has certainly been evidence of a new tendency to construct the Brotherhood as part of the same terroristic threat as al-Qaeda and ISIS in many European and other Western capital cities. It is the case that the Western media now plays its part in the construction of terroristic narratives that frame the Muslim Brotherhood in the same way that ISIS and al-Qaeda and its offshoots are. Hence, the important distinctions between the Muslim Brotherhood and al-Qaeda in Yemen, for instance, are lost to such audiences. The Brotherhood's acceptance of democracy, electoral politics, and disavowal of violence is completely overlooked.

Narrow options

This limits options for support for the Brotherhood and pushes it inexorably towards state actors such as Turkey and Qatar who have their own agendas and ideological positions on the nature of the Middle East region and the place of Islamism in it. The Gulf-promoted Salafi strategy to delimit and curtail the Brotherhood also narrows its place but, one could argue, with dangerous portents for the future. Does this push the Brotherhood closer to outliers of violent extremism in the region in increasingly unstable states such as Libya, Syria, Iraq, Egypt, and Yemen and in territories such as the Gaza Strip? Furthermore, the Salafists are being funded to hold the banner of Islam as part of the Gulf-state-driven pushback against the Brotherhood across the Middle East creating new dividing lines, tensions, and conflicts which can barely be contained. Islamists are now engaged in bidding and outbidding each other in competition to win the support of the 'people' and the grace and resources of powerful state actors such as Kuwait, Saudi Arabia, Qatar, Iran, and Turkey.

The events of the Arab Spring compelled the Islamists to act, and sometimes they grabbed power whether they were ready for it or not. Democracy became less important than the politics of majoritarianism delivered powerfully through the ballot box outcomes in Tunisia and Egypt. This encouraged the Brotherhood away from seeking consensus and to continue to trust only its own even if this meant compacts which restored the status quo ante as Islah did in Yemen. The movement trod the inevitable path of exclusion rather than inclusion appearing to forget the breadth of diversity represented in the populous movements which had swelled on the streets of cities, towns, and villages to oppose authoritarian politics, corruption, and revenge irrespective of what political cover or label was attached to it. Decades in opposition and of sitting on the outside of structures and institutions of power, had not, in fact, equipped it as well as many had predicted it would for power. The Brotherhood in Egypt and Tunisia, like Hamas before it in the Palestinian Territories in 2006, may have demanded power or a role in the legislative process, but they neither expected nor were prepared for governing power over complex, failing, corrupt, and bankrupt state entities which were supposed to serve the citizens of their countries. It is apparent that there are some differences in the approach to democracy of the Brotherhood depending on whether it is governing alone as opposed to simply serving in the legislature or sharing governing powers and responsibilities

194 Epilogue

with other actors. In government it is the case that the Brotherhood and its affiliate organizations have paid less respect for democracy and constitutionalism and attendant human rights norms than they should have. Their failure may lead other more hardline and radical elements though to fill the space of reflecting and articulating populist grievances as refracted through the lens of Islamism.

There is an emerging consensus that since the Arab Spring the Islamist project as spearheaded by the Muslim Brotherhood across the region has, with the exception of Tunisia, proved to be a failure, particularly with respect to the practice of party politics, participation in a multiparty system, constitutional politics, the politics of governance and governing and mediating the politics of state management, bureaucracy, and the deep state in the Middle East. It is also the case that the Muslim Brotherhood has struggled to work in alliance and cooperation with other political elements, even if they are fellow Islamists. It has become evident that they are absolutists preferring zero-sum politics. The political space which opened up during the Arab Spring allowing for social elements to have a voice and break the taboo of fear of the authoritarian narrowed again under Brotherhood rule and governance. The public space became a suffocating place again where a vision of a particular social order was quickly being established by the Brotherhood. The case of Tunisia and the role played by Ennahda may prove to be either the exception or a way forward, the difference being that Ennahda has been compelled to learn to reach out and seek to build alliances with its political partners in government rather than within the Islamist tent. But in Egypt the Brotherhood failed to understand that the Arab Spring had created a new spirit of inclusivity that was about sharing a future rather than a repetition of the traditional zero-sum game of power holding which had characterized Egyptian politics. It was also the case that the Brotherhood had forgotten that the lens through which the Arab Spring should be viewed was primarily socioeconomic; the grievances that led vendor Mohammed Bouazizi to immolate himself and for others to protest were not Islamic.[12] The youth that comprised the majority of the voices raised across the Arab world as the protests of the Arab Spring broke out did not call in the name of Islam. The youth and other protesters did not chant 'Islam is the solution' but instead demanded leaders to '*Erhal!*' (Leave) or chanted 'Game over' or '*Ash-sha'b yurīd isqāt an-nizām*' (The people want to bring down the regime).

Opening of the political space leads to compromise if survival is to be an option, but given the choice of inclusivity, the Muslim Brotherhood struggled in a variety of post–Arab Spring contexts to choose this route of alliance and cooperation. It is as if the Brotherhood saw protest across the Arab world not as truly multifaceted uprising representing a plethora of social groups, political interests, and religious attachments but something quite singular. In this singularity the Brotherhood believed that there were signs that its long-held ambitions for control over governance and society, politics, and economy could at last be realized in the state project in the Middle East. But the Brotherhood failed to see the obstacles in its way or to truly mobilize the middle ground which was willing to work with the Brotherhood in transitioning from tyranny to democracy. The careful husbandry required of constitution making, revision, and rebuilding was also weak and clumsy when placed in the hands of the Muslim Brotherhood. Moreover, there was no uniform pattern of Brotherhood response and action. In Tunisia, for example, Ennahda did not have to contend with a strong, powerful, and deeply embedded military which had played such a deeply effective historic role in shaping politics and the state for many decades, but it did have a well organized secular and leftist movement that was prepared to challenge it and compete with it politically and in terms of the opinion of the street. Tunisia is much more secular than other states in the region, and Ennahda has always understood, under Ghannouchi's leadership, that compromise with others including such elements as the labour unions and workers associations in Tunisia, women's movements, and secular-inspired student groups would be required in the quest for influence and power. In Tunisia, however, and elsewhere such as Egypt, the Brotherhood has also had to compete within the Islamist arena with the Salafi-driven agenda which has played an increasingly important part in iterations of political Islam since the Arab Spring.

Ignition failure

The Muslim Brotherhood had hoped to ignite a new trend in politics in the Middle East. It saw the Arab Spring as the opportunity to realize its long-held dreams and ambitions. It failed. It failed as a result of its own weaknesses and the resistance of other powerful actors to its goals. It failed to translate the youth revolution that symbolized the Arab Spring into what the Muslim Brotherhood itself could and should have stood for. Within their own movements the Old Guard pushed back on the challenges of the younger generations and failed to reward the youth's efforts and their responsiveness during the Arab Spring. They were not made partners to the transition of power but were excluded by their own senior leaders. The glimmer of hope that also appeared to open up for women and the role that they played during the Arab Spring was also extinguished by the patriarchal hegemony that characterizes the Muslim Brotherhood wherever it is. Archaic structures within the Muslim Brotherhood still deny women power at the highest echelons of the organization. This is not to dismiss the role played by women in the Muslim Brotherhood, particularly that of notable individual figures such as Nobel Peace Prize winner Tawakkul Karman from Yemen or the mobilization of the Muslim Sisters in the Tahrir Square uprising, but it is to note that the Brotherhood has not sought a social revolution in the wake of such events.[13]

So what did the impact of the Arab Spring have on the Muslim Brotherhood? Definitively it demonstrated the art of the possible for the Brotherhood in relation to its ability, in a number of contexts, to successfully capitalize on its position as well-organized and largely cohesive opposition movements. The experiences of the Muslim Brotherhood regime in Egypt are unlikely to be repeated for the foreseeable future, and as in the past, the Brotherhood and its leaders are literally condemned to languish in Egyptian jails again indefinitely.

196 Epilogue

The collective expression of modern Muslim identity which the Muslim Brotherhood could claim across the region and for which it was understood as representing is also now significantly diminished in the post–Arab Spring era. The Brotherhood is challenged by other forms of Islamism on a variety of fronts. Some emanating from the radical end of the Islamist spectrum like al-Qaeda and its offshoots are familiar competitors, but others are not. The Brotherhood and its branches in countries such as Yemen, Jordan, Egypt, Libya, Syria, and Tunisia have had to contend with the jihadification of their cause manifest in the proliferation of violent and extremist militias which have been highly critical of the political path Brotherhood branches have taken since the Arab Spring. Jihadi discourse in the wake of the Arab Spring has excoriated the Muslim Brotherhood for the path it has taken and the direction in which it has led contemporary political Islam. Al-Qaeda's Ayman al-Zawahiri, for example, had warned the Brotherhood in Egypt from contesting power through the ballot box, arguing that to do so was to reject the founding principles of this particular modern Islamist movement and its historic commitment to jihad.[14] Following the removal of Brotherhood in power in Egypt in July 2013, al-Zawahiri argued that the Brotherhood had paid the price for sacrificing its principles and in essence contended that it had got what it deserved. In a piece titled 'Bitter Harvest; the Muslim Brotherhood in Sixty Years', Zawahiri wrote of the 'perversions' committed by the Brotherhood, demanding they renounce democracy and parliamentary politics.[15]

Whatever its future face, the Brotherhood, despite the most vehement wishes of its opponents and enemies, will not simply wither and die. Its political impact, even if diminished, will endure. Western governments will still be preoccupied with the Brotherhood as both a domestic and foreign policy issue. The desire to understand the Brotherhood in terms of its philosophy, activities, impact, and influence on national interests, at home and abroad, and of Western government policies towards it will continue to preoccupy policymakers. There have been enormous challenges for many Western governments in the wake of the Arab Spring to analyse and come to terms with. This includes the initial rise and fall of the Brotherhood while at the same time Salafist and Salafi-jihadi elements have continued to rise and rain insecurity and violence across the Middle East and threaten national security agendas in Europe, the United States, Canada, Australia, and beyond. If the belief is that events in Egypt, including the violence and repression of 2013 and the election victory of General al-Sisi following the army's removal from power of the democratically elected President Morsi, will be without eventual repercussion in terms of the stability stakes of the wider Middle East, then this is mistaken. Concerns will persist that the Brotherhood will survive, adapt, but also reemerge headed and steered by more radical elements. Certainly there is little to no sympathy in the West for the Brotherhood. They are certainly not viewed by many governments or policymakers as victims of violent power struggles but the perpetrator of an agenda which is still regarded as inherently tied to jihadist and violent, fanatic energies and values. The orientalist trope that political Islam can never be anything other than violent, authoritarian, and anti-democratic ultimately informed and coloured the ways in which the Brotherhood would be perceived throughout the Arab Spring era. As the UK's former director of public prosecutions noted, when 'democracy had come at last to Egypt, [and] when the army kicked it down, we didn't hear too much gnashing of teeth in the citadels of freedom in the West'.[16] The suspicion remained that the Brotherhood's bid for power through the ballot box was nothing more than instrumental.

Future face

The fate of the Brotherhood in the Middle East is also centred on wider power struggles and discourses in the region about the place and role of Islamism, the dynamic version of Islam, and its impact on the politics of the mass and its exclusion from elite power circles. The views of powerful regional actors such as Saudi Arabia have been a key determinant in deciding the extent to which the Brotherhood in the wake of the Arab Spring has been excluded and criminalized. Declaring the Brotherhood a terrorist organization has placed it shoulder to shoulder with its violent enemies in al-Qaeda and other Salafi-jihadis. Instead of encouraging the region's largest Islamist organization, actively steering it, and incentivizing it to continue down the path of governance and democracy, the opposite effect has happened. Ultimately, the endurance of the organization and its future face will remain tied to the intrinsic attachment of Islam and the shelter this provides. It is to this ultimate refuge of Islam that the Brotherhood will return, where it will remain as protected as it can be and where it will regenerate to impact on the political space once more.

Notes

1 H. al-Banna, *Kitab ul Jihad*, n.p., n.d., p. 220, https://books.google.co.uk/books?id=wZ ALAwAAQBAJ&pg=PA219&dq (accessed 31 May 2015).
2 C.R. Wickham, *The Muslim Brotherhood: Evolution of an Islamist Movement*, Princeton, NJ: Princeton University Press, 2013, p. 187.
3 See Human Rights Watch, *All According to Plan: The Rab'a Massacre and Mass Killings of Protesters in Egypt*, New York: Human Rights Watch, 2014, http://www.hrw.org/sites/default/files/reports/egypt0814web_0.pdf (accessed 30 May 2015); Al Quds al-Arabi, 'MB Guide in Red Death Row Outfit', *Al-Quds al-Arabi*, 20 April 2015, http://www.alquds.co.uk/?p=329132 (accessed 21 April 2015).
4 See M. Azzam, 'There Is Still Time to Side with Those Committed to Democracy in Egypt', *Guardian*, 15 August 2013, http://www.theguardian.com/commentisfree/2013/aug/15/democracy-egypt-irony-muslim-brotherhood (accessed 15 August 2013); N. Morris and I. Johnston, 'Muslim Brotherhood: Government Report Concludes They Should Not Be Classified as a Terrorist Organization', *Independent*, 15 March 2015, http://www.independent.co.uk/news/uk/home-news/muslim-brotherhood-government-report-concludes-they-should-not-be-classified-as-a-terrorist-organisation-10109730.html (accessed 15 March 2015).
5 See Pew Research Center, 'One Year After Morsi's Ouster, Divides Persist over el-Sisi and the Muslim Brotherhood', *Pew Research Center*, 22 May 2014, http://www.pewglobal.org/2014/05/22/one-year-after-morsis-ouster-divides-persist-on-el-sisi-muslim-brotherhood/ (accessed 31 May 2015).

198 Epilogue

6 See Pew Research Center, 'Tunisian Confidence in Democracy Wanes, Ratings for Islamist Ennahda Party Have Declined Since Revolution', *Pew Research Center*, 15 October 2014, http://www.pewglobal.org/2014/10/15/tunisian-confidence-in-democracy-wanes/ (accessed 31 May 2015).

7 See Pew Research Center, 'One Year After Morsi's Ouster, Divides Persist over el-Sisi and the Muslim Brotherhood', *Pew Research Center*, 22 May 2014, http://www.pewglobal.org/2014/05/22/one-year-after-morsis-ouster-divides-persist-on-el-sisi-muslim-brotherhood/ (accessed 31 May 2015).

8 See Ennahda and Nidaa Tounes in Tunisia: J. Lawrence, 'Tunisia, the Courage of Compromise', *Brookings Institution*, 5 February 2015, http://www.brookings.edu/research/opinions/2015/02/05-tunisia-courage-compromise-laurence (accessed 31 May 2015); and the Muslim Brotherhood and Salafists in Egypt: K. Al-Anani, 'The Salafi-Brotherhood Feud in Egypt', *Al-Monitor*, 21 February 2013, http://www.al-monitor.com/pulse/originals/2013/02/muslim-brotherhood-salafist-feud-in-egypt.html# (accessed 31 May 2015).

9 See J. Stacher, *Adaptable Autocrats: Regime Power in Egypt and Syria*, Stanford, CA: Stanford University Press, 2012.

10 See B. Milton-Edwards, 'Hamas and the Arab Spring: Strategic Shifts?' *Middle East Policy*, Vol. 20:3, Fall 2013, pp. 60–72, http://onlinelibrary.wiley.com/doi/10.1111/mepo.12033/abstract (accessed 31 May 2015).

11 A.M.S. Aly, *Middle East Brief: Post-revolution Egyptian Foreign Policy*, Waltham, MA: Brandeis University Crown Center for Middle East Studies, 2014, http://www.brandeis.com/crown/publications/meb/MEB86.pdf (accessed 31 May 2015).

12 J.P. Filiu, *The Arab Revolution: Ten Lessons from the Democratic Uprising*, London: Hurst, 2011; D. Lagraffe, 'The Youth Bulge in Egypt: An Intersection of Demographics, Security and the Arab Spring', *Journal of Strategic Security*, Vol. 5:2, 2012, pp. 65–80, http://scholarcommons.usf.edu/jss/vol5/iss2/9/ (accessed 31 May 2015); D. Singerman, 'Youth, Gender and Dignity in the Egyptian Uprising', *Journal of Middle Eastern Women's Studies*, Vol. 9:3, 2013, pp. 1–27, http://muse.jhu.edu/journals/journal_of_middle_east_womens_studies/v009/9.3.singerman.html (accessed 31 May 2015).

13 See M. Farag, 'The Muslim Sisters and the January 25th Revolution,' *Journal of International Women's Studies*, Vol. 13:5, October 2012, pp. 228–37, http://vc.bridgew.edu/jiws/vol13/iss5/19 (accessed 31 May 2015).

14 See B. Milton-Edwards, 'Revolt and Revolution: The Place of Islamism', *Critical Studies in Terrorism*, Vol. 5:2, August 2012, pp. 219–36, http://dx.doi.org/10.1080/17539153.2012.686658 (accessed 7 May 2015).

15 See A. Zawahiri, 'Bitter Harvest; the Muslim Brotherhood in Sixty Years', *Tawhed*, 1991, http://www.tawhed.ws/r?i=2gxseb4t (accessed 27 April 2015).

16 K. McDonald, 'Britain's Treatment of the Muslim Brotherhood Is Spectacularly Cack-Handed', *Telegraph*, 2 July 2014, http://www.telegraph.co.uk/news/uknews/terrorism-in-the-uk/10938780/Britains-treatment-of-the-Muslim-Brotherhood-is-spectacularly-cack-handed.html (accessed 2 July 2014).

BIBLIOGRAPHY

Abidi, A.H. *Jordan: A Political Study, 1948–1957*, London: Asia Publishing House, 1965.

Abou El Fadl, K. 'Failure of a Revolution: The Military, Secular Intelligentsia and Religion in Egypt's Pseudo-Secular State', in L. Sadiki (ed.) *Routledge Handbook of the Arab Spring: Rethinking Democratization*, Abingdon, Oxon: Routledge, 2015.

Abou el-Fotouh, A.M. 'Democracy Supporters Should Not Fear the Muslim Brotherhood', *Washington Post*, 9 February 2011, http://www.washingtonpost.com/wp-dyn/content/article/2011/02/09/AR2011020905222.html (accessed 14 April 2015).

Abu Amer, A. 'Hamas Ties to Qatar Have Cost', *Al-Monitor*, 22 April 2013, http://www.al-monitor.com/pulse/originals/2013/04/hamas-qatar-relationship-independence.html (accessed 23 April 2013).

Abu Amr, Z. 'Hamas: A Historical and Political Background', *Journal of Palestine Studies*, Vol. 22:4, Summer 1993, pp. 5–19, http://www.jstor.org/stable/2538077 (accessed 1 May 2015).

Abu Amr, Z. *Islamic Fundamentalism in the West Bank and Gaza Strip*, Bloomington: University of Indiana Press, 1994.

Abul-Magd, Z. 'The Egyptian Military in Politics and the Economy: Recent History and Current Transition Status', *Chr. Michelsen Institute*, Vol. 2013:2, October 2013, http://www.cmi.no/publications/file/4935-the-egyptian-military-in-politics-and-the-economy.pdf (accessed 28 April 2015).

Abu Mohammed. Author interview, Nusseirat Refugee Camp, Gaza Strip, 6 September 1993.

Abu Nowar, M. *The History of the Hashemite Kingdom of Jordan*, Vol. 1 of *The Creation and Development of Transjordan, 1920–29*, Reading: Ithaca Press, 1989.

Abuqudairi, A. 'Jordan Releases Anti-ISIL Salafi Leader', *Al Jazeera*, 17 June 2014, http://www.aljazeera.com/news/middleeast/2014/06/jordan-releases-anti-isil-salafi-leader-2014617121457552506.html (accessed 31 May 2015).

Abu-Rabi, I. *Intellectual Origins of Islamic Resurgence in the Modern Arab World*, Albany: State University of New York Press, 1996.

Abu-Rish, Z. 'Jordan's Current Political Opposition Movements and the Need for Further Research: An Interview with Tariq Tell (Part 2)', *Jadaliyya*, 24 August 2012, http://www.jadaliyya.com/pages/index/7007/jordans-current-political-opposition-movements-and (accessed 3 March 2015).

200 Bibliography

Abu Rumman, M. *The Muslim Brotherhood in the 2007 Jordanian Parliamentary Elections: A Passing 'Political Setback' or Diminished Popularity?*, Amman: Friedrich-Ebert-Stiftung, 2007, http://library.fes.de/pdf-files/bueros/amman/05320/05320-eng.pdf (accessed 3 March 2015).

Abu Rumman, M. and Abu Hanieh, H. *The 'Islamic Solution' in Jordan: Islamists, the State, and the Ventures of Democracy and Security*, Amman: Friedruch-Ebert-Stiftung, 2013, http://library.fes.de/pdf-files/bueros/amman/10360.pdf (accessed 3 March 2015).

Agence France-Presse, 'Egypt: Palestinians in Gaza Celebrate Muslim Brotherhood Election Win', *Telegraph*, 24 June 2012, http://www.telegraph.co.uk/news/worldnews/africaandindianocean/egypt/9352563/Egypt-Palestinians-in-Gaza-celebrate-Muslim-Brotherhood-election-win.html (accessed 30 April 2015).Agence France-Presse, 'Hassan Al-Banna, Founding Father of Egypt's Muslim Brotherhood', *IkhwanWeb*, 14 October 2006, http://www.ikhwanweb.com/article.php?id=3272 (accessed 28 February 2014).

Agence France-Press, 'Saleh Supporters Take Over Yemen Protest Site', *Hindustan Times*, 3 February 2011, http://www.hindustantimes.com/world-news/saleh-supporters-take-over-yemen-protest-site/article1-658245.aspx (accessed 27 May 2015).

Agence France-Presse, 'Tensions Brew in Jordan over Muslim Brotherhood Rift', *Gulf News*, 2 May 2015, http://gulfnews.com/news/mena/jordan/tensions-brew-in-jordan-over-muslim-brotherhood-rift-1.1502999 (accessed 30 May 2015).

Ahram Online, 'El-Sisi Wins Egypt's Presidential Race with 96.91%', *Ahram Online*, 3 June 2014, http://english.ahram.org.eg/NewsContent/1/64/102841/Egypt/Politics-/BREAKING-PEC-officially-announces-AbdelFattah-ElSi.aspx (accessed 20 May 2015).

Ahram Online, 'Egypt Imposes Media Gag Order on Ansar Beit Al-Maqdis Case', *Ahram Online*, 21 February 2015, http://english.ahram.org.eg/NewsContent/1/64/123586/Egypt/Politics-/Egypt-imposes-media-gag-order-on-Ansar-Beit-AlMaqd.aspx (accessed 23 February 2015).

Ahram Online, 'Morsi's First 100 Days: A Report Card', *Ahram Online*, 9 October 2012, http://english.ahram.org.eg/NewsContent/1/140/55089/Egypt/The-Balance-Sheet/Morsis-first—days-A-report-card.aspx (accessed 20 May 2015).

Ajami, F. 'The End of Pan-Arabism', *Foreign Affairs*, Vol. 57:2, Winter 1978, pp. 355–73, https://www.foreignaffairs.com/articles/yemen/1978-12-01/end-pan-arabism (accessed 31 May 2015).

Al-Akayila, Dr Abdullah. Author interview, Amman, 22 June 1989.

Alami, A. 'Women Face Fight to Keep Their Rights in Tunisia', *New York Times*, 20 February 2013, http://www.nytimes.com/2013/02/21/world/middleeast/women-face-fight-to-keep-their-rights-in-tunisia.html (accessed 3 March 2015).

Al-Amir, M. 'Jordanian Muslim Brotherhood to Split from Egypt Parent: Sources', *Asharq al-Awsat*, 2 March 2015, http://www.aawsat.net/2015/03/article55341956/jordanian-muslim-brotherhood-to-split-from-egypt-parent-sources (accessed 12 May 2015).

Al-Anani, K. 'Future Remains Unclear for Egypt's Muslim Brotherhood', *Al-Monitor*, 17 April 2014, http://www.al-monitor.com/pulse/politics/2014/04/egypt-muslim-brotherhood-challenges-future.html (accessed 28 April 2015).

Al-Anani, K. *The Muslim Brotherhood after Morsi*, Doha: Arab Center for Research and Policy Studies, 2013, http://english.dohainstitute.org/release/eca3b305-1038-473b-a67e-b2a63af9ef21 (accessed 21 February 2015).

Al-Anani, K. 'The Salafi-Brotherhood Feud in Egypt', *Al-Monitor*, 21 February 2013, http://www.al-monitor.com/pulse/originals/2013/02/muslim-brotherhood-salafist-feud-in-egypt.html# (accessed 31 May 2015).

Al-Anani, K. 'The Young Brotherhood in Search of a New Path', *Current Trends in Islamist Ideology*, Vol. 9, October 2009, pp. 96–109, http://www.hudson.org/content/researchattachments/attachment/1306/al_anani_vol9.pdf (accessed 28 April 2015).

Bibliography **201**

Al-Ariqi, S. 'How Change Square Became the Birthplace of an Uprising', *Yemen Times*, 11 February 2014, http://www.yementimes.com/en/1754/report/3465/How-Change-Square-became-the-birthplace-of-an-uprising.htm (accessed 27 May 2015).

al-Athm, Yousef. Author interview, Amman, 20 June 1989.

Al-Badarin, B. 'Split in Jordan's "Brothers" as 7 Leaders Are Expelled', *Al-Quds Al-Arabi*, 15 February 2015, http://www.alquds.co.uk/?p=296147 (accessed 17 February 2015).

al-Banna, H. 'Toward the Light', BDIslam, May–June 1947, http://bdislam.com/manhaj/books/Towards%20the%20Light.pdf (accessed 26 March 2015).

al-Banna, H. 'To What Do We Invite Humanity?', *The Quran Blog*, https://thequranblog.files.wordpress.com/2008/06/_2_-to-what-do-we-invite-humanity.pdf (accessed 26 March 2015).

al-Banna, H. *Kitab ul Jihad*, n.p., n.d., p. 220, https://books.google.co.uk/books?id=wZALAwAAQBAJ&pg=PA219&dq (accessed 31 May 2015).

Albrecht, H. and Bishara, D. 'Back on Horseback: The Military and Political Transformation in Egypt', *Middle East Law and Governance*, Vol. 3:1–2, 2011, pp. 13–23, http://heinonline.org/HOL/Page?handle=hein.journals/measterna3&div=5&g_sent=1&collection=journals#17 (accessed 28 April 2015).

Al-Daameh, M. 'No Change in Jordan Muslim Brotherhood Status: PM', *Asharq al-Awsat*, 7 March 2015, http://www.aawsat.net/2015/03/article55342099/no-change-in-jordan-muslim-brotherhood-status-pm (accessed 7 March 2015).

Alexander, C. 'Tunisia's Protest Wave: Where It Comes From and What It Means for Ben Ali', *Foreign Policy*, 3 January 2011, http://foreignpolicy.com/2011/01/03/tunisias-protest-wave-where-it-comes-from-and-what-it-means/ (accessed 28 May 2015).

Alexandrani, I. 'The Politics of the Egypt-Gaza Buffer Zone', *Carnegie Endowment for International Peace*, 25 November 2014, http://carnegieendowment.org/sada/2014/11/25/politics-of-egypt-gaza-buffer-zone/hvdh (accessed 4 May 2015).

Al-Fathali, H. 'Ennahda's Ghannouchi Plays Mediator in Tunisia', *Al-Monitor*, 1 December 2014, http://www.al-monitor.com/pulse/politics/2014/12/ennahda-mediator-tunisia-president-elections-nidaa-tunis.html (accessed 2 February 2015).

Alfred, C. 'Who's Behind the Islamic State's Propaganda on Twitter?', *Huffington Post*, 6 March 2015, http://www.huffingtonpost.com/2015/03/06/isis-twitter-census_n_6817308.html (accessed 28 May 2015).

Al-Hayat, 'The Fall of Amran Robs "Brotherhood" and Puts Huthi Stronghold at the Gates of Sana', *Al-Hayat*, 20 July 2014, http://alhayat.com/Articles/3683172 (accessed 14 August 2014).

Ali, M. 'Finally, Egypt's Parties Set to Begin the Battle for Post-Mubarak Parliament', *Ahram Online*, 25 October 2011, http://english.ahram.org.eg/News/25030.aspx (accessed 3 March 2015).

Al-Jabari, R. 'Jordan and the Brotherhood: A Soft Divorce?', *As-Safir*, 28 November 2014, http://assafir.com/Article/1/386832 (accessed 4 March 2015).

Al-Jalil, W. 'Yemen's Political Stalemate Persists, as Houthis Gain Influence', *Al-Monitor*, 25 May 2014, http://www.al-monitor.com/pulse/politics/2014/05/yemen-political-stalemate-houthis-gain-influence.html (accessed 21 April 2015).

Al Jazeera, 'Ansar al-Sharia Blamed for Tunisia Killings', *Al Jazeera*, 27 August 2013, http://www.aljazeera.com/news/africa/2013/08/2013827131811488516.html (accessed 2 September 2013).

Al Jazeera, 'Egyptian Court Declares Hamas a "Terrorist" Entity', *Al Jazeera*, 28 February 2012, http://www.aljazeera.com/news/2015/02/egyptian-court-declares-hamas-terrorist-group-150228122454458.html (accessed 1 March 2015).

Al Jazeera, 'Global Condemnation of Egypt Crackdown', *Al Jazeera*, 15 August 2013, http://www.aljazeera.com/news/middleeast/2013/08/201381505130985967.html (accessed 20 April 2015).

202 Bibliography

Al Jazeera, 'Profile: Sheikh Sadiq al-Ahmar', *Al Jazeera*, 26 May 2011, http://www.aljazeera.com/indepth/features/2011/05/2011526112624960404.html (accessed 19 May 2015).

Al Jazeera, 'The Houthis Reject the Appointment of bin Mabarak as Prime Minster', *Al Jazeera*, 8 October 2014, http://goo.gl/D0s8dw (accessed 30 May 2015).

Al Jazeera, 'Who's Who in Yemen's Opposition?', *Al Jazeera*, 10 March 2014, http://www.aljazeera.com/indepth/spotlight/yemen/2011/02/2011228141453986337.html (accessed 29 May 2015).

Al Jazeera, 'Yemen's Saleh Declares an Alliance with Houthis, *Al Jazeera*, 11 May 2015, http://www.aljazeera.com/news/2015/05/cloneofcloneofcloneofstrikes-yemen-saada-breach-150510143647004.html (accessed 30 May 2015).

Al Jazeera and Agencies, 'Egypt's Military Shuts Down News Channels', *Al Jazeera*, 4 July 2013, http://www.aljazeera.com/news/middleeast/2013/07/2013740531685326.html (accessed 31 May 2015).

Al Jazeera and Agencies, 'Egypt Vows Strong Response to Sinai Attack', *Al Jazeera*, 6 August 2012, http://www.aljazeera.com/news/middleeast/2012/08/20128523429347102.html (accessed 22 February 2015).

Al Jazeera English, 'Talk to Al Jazeera – Mohamed Saad Katatni: "Not a Religious Party"', *Al Jazeera English*, 27 November 2011, https://www.youtube.com/watch?v=aXVr00yJ420 (accessed 15 April 2015).

Allers, S. '[CT] MORE EGYPT/CT/CYBER – Anonymous to Target Egypt's Muslim Brotherhood', *Wikileaks*, 9 November 2011, https://wikileaks.org/gifiles/docs/12/1276191_-ct-more-egypt-ct-cyber-anonymous-to-target-egypt-s-muslim.html (accessed 1 June 2014).

Alley, A.L. 'The Rules of the Game: Unpacking Patronage Politics in Yemen', *Middle East Journal*, Vol. 64:3, Summer 2010, pp. 385–409, http://www.jstor.org/stable/40783106 (accessed 8 May 2015).

Alley, A.L. 'Yemen Changes Everything . . . and Nothing', *Journal of Democracy*, Vol. 24:4, October 2013, pp. 74–85, http://muse.jhu.edu/journals/journal_of_democracy/v024/24.4.alley.html (accessed 30 May 2015).

Al-Moshki, A.I. 'Saudi Arabia Blacklists Yemeni Groups', *Yemen Times*, 13 March 2014, http://www.yementimes.com/en/1763/news/3590/Saudi-Arabia-blacklists-Yemeni-groups.htm (accessed 27 May 2015).

Al-Muslimi, F. 'A New Deal in Yemen?', *Carnegie Endowment for International Peace*, 31 October 2014, http://carnegieendowment.org/syriaincrisis/?fa=57091 (accessed 31 May 2015).

Al-Naimat, T. 'Zamzam and the Jordanian Brotherhood', *Carnegie Endowment for International Peace*, 4 February 2014, http://carnegieendowment.org/sada/2014/02/04/zamzam-and-jordanian-brotherhood/h03b (accessed 24 February 2015).

Al Quds al-Arabi, 'MB Guide in Red Death Row Outfit', *Al-Quds al-Arabi*, 20 April 2015, http://www.alquds.co.uk/?p=329132 (accessed 21 April 2015).

Al-Resalah, 'Bardawil: Egyptians Rule Out Any Attack Against Gaza', *Al-Resalah*, 23 February 2015, http://alresalah.ps/ar/post/110028/البردويل-نستبعد-أي-هجوم-مصري-ضد-غزة (accessed 23 February 2015).

Al-Resalah, 'Blair's Visit to Gaza Is to Test Hamas' Reactions Internationally', *Al-Resalah*, 23 February 2015, http://english.alresalah.ps/en/post.php?id=4532 (accessed 23 February 2015).

Al-Resalah, 'Hamas: Rabah's Comments Interference in Egyptian Affairs', *Al-Resalah*, 23 February 2015, http://alresalah.ps/ar/post/110025/حماس-تصريحات-رباح-تدخل-في-الشأن-المصري (accessed 23 February 2015).

Al-Resalah, 'Hamas Rejects Blair's Conditions', *Al-Resalah*, 23 February 2015, http://english.alresalah.ps/en/post.php?id=4528 (accessed 23 February 2015).

Al-Sabiri, A. 'Al-Nahda Leader Ghannouchi: Tunisia Heading Towards "Muslim democratic state"', *Al-Akhbar English*, 29 September 2014, http://english.al-akhbar.com/node/21749 (accessed 7 May 2015).

Al-Sakkaf, N. 'The Politicization of Yemen's Youth Revolution', *Carnegie Endowment for International Peace*, 27 April 2011, http://carnegieendowment.org/2011/04/27/politicization-of-yemen-s-youth-revolution/6b7t (accessed 21 April 2015).

Al Sharif, O. 'Is Jordan's "Arab Spring" Over?', *Al-Monitor*, 15 September 2013, http://www.al-monitor.com/pulse/originals/2013/09/jordan-arab-spring-over.html (accessed 24 February 2015).

Al-Sharif, O. 'Jordan Takes Sides in Islamist Rift', *Al-Monitor*, 12 May 2015, http://www.al-monitor.com/pulse/originals/2015/05/jordan-government-side-muslim-brotherhood-society-split.html# (accessed 29 May 2015).

Al Sharif, O. 'Zamzam Rattles Jordan's Muslim Brothers', *Al-Monitor*, 6 October 2013, http://www.al-monitor.com/pulse/originals/2013/10/zamzam-jordan-brotherhood-sharif.html (accessed 24 February 2015).

Al-Shrhabi, A.M. 'Houthi Victory Is Defeat for Yemen's Islah', *Al Monitor*, 29 September 2014, http://www.al-monitor.com/pulse/politics/2014/09/yemen-coup-agreement-political-shift-houthi-saleh-end-wars.html# (accessed 29 May 2015).

Al-Smadi, T. 'JMB Investigate Existence of Secret Organization', *al-Hayat*, 1 July 2014, http://alhayat.com/Articles/3322248/--داخل—سري-تنظيم—بوجود-يحقّقون—الأردن-إخوان الجماعة (accessed 9 December 2014).

Alvdellat, M. 'Majeed Thunaibat for "New Arab": "Brotherhood" Ozajua State and Missed the Train', *al-Araby al-Jadid*, 13 May 2015, http://www.alaraby.co.uk/politics/2015/5/12/القطار-ووفاتهم-الدولة-عجوا-أز-الإخوان-الجديد-العربي-الذنيبات-المجيد-عبد (accessed 15 May 2015).

Aly, A.M.S. *Middle East Brief: Post-revolution Egyptian Foreign Policy*, Waltham, MA: Brandeis University Crown Center for Middle East Studies, 2014, http://www.brandeis.com/crown/publications/meb/MEB86.pdf (accessed 31 May 2015).

Al Yafai, F. 'A Losing Battle as Ennahda Tries to Define Tunisian Women's Role', *National UAE*, 21 August 2012, http://www.thenational.ae/thenationalconversation/comment/a-losing-battle-as-ennahda-tries-to-define-tunisian-womens-role (accessed 3 March 2015).

Al-Yemeni, A.A.H. *The Dynamic of Democratisation – Political Parties in Yemen*, Bonn: Friedrich-Ebert-Stiftung, 2003, http://library.fes.de/pdf-files/iez/01459.pdf (accessed 21 April 2015).

Amara, T. 'Tunisia Approves Secular-Islamist Coalition Government', *Reuters*, 5 February 2015, http://www.reuters.com/article/2015/02/05/us-tunisia-government-idUSKBN0L91KB20150205 (accessed 14 May 2015).

Amara, T. 'Tunisia's Islamist Party Agrees to Join Coalition Government', *Reuters*, 1 February 2015, http://www.reuters.com/article/2015/02/01/us-tunisia-politics-idUSKBN0L51OB20150201 (accessed 29 May 2015).

Amara, T. 'Two Dead as Protesters Attack U.S. Embassy in Tunisia', *Reuters*, 14 September 2012, http://uk.reuters.com/article/2012/09/14/us-protests-tunisia-school-idUSBRE88D18020120914 (accessed 18 May 2015).

Amirah-Fernandez, H. 'Jordan: A Delicate Domestic and Regional Equilibrium', in F. Brichs (ed.) *Political Regimes in the Arab World: Society and the Exercise of Power*, Abingdon, Oxon: Routledge, 2013.

Amis, J. 'The Jordanian Brotherhood in the Arab Spring', *Current Trends in Islamist Ideology*, Vol. 14, January 2013, http://www.hudson.org/content/researchattachments/attachment/1145/20130124_ct14final.pdf (accessed 24 February 2015).

204 Bibliography

Angrist, M.P. 'Understanding the Success of Mass Civic Protest in Tunisia', *Middle East Journal*, Vol. 67:4, Autumn 2013, pp. 547–64, http://muse.jhu.edu.queens.ezp1.qub.ac.uk/journals/the_middle_east_journal/v067/67.4.angrist.html (accessed 28 May 2015).Anonymous, 'Operation Brotherhood Takedown Is Engaged', *Anonymous DGAF*, 7 November 2011, https://www.youtube.com/watch?v=s6MWJ2YYitc (accessed 1 June 2015).

Anonymous blogger, n.t., *Al Kotla*, n.d., http://www.alkotla.ps (accessed 19 November 2012).

Arabiyat, A.L. Author interview, Amman, 5 April 1997.

Asal, V., et al. 'Gender Ideologies and Forms of Contentious Mobilization in the Middle East', *Journal of Peace Research*, Vol. 50:3, May 2013, pp. 305–18, http://jpr.sagepub.com/content/50/3/305.full.pdf+html (accessed 28 April 2015).

Associated Press, 'Egypt Declares Muslim Brotherhood a Terrorist Group', *Guardian*, 25 December 2013, http://www.theguardian.com/world/2013/dec/25/egypt-declares-muslim-brotherhood-terrorist-group (accessed 4 March 2015).

Associated Press, 'Egypt Shuts Down Muslim Brotherhood Newspaper', *Huffington Post*, 25 September 2013, http://www.huffingtonpost.com/2013/09/25/egypt-shuts-down-muslim-brotherhood-newspaper_n_3987152.html (accessed 30 May 2015).

Associated Press, 'Head of Hamas, Khaled Mashaal, to Step Down', *Guardian*, 25 September 2012, http://www.theguardian.com/world/2012/sep/25/hamas-khaled-mashaal-step-down (accessed 30 April 2015).

Associated Press, 'Mohammed Badei, Egypt Muslim Brotherhood Leader, Blasts Israel–Gaza Peace Deal', *Huffington Post*, 22 November 2012, http://www.huffingtonpost.com/2012/11/22/mohammed-badei-egypt-muslim-brotherhood-israel-gaza-peace_n_2175371.html (accessed 20 May 2015).

Associated Press, 'UAE Backs Saudis with Muslim Brotherhood Blacklist', *Fox News*, 9 March 2014, http://www.foxnews.com/world/2014/03/09/united-arab-emirates-backs-saudi-arabia-move-to-label-muslim-brotherhood/ (accessed 30 May 2015).

Atlas, T. 'Obama Caught Between Polarized Allies in Egypt Crisis', *Bloomberg*, 19 August 2013, http://www.bloomberg.com/news/articles/2013-08-18/obama-caught-between-polarized-allies-in-egypt-crisis (accessed 20 April 2015).

Avni, B. 'Is This the Last Stand for Hamas?', *Newsweek*, 8 July 2014, http://www.newsweek.com/last-stand-hamas-257942 (accessed 28 May 2015).

Awad, M. and Brown, N.J. 'Mutual Escalation in Egypt', *Washington Post*, 9 February 2015, http://www.washingtonpost.com/blogs/monkey-cage/wp/2015/02/09/mutual-escalation-in-egypt/ (accessed 20 May 2015).

Awad, M. and Dixon, H. 'Special Report: Inside the Egyptian Revolution', *Reuters*, 13 April 2011, http://www.reuters.com/article/2011/04/13/us-egypt-revolution-idUSTRE73C18E20110413 (accessed 28 April 2015).

Awad, M. and El-Madany, S. 'In U-turn, Egypt's Brotherhood Names Presidential Candidate', *Reuters*, 31 March 2012, http://uk.reuters.com/article/2012/03/31/uk-egypt-brotherhood-presidency-idUKBRE82U0DQ20120331 (accessed 16 April 2015).

Ayubi, N. *Political Islam: Religion and Politics in the Arab World*, London: Routledge, 2003.

Azzam, M. 'There Is Still Time to Side with Those Committed to Democracy in Egypt', *Guardian*, 15 August 2013, http://www.theguardian.com/commentisfree/2013/aug/15/democracy-egypt-irony-muslim-brotherhood (accessed 15 August 2013).

Bakker, E. and Meijer, R. (eds) *The Muslim Brotherhood in Europe*, London: Hurst, 2012.

Bakri, N. and Goodman, J.D. 'Thousands in Yemen Protest Against the Government', *New York Times*, 27 January 2011, http://www.nytimes.com/2011/01/28/world/middleeast/28yemen.html (accessed 30 May 2015).

Balousha, H. 'Hamas Mitigates Fallout after Muslim Brotherhood Defeat', *Al-Monitor*, 18 July 2013, http://www.al-monitor.com/pulse/originals/2013/07/gaza-hamas-egypt-political-crisis.html#ixzz3YuMeLmXR (accessed 7 May 2015).

Bar, S. *The Muslim Brotherhood in Jordan*, Tel Aviv: Moshe Dayan Center for Middle Eastern and African Studies, 1998.

Barany, Z. 'Comparing the Arab Revolts: The Role of the Military', *Journal of Democracy*, Vol. 22:4, Oct. 2011, pp. 28–39.

Bardhan, S. 'Egypt, Islamists, and the Internet: The Case of the Muslim Brotherhood and Its Rhetoric of Dialectics in Ikhwanweb', *Digest of Middle East Studies*, Vol. 23:2, Fall 2014, pp. 235–61, http://dx.doi.org/10.1111/dome.12049 (accessed 30 May 2015).

Barnea, N. 'Entire World Is Responsible for Gaza's Fate, Says Blair', *Yedioth Ahronoth*, 21 February 2015, http://www.ynetnews.com/articles/0,7340,L-4629149,00.html (accessed 23 February 2015).

Bassiouni, M. 'Ansar Bayt Maqdis Joins Islamic State', *al-Safir*, 11 November 2014, http://assafir.com/Article/1/383372 (accessed 27 May 2015).

Bayoumi, A. 'Egypt's Salafi Party Faces Growing Isolation', *Al Jazeera*, 18 May 2014, http://www.aljazeera.com/news/middleeast/2014/05/egypt-salafi-party-faces-growing-isolation-2014514111139164795.html (accessed 31 May 2015).

BBC News, 'Egypt Army Arrests Key Muslim Brotherhood Figures', *BBC News*, 4 July 2013, http://www.bbc.co.uk/news/world-middle-east-23189180 (accessed 16 April 2015).

BBC News, 'Egypt Court Bans Muslim Brotherhood "Activities"', *BBC News*, 23 September 2013, http://www.bbc.co.uk/news/world-middle-east-24208933 (accessed 30 May 2015).

BBC News, 'Egyptian State TV Explains Court Verdict Banning Brotherhood Activities,' *BBC Monitoring International Reports*, 23 September 2013.

BBC News, 'Egypt Muslim Brotherhood "Quits Election"', *BBC News*, 1 December 2010, http://www.bbc.co.uk/news/world-middle-east-11890726 (accessed 8 May 2015).

BBC News, 'Egypt's Brotherhood Expands Media Machine', *BBC Monitoring International Reports*, 8 December 2014, http://www.bbc.co.uk/monitoring/egypts-brotherhood-expands-media-machine (accessed 31 May 2015).

BBC News, 'Egypt's Islamist Parties Win Elections to Parliament', *BBC News*, 21 January 2012, http://www.bbc.co.uk/news/world-middle-east-16665748 (accessed 30 May 2015).

BBC News, 'Gaza Crisis: Toll of Operations in Gaza', *BBC News*, 1 September 2014, http://www.bbc.co.uk/news/world-middle-east-28439404 (accessed 28 May 2015).

BBC News, 'Saudi Arabia Declares Muslim Brotherhood "Terrorist Group"', *BBC News*, 7 March 2014, http://www.bbc.co.uk/news/world-middle-east-26487092 (accessed 9 September 2014).

BBC News, 'Top Yemeni General, Ali Mohsen, Backs Opposition', *BBC News*, 21 March 2011, http://www.bbc.co.uk/news/world-middle-east-12804552 (accessed 29 May 2015).

BBC News, 'Tunisia's Islamist Ennahda Party Wins Historic Poll', *BBC News*, 27 October 2011, http://www.bbc.co.uk/news/world-africa-15487647 (accessed 5 May 2015).

Bel Aiba, I. 'Ennahda Leader Says "Tunisia Model" Way to Defeat Islamic State', *Agence France-Presse*, 23 October 2014, http://news.yahoo.com/ennahda-leader-says-tunisia-model-way-defeat-islamic-000837755.html (accessed 7 May 2015).

Bellin, E. 'Reconsidering the Robustness of Authoritarianism in the Middle East: Lessons from the Arab Spring', *Comparative Politics*, Vol. 44:2, January 2012, pp. 127–49, http://dx.doi.org/10.5129/001041512798838021 (accessed 29 May 2015).

206 Bibliography

Ben Bouazza, B. 'Tunisia Manouba University Students Face Off Over Islamic Veil on Campus', *Associated Press*, 1 April 2012, http://www.huffingtonpost.com/2012/01/04/tunisia-manouba-university-veil_n_1184117.html (accessed 7 May 2015).

Ben Bouazza, B. 'Tunisia: Attackers Set Fire to Muslim Saint Shrine', *Associated Press*, 16 October 2012, http://news.yahoo.com/tunisia-attackers-set-fire-muslim-saint-shrine-174125155.html (accessed 18 May 2015).

Ben Khalifa, G. 'The Secret of the Salafists' Appeal in Tunisia', *Al-Monitor*, 1 May 2013, http://www.al-monitor.com/pulse/culture/2013/05/disadvantaged-tunisian-youth-embrace-salafism.html#ixzz3bTpwvZm0 (accessed 28 May 2015).

Berkley Center for Religion, Peace & World Affairs, 'Al-Wasat Islamic Party', *Georgetown University*, 2014, http://berkleycenter.georgetown.edu/organizations/al-wasat-islamic-party (accessed 12 May 2015).

Black, I. 'UN Envoy: Anti-Hamas Rhetoric Undermines Democracy', *Guardian*, 13 June 2007, http://www.theguardian.com/world/2007/jun/13/israel5 (accessed 28 May 2015).

Bohn, L.E. 'The Muslim Brotherhood Takes Twitter', *Foreign Policy*, 18 November 2011, http://mideast.foreignpolicy.com/posts/2011/11/18/the_muslim_brotherhood_takes_twitter (accessed 27 May 2015).

Borger, J. 'Tunisian President Vows to Punish Rioters after Worst Unrest in a Decade', *Guardian*, 29 December 2010, http://www.theguardian.com/world/2010/dec/29/tunisian-president-vows-punish-rioters (accessed 28 May 2015).

Boukhars, A., et al. 'The Egypt Effect: Sharpened Tensions, Reshuffled Alliances', *Carnegie Endowment for International Peace*, 13 February 2014, http://carnegieendowment.org/2014/02/13/egypt-effect-sharpened-tensions-reshuffled-alliances# (accessed 30 May 2015).

Boulby, M. 'The Islamic Challenge: Tunisia Since Independence', *Third World Quarterly*, Vol. 10:2, April 1988, http://www.jstor.org/stable/3992658 (accessed 7 May 2015).

Boulby, M. *The Muslim Brotherhood and the Kings of Jordan, 1945–1993*, Atlanta: Scholars Press, 1999.

Brooks, R. 'Abandoned at the Palace: Why the Tunisian Military Defected from the Ben Ali Regime in January 2011', *Journal of Strategic Studies*, Vol. 36:2, April 2013, pp. 205–20.

Brown, B. 'Egypt Crowds Cheer Tahrir Square Military Flypast', *BBC News*, 4 July 2013, http://www.bbc.co.uk/news/world-middle-east-23190817 (accessed 16 April 2015).

Brown, J. *Salafis and Sufis in Egypt*, Washington, DC: Carnegie Endowment for International Peace, 2011, http://carnegieendowment.org/files/salafis_sufis.pdf (accessed 7 May 2015).

Brown, L.C. 'The Islamic Reformist Movement in North Africa', *Journal of Modern African Studies*, Vol. 2:1, March 1964, pp. 55–63, http://dx.doi.org/10.1017/S0022278X00003669 (accessed 7 May 2015).

Brown, N.J. 'Egypt's Failed Transition', *Journal of Democracy*, Vol. 24:4, October 2013, pp. 45–58, http://www.journalofdemocracy.org/sites/default/files/Brown-24-4.pdf (accessed 8 January 2015).

Brown, N.J. 'Political Islam Becomes Less Political', *Immanent Frame*, 11 March 2014, http://blogs.ssrc.org/tif/2014/03/11/political-islam-becomes-less-political/ (accessed 20 May 2015).

Brownlee, J. *Democracy Prevention: The Politics of the U.S.-Egyptian Alliance*, New York: Cambridge University Press, 2012.

Burgat, F. 'Les islamistes au révélateur de la crise', *Annuaire de l'Afrique du Nord*, Vol. 31, 1992, pp. 201–13, http://aan.mmsh.univ-aix.fr/Pdf/AAN-1992-31_45.pdf (accessed 28 May 2015).

Burrowes, R.D. and Kasper, C.M. 'The Salih Regime and the Need for a Credible Opposition', *Middle East Journal*, Vol. 61:2, Summer 2007, pp. 263–80, http://www.jstor.org/stable/4330388 (accessed 8 May 2015).

Bibliography **207**

Calvert, J. *Islamism: A Documentary and Reference Guide*, Westport: Greenwood, 2008.

Calvert, J. *Sayyid Qutb and the Origins of Radical Islamism*, New York: Oxford University Press, 2009.

Campbell, L. 'Yemen: The Tribal Islamists', in R. Wright (ed.) *The Islamists Are Coming: Who They Really Are*, Herndon, VA: United States Institute of Peace Press, 2012, http://theislamistsarecoming.wilsoncenter.org/islamists/node/23190 (accessed 27 May 2015).

Carapico, S. 'Elections and Mass Politics in Yemen', *Middle East Report*, Vol. 23:185, November/December 1993, http://www.merip.org/mer/mer185/elections-mass-politics-yemen (accessed 28 April 2015).

Carapico, S. 'No Exit: Yemen's Existential Crisis', in D. McMurray and A. Ufheil-Somers (eds) *The Arab Revolts: Dispatches on Militant Democracy in the Middle East*, Bloomington: Indiana University Press, 2013.

Caton, S.C. (ed.) *Yemen*, Santa Barbara, CA: ABC-CLIO, 2013.

Cavatorta, F. and Merone, F. 'Moderation through Exclusion? The Journey of the Tunisian Ennahda from Fundamentalist to Conservative Party', *Democratization*, Vol. 20:5, 2013, pp. 857–75, http://dx.doi.org/10.1080/13510347.2013.801255 (accessed 28 May 2015).

Charrad, M.M. 'Cultural Diversity within Islam: Veils and Laws in Tunisia', in H.L. Bodman and N. Tohidi (eds) *Women in Muslim Societies: Diversity within Unity*, Boulder, CO: Lynne Rienner, 1998.

Chehab, Z. *Inside Hamas: The Untold Story of Militants, Martyrs and Spies*, London and New York: I.B. Tauris, 2007.

Clark, J. *Islam, Charity, and Activism: Middle-Class Networks and Social Welfare in Egypt, Jordan, and Yemen*, Bloomington: Indiana University Press, 2004.

Claudet, S. and Jadallah, S. 'Will Morsi Offer Change for Gaza?', *Al-Monitor*, 9 September 2012, http://www.al-monitor.com/pulse/originals/2012/al-monitor/do-not-publish-hed-to-come.html (accessed 30 April 2015).

Committee to Protect Journalists, 'Al-Jazeera Station Raided, 3 Others Shut in Egypt', *Committee to Protect Journalists*, 3 July 2013, http://www.cpj.org/2013/07/al-jazeera-raided-3-others-shut-egypt.php (accessed 30 May 2015).

Coughlin, C. 'Iran Rekindles Relations with Hamas', *Wall Street Journal*, 21 April 2015, http://www.wsj.com/articles/iran-rekindles-relations-with-hamas-1429658562 (accessed 4 May 2015).

Cunningham, E. 'Egypt's Military Backed Government Declares Muslim Brotherhood a Terrorist Organization', *Washington Post*, 25 December 2013, http://www.washingtonpost.com/world/middle_east/egypts-military-backed-government-declares-muslim-brotherhood-a-terrorist-organization/2013/12/25/7cf075ca-6da0-11e3-aecc-85cb037b7236_story.html (accessed 30 May 2015).

Dandashly, A. 'The EU Response to Regime Change in the Wake of the Arab Revolt: Differential Implementation', *Journal of European Integration*, Vol. 37:1, 2015, pp. 37–56, http://dx.doi.org/10.1080/07036337.2014.975988 (accessed 28 April 2015).

David, A. 'The Revolt of Jordan's Military Veterans', *Foreign Policy*, 16 June 2010, http://mideast.foreignpolicy.com/articles/2010/06/15/the_revolt_of_jordans_military_veterans (accessed 12 November 2013).

Davies, M. 'Egypt Analysts Optimistic for Post-Morsi Economy', *BBC News*, 5 July 2013, http://www.bbc.co.uk/news/business-23183838 (accessed 16 April 2015).

Davies, W. 'Tunisia: President Zine al-Abidine Ben Ali Forced Out', *BBC News*, 15 January 2011, http://www.bbc.co.uk/news/world-africa-12195025 (accessed 23 May 2015).

Davis, J. 'The Re-emergence of the Jihadist Salafis in Jordan', *Jadaliyya*, 28 July 2011, http://arabic.jadaliyya.com/pages/index/2256/the-reemergence-of-the-jihadist-salafis-in-jordan (accessed 3 March 2015).

208 Bibliography

Day, S.W. *Regionalism and Rebellion in Yemen: A Troubled National Union*, Cambridge: Cambridge University Press, 2012.

Dehghanpisheh, B. 'Mohammad Badie on Egypt's Muslim Brotherhood', *Newsweek*, 29 November 2010, http://www.newsweek.com/mohammad-badie-egypts-muslim-brotherhood-70113 (accessed 1 November 2013).

Dekmejian, R.H. *Islam in Revolution: Fundamentalism in the Arab World*, Syracuse, NY: Syracuse University Press, 1995.

Dessouki, A.E.H. (ed.) *Islamic Resurgence in the Arab World*, New York: Praeger, 1982.

Dickens, C. *A Tale of Two Cities*, London: Chapman & Hall, 1898.

Diehl, J. 'Tunisia Boldly Embraces Democracy', *Washington Post*, 26 October 2014, http://www.washingtonpost.com/opinions/jackson-diehl-tunisia-boldly-embraces-democracy/2014/10/26/8d86b19a-5adc-11e4-b812-38518ae74c67_story.html (accessed 26 May 2015).

Dresch, P. *Tribes, Government, and History in Yemen*, New York: Oxford University Press, 1989.

Dresch, P. and Haykel, B. 'Stereotypes and Political Styles: Islamists and Tribesfolk in Yemen', *International Journal of Middle East Studies*, Vol. 27:4, November 1995, 405–31, http://journals.cambridge.org/article_S0020743800062486 (accessed 8 May 2015).

Droz-Vincent, P. 'From Fighting Formal Wars to Maintaining Civil Peace?', *International Journal of Middle East Studies*, Vol. 43, 2011, pp. 392–4.

Dunn, M.C. 'The Political and the Religious in the Modern History of the Maghrib', in J. Ruedy (ed.) *Islamism and Secularism in North Africa*, Houndmills and London: Macmillan and the Center for Contemporary Arab Studies, 1994.

Durac, V. *Islamic Modernism in Contemporary Egypt: An Evaluation*, PhD thesis, Queen's University Belfast, 2000.

Durac, V. 'The Joint Meeting Parties and the Politics of Opposition in Yemen', *British Journal of Middle Eastern Studies*, Vol. 38:3, December 2011, pp. 343–65, http://dx.doi.org/10.1080/13530194.2011.621697 (accessed 27 May 2015).

Economist, 'The Secularist Comeback', *Economist*, 29 October 2014, http://www.economist.com/news/middle-east-and-africa/21628920-surprising-defeat-islamist-nahda-party-secularists-comeback (accessed 26 May 2015).

Edwards, R.D. 'Dreaming of an Islamist Ireland', *Standpoint*, 25 May 2010, http://standpointmag.co.uk/node/2937/full (accessed 30 May 2015).

El-Amrani, T. and Lindsey, U. 'Tunisia Moves to the Next Stage', *Middle East Research and Information Project*, 8 November 2011, http://www.merip.org/mero/mero110811 (accessed 20 May 2015).

El-Awaisi, A. *The Muslim Brothers and the Palestine Question, 1928–47*, London: I.B. Tauris, 1998.

El-Behairy, N. and Hamed, S. 'Timeline of Morsi and the Judiciary: One Year in Power', *Daily News Egypt*, 29 June 2013, http://www.dailynewsegypt.com/2013/06/29/timeline-of-morsi-and-the-judiciary-one-year-in-power/ (accessed 15 April 2015).

Eldar, S. 'Dahlan-Hamas Reconciliation to Open Doors in Egypt', *Al-Monitor*, 7 March 2014, http://www.al-monitor.com/pulse/en/originals/2014/03/mohammed-dahlan-fatah-hamas-reconciliation-meeting-egypt.html (accessed 4 May 2015).

Eldar, S. 'Hamas Isolated After Coup in Egypt', *Al-Monitor*, 4 July 2013, http://www.al-monitor.com/pulse/originals/2013/07/fall-egyptian-brotherhood-trouble-hamas.html# (accessed 30 April 2015).

El-Dine, C.C. *Fragile Alliances in Egypt's Post Revolutionary Order: The Military and Its Partners*, Berlin: Stiftung Wissenschaft und Politik (German Institute for International and Security Affairs), 2014, http://www.swp-berlin.org/fileadmin/contents/products/comments/2014C46_chams_el_dine.pdf (accessed 30 May 2015).

El-Din Shahin, E. 'Sentenced to Death in Egypt', *Atlantic*, 19 May 2015, http://www.theatlantic.com/international/archive/2015/05/death-sentence-egypt-emad-shahin/393590/ (accessed 28 May 2015).

El-Din Shahin, E. 'The Egyptian Revolution: The Power of Mass Mobilization and the Spirit of Tahrir Square', in R.R. Larémont (ed.) *Revolution, Revolt, and Reform in North Africa: The Arab Spring and Beyond*, Abingdon, Oxon and New York: Routledge, 2014.

Eleiba, A. 'Interview: Mohammed Qahtan, Senior Member of Yemen's Islah', *Ahram Online*, 27 November 2014, http://english.ahram.org.eg/NewsContent/2/8/116588/World/Region/Interview-Mohammed-Qahtan,-senior-member-of-Yemens.aspx (accessed 27 May 2015).

El-Errian, E. 'What the Muslim Brothers Want', *New York Times*, 9 February 2011, http://www.nytimes.com/2011/02/10/opinion/10erian.html (accessed 14 April 2015).

El Gamal, R. 'UAE Lists Muslim Brotherhood as Terrorist Group', *Reuters*, 15 November 2014, http://www.reuters.com/article/2014/11/15/us-emirates-politics-brotherhood-idUSKCN0IZ0OM20141115 (accessed 4 March 2015).

El-Ghobashy, M. 'The Metamorphosis of the Egyptian Muslim Brothers', *International Journal of Middle East Studies*, Vol. 37:3, August 2005, pp. 373–95, http://dx.doi.org/10.1017/S0020743805052128 (accessed 30 May 2015).

El-Haddad, G. 'Gehad El-Haddad', Twitter post, 12 September 2013, https://twitter.com/gelhaddad (accessed 27 May 2015).

El-Issawi, F. 'Islamists of Tunisia: Reconciling National Contradictions', *London School of Economics*, 13 April 2012, http://blogs.lse.ac.uk/ideas/2012/04/islamists-of-tunisia-reconciling-national-contradictions/ (accessed 7 May 2015).

El-Shenawi, E. 'Four-Finger Salute: Egypt Rivals Use 'Rabaa Hand' to Turn Facebook Yellow', *Al Arabiya*, 22 August 2013, http://english.alarabiya.net/en/media/2013/08/21/Four-finger-salute-Egypt-rivals-use-Rabaa-symbol-to-turn-Facebook-yellow.html (accessed 30 May 2015).

El-Sherif, A. *The Muslim Brotherhood and the Future of Political Islam in Egypt*, Washington, DC: Carnegie Endowment for International Peace, 2014, http://carnegieendowment.org/files/mb_future_egypt1.pdf (accessed 28 April 2015).

Enayat, H. *Modern Islamic Political Thought*, London: I.B. Tauris, 2005.

Ennarah, K.M. 'The End of Reciprocity: The Muslim Brotherhood and the Security Sector', *South Atlantic Quarterly*, Vol. 113:2, 2014, http://saq.dukejournals.org/content/113/2/407.full.pdf+html (accessed March 24, 2015).

Esparza, L. 'Sheik Hashim Al Ahmar: One Year after Hasaba.English.', YouTube video, posted 2 June 2012, https://www.youtube.com/watch?v=1TajuCbSJYA (accessed 19 May 2015).

Esposito, J.L. *Islam and Politics*, 3rd ed., Syracuse, NY: Syracuse University Press, 1991.

Esposito, J.L. *Islam: The Straight Path*, New York: Oxford University Press, 1988.

Esposito, J.L. *The Islamic Threat: Myth or Reality?*, 3rd ed., New York: Oxford University Press, 1999.

Esposito, J.L. (ed.) *Voices of Resurgent Islam*, New York: Oxford University Press, 1983.

ES Press, 'The Houthi-Islahi Conflict and Its Danger for the Future of Yemen,' *Wefaq Press*, 8 September 2014, http://wefaqpress.net/news_details.php?sid=19125 (accessed 30 May 2015).

Ezzat, D. 'Egyptian Islamists, Along with NDP, Campaign Hard for a "Yes" Vote on Constitutional Amendments', *Ahram Online*, 17 March 2011, http://english.ahram.org.eg/NewsContent/1/64/7971/Egypt/Politics-/Egyptian-Islamists,-along-with-NDP,-campaign-hard-.aspx (accessed 14 November 2014).

Fahim, K. 'Yemen's Opposition May Be Caught by Its Own Double Game,' *New York Times*, 2 December 2011, http://www.nytimes.com/2011/12/03/world/middleeast/yemens-opposition-party-islah-faces-credibility-gap.html?_r=1 (accessed 30 May 2015).

210 Bibliography

Fahim, K. and El-Naggar, M. 'Violent Clashes Mark Protests Against Mubarak's Rule', *New York Times*, 25 January 2011, http://www.nytimes.com/2011/01/26/world/middleeast/26egypt. html (accessed 7 May 2015).

Farag, M. 'The Muslim Sisters and the January 25th Revolution,' *Journal of International Women's Studies*, Vol. 13:5, October 2012, pp. 228–37, http://vc.bridgew.edu/jiws/vol13/iss5/19 (accessed 31 May 2015).

Farham, Ishaq. Author interview, Amman, 5 April 1997.

Fattah, K. 'Yemen: A Social Intifada in the Republic of Sheikhs', *Middle East Policy*, Vol. 18:3, Fall 2011, pp. 79–85, http://www.mepc.org/journal/middle-east-policy-archives/yemen-social-intifada-republic-sheikhs (accessed 27 May 2015).

Federation of Islamic Organisations in Europe, 'Muslims of Europe Charter', *Federation of Islamic Organisations in Europe*, 2008, http://www.cie.ugent.be/documenten/muslim_charter.pdf (accessed 26 May 2015).

Filiu, J.P. *The Arab Revolution: Ten Lessons from the Democratic Uprising*, London: Hurst, 2011.

Financial Times, 'Cameron Acts Clumsily on the Muslim Brothers', *Financial Times*, 17 March 2015, http://www.ft.com/cms/s/0/5dbeaf8e-cc9d-11e4-b5a5-00144feab7de. html#axzz3bbhguuTv (accessed 30 May 2015).

Finn, T. 'With Democracy in Mind Yemen's Youth Are Revolting', *Global Post*, 13 May 2011, http://www.globalpost.com/dispatch/news/regions/middle-east/110512/yemen-protests-youth-revolution-Salih (accessed 2 February 2014).

Ford, D., et al. 'Egypt's President Calls for a "Religious Rvolution"', *CNN*, 6 January 2015, http://edition.cnn.com/2015/01/06/africa/egypt-president-speech/ (accessed 20 April 2015).

Francona, R. 'Egyptian Military Embracing the Muslim Brotherhood?', *Middle East Perspectives by Rick Francona*, 15 February 2011, http://francona.blogspot.co.uk/2011/02/egyptian-military-embracing-muslim.html (accessed 1 March 2014).

Freeman, J. 'The al Houthi Insurgency in the North of Yemen: An Analysis of the Shabab al Moumineen', Studies in Conflict and Terrorism, Vol. 32:11, 2009, pp. 1008–19, http://dx.doi.org/10.1080/10576100903262716 (accessed 30 May 2015).

Friedman, T.L. 'Political Islam Without Oil', *New York Times*, 10 January 2012, http://www.nytimes.com/2012/01/11/opinion/friedman-political-islam-without-oil.html?_r=0 (accessed 31 May 2015).

Gartenstein-Ross, D., et al. *Raising the Stakes: Ansar al-Sharia in Tunisia's Shift to Jihad*, ICCT Research Paper, International Centre for Counter-Terrorism, The Hague, February 2014, http://www.icct.nl/download/file/ICCT-Gartenstein-Ross-Moreng-Soucy-Raising-the-Stakes-ASTs-Shift-to-Jihad-Feb-2014 (accessed 20 May 2015).

Gelvin, J.L. *The Arab Uprisings: What Everyone Needs to Know*, New York: Oxford University Press, 2012.

Georgy, M. 'Egyptian Court Bans Hamas' Armed Wing, Lists as Terrorist Organization', *Reuters*, 31 January 2015, http://www.reuters.com/article/2015/01/31/us-egypt-hamas-idUSKBN0L40BS20150131 (accessed 30 April 2015).

Gerges, F. *The Rise and Fall of Al Qaeda*, New York: Oxford University Press, 2011.

Ghannouchi, R. 'A Day to Inspire All Tunisians – Whether Islamic or Secular', *Guardian*, 17 October 2011, http://www.theguardian.com/commentisfree/2011/oct/17/tunisians-islamic-secular-ennahda-election (accessed 3 March 2015).

Ghannouchi, R. 'The Battle Against Islam', *Middle East Affairs Journal*, Vol. 1:2, Winter 1992, pp. 1–15.

Ghannouchi, R. 'Tunisia Shows There Is No Contradiction between Democracy and Islam', *Washington Post*, 24 October 2014, http://www.washingtonpost.com/opinions/tunisia-shows-there-is-no-contradiction-between-democracy-and-islam/2014/10/24/2655e55 2-5a16-11e4-bd61-346aee66ba29_story.html (accessed 7 May 2014).

Bibliography **211**

Gilligan, A. 'How the Muslim Brotherhood Fits into a Network of Extremism', *Telegraph*, 8 February 2015, http://www.telegraph.co.uk/news/worldnews/middleeast/11398538/How-the-Muslim-Brotherhood-fits-into-a-network-of-extremism.html (accessed 31 May 2015).

Gleis, J.L. and Berti, B. *Hezbollah and Hamas: A Comparative Study*, Baltimore: John Hopkins University Press, 2012.

Gold, Z. *Sinai Security: Opportunities for Unlikely Cooperation among Egypt, Israel, and Hamas*, Washington, DC: Brookings Institution, 2013, http://www.brookings.edu/~/media/research/files/papers/2013/10/22-sinai-egypt-israel-hamas-gold/22-sinai-hamas-egypt-israel-gold.pdf (accessed 20 May 2015).

Goldberg, J. 'The Modern King in the Arab Spring', *Atlantic*, 18 March 2013, http://www.theatlantic.com/magazine/archive/2013/04/monarch-in-the-middle/309270/?single_page=true (accessed 5 January 2015).

Greenhouse,E.'HowtoProvoke NationalUnrestwithaFacebookPhoto',*NewYorker*,8April2013, http://www.newyorker.com/tech/elements/how-to-provoke-national-unrest-with-a-facebook-photo (accessed 22 February 2015).

Guardian, 'Assassination of King Abdullah', *Guardian*, 21 July 1951, http://www.theguardian.com/theguardian/1951/jul/21/fromthearchive (accessed 29 November 2014).

Guazzone, L. 'Ennahda Islamists and the Test of Government in Tunisia', *The International Spectator: Italian Journal of International Affairs*, Vol. 48:4, December 2013, pp. 30–50, http://dx.doi.org/10.1080/03932729.2013.847677 (accessed 5 May 2015).

Guazzone, L. (ed.) *The Islamist Dilemma*, London: Ithaca Press, 1995.

Gunning, J. *Hamas in Politics: Democracy, Religion, Violence*, London: Hurst, 2007.

Gupte, P.B. 'A Look into the Muslim Brotherhood: Antipathy for Syria, Praise for Jordan', *New York Times*, 7 December 1980, p. 14.

Haddad, Y. 'Islamists and the "Problem of Israel": The 1967 Awakening', *Middle East Journal*, Vol. 46:2, Spring 1992, http://www.jstor.org/stable/4328433 (accessed 13 May 2015).

Haidar, M. 'Thousands of Yemenis Stage Rallies Against President', *Al-Manar*, 27 January 2011, http://31.24.33.46/english/adetails.php?fromval=3&cid=20&frid=23&seccatid=31&eid=651 (accessed 30 May 2015).

Halliday, F. 'Tunisia's Uncertain Future', *Middle East Report*, Vol. 20:163, March–April 1990, http://www.jstor.org/stable/3012554 (accessed 7 May 2015).

Halliday, F. *Arabia Without Sultans*, Harmondsworth: Penguin, 1974.

Halliday, F. *Nation and Religion in the Middle East*, London: Saqi Books, 2000.

Hamas, 'Hamas Covenant 1988', *Yale Law School Lillian Goldman Law Library*, 18 August 1988, http://avalon.law.yale.edu/20th_century/hamas.asp (accessed 10 March 2014).

Hamid, S. 'A Future Worse Than Mubarak's Reign', *New York Times*, August 21, 2013, http://www.nytimes.com/roomfordebate/2013/08/14/is-this-the-end-of-the-arab-spring/a-future-worse-than-mubaraks-reign (accessed 28 April 2015).

Hamid, S. 'Islamists Struggle to Match Religious Values to Politics', *Woodrow Wilson International Center for Scholars*, 28 May 2014, http://www.wilsoncenter.org/islamists/article/islamists-struggle-to-match-religious-values-to-politics (accessed 28 May 2015).

Hamid, S. *Temptations of Power: Islamists and Illiberal Democracy in a New Middle East*, New York: Oxford University Press, 2014.

Hamid, S. 'The Brotherhood Will Be Back', *New York Times*, 24 May 2014, http://www.nytimes.com/2014/05/24/opinion/more-democratic-less-liberal.html (accessed 28 April 2015).

Hamid, S. 'Tunisia Field Report: The Islamist Balancing Act', *Brookings Institution*, 12 February 2015, http://www.brookings.edu/blogs/markaz/posts/2015/02/12-tunisia-islamists-ennahda-hamid (accessed 31 May 2015).

212 Bibliography

Hamid, S. and Wheeler, M. 'Was Mohammed Morsi Really an Autocrat?', *Atlantic*, 31 March 2014, http://www.theatlantic.com/international/archive/2014/03/was-mohammed-morsi-really-an-autocrat/359797/ (accessed 28 April 2015).

Hamza, K. 'Faith and Media: Muslim Brotherhood's Media, from the Missionary to the Political Discourse: Ikhwanweb as an Example', *IkhwanWeb*, 16 June 2009, http://www.ikhwanweb.com/article.php?id=20546 (accessed 27 May 2015).

Hamzawy, A. 'Islamist Participation in Arab Politics: The Case of the Yemeni Congregation for Reform', *Taiwan Journal of Democracy*, Vol. 6:1, July 2010, pp. 25–54, http://www.tfd.org.tw/export/sites/tfd/files/publication/journal/dj0601/002.pdf (accessed 8 May 2015).

Harb, I. 'The Egyptian Military in Politics: Disengagement or Accommodation', *Middle East Journal*, Vol. 57:2, Spring 2003, http://www.jstor.org/stable/4329881 (accessed 20 May 2015).

Harrera, L. *Revolution in the Age of Social Media: The Egyptian Popular Insurrection and the Internet*, London: Verso, 2014.

Hartman, B. '2012 Story of the Year: Operation Pillar of Defense', *Jerusalem Post*, 2 January 2013, http://www.jpost.com/Features/In-Thespotlight/2012-story-of-the-year-Operation-Pillar-of-Defense (accessed 1 May 2015).

Hashem, M. 'A Generational Battle among Brothers', *Carnegie Endowment for International Peace*, 29 January 2015, http://carnegieendowment.org/sada/2015/01/29/generational-battle-among-brothers/i7w0 (accessed 1 February 2015).

Hashemi, N. 'The Arab Spring Two Years On: Reflections on Dignity, Democracy, and Devotion', *Ethics & International Affairs*, Vol. 27:2, Summer 2013, http://dx.doi.org/10.1017/S0892679413000099 (accessed 7 May 2015).

Hattar, M. 'Tensions Brew in Jordan over Muslim Brotherhood Rift', *Agence France-Presse*, 2 May 2015, http://news.yahoo.com/tensions-brew-jordan-over-muslim-brotherhood-rift-134051523.html (accessed 29 May 2015).

Hattar, S. 'Jordan's Brotherhood Schism Presents a Mirror of Society', *Bitter Lemons*, Vol. 8:36, September 17, 2009, http://www.bitterlemons-international.org/previous.php?opt=1&id=290 (accessed 5 January 2015).

Hearst, D. 'Saudi Crapshoot in Yemen', *Huffington Post*, 28 September 2014, http://www.huffingtonpost.com/david-hearst/saudi-high-risk-bet-in-ye_b_5895984.html (accessed 19 May 2015).

Heikal, M. *The Cairo Documents*, New York: Doubleday, 1973.

Hermassi, A. 'The Political and the Religious in the Modern History of the Maghrib', in J. Ruedy (ed.) *Islamism and Secularism in North Africa*, Houndmills and London: Macmillan and the Center for Contemporary Arab Studies, 1994.

Heydemann, S. *Upgrading Authoritarianism in the Arab World*, Washington, DC: Brookings Institution, 2007, http://www.brookings.edu/~/media/research/files/papers/2007/10/arabworld/10arabworld.pdf (accessed 7 May 2015).

Heydemannm, S. and Leenders, R. 'Authoritarian Learning and Authoritarian Resilience: Regime Responses to the "Arab Awakening"', *Globalizations*, Vol. 8:5, 2011, pp. 647–53, http://dx.doi.org/10.1080/14747731.2011.621274 (accessed 31 May 2015).

Hinnebusch, R. 'A Historical Sociology Approach to Authoritarian Resilience in Post-Arab Uprising MENA', *Project on Middle East Political Science*, 19 December 2014, http://pomeps.org/2014/12/19/a-historical-sociology-approach-to-authoritarian-resilience/#sthash.F73yNrUs.dpuf (accessed 29 May 2015).

Holzapfel, P.B. *Yemen's Transition Process: Between Fragmentation and Transformation*, Washington, DC: United States Institute of Peace, 2014, http://www.usip.org/sites/default/files/PW95-Yemen%20in%20Transition-Between%20Fragmentation%20and%20Transformation.pdf (accessed 27 May 2015).

Bibliography **213**

Hopwood, D. *Egypt 1945–1990: Politics and Society*, 3rd ed., London and New York: Routledge, 1991.

Hourani, A. *A History of the Arab Peoples*, London: Faber and Faber, 1991.

Howard, P.N. *The Digital Origins of Dictatorship and Democracy: Information Technology and Political Islam*, New York: Oxford University Press, 2011.

Human Rights Watch, *All According to Plan: The Rab'a Massacre and Mass Killings of Protesters in Egypt*, New York: Human Rights Watch, 2014, http://www.hrw.org/sites/default/files/reports/egypt0814web_0.pdf (accessed 30 May 2015).

Human Rights Watch, 'Egypt: Mass Killings by Security Forces', *Human Rights Watch*, 11 August 2014, https://www.youtube.com/watch?v=AUtFM9L6ago (accessed 20 April 2015).

Human Rights Watch, 'Egypt: Terrorist Tag Politically Driven', *Human Rights Watch*, 28 December 2013, http://www.hrw.org/news/2013/12/28/egypt-terrorist-tag-politically-driven (accessed 28 May 2015).

Human Rights Watch, 'Jordan: Arrest Wave Signals Growing Intolerance for Dissent', *Human Rights Watch*, 14 September 2012, http://www.hrw.org/news/2012/09/14/jordan-arrest-wave-signals-growing-intolerance-dissent (accessed 15 September 2012).

Human Rights Watch, *World Report 2014*, New York: Human Rights Watch, 2014, pp. 532–8, http://www.hrw.org/sites/default/files/wr2014_web_0.pdf (accessed 16 April 2015).

Huntington, S. *The Clash of Civilizations and the Remaking of World Order*, New York: Simon & Schuster, 1996.

Hussein, M. 'We Persist in Tahrir Square to Fulfil Demands, Expedite Presidential Elections via Proper Procedures', *IkhwanWeb*, 28 January 2012, http://www.ikhwanweb.com/article.php?id=29606&ref=search.php (accessed 14 January 2013).

Ikhwan Jordan, 'Audio Jordan Friday Rescue', *Ikhwan Jordan*, 13 October 2012, https://www.youtube.com/watch?v=sPEvAVVgC0E (accessed 1 June 2015).

IkhwanOnline, 'The Muslim Brotherhood's Decision of a Run-Off Parliamentary Elections in 2010', *IkhwanOnline*, 1 December 2010, https://www.youtube.com/watch?v=iSpIemEtSts (accessed 8 May 2015).

IkhwanWeb, 'FJP – No Alliance with Salafist al Noor Party', *IkhwanWeb*, 1 December 2011, http://www.ikhwanweb.com/article.php?id=29279 (accessed 15 April 2015).

IkhwanWeb, 'Jordanian MB Forms Political Alliance to Fight Corruption', *IkhwanWeb*, 2 June 2011, http://www.ikhwanweb.com/article.php?id=28664 (accessed 12 December 2014).

IkhwanWeb, 'MB Chairman: We Seek to Participate, Not Dominate Elections', *IkhwanWeb*, 20 April 2011, http://www.ikhwanweb.com/article.php?id=28432 (accessed 19 October 2011).

IkhwanWeb, 'Statement: Friday of Rage', *IkhwanWeb*, 16 August 2013, http://www.ikhwanweb.com/article.php?id=31245 (accessed 19 December 2014).

Immanuel, J. 'Hamas Sends Mission to Sudan', *Jerusalem Post*, 8 October 1995.

International Crisis Group, *Light at the End of their Tunnels? Hamas & the Arab Uprisings – Middle East Report N°129*, Gaza City: International Crisis Group, 2012, http://www.crisisgroup.org/~/media/Files/Middle%20East%20North%20Africa/Israel%20Palestine/129-light-at-the-end-of-their-tunnels-hamas-and-the-arab-uprisings.pdf (accessed 28 May 2015).

International Crisis Group, *Popular Protest in North Africa and the Middle East (IX): Dallying with Reform in a Divided Jordan*, Amman/Brussels: International Crisis Group, 2012, http://www.crisisgroup.org/~/media/Files/Middle%20East%20North%20Africa/Iran%20Gulf/Jordan/118-popular-protest-in-north-africa-and-the-middle-east-ix-dallying-with-reform-in-a-divided-jordan.pdf (accessed 3 March 2015).

International Crisis Group, *Tunisia: Violence and the Salafi Challenge – Middle East and North Africa Report N°137*, Tunis/Brussels: International Crisis Group, 2013, http://www.crisisgroup.org/en/regions/middle-east-north-africa/north-africa/tunisia/137-tunisia-violence-and-the-salafi-challenge.aspx (accessed 19 May 2015).

214 Bibliography

Iskander, A. 'Tamarod: Egypt's Revolution Hones Its Skill', *Jadiliyya*, 30 June 2013, http://www.jadaliyya.com/pages/index/12516/tamarod_egypts-revolution-hones-its-skills (accessed 20 May 2015).

Islamic Movement Ajloun, 'The Islamic Movement of Ajloun Calls to Stop the Policy of Arrests', *Muslim Brotherhood (Jordan)*, 14 December 2014, http://www.ikhwan-jor.com/Portals/Content/?info=YVdROU5UVTJPU1p6YjNWeVkyVTlVM1ZpY0dGblpTWj BlWEJsUFRFbSt1 (accessed 12 May 2015).

Issacharoff, A. 'Truce Offer May Signal Hamas Has Reached Breaking Point', *Times of Israel*, 27 July 2014, http://www.timesofisrael.com/ceasefire-offer-may-signal-hamas-has-reached-breaking-point/ (accessed 28 May 2015).

Jacinto, L. 'Tunisia's Islamist Ennahda Party Turns on Salafists', *France 24*, 22 May 2013, http://www.france24.com/en/20130522-tunisia-islamist-ennahda-party-salafist-ansar-sharia (accessed 29 May 2015).

Jadaliyya and Ahram Online, 'Mohamed Al-Beltagy', *Jadaliyya*, 18 November 2011, http://www.jadaliyya.com/pages/index/3179/mohamed-al-beltagy (accessed 20 April 2015).

Jensen, M.I. *The Political Ideology of Hamas: A Grassroots Perspective*, London: I.B. Tauris, 2009.

Jerusalem Post, 'Mashaal Admits Hamas Members Kidnapped and Murdered Naftali, Gilad and Eyal', *Jerusalem Post*, 23 August 2014, http://www.jpost.com/Arab-Israeli-Conflict/Mashaal-admits-Hamas-members-kidnapped-and-murdered-Naftali-Gilad-and-Eyal-371997 (accessed 28 May 2015).

Joint statement of Hamas and Palestinian Islamic Jihad, 21 November 2012.

Jones, J.P. 'The Constitution of Tunisia', *University of Richmond School of Law*, 2014, http://confinder.richmond.edu/admin/docs/Tunisiaconstitution.pdf (accessed 26 February 2015).

Jordan Muslim Brotherhood, Covenant, Jordan Muslim Brotherhood, Amman, 1993.

JoSat TV, 'MEMRI: Jordanian Muslim Brotherhood Leader Hamza Mansour Refuses to Acknowledge That ISIS Are Terrorists', *Middle East Media Research Institute*, 2 February 2015, http://www.memritv.org/clip/en/4765.htm (accessed 25 February 2015).

Joscelyn, T. 'Ansar al-Sharia Responds to Tunisian Government', *Long War Journal*, 3 September 2013, http://www.longwarjournal.org/archives/2013/09/ansar_al_sharia_tuni_6.php (accessed 4 September 2013).

Joscelyn, T. 'War of Words Escalates in Tunisia', *Long War Journal*, 27 March 2013, http://www.longwarjournal.org/archives/2013/03/war_of_words_escalat.php (accessed 29 May 2015).

Kallab, S. 'The Expected End of the Muslim Brothers', *al-Jarida*, 4 March 2015, http://www.aljarida.com/news/index/2012721563/ (accessed 4 March 2015).

Kandil, H. *Inside the Brotherhood*, Cambridge: Polity Press, 2014.

Keddie, N.R. *An Islamic Response to Imperialism: Political and Religious Writings of Sayyid Jamāl Ad-Dīn 'al-Afghānī'*, Berkeley: University of California Press, 1983.

Keddie, N.R. 'The Origins of the Religious-Radical Alliance in Iran', *Past and Present*, Vol. 34:1, July 1966, http://www.jstor.org/stable/650055 (accessed 30 May 2015).

Keinon, H. 'Netanyahu: Toppling Hamas Remains an Option', *Jerusalem Post*, 30 August 2014, http://www.jpost.com/Israel-News/Politics-And-Diplomacy/Netanyahu-Toppling-Hamas-remains-an-option-372828 (accessed 28 May 2015).

Kepel, G. *Muslim Extremism in Egypt: The Prophet and the Pharaoh*, London: Saqi Books, 1985.

Kepel, G. *The Roots of Radical Islam*, London: Saqi Books, 2005.

Kerr, M. *Islamic Reform: The Political and Legal Theories of Muhammed 'Abduh and Rashid Rida*, Berkeley and Los Angeles: University of California Press, 1966.

Kerr, M. The Arab Cold War: Gamal 'Abd al-Nasir and His Rivals, 1958–1970, 3rd ed., Oxford: Oxford University Press, 1971.

Khalid, A. 'Pan-Islamism in Practice: The Rhetoric of Muslim Unity and Its Uses', in Elizabeth Özdalga (ed.) *Late Ottoman Society: The Intellectual Legacy*, Abingdon: RoutledgeCurzon, 2005.

Khayrallah, K. 'Hamas Fell in Egypt and So Did the MB Project', *al-Rai al-Aam*, 19 September 2014.

Khoury, J. 'Hamas Rebuilding Gaza Forces as Military Leader Returns to the Helm', *Haaretz*, 29 April 2015, http://www.haaretz.com/news/diplomacy-defense/.premium-1.654029 (accessed 28 May 2015).

Kingsley, P. 'Abdel Fatah al-Sisi Sweeps to Victory in Egyptian Presidential Election', *Guardian*, 29 May 2014, http://www.theguardian.com/world/2014/may/29/abdel-fatah-al-sisi-sweeps-victory-egyptian-election (accessed 20 April 2015).

Kingsley, P. 'Egyptian TV Satirist Bassem Youssef Bailed after Police Questioning', *Guardian*, 1 April 2013, http://www.theguardian.com/world/2013/mar/31/egypt-orders-arrest-tv-satirist (accessed 3 April 2013).

Kingsley, P. 'Will #SisiLeaks Be Egypt's Watergate for Abdel Fatah al-Sisi?', *Guardian*, 5 March 2015, http://www.theguardian.com/world/2015/mar/05/sisileaks-egypt-watergate-abdel-fatah-al-sisi (accessed 31 May 2015).

Kingsley, P. and Beaumont, P. 'Gaza Wants Back in from the Darkness as Hamas Feels the Isolation', *Guardian*, 25 April 2014, http://www.theguardian.com/world/2014/apr/25/gaza-back-in-hamas-isolation-egypt-unity-palestinian (accessed 30 April 2015).

Kirkpatrick, D.D. 'As Moderate Islamists Retreat, Extremists Surge Unchecked', *New York Times*, 18 June 2014, http://www.nytimes.com/2014/06/19/world/middleeast/as-moderate-islamists-retreat-extremists-surge-unchecked.html (accessed 26 February 2015).

Kirkpatrick, D.D. 'In Leaked Video, Egyptian Army Officers Debate How to Sway News Media', *New York Times*, 3 October 2013, http://www.nytimes.com/2013/10/04/world/middleeast/in-leaked-video-egyptian-army-officers-debate-how-to-sway-news-media.html (accessed 28 May 2015).

Kirkpatrick, D.D. 'Leaks Gain Credibility and Potential to Embarrass Egypt's Leaders', *New York Times*, 12 May 2015, http://www.nytimes.com/2015/05/13/world/middleeast/leaks-gain-credibility-and-potential-to-embarrass-egypts-leaders.html (accessed 28 May 2015).

Kirkpatrick, D.D. 'Prominent Muslim Brotherhood Leader Is Seized in Egypt', *New York Times*, 30 October 2013, http://www.nytimes.com/2013/10/31/world/middleeast/high-ranking-muslim-brotherhood-leader-is-seized-in-egypt.html (accessed 28 April 2015).

Kirkpatrick, D.D. 'Recordings Suggest Emirates and Egyptian Military Pushed Ousting of Morsi', *New York Times*, 1 March 2015, http://www.nytimes.com/2015/03/02/world/middleeast/recordings-suggest-emirates-and-egyptian-military-pushed-ousting-of-morsi.html (accessed 28 May 2015).

Kirkpatrick, D.D. 'Saudis Put Terrorist Label on Muslim Brotherhood', *New York Times*, 7 March 2014, http://www.nytimes.com/2014/03/08/world/middleeast/saudis-put-terrorist-label-on-muslim-brotherhood.html (accessed 12 May 2015).

Kirkpatrick, D.D. 'Top Challenger in Egypt Vote Is an Islamist, and a Moderate', *New York Times*, 12 March 2012, http://www.nytimes.com/2012/03/14/world/middleeast/top-challenger-in-egypt-vote-is-an-islamist-and-moderate.html?_r=0 (accessed 28 May 2015).

Kirkpatrick, D.D. and Rudoren, J. 'Israel and Hamas Agree to a Cease-Fire, After a U.S.-Egypt Push', *New York Times*, 21 November 2012, http://www.nytimes.com/2012/11/22/world/middleeast/israel-gaza-conflict.html (accessed 22 February 2015).

Kortam, H. 'Complaint Brought Against Al-Nas Channel', *Daily News Egypt*, 9 September 2012, http://thedailynewsegypt.com/2012/09/09/complaint-brought-against-al-nas-channel/ (accessed 31 May 2015).

216 Bibliography

Kortam, H. 'Qaradwi's Friday Speech in Al-Azhar', *Daily News Egypt*, 16 November 2012, http://www.dailynewsegypt.com/2012/11/16/qaradwis-friday-speech-in-al-azhar/ (accessed 1 May 2015).

Kristianasen, W. 'Muslim Brotherhood, a Row in the Family', *Le Monde diplomatique*, April 2000, http://mondediplo.com/2000/04/03tanzim (accessed 30 May 2015).

Kurzman, C. Ennahda Movement Programme: For Freedom, Justice and Development in Tunisia, Ennahda Electoral Programme 2011, University of North Carolina at Chapel Hill, 30 April 2015, http://kurzman.unc.edu/files/2011/06/Nahda_2011_summary_in_English.pdf (accessed 7 May 2015).

Lafraain Channel, 'Video. Tawfiq Okasha: Sisi Decided an Air Strike on the Gaza Strip', *Klmty.net*, 18 February 2015, http://klmty.net/322285-_السيسي_عكاشة_توفيق___بالفيديو غزة_لقطاع_جوية_ضربة_توجيه_قرر».html (accessed 23 February 2015).

Lagraffe, D. 'The Youth Bulge in Egypt: An Intersection of Demographics, Security and the Arab Spring', *Journal of Strategic Security*, Vol. 5:2, 2012, pp. 65–80, http://scholarcommons.usf.edu/jss/vol5/iss2/9/ (accessed 31 May 2015).

Larzillière, P. 'Political Commitment under an Authoritarian Regime: Professional Associations and the Islamist Movement as Alternative Arenas in Jordan', *International Journal of Conflict and Violence*, Vol. 6:1, 2012, pp. 11–25, http://www.ijcv.org/index.php/ijcv/article/view/186/pdf_47 (accessed 12 May 2015).

Lawrence, J. 'Tunisia, the Courage of Compromise', *Brookings Institution*, 5 February 2015, http://www.brookings.edu/research/opinions/2015/02/05-tunisia-courage-compromise-laurence (accessed 31 May 2015).

Lefèvre, R. *Ashes of Hama: The Muslim Brotherhood in Syria*, London: Hurst, 2013.

Lefèvre, R. 'The Syrian Brotherhood's Islamic State Challenge', *Project on Middle East Political Science*, 11 February 2015, http://pomeps.org/2015/02/11/the-syrian-brotherhoods-islamic-state-challenge/ (accessed 4 May 2015).

Legge, J. 'Tunisia Shocked by Assassinations: Opposition Leaders Mohamed Brahmi and Chokri Belaid Killed with the Same Gun', *Independent*, 26 July 2013, http://www.independent.co.uk/news/world/africa/tunisia-shocked-by-assassinations-opposition-leaders-mohamed-brahmi-and-chokri-belaid-killed-with-the-same-gun-8733972.html (accessed 20 September 2013).

Lewis, B. 'Islam and Liberal Democracy', *Atlantic*, February 1993, http://www.theatlantic.com/magazine/archive/1993/02/islam-and-liberal-democracy/308509/ (accessed 22 April 2015).

Lia, B. *The Society of the Muslim Brothers in Egypt: The Rise of an Islamic Mass Movement, 1928–1982*, Reading: Ithaca Press, 1998.

Lindenstrauss, G. and Süfyan, K. 'Turkish-Hamas Relations: Between Strategic Calculations and Ideological Affinity', *Strategic Assessment*, Vol. 17:2, July 2014, pp. 7–16, http://www.inss.org.il/uploadImages/systemFiles/adkan17_2ENG4_Lindenstrauss%20and%20Kivam.pdf (accessed 28 May 2015).

Lombardi, C. and Brown, N.J. 'Islam in Egypt's New Constitution', *Foreign Policy*, 13 December 2012, http://foreignpolicy.com/2012/12/13/islam-in-egypts-new-constitution (accessed 10 April 2013).

Longley, A. 'The High Water Mark of Islamist Politics? The Case of Yemen', *Middle East Journal*, Vol. 61:2, Spring 2007, http://www.jstor.org/stable/4330387 (accessed 8 May 2015).

Luck, T. 'In Hamas Leader's Exit from Qatar, Signs of Growing Saudi-Egyptian Influence', *Christian Science Monitor*, 26 January 2015, http://www.csmonitor.com/World/Middle-East/2015/0126/In-Hamas-leader-s-exit-from-Qatar-signs-of-growing-Saudi-Egyptian-influence (accessed 4 May 2015).

Luck, T. 'Muslim Brotherhood Expels Three over "Zamzam" Initiative', *Jordan Times*, 21 April 2014, http://jordantimes.com/muslim-brotherhood-expels-three-over-zamzam-initiative (accessed 6 January 2015).

Lust-Okar, E. and Zerhouni, S. (eds) *Political Participation in the Middle East*, Boulder, CO: Lynne Rienner, 2008.

Lutterbeck, D. 'Arab Uprising, Armed Forces, and Civil-Military Relations', *Armed Forces and Society*, 13 April 2012, pp. 1–25.

Lynch, M. 'Spoilt Ballots,' *National UAE*, 30 October 2009, http://www.ikhwanweb.com/article.php?id=21399 (accessed 2 February 2015).

Lynch, M. *The Arab Uprising: The Unfinished Revolutions of the New Middle East*, New York: PublicAffairs, 2012.

Lynch, M. 'Tunisia's New al-Nahda', *Foreign Policy*, 29 June 2011, http://foreignpolicy.com/2011/06/29/tunisias-new-al-nahda/ (accessed 3 March 2015).

Lynch, M. 'Young Brothers in Cyberspace', *Middle East Report*, Vol. 37:245, Winter 2007, pp. 26–33, http://www.merip.org/mer/mer245/young-brothers-cyberspace (accessed 28 April 2015).

Madabish, A. 'Yemen: National Dialogue Calls for Immediate End to Dammaj Conflict', *al-Sharq al-Awsat*, 14 November 2013, http://www.aawsat.net/2013/11/article55322399/yemen-national-dialogue-calls-for-immediate-end-to-dammaj-conflict (accessed 30 May 2015).

Malkawi, K. 'Legislation Bureau Says Newly Licensed Brotherhood Entitled to Manage Group's Assets', *Jordan Times*, 28 May 2015, http://jordantimes.com/legislation-bureau-says-newly-licensed-brotherhood-entitled-to-manage-groups-assets (accessed 29 May 2015).

Malmström, M.F. 'The Sound of Silence in Cairo: Affects, Politics and Belonging', *Anthropology Now*, Vol. 6:2, September 2014, pp. 23–34, http://www.jstor.org/stable/10.5816/anthropologynow.6.2.0023 (accessed 28 April 2015).

Malsin, J. 'Egyptian Court Sentences Ousted President Morsi to Death', *New York Times*, 16 May 2015, http://www.nytimes.com/2015/05/17/world/middleeast/egyptian-court-sentences-ousted-president-morsi-to-death.html (accessed 31 May 2015).

Mandraud, I. 'La Tunisie tourne le dos à la charia', *Le Monde*, 7 January 2014, http://www.lemonde.fr/international/article/2014/01/07/la-tunisie-officialise-le-renoncement-a-la-charia_4343892_3210.html (accessed 3 March 2015).

Manwire, T. (ed.) *The Arab Spring: Rebellion, Revolution, and a New World Order*, London: Guardian Books, 2012.

Maréchal, B. 'Universal Aspirations the Muslim Brotherhood in Europe', *ISIM Review*, Vol. 22, Autumn 2008, https://openaccess.leidenuniv.nl/bitstream/handle/1887/17269/ISIM_22_Universal_Aspirations_The_Muslim_Brotherhood_in_Europe.pdf?sequence=1 (accessed 30 May 2015).

Maréchal, B. *The Muslim Brothers in Europe: Roots and Discourse*, Boston: Brill, 2008.

Marks, M. *Convince, Coerce, or Compromise? Ennahda's Approach to Tunisia's Constitution*, Doha: Brookings Doha Center, 2014, http://www.brookings.edu/~/media/research/files/papers/2014/02/10-ennahda-tunisia-constitution-marks/ennahda-approach-tunisia-constitution-english.pdf (accessed 6 May 2015).

Marks, M. 'Youth Politics and Tunisian Salafism: Understanding the Jihadi Current', *Mediterranean Politics*, Vol. 18:1, 2013, pp. 104–11, http://dx.doi.org/10.1080/13629395.2013.764657 (accessed 28 May 2015).

Mashour, M. *Bayna al-qiyadah wa-al-jundiyah ala tariq al-dawah (Min fiqh al-dawah)* [Jihad is the way (from the laws of Da'wa)], Cairo: Dar al-Tawziah wal-Nashr al-Islamia, 1995.

McDonald, K. 'Britain's Treatment of the Muslim Brotherhood Is Spectacularly Cack-Handed', *Telegraph*, 2 July 2014, http://www.telegraph.co.uk/news/uknews/terrorism-in-the-uk/

10938780/Britains-treatment-of-the-Muslim-Brotherhood-is-spectacularly-cack-handed.html (accessed 2 July 2014).

McGeough, P. *Kill Khalid: The Failed Mossad Assassination of Khalid Mishal and the Rise of Hamas*, London: Quartet Books, 2009.

MEE Staff, 'MEE INTERVIEW: Yemen's "Mother of the Revolution" on the Way Forward', *Middle East Eye*, 8 May 2015, http://www.middleeasteye.net/news/mee-interview-yemens-mother-revolution-speaks-exile-about-way-forward-558001274#sthash.aWX9pTfj.dpuf (accessed 30 May 2015).

Melkonian, E. 'Women's Rights in Tunisia: Promising Future or Religio-political Game?', *Open Democracy*, 16 January 2015, https://www.opendemocracy.net/openglobalrights/elsy-melkonian/women%E2%80%99s-rights-in-tunisia-promising-future-or-religiopolitical-game (accessed 28 May 2015).

Merone, F. 'Salafism in Tunisia: An Interview with a Member of Ansar al-Sharia', *Jadaliyya*, 11 April 2013, http://www.jadaliyya.com/pages/index/11166/salafism-in-tunisia_an-interview-with-a-member-of- (accessed 28 May 2015).

Middle East Monitor, 'Al-Sisi: "We Destroyed 80% of Tunnels with Gaza"', *Middle East Monitor*, 13 May 2015, https://www.middleeastmonitor.com/news/africa/18593-al-sisi-we-destroyed-80-of-tunnels-with-gaza (accessed 13 May 2015).

Middle East Monitor, 'Egypt Urges European Ambassadors to Close Pro-Muslim Brotherhood Satellite Channels', *Middle East Monitor*, 4 February 2015, https://www.middleeastmonitor.com/news/africa/16780-egypt-urges-european-ambassadors-to-close-pro-muslim-brotherhood-satellite-channels (accessed 31 May 2015).

Middle East Monitor, 'Iran Severs Ties with Palestinian Islamic Jihad', *Middle East Monitor*, 20 May 2015, https://www.middleeastmonitor.com/news/middle-east/18749-iran-severs-ties-with-palestinian-islamic-jihad (accessed 28 May 2015).

Middle East Monitor, 'Tunisia's Ennahda Party Will Not Run a Candidate in the Presidential Election', *Middle East Monitor*, 8 September 2014, https://www.middleeastmonitor.com/news/africa/13979-tunisias-ennahda-party-will-not-run-a-candidate-in-the-presidential-election (accessed 29 May 2015).

Mideast Mirror, 'Muslim Brotherhood Joins Cabinet in Long-Awaited Reshuffle, *Mideast Mirror*, 2 January 1991, p. 10.

Miller, G. 'Former CIA Official Cites Agency's Failure to See al-Qaeda's Rebound', *Washington Post*, 3 May 2015, http://www.washingtonpost.com/world/national-security/former-cia-official-cites-agencys-failure-to-see-al-qaedas-rebound/2015/05/03/d68e7292-f028-11e4-8abc-d6aa3bad79dd_story.html (accessed 1 June 2015).

Milton-Edwards, B. 'A Temporary Alliance with the Crown: The Islamic Response in Jordan', J. Piscatori (ed.) *Islamic Fundamentalisms and the Gulf Crisis*, Chicago: AAAS, 1991.

Milton-Edwards, B. 'Climate of Change in Jordan's Islamist Movement', in A.S. Sidahemed and A. Etshesami (eds) *Islamic fundamentalism*, Boulder, CO: Westview Press, 1996.

Milton-Edwards, B. 'Hamas and the Arab Spring: Strategic Shifts?' *Middle East Policy*, Vol. 20:3, Fall 2013, pp. 60–72, http://onlinelibrary.wiley.com/doi/10.1111/mepo.12033/abstract (accessed 31 May 2015).

Milton-Edwards, B. *Islamic Fundamentalism since 1945*, 2nd ed., Abingdon: Routledge, 2014.

Milton-Edwards, B. *Islamic Politics in Palestine*, London: I.B. Tauris, 1996.

Milton-Edwards, B. 'Islamist Versus Islamist: Rising Challenge in Gaza', *Terrorism and Political Violence*, Vol. 26:2, 2014, pp. 259–76, http://dx.doi.org/10.1080/09546553.2012.690791 (accessed 30 April 2015).

Milton-Edwards, B. 'Perpetual Struggle: The Significance of the Arab-Israeli Conflict for Islamists', in S. Akbarzadeh (ed.) *Routledge Handbook of Political Islam*, London: Routledge, 2012.

Milton-Edwards, B. 'Revolt and Revolution: The Place of Islamism', *Critical Studies in Terrorism*, Vol. 5:2, August 2012, pp. 219–36, http://dx.doi.org/10.1080/17539153.2012.686 658 (accessed 7 May 2015).

Milton-Edwards, B. 'Temporary Alliances: The Islamic Response in Jordan', in J. Piscatori (ed.) *Islamic Fundamentalisms and the Gulf Crisis*, Chicago: University of Chicago Press, 1991.

Milton-Edwards, B. *The Israeli-Palestinian Conflict: A People's War*, Abingdon: Routledge, 2009.

Milton-Edwards, B. and Farrell, S. *Hamas: The Islamic Resistance Movement*, Cambridge: Polity Press, 2010.

Milton-Edwards, B. and Hinchcliffe, P. 'Abdullah's Jordan: New King, Old Problems', *Middle East Report*, Vol. 29:213, Winter 1999, pp. 28–31, http://www.jstor.org/stable/3013387 (accessed 12 May 2015).

Milton-Edwards, B. and Hinchcliffe, P. *Jordan: A Hashemite Legacy*, 2nd ed., Abington: Routledge, 2009.

Mishal, S. and Sela, A. *The Palestinian Hamas: Vision, Violence and Coexistence*, New York: Columbia University Press, 2000.

Mitchell, R.P. *The Society of the Muslim Brothers*, Oxford: Oxford University Press, 1969.

Moaddel, M. *Islamic Modernism, Nationalism, and Fundamentalism: Episode and Discourse*, Chicago: University of Chicago Press, 2005.

Moghadam, V.M. 'What Is Democracy? Promises and Perils of the Arab Spring', *Current Sociology*, Vol. 61:4, July 2013, pp. 393–408, http://csi.sagepub.com/content/early/2013 /04/16/001139211347973 (accessed 8 May 2015).

Mohns, E. and Bank, A. 'Syrian Revolt Fallout: End of the Resistance Axis?', *Middle East Policy*, Vol. 19:3, Fall 2012, pp. 25–35, http://dx.doi.org/10.1111/j.1475-4967.2012.00545.x (accessed 28 May 2015).

Mohsen, M. 'Health Ministry Raises Death Toll of Wednesday's Clashes to 638', *Daily News Egypt*, 16 August 2013, http://www.dailynewsegypt.com/2013/08/16/health-ministry-raises-death-toll-of-wednesdays-clashes-to-638/ (accessed 13 April 2015).

Moore, C.H. *Tunisia Since Independence: The Dynamics of One-Party Government*, Berkeley and Los Angeles: University of California Press, 1965.

Moore, P. 'Why Not Jordan?', *Middle East Research and Information Project*, 13 November 2012, http://www.merip.org/why-not-jordan (accessed 13 December 2014).

Morris, N. and Johnston, I. 'Muslim Brotherhood: Government Report Concludes They Should Not Be Classified as a Terrorist Organization', *Independent*, 15 March 2015, http://www.independent.co.uk/news/uk/home-news/muslim-brotherhood-government-report-concludes-they-should-not-be-classified-as-a-terrorist-organisation-10109730.html (accessed 15 March 2015).

Morsi, M. 'President Mohamed Morsi's Speech in Tahrir Square', *IkhwanWeb*, 29 June 2012, http://www.ikhwanweb.com/article.php?id=30153 (accessed 3 March 2014).

Munson, Z. 'Islamic Mobilization: Social Movement Theory and the Egyptian Muslim Brotherhood', *Sociological Quarterly*, Vol. 42:4, Fall 2001, pp. 487–510, http://www.jstor.org/stable/4121130 (accessed 14 May 2015).

Mura, A. 'A Genealogical Inquiry into Early Islamism: The Discourse of Hasan al-Banna', *Journal of Political Ideologies*, Vol. 17:1, February 2012, http://dx.doi.org/10.1080/135693 17.2012.644986 (accessed 30 May 2015).

Murphy, D. 'Egypt Revolution Unfinished, Qaradawi Tells Tahrir Masses', *Christian Science Monitor*, 18 February 2011, http://www.csmonitor.com/World/Middle-East/2011/0218/Egypt-revolution-unfinished-Qaradawi-tells-Tahrir-masses (accessed 1 March 2014).

Mushtaha, Rawhi. Author interview, Gaza City, 30 April 2013.

220 Bibliography

Muslim Brotherhood, 'Brotherhood around the World', *Muslim Brotherhood*, 2015, http://ikhwanwiki.com/index.php?title=تصنيف:الإخوان_حول_العالم (accessed 27 May 2015).

Muslim Brotherhood, 'Ikhwan Wiki', *Muslim Brotherhood*, 2015, http://ikhwanwiki.com/index.php (accessed 27 May 2015).

Nader, E. 'Hamas Terrorist Case Postponed to 28 February, Spokesperson Blasts Media "Incitement"', *Daily News Egypt*, 23 February 2015, http://www.dailynewsegypt.com/2015/02/22/hamas-terrorist-case-postponed-28-february-spokesperson-blasts-media-incitement/ (accessed 23 February 2015).

Nagel, J. 'Masculinity and Nationalism: Gender and Sexuality in the Mmaking of Nations', *Ethnic and Racial Studies*, Vol. 21:2, March 1998, pp. 242–69, http://dx.doi.org/10.1080/014198798330007 (accessed 28 April 2015).

National Democratic Institute, *Final Report on the Tunisian National Constituent Assembly Elections*, Washington, DC: National Democratic Institute, 2011, https://www.ndi.org/files/tunisia-final-election-report-021712_v2.pdf (accessed 28 May 2015).

Nepstead, S. 'Nonviolent Resistance in the Arab Spring: The Critical Role of Military-Opposition Alliances', *Swiss Political Science Review*, Vol. 17:4, 2011, pp. 485–91.

New York Times, 'Syria Reports Killing Nine in Raid on Moslem Brotherhood Hideout', *New York Times*, 21 December 1980.

New York Times, 'Yemeni President Wins Re-election', *New York Times*, 24 September 2006, http://www.nytimes.com/2006/09/24/world/middleeast/24yemen.html (accessed 30 May 2015).

Noozz.com, 'A. Kotti "Ennahda Does Not Go Out the Window . . . "', *Noozz*, 13 January 2015, http://noozz.com/Tunisia/Articles/ViewNews/364851 (accessed 7 May 2015).

Noueihed, L. and Warren, A. *The Battle for the Arab Spring: Revolution, Counter-Revolution and the Making of a New Era*, London: Yale University Press, 2012.

O'Neill, B. 'Yemen, a Prisoner of Its Own History', *National UAE*, 7 May 2010, http://www.thenational.ae/arts-culture/yemen-a-prisoner-of-its-own-history#full (accessed 21 April 2015).

Owen, R. *The Rise and Fall of Arab Presidents for Life*, Cambridge, MA: Harvard University Press, 2012.

Pargeter, A. *The Muslim Brotherhood: The Burden of Tradition*, London: Saqi Books, 2010.

Pelham, N. 'Gaza's Tunnel Complex', *Middle East Report*, Vol. 41:261, Winter 2011, pp. 30–5, http://www.jstor.org/stable/41408031 (accessed 3 March 2012).

Pelham, N. *Sinai: The Buffer Erodes*, London: Royal Institute of International Affairs (Chatham House), 2012, pp. 13–16, http://www.chathamhouse.org/sites/files/chathamhouse/public/Research/Middle%20East/pr0912pelham.pdf (accessed 21 May 2015).

Pelletiere, S.C. *Hamas and Hizbollah: The Radical Challenge to Israel in the Occupied Territories*, Carlisle, PA: US Army War College Press, 1994, http://www.strategicstudiesinstitute.army.mil/pubs/download.cfm?q=196 (accessed 1 May 2015).

Perkins, K. *A History of Modern Tunisia*, New York: Cambridge University Press, 2005.

Pew Research Center, 'One Year After Morsi's Ouster, Divides Persist over el-Sisi and the Muslim Brotherhood', *Pew Research Center*, 22 May 2014, http://www.pewglobal.org/2014/05/22/one-year-after-morsis-ouster-divides-persist-on-el-sisi-muslim-brotherhood/ (accessed 31 May 2015).

Pew Research Center, *The Future of World Religions: Population Growth Projections, 2010–2050*, Washington, DC: Pew Research Center, 2015, http://www.pewforum.org/files/2015/03/PF_15.04.02_ProjectionsFullReport.pdf (accessed 30 May 2015).

Pew Research Center, 'Tunisian Confidence in Democracy Wanes, Ratings for Islamist Ennahda Party Have Declined Since Revolution', *Pew Research Center*, 15 October 2014, http://www.pewglobal.org/2014/10/15/tunisian-confidence-in-democracy-wanes/ (accessed 31 May 2015).

Bibliography **221**

Phillips, J. 'The Arab Spring Descends into Islamist Winter: Implications for U.S. Policy', *Heritage Foundation*, 20 December 2012, http://www.heritage.org/research/reports/2012/12/the-arab-spring-descends-into-islamist-winter-implications-for-us-policy (accessed 7 May 2015).

Pickard, D. *Lessons from Constitution-Making in Tunisia*, Washington, DC: Atlantic Council of the United States, 2012, http://www.atlanticcouncil.org/images/files/publication_pdfs/403/mec121213tunisia.pdf (accessed 26 May 2015).

Pioppi, D. 'Playing with Fire: The Muslim Brotherhood and the Egyptian Leviathan', *The International Spectator: Italian Journal of International Affairs*, Vol. 48:4, 2013, http://dx.doi.org/10.1080/03932729.2013.847680 (accessed 28 April 2015).

Piscatori, J.P. *Islam in a World of Nation States*, Cambridge: Cambridge University Press, 1986.

Pratt, N. *Democracy and Authoritarianism in the Arab World*, Boulder, CO: Lynne Rienner, 2007.

Prime Ministry, the Hashemite Kingdom of Jordan, 'Prime Minister Meets Leaders of Islamic Movement', *Prime Ministry, The Hashemite Kingdom of Jordan*, 31 May 2007, http://www.pm.gov.jo/english/index.php?page_type=news&part=1&id=3081 (accessed 2 February 2015).

Public Records Office file CO733/257/12, Situation in Palestine 1935, and Tegart Papers, Box 1, File 3c, from report on Terrorism 1936–37, p. 7, Kew, London.

Ramadan, A.A. 'Fundamentalist Influence in Egypt: The Strategies of the Muslim Brotherhood and the Takfir Groups', in M.E. Marty and R.S. Appleby (eds) *Fundamentalisms and the State, Remarking Polities, Economies and Militance*, Chicago: University of Chicago Press, 1993.

Rashwan, N.H. 'Morsi's Coup Against SCAF: The Hows and the Whys', *Ahram Online*, 14 August 2012, http://english.ahram.org.eg/NewsContent/1/140/50324/Egypt/First-days/Morsis-coup-against-SCAF-The-hows-and-the-whys.aspx (accessed 20 May 2015).

Reed, J. 'Jordan Tackles Homegrown Islamists as It Joins Attacks on Isis', *Financial Times*, 5 October 2014, http://www.ft.com/cms/s/0/08fc027c-4a29-11e4-bc07-00144feab7de.html#axzz3bbhguuTv (accessed 31 May 2015).

Reuters, 'Egyptian Court Sentences Muslim Brotherhood Leader to Death', *Guardian*, 11 April 2015, http://www.theguardian.com/world/2015/apr/11/egyptian-court-muslim-brotherhood-death-sentences-mohammed-badie (accessed 11 April 2015).

Reuters, 'Protests Erupt in Tunis after Opposition Leader Shot Dead', *France 24*, 26 July 2013, http://www.france24.com/en/20130725-tunisia-thousands-protest-after-tunisian-opposition-leader-brahmi-shot-dead/ (accessed 7 May 2015).

Reuters, 'Tribal Leader Says Salih Will Leave Yemen Barefoot', *Reuters*, 26 May 2011 http://www.reuters.com/article/2011/05/26/yemen-tribe-idUSLDE74P0VJ20110526 (accessed 21 April 2015).

Richter, C. 'Media Strategies of the Major Social Movement in Egypt: The Muslim Brothers' Website ikhwanonline.net', in N. Schneider and B. Gräf (eds) *Social Dynamics 2.0: Researching Change in Times of Media Convergence: Case Studies from the Middle East and Asia*, Berlin: Frank & Timme, 2011.

Richter, C. 'The Egyptian Muslim Brotherhood Movement and Its Media Strategies: The Mobilising Effect of Religion in Contentious Politics', in J. Haynes and A. Hennig (eds) *Religious Actors in the Public Sphere, Means, Objectives and Effects*, Abingdon: Routledge, 2011.

Rida, M.R. 'Renewal, Renewing and Renewers', in C. Kurzman (ed.) *Modernist Islam, 1840–1940: A Sourcebook*, New York: Oxford University Press, 2002, http://home.zcu.cz/~dkrizek/SBV1/Texty%202/Rida-Renewal_renewing_and_renewers.pdf (accessed 7 May 2015).

Risheq, I. Statement to the author, 21 November 2012.

Rogan, E. *The Arabs: A History*, London: Penguin, 2011.

222 Bibliography

Rogan, E.L. 'Jordan and 1948: The Persistence of an Official History', in E.L. Rogan and A. Shlaim (eds) *The War for Palestine*, 2nd ed., New York: Cambridge University Press, 2007.

Rose, D. 'The Gaza Bombshell', *Vanity Fair*, April 2008, http://www.vanityfair.com/news/2008/04/gaza200804 (accessed 4 May 2015).

Roy, O. 'Has Islamism a Future in Afghanistan?', in W. Maley (ed.) *Fundamentalism Reborn? Afghanistan and the Taliban*, London: Hurst, 2001.

Roy, O. 'The Myth of the Islamist Winter', *New Statesman*, 13 December 2013, http://www.newstatesman.com/world-affairs/world-affairs/2012/12/myth-islamist-winter (accessed 20 May 2015).

Roy, S. *Hamas and Civil Society in Gaza: Engaging the Islamist Social Sector*, Princeton, NJ: Princeton University Press, 2011.

Rubin, B. (ed.) *The Muslim Brotherhood: The Organization and Policies of a Global Islamist Movement*, Basingstoke: Palgrave Macmillan, 2010.

Rudoren, J. 'Qatar's Emir Visits Gaza, Pledging $400 Million to Hamas', *New York Times*, 23 October 2012, http://www.nytimes.com/2012/10/24/world/middleeast/pledging-400-million-qatari-emir-makes-historic-visit-to-gaza-strip.html (accessed 30 April 2015).

Rutherford, B. 'Explaining the Ideological Change in Egypt's Muslim Brotherhood during the Mubarak Regime', in S. Arjomand and N. Brown (eds) *The Rule of Law, Islam, and Constitutional Politics in Egypt and Iran*, Albany, NY: State University of New York Press, 2013.

Ryan, C.R. *Jordan in Transition: From Hussein to Abdullah*, London: Lynne Rienner, 2002.

Saleh, M. 'Political Islam: One Step Backwards Towards a Leap Forward', *Current Trends in Islamist Ideology*, Vol. 16, March 2014, pp. 42–8, http://www.hudson.org/content/researchattachments/attachment/1393/ct_16_posting.pdf (accessed 22 February 2015).

Saleh, Y. and Kalin, S. 'Sisi Won 96.91 Percent in Egypt's Presidential Vote-Commission', *Reuters*, 3 June 2014, http://www.reuters.com/article/2014/06/03/us-egypt-election-results-idUSKBN0EE1UO20140603 (accessed 20 May 2015).

Salem, M. 'Hamas Says Media Falsely Implicating It in Egyptian Affairs' *Daily News Egypt*, 5 November 2013, http://www.dailynewsegypt.com/2013/11/05/hamas-says-media-falsely-implicating-it-in-egyptian-affairs/ (accessed 28 May 2015).

Salmoni, B.A., et al. *Regime and Periphery in Northern Yemen: The Huthi Phenomenon*, Santa Monica, CA: RAND Corporation, 2010, http://www.rand.org/content/dam/rand/pubs/monographs/2010/RAND_MG962.pdf (accessed 8 May 2015).

Samak, D. and Eleiba, A. 'Egypt Still Considering Free-Trade Zone with Gaza: Hamas Official', *Ahram Online*, 27 September 2012, http://english.ahram.org.eg/NewsContent/1/64/54018/Egypt/Politics-/Egypt-still-considering-freetrade-zone-with-Gaza-H.aspx (accessed 30 April 2015).

Samir, S. 'Pro-MB Turkish Channel Incites Attack on Police Forces', *Cairo Post*, 25 January 2015, http://www.thecairopost.com/news/134794/inside_egypt/pro-mb-turkish-channel-incites-attack-on-police-forces (accessed 31 May 2015).

Saudi Gazette Editorial Board,'Libyan Conflict Nearing the Endgame?',*Saudi Gazette*,21 May 2015,http://www.saudigazette.com.sa/index.cfm?method=home.regcon&contentid=20150522244604 (accessed 26 May 2015).

Schachtel, J. 'Czech President at AIPAC: World Must Unite to Destroy Muslim Brotherhood', *Breitbart*, 2 March 2015, http://www.breitbart.com/national-security/2015/03/02/czech-president-at-aipac-world-must-unite-to-destroy-muslim-brotherhood/ (accessed 3 March 2015).

Schenker, D. 'Down and Out in Amman: The Rise and Fall of the Jordanian Muslim Brotherhood', *Foreign Affairs*, 3 October 2013, http://www.foreignaffairs.com/articles/139982/david-schenker/down-and-out-in-amman (accessed 24 February 2015).

Bibliography 223

Schmitz, C. 'Yemen's National Dialogue', *Middle East Institute*, 10 March 2014, http://www.mei.edu/content/yemens-national-dialogue (accessed 9 March 2015).

Schwedler, J. *Faith in Moderation: Islamist Parties in Jordan and Yemen*, New York: Cambridge University Press, 2006.

Schwedler, J. 'Jordan: The Quiescent Opposition', in R. Wright (ed.) *The Islamists Are Coming: Who They Really Are*, Herndon, VA: United States Institute of Peace Press, 2012, http://theislamistsarecoming.wilsoncenter.org/islamists/node/23188 (accessed 5 January 2015).

Schwedler, J. 'The Politics of Protest in Jordan', *Foreign Policy Research Institute*, March 2012, http://www.fpri.org/footnotes/1701.201203.schwedler.politicsprotestjordan.html (accessed 14 December 2014).

Shadid, A., et al. 'Waves of Unrest Spread to Yemen, Shaking a Region, *New York Times*, 27 January 2011, http://www.nytimes.com/2011/01/28/world/middleeast/28unrest.html (accessed 3 May 2014).

Shakarian, P., et al. *Introduction to Cyber-Warfare: A Multidisciplinary Approach*, Waltham, MA: Elsevier, 2013.

Shehata, D. *Islamists and Secularists in Egypt: Opposition, Conflict & Cooperation*, London and New York: Routledge, 2009.

Shehata, D. 'The Fall of the Pharaoh: How Hosni Mubarak's Reign Came to an End', *Foreign Affairs*, Vol. 90:3, May/June 2011, https://www.foreignaffairs.com/articles/north-africa/2011-04-14/fall-pharaoh (accessed 20 May 2015).

Shehata, S. 'The Military vs. the Islamists', *Woodrow Wilson International Center for Scholars*, 4 November 2013, http://www.wilsoncenter.org/islamists/article/the-military-vs-the-islamists (accessed 28 May 2015).

Shehata, S. and Stacher, J. 'Boxing in the Brothers', *Middle East Research and Information Project*, 8 August 2007, http://merip.org/mero/mero080807 (accessed 7 May 2015).

Shikaki, K. and Ladadweh, W. 'Palestinian Public Opinion Poll No 54', *Palestinian Center for Policy and Survey Research*, 15 January 2015, http://www.pcpsr.org/en/node/600 (accessed 31 January 2015).

Shlaim, A. *Collusion across the Jordan: King Abdullah, the Zionist Movement, and the Partition of Palestine*, New York: Columbia University Press, 1988.

Shukrallah, S. and Gaber, Y. 'What Was Religion Doing in the Debate on Egypt's Constitutional Amendments?', *Ahram Online*, 22 March 2011, http://english.ahram.org.eg/NewsContent/1/64/8267/Egypt/Politics-/What-was-religion-doing-in-the-debate-on-Egypts-Co.aspx (accessed 19 October 2011).

Singerman, D. 'Youth, Gender and Dignity in the Egyptian Uprising', *Journal of Middle Eastern Women's Studies*, Vol. 9:3, 2013, pp. 1–27, http://muse.jhu.edu/journals/journal_of_middle_east_womens_studies/v009/9.3.singerman.html (accessed 31 May 2015).

Smith, B. 'Egypt's Presidential Election 2012', SNIA/6338, *House of Commons Library*, 23 May 2012, http://www.parliament.uk/briefing-papers/SN06338.pdf (accessed 28 April 2015).

Solberg, K. 'Cairo Mourns the Dead after Violent Crackdown', *Lancet*, Vol. 382:9895, 7 September 2013, pp. 847–8, http://dx.doi.org/10.1016/S0140-6736(13)61849-8 (accessed 28 April 2015).

Spencer, R. 'Middle East Review of 2012: The Arab Winter', *Telegraph*, 31 December 2012, http://www.telegraph.co.uk/news/worldnews/middleeast/9753123/Middle-East-review-of-2012-the-Arab-Winter.html (accessed 7 May 2015).

Stacher, J. *Adaptable Autocrats: Regime Power in Egypt and Syria*, Stanford, CA: Stanford University Press, 2012.

Stacher, J. 'SCAF and the Muslim Brotherhood', *Middle East Institute*, 14 April 2013, http://www.mei.edu/content/scaf%C2%A0and%C2%A0the%C2%A0muslim-brotherhood (accessed 20 May 2015).

224 Bibliography

Stuster, J.D. 'Rick Sanchez Wages Flame War Against Muslim Brotherhood Twitter Feed', *Foreign Policy*, 4 April 2013, http://foreignpolicy.com/2013/04/04/rick-sanchez-wages-flame-war-against-muslim-brotherhood-twitter-feed/ (accessed 27 May 2015).

Sweis, R. 'Brotherhood Leader's Arrest in Jordan Is Seen as Warning from Monarchy', *New York Times*, 7 December 2014, http://www.nytimes.com/2014/12/08/world/brotherhood-leaders-arrest-in-jordan-is-seen-as-warning-from-monarchy.html (accessed 24 February 2015).

Tadros, S. 'The Muslim Brotherhood's Shrewd Election Tactics', *National Review*, 31 October 2011, http://www.nationalreview.com/corner/281746/muslim-brotherhoods-shrewd-election-tactics-samuel-tadros (accessed 14 May 2015).

Tal, L. 'Dealing with Radical Islam: The Case of Jordan', *Survival: Global Politics and Strategy*, Vol. 37:3, pp. 139–56, 1995, http://dx.doi.org/10.1080/00396339508442807 (accessed 12 May 2015).

Tamimi, A. *Hamas: Unwritten Chapters*, London: Hurst, 2007.

Tamimi, A.S. *Rachid Ghannouchi: A Democrat within Islamism*, New York: Oxford University Press, 2001.

Taraki, L. 'The Islamic Resistance Movement in the Palestinian Uprising', *Middle East Report*, Vol. 19:156, January–February 1989, pp. 30–2, http://www.jstor.org/stable/3012813 (accessed 28 April 2015).

Thiel, T. *Yemen's Arab Spring: From Youth Revolution to Fragile Political Transition*, London: London School of Economics IDEAS, 2012, http://www.lse.ac.uk/IDEAS/publications/reports/pdf/SR011/FINAL_LSE_IDEAS__YemensArabSpring_Thiel.pdf (accessed 9 June 2014).

Thompson, E.F. *Justice Interrupted: The Struggle for Constitutional Government in the Middle East*, Cambridge, MA: Harvard University Press, 2013.

Thrall, N. 'Whose Palestine?', *New York Review of Books*, 19 June 2014, http://www.nybooks.com/blogs/nyrblog/2014/jun/19/whose-palestine/ (accessed 20 July 2014).

Tibi, B. *The Sharia State: Arab Spring and Democratization*, New York: Routledge, 2013.

Time, 'TUNISIA: Breaking the Fast', *Time*, 22 February 1960, p. 28, http://content.time.com/time/magazine/article/0,9171,939596,00.html (accessed 14 November 2014).

Times, 'Many Arrests in Egypt', *Times*, 14 January 1954, p. 8.

Tomlinson, H. 'Islamist Leaders Arrested as Egypt's Army Tightens Grip', *Times*, 5 July 2013, pp. 26–7.

Topol, S.A. 'Meet Radical Islam's Tech Guru', *Daily Beast*, 26 December 2010, http://www.thedailybeast.com/articles/2010/12/26/meet-radical-islams-tech-guru-the-muslim-brotherhood-creates-a-media-savvy-machine.html (accessed 30 May 2015).

Touati, Z. and Zlitni, S. 'Social Networks and Women's Rights Activism in Post-Revolutionary Tunisia', in M.S. Olimat (ed.) *Arab Spring and Arab Women: Challenges and Opportunities*, Abingdon, Oxon and New York: Routledge, 2014.

Trager, E. 'Egypt's Invisible Insurgency', *New Republic*, 19 March 2014, http://www.newrepublic.com/article/117072/egypts-young-islamists-use-facebook-organize-violence (accessed 31 May 2014).

US Department of State, *Yemen 2012 International Religious Freedom Report*, Washington, DC: US Department of State, Bureau of Democracy, Human Rights and Labor, 2013, http://www.state.gov/documents/organization/208632.pdf (accessed 27 May 2015).

US Embassy Amman, 'Credible Muslim Voices in Jordan', *Wikileaks*, 12 September 2007, https://cablegatesearch.wikileaks.org/cable.php?id=07AMMAN3797 (accessed 6 January 2015).

US Embassy Amman, 'Jordanian Islamists' Relationship with Hamas', *Wikileaks*, 21 September 1998, https://wikileaks.org/plusd/cables/98AMMAN8578_a.html (accessed 12 May 2015).

Bibliography 225

US Embassy Sanaa, 'JMP's "National Salvation Plan" Just Another Detour on the Road to the 2011 Elections', *Wikileaks*, 19 September 2009, http://www.wikileaks.org/plusd/cables/09SANAA1687_a.html (accessed 20 October 2014).

US Embassy Sanaa, 'US Embassy Cables: Who Will Succeed Salih in Yemen?', *Guardian*, 21 March 2011, http://www.theguardian.com/world/us-embassy-cables-documents/40815 (accessed 16 June 2014).

US Embassy Sanaa,'Yemen:Hamid Al-Ahmar Sees Saleh as Weak and Isolated,Plans NextSteps', *Wikileaks*, 31 August 2009 https://search.wikileaks.org/plusd/cables/09SANAA1617_a.html (accessed 20 October 2014).

United Nations Office for the Coordination of Humanitarian Affairs, *Gaza Initial Rapid Assessment*, Jerusalem: United Nations Office for the Coordination of Humanitarian Affairs occupied Palestinian territory, 2014, http://www.ochaopt.org/documents/gaza_mira_report_9september.pdf (accessed 28 May 2015).

United Nations, 'QDi.156 ABD-AL-MAJID AZIZ AL-ZINDANI', *United Nations Al-Qaida Sanctions Committee*, 10 June 2013, http://www.un.org/sc/committees/1267/NSQDi156E.shtml (accessed 21 April 2015).

Van Tets, F. 'After the Death of Mu'ath al-Kasasbeh the Tide May Be Turning Against Isis in Jordan', *Independent*, 6 February 2015, http://www.independent.co.uk/news/world/middle-east/after-the-death-of-muath-alkasaesbeh-the-tide-may-be-turning-against-isis-in-jordan-10030151.html (accessed 17 February 2015).

Vatikiotis, P. *The History of Modern Egypt from Muhammad Ali to Mubarak*, London: Weidenfeld, 1991.

Vidino, L. 'The Muslim Brotherhood's Conquest of Europe', *Middle East Quarterly*, Vol. 12:1, Winter 2005, pp. 25–34, http://www.meforum.org/687/the-muslim-brotherhoods-conquest-of-europe (accessed 26 May 2015).

Vidino, L. *The New Muslim Brotherhood in the West*, New York: Columbia University Press, 2010.

Wagemakers, J. 'Legitimizing Pragmatism: Hamas' Framing Efforts from Militancy to Moderation and Back?', *Terrorism and Political Violence*, Vol. 22:3, 2010, pp. 357–77, http://dx.doi.org/10.1080/09546551003765942 (accessed 4 May 2015).

Ware, L.B. 'Ben Ali's Constitutional Coup in Tunisia', *Middle East Journal*, Vol. 42:4, Autumn 1988, pp. 587–601, http://www.jstor.org.queens.ezp1.qub.ac.uk/stable/4327834 (accessed 28 May 2015).

Washington Times Editorial Board, 'From Arab Spring to Islamist Winter', *Washington Times*, 25 October 2011, http://www.washingtontimes.com/news/2011/oct/25/from-arab-spring-to-islamist-winter/ (accessed 7 May 2015).

Wehrey, F. 'The Authoritarian Resurgence: Saudi Arabia's Anxious Autocrats', *Journal of Democracy*, Vol. 26:2, April 2015, http://muse.jhu.edu/journals/journal_of_democracy/v026/26.2.wehrey.pdf (accessed 27 May 2015).

Wells, M. 'Yemen's Houthi Movement and the Revolution', *Foreign Policy*, 27 February 2012, http://foreignpolicy.com/2012/02/27/yemens-houthi-movement-and-the-revolution/ (accessed 21 April 2015).

Wickham, C.R. *The Muslim Brotherhood: Evolution of an Islamist Movement*, Princeton, NJ: Princeton University Press, 2013.

Wiktorowicz, Q. 'The New Global Threat: Transnational Salafis and Jihad', *Middle East Policy*, Vol. 8:4, December 2001, pp. 18–38, http://dx.doi.org/10.1111/j.1475-4967.2001.tb00006.x (accessed 27 May 2015).

Wiktorowicz, Q. *The Management of Islamic Activism: Salafis, the Muslim Brotherhood, and State Power in Jordan*, Albany: State University of New York Press, 2001.

Wilke, C. 'Flaws in Jordan's Largest Terrorism Trial', *Human Rights Watch*, 21 November 2011, http://www.hrw.org/news/2011/11/21/flaws-jordan-s-largest-terrorism-trial (accessed 29 May 2015).

226 Bibliography

Williams, C. 'How Egypt Shut Down the Internet', *Telegraph*, 28 January 2011, http://www.telegraph.co.uk/news/worldnews/africaandindianocean/egypt/8288163/How-Egypt-shut-down-the-internet.html (accessed 7 May 2015).

Willis, M. *Politics and Power in the Maghreb: Algeria, Tunisia and Morocco from Independence to the Arab Spring*, London: Hurst, 2012.

Wilson, M. *King Abdullah, Britain and the Making of Jordan*, New York: Cambridge University Press, 1987.

Winter, L. 'Conflict in Yemen: Simple People, Complicated Circumstances', *Middle East Policy*, Vol. 18:1, Spring 2011, pp. 102–20, http://dx.doi.org/10.1111/j.1475-4967.2011.00476.x (accessed 27 May 2015).

Witte, G., et al. 'In Egypt Muslim Brotherhood Reverses Course, Agrees to Talks on Transition', *Washington Post*, 6 February 2011, http://www.washingtonpost.com/wp-dyn/content/article/2011/02/05/AR2011020501707.html (accessed 20 May 2015).

Wittes, T.C. 'The Politics of Restoring Egypt's Military Aid', *Washington Post*, 2 April 2015, http://www.washingtonpost.com/blogs/monkey-cage/wp/2015/04/02/the-politics-of-restoring-egypts-military-aid/ (accessed 24 February 2015).

Wolf, A. 'Can Nidaa Tounes Lead Tunisia?', *Middle East Institute*, 21 November 2014, http://www.mei.edu/content/article/can-nidaa-tounes-lead-tunisia (accessed 20 May 2015).

Wolf, A. 'The Future of Tunisia's Nidaa Tounes Party', *Middle East Institute*, 25 July 2014, http://www.mei.edu/content/at/future-tunisias-nidaa-tounes-party (accessed 12 December 2014).

Wright, L. *Thirteen Days in September: Carter, Begin, and Sadat at Camp David*, New York: Knopf, 2014.

Wright, R. 'Islam, Democracy and the West, *Foreign Affairs*, Vol. 71:3, Summer 1992, pp. 131–45.

Yadav, S.P. and Carapico, S. 'The Breakdown of the GCC Initiative', *Middle East Report*, Vol. 44:273, Winter 2014, http://www.merip.org/mer/mer273/breakdown-gcc-initiative (accessed 29 May 2015).

Yasushi, K. 'Al-Manar Revisited, the "Lighthouse" of the Islamic Revival', in S.A. Dudoignon, K. Hisao and K. Yasushi (eds) *Intellectuals in the Modern Islamic World, Transmission, Transformation and Communication*, Abingdon, Oxon: Routledge, 2006.

Yemen Post Staff, 'Houthi Militants Clash with Armed Forces in Amran', *Yemen Post*, 27 May 2014, http://www.yemenpost.net/Detail123456789.aspx?ID=3&SubID=7876 (accessed 16 June 2014).

Yemen Post Staff, 'Islah Leader Calls for Unity', *Yemen Post*, 4 December 2013, http://www.yemenpost.net/Detail123456789.aspx?ID=3&SubID=7405 (accessed 2 March 2014).

Yemeni Congregation for Reform, 'Islah Party Announces Decisive Storm Support', *IkhwanWeb*, 4 April 2015, http://www.ikhwanweb.com/article.php?id=32080 (accessed 29 April 2015).

Yemeni Congregation for Reform, 'Islah Refutes the Allegations of the Former President', *AlIslah.net*, 31 October 2013, http://al-islah.net/new/EN/view_en.aspx?id=3669 (accessed 30 May 2015).

Ynet, 'Rockets Fired at Tel Aviv Area for First Time Since Gulf War', *Yedioth Ahronoth*, 15 November 2012, http://www.ynetnews.com/articles/0,7340,L-4306249,00.html (accessed 30 April 2015).

Yom, S. 'Don't Forget about Jordan: A Regime Caught between Contagion and Consent', *Foreign Policy*, February 2, 2011, http://foreignpolicy.com/2011/02/02/dont-forget-about-jordan-a-regime-caught-between-contagion-and-consent/ (accessed 3 March 2015).

Yom, S., et al. *Arab Uprisings – Jordan: Forever on the Brink*, Washington, DC: Project on Middle East Political Science, 2012, http://pomeps.org/wp-content/uploads/2012/05/POMEPS_BriefBooklet11_Jordan_Web.pdf (accessed 3 March 2015).

Younis, M. 'Egyptians to Government: Focus on Jobs', *Gallup*, 16 July 2012, http://www.gallup.com/poll/155732/egyptians-government-focus-jobs.aspx (accessed 20 May 2015).

Yousef, A. Author interview, Gaza City, 11 February 2013.Zahar, Dr Mahmoud. Author interview, Gaza City, 27 November 1989.

Zahar, Dr Mahmoud. Author interview, Gaza City, 8 December 2011.

Zahar, Dr Mahmoud. Author interview, Gaza City, 9 July 2012.

Zahar, Dr Mahmoud. Author interview, Gaza City, 11 February 2013.

Zahar, Dr Mahmoud. Author interview, Gaza City, 2 September 2013.

Zahid, M. *The Muslim Brotherhood and Egypt's Succession Crisis: The Politics of Liberalisation and Reform in the Middle East*, London: I.B. Tauris, 2010.

Zawahiri, A. 'Bitter Harvest; the Muslim Brotherhood in Sixty Years', *Tawhed*, 1991, http://www.tawhed.ws/r?i=2gxseb4t (accessed 27 April 2015).

Zollner, B. 'Prison Talk: The Muslim Brotherhood's Internal Struggle during Gamal Abdel Nasser's Persecution, 1954–1971', *International Journal of Middle East Studies*, Vol. 39:3, August 2007, pp. 411–33, http://dx.doi.org/10.1017/S0020743807070535 (accessed 13 May 2015).

Zollner, B. *The Muslim Brotherhood: Hasan al-Hudaybi and Ideology*, London and New York: Routledge, 2009.

INDEX

Abbas, Mahmoud 70, 75
Abdelaziz, Sheikh Yassin 142, 144
Abduh, Mohammed 14, 64
Abdullah I of Jordan 87, 88, 89
Abdullah II of Jordan 8, 46, 89, 94, 95, 97, 98, 101, 102, 104
Abu Qura, 'Abd al-Latif 87, 88, 89
Abu Rumman, Mohammed 96
Afek Tounes 128
Afghani, Jamal al-Din al- 14, 162, 163
Afghanistan 5, 120, 142, 143, 167, 187
Ahmar, Ali Mohsen al- 149, 155, 156
Ahmar, family 9, 144, 151, 152, 154
Ahmar, Hamid 149
Ahmar, Hussein 150
Ahmar, Himyar 150
Ahmar, Sheikh Abdullah Ibn Husayn al- 140, 141, 144, 145–6, 148
Ahmar, Sheikh Sadiq bin Abdullah al- 141, 150, 151
Akayila, Abdullah al- 94, 96
Akef, Mohammed 22
Al-Aqsa mosque 27, 63, 89
Al-Azhar University 15–16, 38, 49, 63, 64, 73
Ali, Mohammed (19th century Egyptian ruler) 14
Al-Nas (television channel) 173
al-Nour party 43, 44, 49, 51, 178
al-Qaeda 23, 54, 95, 120, 121, 138, 143, 144, 148, 149, 166, 177, 180, 181, 187, 188, 193, 196, 197
al-Qaeda in the Arab Peninsula (AQAP) 137, 139, 142, 153, 154, 187

al-Qiddissin Church attack 36
al-Wasat party Egypt 29, 42–3
al-Wasat party Jordan 100, 101
Algeria 5, 120, 167
Aly, Abdel Monem Said 191
Ansar Allah 142, 151
Ansar Bayt al- Maqdis 51, 70, 75, 179
Ansar al-Shari'a 124–5
Ansi, Abdelwahab al- 144, 147, 155
Arab Cold War 166–7
Arab-Israeli war 66, 88
Arabiyat, Abdel Latif 95, 96
Arab Legion 88, 91
Arab Spring: democracy and 4–5; in Egypt 36–41; Hamas and 79–80; impact of 195–6; Islamism and 193–4; Jordan and 97–9, 104–5; Morsi in 19–20; Muslim Brotherhood and 3, 5, 37–8; in Tunisia 121–6; as turning point 4; in Yemen 137; Zahar and 2
Askar, Khalil 102
Assad, Bashar al- 72, 78
Assad, Hafez al- 92, 177
Athm, Yousef al- 88, 91–2
Attaturk, Kemal 15
Azzam, Abdullah 91, 106n25, 167

Badie, Mohammed 35, 42, 51, 73
Baghdad Pact 91
Bahrain 5, 40, 102, 150
Banna, Hassan al- 1, 6, 12, 16, 23, 28, 49, 169, 183; aim of 18; background of 12–14; father of 13; Ghannouchi

and 116; Hamas and 61, 63, 64, 66; impact of 21–2; on Islam 30, 187; jihad and 20–1; Jordan and 116; *Manar, Al-* (The lighthouse) (newspaper) and 14–15; on Muslim Brotherhood 16, 18; on nationalism 165; Rida and 14; Secret Apparatus and 20; secularism and 17; transnationalism and 163–4; Wafdists and 19

Banna al-Sa'ti, Sheikh Ahmad Abd al-Rahman al- 13

Barqawi, Jamil al- 87

Barqawi, Yousuf al- 87

Belaid, Chokri 124, 125, 128

Believing Youth 143

Beltagy, Mohammed el- 44, 51

Ben Ali, Zine El Abidine 8, 36, 37, 95, 111–12, 118, 119, 120, 121, 122, 125, 126, 128, 129, 130, 138, 147, 150

Ben Youssef, Salah 112

Bin Laden, Usama 143, 187

Black September 93

Blair, Tony 77

Bloody Friday 150–1

Bouazizi, Mohammed 121, 174, 194

Bourguiba, Habib 112, 113–15, 117–18, 119, 124

Brahmi, Mohamed 124, 125, 128

Cairo 1, 2, 13–14, 15, 16, 18, 19, 21, 23, 27, 37, 39, 49, 61, 62, 63, 64, 65, 66, 68, 70, 71, 72, 75, 79, 80, 87, 90, 99, 102, 117, 127, 141, 165, 166, 192

caliphate, in Turkey 15, 163

Caton, Steven C. 140

Change and Reform Party 42

Christians 36, 42

Civil Coalition of Revolutionary Youth (CCRY) 149–50

Congrès pour la République (CPR) 122, 127, 147

Consultative Assembly 24

Dahlan, Mohammed 75, 79

Day, Stephen 139, 142

"Day of Rage" 21

Dawa 13, 28, 29, 42, 46, 90

Deaf and Dumb Youth revolution Alliance 137

democracy 127–8, 144–5; Arab Spring and 4–5, 40–1; in Egypt 40–1; Ennahda and 124; Muslim Brotherhood and 40–1

Democratic Alliance (Egypt) 43–4

Dheisat, Jamal 101

Dome of the Rock 27, 63

Duheissat, Jamil 102

economy: in Egypt 35, 36, 47, 53; in Jordan 97–8; in Tunisia 113, 123, 124, 127, 128

Egypt: al-Nour party in 43, 44, 178; al-Wasat party in 42; Arab Spring in 36–41; backlash in 176; coup in 49–51; democracy in 40–1; Democratic Alliance in 43–4; in early 20th century 13; economy of 47; elections in 43–6; Freedom and Justice Party in 42, 43, 44, 47, 176; Free Officers in 22–3, 41, 66; governance by Muslim Brotherhood in 46–8; Hamas and 68–9, 71, 72–3, 75–8; jihad and 28–9; Jordan and 99; judiciary in 48–9; Morsi's victory speech in 19–20; nationalism in 15; Palestine and 66, 77–8; resistance to Muslim Brotherhood in 48; Six Day War and 3; Supreme Council of the Armed Forces in 40, 41, 42, 44, 48; Tamarod group in 49, 51; transnationalism and 166; United Kingdom and 22; Wafd party in 15, 19, 53

Egypt-Israel Peace Treaty 70

Eid al-Adha 115

Eid al-Fitr 115

elections: in Egypt 43–6; in Palestine 69; in Tunisia 119, 122–3, 127; in Yemen 146–7

Ennahda 2, 9; Arab Spring and 122–6; at Beirut conference 120; democracy and 124, 127–8; elections and 119, 122–3, 127; in Europe 120; future of 129–31; Ghannouchi and 116–17, 120; inception of 115–16; Islamism and 123–4; jihad and 124–5; Mourou and 120; Mouvement de la Tendance Islamique and 117–19; Nidaa Tounes and 129; Salafism and 125

Ensour, Abdullah 103

Erdogan, Recep Tayyip 79

Erian, Essam el- 5, 40, 51

Esposito, John 14

Essebsi, Beji Caid 127, 128

Essid, Habib 129

Europe 167–9, 192–3

Ezz, Ibrahim Abu el- 102

Facebook 36, 52, 102, 121, 171, 173

Fadil, Abdel Rahman 155

Falahat, Salem 94, 96

Farhan, Ishaq 95

Fatah 62, 67, 69, 70–1, 72, 74, 75, 76, 77, 78, 79, 177

First World War 64, 65
Forum Démocratique pour le Travail et les Libertés (Ettakatol) 122–3
Fotouh, Abdel Moneim Abou el- 45
France 64, 169; Tunisia and 112–13
Freedom and Justice Party (FJP) 42, 43, 44, 47, 49, 50, 51, 53, 176, 178
Free Officers 22–3, 41, 66, 114
Free Patriotic Union 128, 129

Gaza Strip: 1, 2, 7, 12, 25, 27, 46, 53, 61; Brotherhood in 67; Hamas and 61, 62; Morsi and 69–72; Operation Pillar of Defence and 72–4; tunnels in 71–2, 74
General People's Congress (GPC) 138, 139, 141, 144, 145, 146, 147, 148, 149, 150, 154
Ghannouchi, Rachid 8, 111, 112, 116–17, 118–20, 122, 123, 124, 125, 126, 130, 179, 189–90, 195
Gharaibeh, Ruhayil 101, 102, 103
Guidance Bureau 25, 38, 47, 51
Gulf Cooperation Council (GCC) 138, 151, 152, 155
Gulf Initiative 138

Haddad, Gehad El- 171
Haddad, Yvonne 27
Hadi, Ibrahim Abdel 21
Hadi, Abd Rabbo Mansour 9, 138, 139, 152, 153, 154–5
Halliday, Fred 140
Hamas 7; in 2006 elections 69; al- Banna and 61, 63; Arab Spring and 79–80; charter 67; Egypt and 68–9, 71, 72–3, 75–8; Fatah and 70–1, 74, 75, 78, 79; founding of 61; future of 79–80; ISIS and 75; Islamism and 61–2, 62–3; Jordan and 68–9, 93–4; leadership problems 78–9; on Muslim Brotherhood 67; Operation Pillar of Defence and 72–4; Operation Protective Edge and 75; Operation Stones of Shale and 73; Palestine Liberation Organization and 68; Qatar and 78, 79, 80; roots of 62–4; Saudi Arabia and 79, 80; Syria and 68, 78; tunnels of 71–2, 74; Turkey and 79; Zahar and 1; Zionism and 62
Hamid, Shadi 50, 53, 171, 175, 176
Haniyeh, Ismail 78
Haram al-Sharif 89; see also Al-Aqsa mosque
Hashemi, Nader 126
Hashemites 87–9, 90

Hashid confederation 9, 140–1, 144, 145, 146, 148, 150, 151
Hayja, Jabr Abu al- 102
Hizballah 68, 79
Holzapfel, Philip 138, 151
Hourani, Albert 13
Houthi, Abdulmalek Badr al-Din al- 143, 152–3
Houthi, Badr al-Din al- 143
Houthi, Husayn 143
Houthi, Mohammed Badr al-Din al- 143
Houthi rebels 9, 137, 139, 142, 143, 152–4
Houthi, Yahya Badr al-Din 143
Hudaybi, Hassan al- 21, 22–3, 25–6, 28, 29
Hussein (King of Jordan) 7, 8, 26, 67, 68, 87, 89, 91, 92, 93, 94, 95
Hussein, Mahmoud 44
Hussein, Mohamed 48
Hussein, Saddam 8, 165
Hussein, Taha 15
Husseini, Haj Amin al- 63, 64, 66

IkhwanWeb 170–1
Ikhwanwiki (web site) 5, 171
Internet 169–74
Intifada 7, 38, 61, 67, 68, 95
Iran 9, 29, 78, 79, 121, 139, 155, 193, 177
Iraq 5, 76, 79, 86, 91, 95, 112, 120, 128, 153, 165, 179, 187, 193
Irsheid, Zaki Bani 101, 102
ISIS 54, 75, 76, 77, 79, 102, 128, 153, 171, 177, 179, 180, 181, 193
Islah 9–10, 137; Arab Spring and 137; backlash against 176; elections and 146–7; Hashid confederation and 140–1; Houthi rebels and 152–4; as political actor 141–2; in transitional government 138; tribes and 140–1; Yemeni unification and 144–6
Islamic Action Front (IAF) 42, 46, 86, 95, 96–7, 98, 99, 100, 102, 104
Islamic Fighting Group 124
Islamism: al-Qassam and 65–6; Arab Spring and 193–4; and backlashes against Brotherhood 177–8; Egypt and 54; Ennahda and 123–4; Hamas and 61–2, 62–3; Islah and 139, 142; Tunisia and 112, 119, 179; see also Salafism
"Islamist winter" 5, 122, 162, 174
Ismailia, Egypt 15
Israel: establishment of 62; Jordan and 8, 88; Operation Pillar of Defence and 72–4; Operation Protective Edge and 75;

232 Index

Operation Stones of Shale and 73; Six Day War and 3–4, 27–9; *see also* Palestine

Izz ad-Din al-Qassam Brigade 73, 76, 78

Jaabari, Ahmad al- 73
Jabhat al-Nusra 79, 128, 177
Jasmine Revolution 36, 112, 131
Jebali, Hamadi 123
Jerusalem 27, 63, 64, 66, 68, 73, 88, 89, 90, 91, 92, 120
jihad: al-Banna and 20–1; Egypt and 28–9; Ennahda and 124–5; Libya and 65; Qutb 24; *see also* Salafism
Joint Meeting Parties (JMP) 138, 148–9, 151, 152, 154
Jordan 7–8; al-Wasat party in 100; Arab Legion in 88; Arab Spring and 97–9, 104–5; backlash in 176–7; in Baghdad Pact 91; economy in 97–8; Egypt and 99; future in 104–5; Hamas and 68–9, 93–4; history of Brotherhood in 86–9; Islamic Action Front in 86; Israel and 8, 88; nationalism in 89; Palestine Liberation Organization and 91, 167; resistance in 89–92; Salafism and 98–9, 178–9; Saudi Arabia and 102; Six Day War and 88; Syria and 92–3; United Arab Emirates and 102; United Kingdom and 90; West Bank and 67, 91, 93; Zamzam Initiative and 101
judiciary, in Egypt 48–9

Karman, Tawakkul 137, 155–6, 195
Kasasbeh, Muath al- 102
Katatni, Mohammed Saad al- 42, 44, 51
Kefaya 36
Khalifa, Mohammed Abd al-Rahman 87, 89, 90, 91
Khartoum conference 69
Khatib, Ahmad al- 87
Khedive Ismail the Magnificent 15
Kofahi, Nabil 101, 102
Kotti, Abdelaziz 128
Kuwait 5, 94, 165, 167, 172, 192, 193

Larayedh, Ali 123, 125
Lebanon 5, 31, 79
Libya 2, 3, 5, 40, 65, 97, 112, 117, 125, 127, 130, 150, 172, 177, 188, 193, 196
Libyan Islamic Fighting Group 124
Lynch, Marc 97

Manar, Al- (The Lighthouse) (newspaper) 14–15; Jordan 92

Mansour, Abdulmalek 144
Mansour, Adly 49
Mansour, Hamza 102
Maqdisi, Abu Mohammed al- 102
Marzouk, Musa Abu 77
Marzouki, Moncef 128
Mashour, Mustafa 29, 166
McGeough, Paul 93
Mecca 88, 89
media 161, 169
Mekameleen (television network) 173
Meshal, Khaled 70–1, 74, 78, 93–4
Misr al-An (television network) 173
Missayami, Hayat al- 98
Morocco 5, 172
Morsi, Mohammed 7; Aly on 191; on Egypt 34; election of 45–6; Gaza and 69–72; Operation Pillar of Defence and 73; ouster of 21, 49–51; presidency and 44–5; victory speech of 19–20; Zahar and 2
Mourou, Abdelfattah 116, 117, 120
Mouvement de la Tendance Islamique (MTI) 111, 116, 117–19
Mouvement des Démocrates Socialistes 119
Mubarak, Hosni 19, 28–9, 34, 35, 36–7, 38, 39, 40, 41, 42, 45, 47, 50, 52, 53, 54, 70, 71, 95, 138, 149, 150, 172, 188
Mushtaha, Rawhi 71
Muslim Brotherhood: al-Banna on 18; backlash against 176–8; founding of 15; future of 29–31, 53–4, 180–1; "global reach" of 5; as political organization 17–18; rise of 13–18; Six Day War and 27–9; structure of 24–5
Muslim Brotherhood Association 103
Muslim World League 143
Mzali, Mohammed 117

Nabulsi, Muslim al- 87
Nasser, Gamal Abdel 1, 3, 114; death of 27; Free Officers and 22–3; Jordan and 90; and marginalization of Muslim Brotherhood 26–7
National Coalition for Reform and Change 147
nationalism: al-Banna on 165; in Egypt 15; in Jordan 89; opposition to, by Brotherhood 164; triumph of 192
National Reform Front (NRF) 100
Nawasi Brigade 177
Nidaa Tounes 111, 127, 128–9
9/11 attacks 120, 187
Nuqrashi, Prime Minister 21, 22

Index **233**

Operation Decisive Storm 9, 154
Operation Pillar of Defence 72–4
Operation Protective Edge 75, 76
Operation Stones of Shale 73
Oslo Accords 69
Ottoman 14, 64, 65, 163

Palestine: al-Qassam and 65–6; backlash in
177; Change and Reform Party in 42;
and early Muslim Brotherhood activity
18–19; Egypt and 66, 77–8; elections
in 69; influence in 64–6; Muslim
Brotherhood in early 63–4; Salafism and
179; Secret Apparatus and 20; Six Day
War and 27; Zionism and 65; *see also*
Gaza; Hamas; West Bank
Palestine Liberation Organization (PLO)
7–8, 38, 68, 69, 70, 80, 91, 167
Palestinian Legislative Council 61
Pan-Islamism i, 3, 162–3
Parti Socialiste Destourien 113
Pasha, Glubb 88, 91
Personal Status Codes 112, 113, 114, 126

Qahtan, Mohammed 139, 147
Qandil, Hesham Mohammed 73
Qaradawi, Yusuf al- 41, 73
Qassam, Sheikh Izz ad-Din al- 63, 64, 65–6;
see also Izz ad-Din al-Qassam Brigade
Qasuss, Abdulmalik 137
Qatar 5, 72, 76, 78, 79, 80, 154, 155, 193
Qutb, Sayyid 13, 23–5, 28, 31, 64, 91, 164,
167, 169

Rabaa (television network) 173
Rabaa Square 31, 44, 49, 52, 173, 179
Rafah 70, 73, 74; attack 71
Ramadan 113, 115, 118, 162
Ramadan, Said 87
Rassemblement Constitutionnel
Démocratique (RCD) 119, 120, 122, 129
Raziq, Ali Abd al- 16
Rida, Rashid 14, 15, 63, 64, 162
Risheq, Izzat 73–4
Rover Troops 21

Saadi, Mohammed al- 147
Sa'd, Muflih al- 87
Sadat, Anwar al- 23, 27–8, 37, 52, 53
Said, Hammam 8, 94, 96, 101, 103, 104
Salafism: Arab Spring and 5; Ennahda and
125; European expansion and 64; Jordan
and 98–9, 178–9; Palestine and 179; *see
also* Islamism

Salih, Ali Abdullah 9, 137, 138, 143, 145,
146, 147, 148, 149, 150, 151–2, 153,
154, 155
Sarayira, Mamduh al- 87
Saudi Arabia: Hamas and 79, 80; Jordan and
102; Yemen and 9, 143
Secret Apparatus 20, 21, 22, 23
secularism 15, 17, 30, 125–6, 179
Shafiq, Ahmed 45
Shallah, Ramadan 74
Shatir, Khairat al- 45, 51
Shehata, Samer 2, 177
Shura Council 47, 94, 95, 96, 98, 141,
166, 175
Sisi, Abdel Fattah al- 7, 23, 48, 49–51, 52,
53, 62, 70, 74, 75, 76, 79, 102, 152, 172,
176, 177, 188, 196
Six Day War 3–4, 27–9, 88
social media 10, 36, 37, 38, 52, 77, 121, 126,
169, 171, 172, 173, 192
Suleiman, Omar 73
Supreme Council of the Armed Forces
(SCAF) (Egypt) 40, 41, 42, 44, 45, 48, 49,
53, 70, 127
Supreme Guide 22, 24, 25, 29, 51, 73, 103,
166
Syria: Arab Spring and 5; backlash in 177;
Hamas and 68, 78; Jordan and 8, 92–3;
Six Day War and 27; Tunisia and 128

Taghir Square 137, 149–52
Tahrir Square 19, 37, 38, 39, 47, 48,
149, 195
Tamarod group 49, 51
Tawadros II, Pope 49
Tayeb, Sheikh Ahmed al- 49
Thunaibat, Abdul Majid 86, 96, 102, 103,
104, 105
Tilmisani, Umar al- 28, 29
transnationalism: al-Banna and 163–4;
Egypt and 166; Internet and 169–74;
Pan-Islamism and 162–3
tribes, in Yemen 138, 140–1, 150, 155
Tunisia 8–9; Arab Spring in 121–6;
Ennahda in 2; France and 112–13;
independence of 112–13; Islamism and
112, 179; secularism in 125–6, 179; Syria
and 128; women in 113, 114; *see also*
Ennahda
Turkey 15, 72, 79, 155, 173, 177, 193
Twitter 36, 52, 171

ummah 17, 73, 89, 162–74, 187
Union Générale des Travailleurs Tunisiens 121

234 Index

United Arab Emirates (UAE) 75, 99, 162, 176, 180, 192; Hamas and 79; Jordan and 102, 105; Yemen and 152, 155
United Kingdom: Brotherhood in media in 161; Egypt and 22; Jordan and 90
USS *Cole* 143

Wafd party 15, 19, 22, 43, 53
waqf 89, 113
West Bank 26, 27, 70, 72, 76, 177; Brotherhood in 67; Jordan and 88, 91, 93
Wickham, Carrie 36, 39, 44, 96, 97, 100
Women 9, 37, 38, 42, 47, 52, 95, 113, 114, 115, 119, 121, 122, 125, 126, 137, 140, 195

Yadoumi, Mohammed al- 9, 138, 147
Yassin, Sheikh Ahmed 1, 27, 94
Yemen 9–10; General People's Congress in 138, 139, 141, 144, 146, 147; Saudi Arabia and 143; tribes in 140–1; unification in 144–6; *see also* Islah
Yemeni Socialist Party (YSP) 146, 147, 148, 152
Yousef, Ahmed 71
Yousef, Bassam 45
YouTube 36, 78, 171, 173–4

Zahar, Mahmoud al- 61; background of 1, 2; Morsi and 70
Zaidan, Nael 102
Zamzam Initiative 101, 102
Zawahiri, Ayman al- 196
Zaydi sect 142, 143, 145, 148, 153
Zaytuna University 113, 114, 116–17, 118
Zeman, Miloš 161
Zindani, Sheikh Abdul Majid al- 141, 142–3, 144, 145, 146, 155, 179
Zionism 7, 62, 63, 65